GOTTLOB FREGE · POSTHUMOUS WRITINGS

GOTTLOB FREGE

Posthumous Writings

Edited by
HANS HERMES
FRIEDRICH KAMBARTEL
FRIEDRICH KAULBACH
with the assistance of Gottfried Gabriel and Walburga Rödding

Translated by
PETER LONG
ROGER WHITE
with the assistance of Raymond Hargreaves

The University of Chicago Press

The University of Chicago Press, Chicago 60637

Published 1979
Printed in Great Britain by Spottiswoode Ballantyne Ltd.

ISBN 0-226-26199-9

Library of Congress Cataloging in Publication Data

Frege, Gottlob, 1848/1925.
  Posthumous writings.
Translation of selections from v. 1. of Nachgelassene Schriften und
Wissenschaftlicher Briefwechsel.
1. Mathematics—Collected works. 2. Logic, Symbolic and
mathematical—Collected works. I. Hermes, Hans. II. Kambartel, Friedrich. III.
Kaulbach, Friedrich. IV. Title.
QA3. F74213   510   79-10986

Originally published in German under the title *Nachgelassene Schriften und
wissenschaftlicher Briefwechsel*, vol. 1, by Felix Meiner (Hamburg, 1969).

TABLE OF CONTENTS

Gottlob Frege, Posthumous Writings

TRANSLATORS' PREFACE

What is printed here is a translation of the first volume of Frege's posthumous writings and correspondence published by Felix Meiner, Hamburg 1969, under the editorship of Hans Hermes, Friedrich Kambartel and Friedrich Kaulbach. Whilst we have naturally translated everything in the volume which is by Frege's hand, we have chosen to omit much of the editorial apparatus. Thus we have not translated the three introductory exegetical essays by the editors, though we have translated their history of the Frege *Nachlaß*—leaving out, however, parts that are taken up with editorial minutiae and a general discussion of the difficulties of deciding on dates and titles for some of the pieces. Again, we have not translated all of their footnotes, many of which are exegetical, though we have translated such as relate to the composition or dating of the individual pieces, or give the provenance of some quotation in the text or (where we think it helpful) the authorship of some view that Frege is discussing. We have, finally, omitted the bibliography of Frege's published work and translations thereof.

We ourselves have added footnotes where some difficulty in translation seemed to call for comment or where we thought one necessary if the reader was to follow the argument. Asterisked footnotes are Frege's own; numbered footnotes are either ours or the editors' and are marked accordingly. Matter within square brackets is either editorial or added by ourselves where we have made some interpolation to assist the reader—as, for instance, where there is some play on words in the German which is inevitably lost in the English translation. It should be clear in each case whether the intervention is ours or the editors'.

We have not thought it necessary to provide the reader with a glossary, but some key terms call for comment here either because of their inherent difficulty or because we have adopted different renderings from previous translators.

First and foremost we have parted company with all previous English translators of Frege by rendering '*bedeuten*' and '*Bedeutung*' as 'mean' and 'meaning'. We have done this throughout, both before and after he formulated his celebrated distinction between *Sinn* (sense) and *Bedeutung* (except of course where the obvious translation of '*Bedeutung*' is 'importance' or 'significance'). And cognate terms such as '*bedeutungsvoll*' and '*gleichbedeutend*' we have accordingly rendered by 'meaningful' and 'having the same meaning'. 'Meaning' is, after all, the natural English equivalent for '*Bedeutung*', and renderings such as 'reference' and 'denotation' are strictly incorrect and have only been adopted by other translators for exegetical reasons. We have thought it better not to beg questions of exegesis by suggesting through translation a certain view of what Frege meant in his later writings by '*Bedeutung*', leaving it rather to the reader to form his own judgement of the contrast Frege intended by his *Sinn-Bedeutung* distinction. If his later use of '*bedeuten*' and '*Bedeutung*' reads oddly in German, this oddness should be reflected in translation and not ironed out by mistranslation.

'*Satz*' we have almost always rendered by 'sentence'. For Frege a *Satz* is a series of sounds or written signs which, unlike the thought or sense expressed by it, can be perceived by the senses. That this is how Frege normally used the word is clear from many passages in these writings; the reader may be referred, for instance, to the discussion of truth at the beginning of the second piece entitled 'Logic' or to his remarks at the beginning of the short piece entitled 'A brief Survey of my logical Doctrines'. Sometimes, however, the word is rather to be translated 'theorem', as in the notes on Hilbert's *Foundations of Geometry*. Where the word creates difficulties, as in certain compound nouns, we have helped the reader by giving the German alongside the English.

'*Vorstellung*' is a notorious crux for translators and we have by and large rendered it by 'idea', preferring this in general to the quasi-technical 'representation' with its Kantian overtones and the too narrow 'image'. Admittedly our rendering reads awkwardly in some contexts and may mislead the unwary. But Frege, again in the second piece entitled 'Logic', helps the reader by explaining how he is there using '*Vorstellung*' and we have occasionally singled out the word for special mention where we thought there was a danger of misunderstanding.

Another term which has occasioned us some difficulty is '*anerkennen*'. It is tempting at first sight to render this by 'acknowledge' or 'accept', reserving 'recognize' for '*erkennen*'. But when Frege says that to assert (*behaupten*) something is to express the *Anerkennen* of a thought, the more natural rendering seems to be 'recognition'. On the other hand, when he says that to reject (*verwerfen*) a thought is to *anerkennen* the opposite thought, the natural rendering seems to be 'accept' or 'acknowledge'.

'*Begriffsschrift*' we have translated 'concept-script', preferring this to the other translations we have seen. For '*beurteilbarer Inhalt*' we have used 'content of possible judgement' in preference to 'possible content of judgement'. For '*vertreten*' as used by Frege of what he calls 'indefinitely indicating letters' we have preferred 'stand in for' to 'represent'. And finally, where '*Anzahl*' ('natural number') occurs in the text, as opposed to '*Zahl*' ('number'), we have usually noted the fact.

Perhaps we should point out, by way of conclusion, that many of the pieces printed here were not written up by Frege for publication. Some, for instance, are preliminary drafts of papers, some merely summarize his views or are in the form of diary notes, and the longest piece in the book—*Logic in Mathematics*—is probably a set of lecture notes. The reader should not therefore hold it against the author if the style is occasionally rough and some of the constructions awkward, or if here and there points are laboured too heavily. Still, throughout these writings, whether polished or not, we find that formidable clarity which distinguishes the work he published. If one chose a motto for the title page of this volume, what could be more apt than Vauvernarques' 'La clarté est la bonne foi des philosophes'?

HISTORY OF THE FREGE *NACHLAß* AND THE BASIS FOR THIS EDITION[1]

When Frege died in Bad Kleinen on 26 July 1925, he left to his adopted son, the engineer Alfred Frege, a quantity of important scientific papers.[2] These included unpublished manuscripts of some length, almost all of which, however, were incomplete or in the form of drafts; notes and drafts of letters, as well as a large number of letters from his most important academic correspondents. In a short note attached to his will dated 1 January 1925 Frege wrote concerning his bequest:

> Dear Alfred,
>
> Do not despise the pieces I have written. Even if all is not gold, there is gold in them. I believe there are things here which will one day be prized much more highly than they are now. Take care that nothing gets lost.
>
> Your loving father.
>
> It is a large part of myself which I bequeath to you herewith.

The papers Frege left remained in Alfred Frege's keeping for more than a decade; on 26 November 1925 he handed over, amongst other things, a series of letters addressed to Frege (these included Russell's letters) to the chemist and historian of science Ludwig Darmstaedter for the latter's collection in the Prussian State Library. He may have been moved to do this by the fact that Darmstaedter had some time previous been in touch with Frege concerning the collection he was compiling, with the result that in 1919 he had received from Frege the piece printed on pp. 253–257. The manuscripts handed over to Darmstaedter in 1925 also included drafts of Frege's letters to Russell and rough copies of the hand-written sheets that Darmstaedter had received in 1919.

---

[1] Cf. the account *Der wissenschaftliche Nachlass von Gottlob Frege* by H. Scholz and F. Bachmann in the *Actes du congrès international de philosophie scientifique, Paris 1935*, Vol. VIII: *Histoire de la logique et de la philosophie scientifique* (published Paris 1936), pp. 24–30 (ed.).

[2] The papers here called 'scientific [*wissenschaftlich*]' dealt of course with logic, philosophy and the foundations of mathematics. We have no equivalent in English for the German term: the noun *'Wissenschaft'*, which in the main text we have sometimes rendered by 'discipline', may be applied to any field of study, and not only to such as we should normally call 'scientific'. At other places in this history we have used the word 'scientific' in the same convenient, if improper, sense (trans.).

In the thirties particular attention was devoted to Frege's writings by what was known at the time as '*Philosophisches Seminar B*' [Department of Philosophy (B)] of the University of Münster; the head of department was H. Scholz and the department later became the well-known first German *Institut für mathematische Logik und Grundlagenforschung* [Institute for Mathematical Logic and Foundation Studies]. It was in this connection that Scholz tried to find out what had become of the writings Frege had left behind at his death [Frege's *Nachlaß*]. In 1935 he discovered where Frege's adopted son was living and entered into correspondence with him. Alfred Frege said that he was prepared to hand over Frege's *Nachlaß* to Scholz and his collaborators 'on the understanding', as Scholz and Bachmann write, 'that we should go over the papers and see whether they were suitable for publication and then deposit them in the library of the University of Münster in Westphalia'. Alfred Frege retained proprietary rights over Frege's *Nachlaß*, but on 26 July 1935 he made a written statement to the effect that in the event of his death Scholz should have the right of disposing of the *Nachlaß* as he thought fit.

Scholz and Bachmann, his collaborator at that time, set to work immediately and were able to report in detail on the Frege *Nachlaß* in their paper to the International Congress for scientific Philosophy which was held in Paris from 15 to 21 September 1935. In their address they issued a request that any letters of Frege's should be made available for the Frege archives in Münster. In the following years Scholz was able to get hold of a large number of Frege's letters, either originals or copies, for the Münster collection. In particular, Russell gave him the letters Frege had written to him.

Once Scholz had achieved an overall picture of the Frege *Nachlaß*, he decided to prepare a selection of shorter writings which was to include important unpublished papers and the correspondence with Russell. Three volumes of roughly 300 pages each were planned. Scholz was able to elicit the support of the *Notgemeinschaft der deutschen Wissenschaft* for this project. The group which then took up work on the edition included, besides Scholz and Bachmann, Dr Albrecht Becker and Marga Tietz. Where reference is made by the present editors to 'previous editors' of the *Nachlaß*, in nearly every case it is this group which is meant.

A letter written to Scholz on 2 March 1936 by the then Librarian of the University Library in Münster reveals that as early as 15 February 1936 Scholz had announced his intention of handing over to the Library, in accordance with the disposition made by Alfred Frege, the pieces entrusted to him. It was quite clear, however, that the *Nachlaß* remained in Department of Philosophy (B) right up to October 1943 and was only then deposited in the University Library because of the danger of its being destroyed by the air raids which were growing more and more frequent. However, this safety precaution proved futile. The Frege *Nachlaß* was destroyed by fire during the bombing of the city of Münster on 25 March 1945, in the course of which the University Library was badly hit. Scholz later wrote 'The work we were engaged on has suffered immeasurably from the bombing. The whole of the original material, which after an initial shock to the foundations in October 1943 had been handed over to the University Library for safe keeping, must be regarded as lost. After months of enquiries this information was communicated to me, a few weeks ago, by the present University Librarian.' Information subsequently obtained from Dr Heinrich Jansen, who had been in charge of the manuscript section of the University Library, confirmed the fact of the destruction of the *Nachlaß* and that it had happened on the date given above.

The Second World War not only led to the loss of the Frege manuscripts deposited at Münster; it brought the work on the three volume edition of Frege's shorter writings to a virtual standstill. Nevertheless, in the course of preparing this edition typescript copies of most of the important pieces from the *Nachlaß* had been made. Scholz has managed to save the majority of these typescripts, either top copies or carbons, from being destroyed. It is these typescripts which have formed the basis of all subsequent projects for editing the *Nachlaß*.

Not long after the end of the war Scholz again took up his plan of preparing a three volume selection of Frege's writings. In 1947, with the support of the *Forderergesellschaft* of Münster University, he had copies made of most of the surviving pieces. The following extract from a letter he wrote gives one some idea of the stringencies of the post-war situation with which Scholz had to contend and the characteristic way in which he tried to cope with them:

Münster, 23.5.47
Westring 17 I

The Rector,
Professor Dr E. Lehnartz

Dear Rector,

I request that, in the event of a supplementary delivery of coal becoming available for next winter, *urgently required heating material* should be allocated to me *for my study* in Melcherstr. 26 II. This is far and away the largest room in our flat. The large library, which I was able to preserve, is kept there. The room is at least 25 metres square and is adjoined on one side by a glass verandah which inevitably acts as a cold-trap in winter. The room is heated by an efficient cylindrical stove.

The reason for my request:

I have to edit Gottlob Frege's 'Shorter Writings' for the occasion of the centenary of his birth in July of next year; these include the large corpus of writings which I unearthed, writings which this great German master, who pioneered work into the foundations of mathematics, left behind at his death. Until the outbreak of war this work was supported by the *Notgemeinschaft der deutschen Wissenschaft*. At that time the material existed in its entirety in carefully prepared transcripts divided into three volumes of around 300 pages each. The outbreak of war prevented this edition from appearing. With the exception of a series of carbon copies, I handed over this valuable material, along with the originals, to the University Library for safe keeping. Nevertheless it was all destroyed. I therefore have to have everything copied out once more from the surviving carbon copies,[1] since I cannot possibly part with the only documents now remaining to me. A few weeks ago I was at last able to obtain a suitable person for the work of copying this material. She is paid out of the funds which have been placed at my disposal for this purpose by the *Förderergesellschaft* of the University acting under your chairmanship. I myself have made the large typewriter in my study available for this purpose. The work has to be done in this room since no other is available. It will, in any event, take up the whole of the winter. It cannot be postponed if the first volume at least is to come out in the course of next year. . . .

Yours sincerely,
Heinrich Scholz

The first volume did not, however, come out in 1948 or later. During the last decade of his life, serious illness made it increasingly difficult for Scholz to do sustained work. And so the edition at which he had laboured so doggedly since 1935 was still incomplete when he died at the end of 1956. Upon Scholz's retirement he was succeeded in the chair of Mathematical Logic and Foundation Studies by his pupil H. Hermes. And so, in accordance with the disposition made by Alfred Frege, Hermes, as Scholz's nominee, became responsible for preparing the edition of Frege's *Nachlaß*.

The first impetus to renew work on this edition came in 1957 when Michael Dummett, the English Frege scholar, spent a period of study in the Institute for Mathematical Logic and Foundation Studies in Münster. Working from the notes Scholz had made in the thirties and the copies to be found in Scholz's *Nachlaß*, he made a preliminary conspectus of the material that Scholz had originally gathered together and the corpus that had survived. In addition, he tried to enlist the support of English trusts for the planned edition. Since this proved fruitless, nothing further came of this first initiative that succeeded Scholz's death. Nevertheless, Dummett's spade-work was an important help to the present editors, which they were thankful to receive. In a second effort to get things moving Hermes succeeded in persuading his two co-editors in 1961 to form a team, and this team has subsequently been engaged in preparing Frege's posthumous writings and his scientific correspondence for publication. In 1962 the *Deutsche Forschungsgemeinschaft* gave its support for the undertaking, with the result that work could be delegated to assistants. Among these assistants Dr Walburga Schwering, now Dr Rödding, and Herr Gottfried Gabriel have

---

[1] Though, as we mentioned earlier, some of the top copies were found in Scholz's *Nachlaß* (ed.).

made such a substantial contribution to the completion of this volume that they are named on the title page.

The first thing the editors decided was that they would depart from the plan that Scholz had followed so consistently. They gave up the idea of a selected edition, and decided upon a *complete* edition of Frege's extant scientific writings and letters whether these were available as originals, copies or transcripts. They made an exception only of drafts that had been written up and published. Since it was expected that a new impression or photomechanical reproduction—now completed—of all Frege's previously published writings would be published by the *Wissenschaftlichen Buchgesellschaft* (Darmstadt) and the publishing house of G. Olms (Hildesheim), the editors were able to exclude these. The editors therefore confined themselves to preparing a complete edition in three volumes of Gottlob Frege's posthumous writings and scientific correspondence, the present first volume of which contains the whole of the extant *Nachlaß*, excluding the letters.

Scholz's death meant that the transcripts of the Frege *Nachlaß* that had survived became in turn part of a *Nachlaß*. Since in the post-war years Scholz had worked alone on his projected edition, all that was known about the history of the material, of how it was arranged and of how complete it was, was lost with him. As a result the editors had first to set to work and classify anew the pieces from amongst Scholz's papers that he had managed to preserve.

It is most unlikely that any scientific writings of Frege that Alfred Frege did not pass on to Scholz could have survived the war. Alfred Frege died in action on 15 June 1944 at Montesson near Paris. What became of his possessions is not known.

The editors thank the *Deutsche Forschungsgemeinschaft* for their financial support in the preparation and printing of this volume, the University Libraries in Constance and Münster for their help in obtaining literature, the publishing house of Meiner for the care and patience it devoted, to such good effect, to this difficult text, Dr Lothar Kreiser (Leipzig) and Dr Heinrich Schepers (Münster) for valuable suggestions, and in particular those who collaborated in preparing this edition, amongst whom special mention must be made of Heinz Albert Veraart, as well as Gottfried Gabriel and Dr Walburga Rödding. Those others who have contributed from the thirties to the present day to the preparation and publication of the Frege *Nachlaß* with advice, information and assistance are too numerous to be listed here. To these, too, we wish to extend our warm gratitude.

H. Hermes   *F. Kambartel*   *F. Kaulbach*

Logic[1]

[between 1879 and 1891]

A. Introduction.
        Essence, subject-matter.
        Different from psychology, related to ethics.
        On method.

B. Content of possible judgement.
        Negation. *duplex negatio*.
        Combining contents of possible judgement into a new content.
        and, *neither–nor* and *not* etc.
        Inferences.

C. Analysis of a judgement. Concept, object.
        Generality, condition, consequence. *Or*. Subordination of
        concepts. Existential judgements. (There is).
        Elimination of auxiliary objects. Inferences involving particular
        judgements. Relation-concepts. Pairs.

D. Definition of concepts.
        By means of characteristic marks. More complicated cases.

E. Definition of objects.
        Indirect by means of concepts. Direct. Judgements in which
        something is recognized as the same again.
        Improper existential judgements.

[A. Introduction]

[2f.] Truth. Judging. Asserting.
        Truth independent of our recognition.
        Grounds that do—and grounds that do not—justify such recognition.
        The latter take place according to psychological laws, have no relation
        to truth.

---

[1] In this piece (cf. Frege's footnote, p. 6) we clearly have a fragment of what was intended as a textbook on logic.

The footnote on p. 6 refers to the *Begriffschrift* (1879). In section B of the table of contents Frege uses the expression 'content of possible judgement'. From a letter to Husserl dated 24.5.1891 it is clear that he had given up using this designation by the first half of 1891 at the latest. Therefore the present piece should be dated between 1879 and 1891 (ed.).

[2f.] Superstitions about the weather have a basis in experience. Furnishing grounds of this kind is no proof.

[3]　Grounds that afford a justification are often found in other truths.

Inference. To establish laws of inference is the task of logic. Logic, like psychology, has for its subject-matter things that cannot be perceived by the senses. There is a sharp divide, however, marked by 'true'. Logic considers its objects in so far as they are true. What is true is true independently of the person who recognizes it to be true, and so is not a product of an inner process.

[4]　Comparison with ethics.

[5]　Comment on technical terms of logic. Rejection of psychological distinctions.

[5f.] Isolating what is psychological, by consciously marking it off. Warning against confusing points of view and switching from one question to another. Danger lies in language. Translation possible? Yes, so far as the logical kernel is concerned. Value of learning languages for one's logical education.

[6]　The formula-language of algebra: analysis of the logically complex. Reducing the laws of logic to one another.

The goal of scientific endeavour is *truth*. Inwardly to *recognize something as true* is to *make a judgement*, and to give expression to this judgement is to make an assertion.

What is true is true independently of our recognizing it as such. We can make mistakes. The grounds on which we make a judgement may justify our recognizing it as true; they may, however, merely give rise to our making a judgement, or make up our minds for us, without containing a justification for our judgement. Although each judgement we make is causally conditioned, it is nevertheless not the case that all these causes are grounds that afford a justification. There is an empirical tendency in philosophy which does not take sufficient heed of this distinction, and so, because our thinking takes its rise from experience, philosophy ends up by declaring all our knowledge to be empirical. The causes which merely give rise to acts of judgement do so in accordance with psychological laws; they are just as capable of leading to error as of leading to truth; they have no inherent relation to truth whatsoever; they know nothing of the opposition of true and false. The farmer whose fortunes are, for good or ill, bound up with the weather, seeks for means of determining what it will be like in advance. Little wonder that he attempts to link phases of the moon with variations in the weather and asks himself whether a full moon does not herald a change in the weather. If this appears to be confirmed—as may well be the case, since by and large the weather does not change abruptly and since it is not altogether easy to say whether the weather has changed—from that moment on he believes the weather is connected with the moon, and this belief takes root because the cases that speak in its favour make a greater impression than those that do not and imprint themselves more firmly on his memory; and he thinks he now knows this from experience. This is exactly what experience is in the case of the said empirical tendency amongst philosophers. And so it is with every superstition. Usually it is possible to make out the psychological causes. Clearly such an account of how men have come to hold something to be true is no proof; and in science, too, the history of how a mathematical law was discovered cannot take the place of the grounds that justify it. These will always be ahistorical; in other words, it will never depend on who first gave them, what provided him with the incentive to follow up such a fruitful line of thought, when and where this occurred, and so forth.

Now the grounds which justify the recognition of a truth often reside in other truths which have already been recognized. But if there are any truths recognized by us at all, this cannot be the only form that justification takes. There must be judgements whose justification rests on something else, if they stand in need of justification at all.

And this is where epistemology comes in. Logic is concerned only with those grounds of judgement which are truths. To make a judgement because we are cognisant of other truths as providing a justification for it is known as *inferring*. There are laws governing this kind of justification, and to set up these laws of valid inference is the goal of logic.

The subject-matter of logic is therefore such as cannot be perceived by the senses and in this respect it compares with that of psychology and contrasts with that of the natural sciences. Instincts, ideas etc. are also neither visible nor tangible. All the same there is a sharp divide between these disciplines, and it is marked by the word 'true'. Psychology is only concerned with truth in the way every other science is, in that its goal is to extend the domain of truths; but in the field it investigates it does not study the property 'true' as, in its field, physics focuses on the properties 'heavy', 'warm', etc. This is what logic does. It would not perhaps be beside the mark to say that the laws of logic are nothing other than an unfolding of the content of the word 'true'. Anyone who has failed to grasp the meaning of this word—what marks it off from others—cannot attain to any clear idea of what the task of logic is.

For psychology it is neither here nor there whether the products of the mental processes it studies may be called true. What is true is true independently of the person who recognizes it as true. What is true is therefore not a product of a mental process or inner act; for the product of one person's mind is not that of another's, however similar they may seem to be, just as the hunger of one person is not that of another or the eye of one person is not that of another, however close the resemblance may be. We do not directly observe the processes in the mind of another, only the effects they have in the physical world. Strictly speaking, therefore, we can only form a superficial judgement of the similarity between mental processes, since we are unable to unite the inner states experienced by different people in *one* consciousness and so compare them. If the content of the sentence $2 + 3 = 5$ is exactly the same, in the strictest sense, for all those who recognize it to be true, this means that it is not a product of the mind of this person and a product of the mind of that person, but that it is grasped and recognized as true by both equally. Even if subjective elements are a necessary part and parcel of this grasping of a content, we shall not include them in what we call 'true'.

Logic has a closer affinity with ethics. The property 'good' has a significance for the latter analogous to that which the property 'true' has for the former. Although our actions and endeavours are all causally conditioned and explicable in psychological terms, they do not all deserve to be called good. Here, too, we can talk of justification, and here, too, this is not simply a matter of relating what actually took place or of showing that things had to happen as they did and not in any other way. Certainly we say '*tout comprendre, c'est tout pardonner*', but we can only pardon what we consider not to be good.

What makes us so prone to embrace such erroneous views is that we define the task of logic as the investigation of the laws of thought, whilst understanding by this expression something on the same footing as the laws of nature: we understand them as laws in accordance with which thinking actually takes place and by whose means we could explain a single thought process in a particular person in a way analogous to that in which we explain, say, the movement of a planet by means of the law of gravity. The laws in accordance with which we actually draw inferences are not to be identified with laws of valid inference; otherwise we could never draw a wrong inference.

In these times when the theory of evolution is marching triumphantly through the sciences and the method of interpreting everything historically threatens to exceed its proper bounds, we must be prepared to face some strange and disconcerting questions. If man, like all other living creatures, has undergone a continuous process of evolution, have the laws of his thinking always been valid and will they always retain their validity? Will an inference that is valid now still be valid after thousands of years and was it already valid thousands of years ago? Clearly, the laws of how men do in fact think are being confounded here with the laws of valid inference. Let us take a somewhat closer look at this question. In the sense in which we speak of natural laws, psychological, mathematical or logical laws, it is, strictly speaking, impossible for laws to change at all. For such a law, expressed in full, must include mention of all relevant conditions, in which case it will hold independently of time and place. The law of inertia, for instance, claims to be valid for all times and regions of space. If it appeared not to be valid in, say, the neighbourhood of Sirius, we should assume that it had not been fully expressed, a condition having been overlooked which is satisfied here but not in the neighbourhood of Sirius. A genuine condition always contains something indefinite, and so, according to how this something is determined, it can assume the form of a true or false proposition. Thus if after some time the law of inertia no longer seemed to hold, this would be an indication that a further condition needed adding, a condition which had been satisfied up to a certain date but not subsequently. The supposed change in the laws of thought would have to be interpreted in this way too; this could be no more than an apparent change and would be an indication that our knowledge of these laws was incomplete. Now if by the laws of thought we understand the laws of logic, it is easy to see the absurdity of a condition relating, say, to the phosphorus content of our brains or to something else in human beings which is subject to change. In that case it would be quite possible that such a change should have taken place in some people, but not in others, so that for some people there would follow from certain truths the opposite to what would follow for others. This is utterly contrary to the nature of a law of logic, since it is contrary to the sense of the word 'true', which excludes any reference to a knowing subject.

If, on the other hand, by the laws of thought we understand psychological laws, then we cannot rule out in advance the possibility that they should contain mention of something that varies with time and place and, accordingly, that the process of thinking is different nowadays from what it was 3000 years ago.

Logic, in common with every science, has its technical terms, words some of which are also used outside the sciences, though not in quite the same sense. It doesn't matter in the least if the meaning we fix on is not altogether in line with the everyday use of the word or it doesn't accord with its etymology; what does matter is that the word should be as appropriate a vehicle as possible for use in expressing the laws. Provided there is no loss of rigour, the more compendious the formulation of the whole system of laws is, the more felicitous is the apparatus of technical terms.

The task of logic being what it is, it follows that we must turn our backs on anything that is not necessary for setting up the laws of inference. In particular we must reject all distinctions in logic that are made from a purely psychological standpoint and have no bearing on inference. Similarly, in pure mechanics we don't distinguish substances according to their chemical properties, but speaks only of 'mass' and physical bodies, so that we don't have, say, to establish a special law for each chemical substance in place of the one law of inertia. Therefore let us only distinguish where it serves our purpose. The so-called deepening of logic by psychology is nothing but a falsification of logic by psychology. In the form in which thinking naturally develops the logical and the psychological are bound up together. The task in hand is precisely that of isolating what is logical. This does not mean that we want to banish any trace of what is psychological from thinking as it naturally takes place, which would be impossible; we only want to become aware of the logical justification for what we think. So the required separation of the logical from the psychological is only a matter of distinguishing in our minds between them. That is why we cannot give too many warnings against the danger of confusing points of view and switching from one question to another, a danger to which we are particularly exposed because we are accustomed to thinking in some language or other and because grammar, which has for speech a significance analogous to that which logic has for thought, is a mixture of the logical and the psychological. Otherwise all languages would necessarily have the same grammar. Can the same thought be expressed in different languages? Without a doubt, so far as the logical kernel is concerned; for otherwise it would not be possible for human beings to share a common intellectual life. But if we think of the kernel with the psychological husk added, a precise translation is impossible. Indeed we may go so far as to doubt whether the outer covering is the same for any two men. From this we can see the value of learning foreign languages for one's logical education; when we see that the same thought can be worded in different ways, our mind separates off the husk from the kernel, though, in any given language, it appears as a natural and integral part of it. This is how the differences between languages can facilitate our grasp of what is logical. But still the difficulties are not wholly removed in this way and our logicians still keep dragging in a number of things which are really of no logical concern, though they belong to the grammar of languages akin to our own, if not to others. For this reason it is useful to be acquainted also with a means of expression of a quite different kind, such as we have, for instance, in the formula-language of algebra.*

But even when we have completely isolated what is logical in some form or phrase from the vernacular or in some combination of words, our task is still not complete. What we obtain will generally turn out to be complex; we have to analyse this, for here as elsewhere we only attain full insight by pressing forwards until we arrive at what is absolutely simple. In this respect, too, logic, because of its attachment to language and grammar, has fallen short in a number of ways. The laws of logic are themselves truths and here again there arises the question how a judgement is justified. If it is not justified in terms of other truths, then logic doesn't need to bother itself with it any further. If, on the other hand, a law of logic can be reduced to other laws by a process of inference, then it is evidently the task of logic to carry out this reduction; for it is only by doing this that we can reach a vantage point from which we can take a conspectus of the laws of logic, and not count as many a law that is one and the same.

To sum up briefly, it is the business of the logician to conduct an unceasing struggle against psychology and those parts of language and

---

* In this connection mention might also be made of my concept-script. I would not be in a position to write this work on logic without benefit of my earlier endeavours to devise a concept-script.

grammar which fail to give untrammelled expression to what is logical. He does not have to answer the question: how does thinking normally take place in human beings? What course does it *naturally* follow in the human mind? What is natural to one person may well be unnatural to another. To see this we need look no further than to the great difference between grammars. There is no reproach the logician need fear less than the reproach that his way of formulating things is unnatural, that the actual process of thinking follows a different course. If you aim to teach a beginner the rudiments of mathematics in as logically rigorous a form as possible, he will, unless he is quite exceptional, find this very unnatural, and for the very reason that such a degree of rigour is employed. As a result, he will understand what he is taught either not at all or only imperfectly. Therefore, one needs to temper the rigour of one's approach in the early stages, and only as one advances try by degrees to arouse a need for it. Even in mathematics we find that the most rigorous work always belongs to the latest stages in the history of the subject. If we were to heed those who object that logic is unnatural, we would run the risk of becoming embroiled in interminable disputes about what is natural, disputes which are quite incapable of being resolved within the province of logic, and which therefore have no place in logic at all. Perhaps definitive answers are simply not to be had, or cannot be given until we have observed primitive peoples and made a scientific study of languages.

[B.] Content of possible judgement

Inwardly to recognize something as true is to make a judgement. Thus an instance of a content of possible judgement is the content of the equation $2 + 3 = 5$. As we have seen, such a content is not the result of an inner process or the product of a mental act which men perform, but something objective: that is to say, it is something that is exactly the same for all rational beings, for all who are capable of grasping it, just as the sun, say, is something objective. But isn't the sun perhaps for some people a beneficent or maleficent deity, for others a shining disk hurled into the heavens from the east and rolling back down again towards the west, and for yet others an immense, spherical white-hot body enveloped by a cloud of incandescent gases? No. To some it may *seem* one thing, to others another; it *is* what it is.

A judgement is often preceded by questions. A mathematician will formulate a theorem to himself before he can prove it. A physicist will accept a law as an hypothesis in order to test it by experience. We grasp the content of a truth before we recognize it as true, but we grasp not only this; we grasp the opposite as well. In asking a question we are poised between opposite sentences. Although it is usually only one side that is expressed when we speak,* the other is still always implied; for the sense of the

---

* Here, of course, we are referring only to sentence-questions, not to word-questions.

question remains the same if we add 'or not?'. It is this very fact which makes possible such verbal economy. Now whatever can thus be posed in a question, we wish to call a content of possible judgement. Therefore the content of any truth is 'a content of possible judgement', but so too is the opposite content. This opposition or conflict is such that we automatically reject one limb as false when we accept the other as true, and conversely. The rejection of the one and the acceptance of the other are one and the same.

Boole's logical Calculus and the Concept-script[1]

[1880/81]

In his writings, Leibniz threw out such a profusion of seeds of ideas that in this respect he is virtually in a class of his own. A number of these seeds were developed and brought to fruition within his own lifetime and with his collaboration, yet more were forgotten, then later rediscovered and developed further. This justifies the expectation that a great deal in his work that is now to all appearance dead and buried will one day enjoy a resurrection. As part of this, I count an idea which Leibniz clung to throughout his life with the utmost tenacity, the idea of a *lingua characterica*, an idea which in his mind had the closest possible links with that of a *calculus ratiocinatur*. That it made it possible to perform a type of computation, it was precisely this fact that Leibniz saw as a principal advantage of a script which compounded a concept out of its constituents rather than a word out of its sounds, and of all hopes he cherished in this matter, we can even today share this one with complete confidence. I will quote just the following from the relevant passages:

'Si daretur vel lingua quaedam exacta, vel genus scripturae vere philosophiae, ... omnia quae ex datis ratione assequi, inveniri possent quodam genere calculi, perinde ac resolvuntur problemata arithmetica aut geometrica.'*

---

* De Scientia universali seu calculo philosophico.

---

[1] In 1881, this article was submitted by Frege in turn to the *Zeitschrift für Mathematik und Physik*, the *Mathematischen Annalen* and the *Zeitschrift für Philosophie und philosophische Kritik*, but was in every case rejected by the editors. It finally remained unpublished.

From the report of H. Scholz and F. Bachmann: *Der wissenschaftliche Nachlass von Gottlob Frege* (Paris 1936) we learn that the lost original was 'a manuscript prepared for publication of 103 closely written sides of quarto'. Scholz and Bachmann mention besides that Frege also submitted the manuscript to R. Avenarius for the *Vierteljahrsschrift für wissenschaftliche Philosophie*. However it could be that what Frege submitted to Avenarius was the essay published in this volume on pp. 47 ff. 'Boole's logical Formula-language and my Concept-Script', since Avenarius in his letter to Frege of 20/4/1882 cites the title of the manuscript returned by him as 'Boole's logical Formula-Language'.

The article can scarcely have been composed before 1880, the year in which the review by Schroder mentioned on p. 11 appeared. A great number of the reflections

Among the various sorties Leibniz made upon his goal, the beginnings of a symbolic logic come closest to what seems to be indicated by the phrase '*calculus ratiocinatur*'. They are to be found in the essays:

Non inelegans specimen demonstrandi in abstractis   and
Addenda ad specimen calculi universalis

In these Leibniz stuck very close to language. Just as the words we use for the attributes of a thing follow one another, so he simply juxtaposes the letters corresponding to properties in order to express the formation of a concept. If, for instance, A means right-angled, B isosceles, C triangle, then Leibniz represents right-angled isosceles triangle by ABC. He uses a sign for identity, ∞, and the sign + with the definition:

$$\text{'}A + B \infty L \quad significat \quad A \ inesse \ ipsi \ L\text{'}.$$

This seems to coincide with the meaning recent logicians have given this sign, according to which $A + B$ represents the class of individuals which belong to A or to B or to both. Since I am passing over less important details, the only other fact I will mention is that Leibniz allows the words '*non*' and '*ens*' to occur in his formulae. In this project he surely has the *lingua characterica* in mind, even though he made no express connection with the attempts he made to represent a content.

This way of setting up a formal logic seems to suggest itself naturally. At any rate recent German and English logicians have arrived at the same conception quite independently of Leibniz, though, as far as I know, in doing so they do not have a general characteristic in mind. However much Boolean logic* may stand out as a systematic working out of the fragmentary hints in Leibniz, it only goes beyond him in one point of fundamental importance—in the way it reduces hypothetical and disjunctive judgements to categorical.** The Leibnizian '*ens*' is left out.

In a short monograph,*** I have now attempted a fresh approach to the Leibnizian idea of a *lingua characterica*. In so doing, I had to treat in part the same subject-matter as Boole, even if in a different way. This has

---

* Boole's main work is *An Investigation of the Laws of Thought on which are founded the mathematical theories of logic and probabilities*. London 1854.

** On one point indeed Boole has taken a retrograde step away from Leibniz, in adding to the Leibnizian meaning of $A + B$ the condition that the classes A and B should have no common element. W. Stanley Jevons, E. Schröder and others have quite rightly not followed him in this.

*** *Begriffschrift, eine der arithmetischen nachgebildete Formelsprache des reinen Denkens*. Halle a S. 1879.   (Note continued, pp. 11–12.)

---

put forward here by Frege are along the same lines as the contents of the essay published in 1882 *Über der Zweck der Begriffsschrift*.

The last two sides of the lost original are preserved on a photostat, which was presented at the Paris Congress in 1935 as a specimen of the Frege *Nachlaß*.

prompted many critics to draw comparisons between the two, of which the most detailed are those set out by E. Schröder in the *Zeitschrift für Math. u. Phys.* Vol. XXV. He will not regard it as detracting from the gratitude which I here express for his thorough study of my monograph and its friendly review, if in what follows I attempt to supplement and correct that comparison.

A few of the signs I introduced there should be explained briefly here:

I deviate from usual practice in drawing a distinction between judgement and content of possible judgement. For me the relation in a hypothetical is not one between judgements but between contents of possible judgement. But if I affirm that this relation holds, I then express a judgement.

(1) The *content-stroke* is horizontal, it is always prefixed to the expression of a content of *possible judgement*, serving to connect it to the judgement and negation-strokes, and also to combine it with other contents of possible judgement by means of the conditional-stroke (§ 2): e.g.

$$—(2 + 3 = 5).$$

(2) The *judgement-stroke* is placed vertically at the left hand end of the content-stroke, it converts the content of possible judgement into a judgement (§ 2): e.g.

$$\vdash—(2 + 3 = 5).$$

(3) the *negation-stroke* is placed vertically under the content-stroke dividing it into two parts. The part to the right of the negation-stroke is the content-stroke of the original content, the part to the left that of its negation (§ 7): e.g.

$$\rightfootline—(2 + 3 = 6).$$

(4) The *conditional stroke* connects two content-strokes by running from the under side of the upper one to the left hand end of the lower. Like the negation-stroke it splits the upper stroke in two, of which the part to the right remains the content-stroke of the upper content, while the part to the left becomes the content-stroke of the whole, which means the negation of the case that the upper content is false, and the lower true (§ 5): e.g.

$$\begin{array}{l} x = 7 \\ x + 3 = 10: \end{array}$$

means: the case that $x + 3 = 10$ without $x = 7$ does not occur. We can say in this case: if $x + 3 = 10$, then $x = 7$. The roman letters such as the x here, confer generality on the content of the judgement by presenting it as true, whatever one may substitute for the roman letter (§ 11, p. 21). If, for instance, we replace x by 2 we obtain

$$\begin{array}{l} 2 = 7 \\ 2 + 3 = 10. \end{array}$$

This is a true judgement, although the upper content, as well as the lower, is false. Here, the rendering 'if' would jar with normal usage. Yet here too, the case is denied that $2 + 3 = 10$ is true and $2 = 7$ false.

If a negation-stroke stands to the left of the conditional stroke, as in

$$\begin{array}{l} 2 = 7 \\ 2 + 3 = 5, \end{array}$$

Above all, if we are not to go astray it is necessary that we should always bear in mind the purpose that governed Boole in his symbolic logic and the one that governed me in my *Begriffsschrift*.

If I understand him aright, Boole wanted to construct a technique for resolving logical problems systematically, similar to the technique of elimination and working out the unknown that algebra teaches. To this end, he represents judgements in the form of equations that he constructs out of letters and arithmetical signs such as +, 0 and 1. Logical laws then assume the form of algorithms, although these only coincide in part with those that hold in arithmetic for the same signs. In all this there is no concern about content whatsoever. In the main these means fulfil their purpose, at least as far as the range of problems that Boole has in mind are concerned. But one may think of logical problems lying outside this range. The use of arithmetical signs for logical purposes has the advantage that one is spared the necessity of learning a completely new algorithm. A large number of the transformations already familiar to our eyes still remain valid.* Higher demands, which however Boole does not set himself, are naturally not met by this enterprise. Anyone demanding the closest possible agreement between the relations of the signs and the relations of the things themselves will always feel it to be back to front when logic, whose concern is correct thinking and which is also the foundation of arithmetic, borrows its signs from arithmetic. To such a person it will seem more appropriate to develop for logic its own signs, derived from the nature of logic itself; we can then go on to use them throughout the other sciences wherever it is a question of preserving the formal validity of a chain of inference.

In contrast we may now set out the aim of my concept-script. Right from the start I had in mind the *expression of a content*. What I am striving after is a *lingua characterica* in the first instance for mathematics, not a *calculus* restricted to pure logic. But the content is to be rendered more exactly than is done by verbal language. For that leaves a great deal to guesswork, even if only of the most elementary kind. There is only an imperfect correspondence between the way words are concatenated and the structure

---

the negation of the case that $2 + 3 = 5$ without $2 = 7$ is thereby converted into its affirmation we may render: $2 + 3 = 5$ and it is not the case that $2 = 7$ (§ 7, p. 13). In

$$\vdash\begin{array}{l} \rule[0.5ex]{0pt}{0pt}2 = 1 + 1 \\ 2 + 3 = 5 \end{array}$$

$\rule[0.5ex]{1em}{0.4pt}\ 2 = 1 + 1$ takes the place of the $2 = 7$ of the preceding example. In rendering this, two denials come together and yield an affirmation:

$$2 + 3 = 5, \textit{and}\ 2 = 1 + 1\ (\text{§ 7. p. 12}).$$

* I should mention that the deviations from arithmetic are for all that so fundamental that solving logical equations is not at all like solving algebraic ones. And this greatly diminishes the value of the agreement in the algorithm.

of the concepts. The words 'lifeboat' and 'deathbed' are similarly constructed though the logical relations of the constituents are different. So the latter isn't expressed at all, but is left to guesswork. Speech often only indicates by inessential marks or by imagery what a concept-script should spell out in full. At a more external level, the latter is distinguished from verbal language in being laid out for the eye rather than for the ear. Verbal script is of course also laid out for the eye, but since it simply reproduces verbal speech, it scarcely comes closer to a concept-script than speech: in fact it is at an even greater remove from it, since it consists in signs for signs, not of signs for the things themselves. A *lingua characterica* ought, as Leibniz says, *peindre non pas les paroles, mais les pensées*. The formula-languages of mathematics come much closer to this goal, indeed in part they arrive at it. But that of geometry is still completely undeveloped and that of arithmetic itself is inadequate for its own domain; for at precisely the most important points, when new concepts are to be introduced, new foundations laid, it has to abandon the field to verbal language, since it only forms numbers out of numbers and can only express those judgements which treat of the equality of numbers which have been generated in different ways. But arithmetic in the broadest sense also forms concepts—and concepts of such richness and fineness in their internal structure that in perhaps no other science are they to be found combined with the same logical perfection. And there are other judgements which arithmetic makes, besides mere equations and inequalities. The reason for this inability to form concepts in a scientific manner lies* in the lack of one of the two components of which every highly developed language must consist. That is, we may distinguish the formal part which in verbal language comprises endings, prefixes, suffixes and auxiliary words, from the material part proper. The signs of arithmetic correspond to the latter. What we still lack is the logical cement that will bind these building stones firmly together. Up till now verbal language took over this role, and hence it was impossible to avoid using it in the proof itself, and not merely in parts that can be omitted without affecting the cogency of the patterns of inference, whose only purpose is to make it easier to grasp connections. In contrast, Boole's symbolic logic only represents the formal part of language, and even that incompletely. The result is that Boole's formula-language and the formula-language of arithmetic each solve only one part of the problem of a concept-script. What we have to do now, in order to produce a more adequate solution, is to supplement the signs of mathematics with a formal element, since it would be inappropriate to leave the signs we already have unused. But on this score alone Boole's logic is already completely unsuited to the task of making this supplementation, since it employs the signs +, 0 and 1 in a sense which diverges from their arithmetical ones. It would lead to great inconvenience if the same signs were to occur in one formula with different meanings. This is not an

---

* In the case of the formula-language of arithmetic.

objection to Boole, since such an application of his formulae obviously lay completely outside his intentions. Thus, the problem arises of devising signs for logical relations that are suitable for incorporation into the formula-language of mathematics, and in this way of forming—at least for a certain domain—a complete concept-script. This is where my booklet comes in.

Despite all differences in our further aims, it is evident from what has been said already that the first problem for Boole and me was the same: the perspicuous representation of logical relations by means of written signs. This implies the possibility of comparing the two. If I now turn to this, it cannot be done in the sense of adjudicating between the two formula-languages, which is to be preferred. To raise such a question would mean referring back to their ultimate aims, which are more ambitious in my case than in Boole's. It would indeed be more than possible that each set of signs was the more appropriate for its own ends. Nevertheless, it seems to me worthwhile to work out the comparison in detail, since in that way many of the peculiarities of my concept-script are thrown into sharper focus.

To begin with, as far as the extent of these sign languages is concerned, one is entitled to expect that these would have to coincide, once everything had been sifted from my concept-script which lies beyond the confines of pure logic. Yet even then, not everything that I express can be translated into Boolean notation, whereas the converse transformation is possible. E. Schröder indeed thinks that my concept-script would only correspond to the second part of Boole's. This is refuted by the fact that I too can easily express such a judgement as 'Every square root of 4 is a fourth root of 16' by

$$\vdash^{\!\alpha}\!\!\top\!\! \begin{array}{l} a^4 = 16 \\ a^2 = 4 \end{array}$$

although Boole would count it as one of the *primary propositions*. I represent all judgements in the first part of Boole in a similar way though in so doing I admittedly construe them quite differently. The real difference is that I avoid such a division into two parts, the first dedicated to the relation of concepts (*primary propositions*), the second to the relation of judgements (*secondary propositions*) and give a homogeneous presentation of the lot. In Boole the two parts run alongside one another, so that one is like the mirror image of the other, but for that very reason stands in no organic relation to it.

On the other hand, Boole had only an inadequate expression for particular judgements such as 'some 4th roots of 16 are square roots of 4'

$$\vdash\!\!\smile\!\!^{\!\alpha}\!\!\top\!\! \begin{array}{l} a^2 = 4 \\ a^4 = 16, \end{array}$$

and for existential judgements such as 'there is at least one 4th root of 16'

$$\vdash\!\!\smile\!\!^{\!\alpha}\!\!\top\, a^4 = 16,$$

apparently no expression at all.

So it transpires that even when we restrict ourselves to pure logic my concept-script commands a somewhat wider domain than Boole's formula-language. This is a result of my having departed further from Aristotelian logic. For in Aristotle, as in Boole, the logically primitive activity is the formation of concepts by abstraction, and judgement and inference enter in through an immediate or indirect comparison of concepts via their extensions.* The only difference is that Aristotle places in the foreground the case where the extension of one concept completely includes that of another—i.e. that of subordination—whereas Boole reduces other cases to the case of equality of extensions.** Here hypothetical and disjunctive judgements are for the moment left on one side. Boole now construes the hypothetical judgement 'If B, then A' as a case of subordination of concepts, by saying 'the class of time instants at which B is included in the class of time instants at which A'.

The full incongruity of the introduction here of the idea of time instants stands out most clearly if you think of eternal truths such as those of mathematics. Schröder seems to want to avoid the artificiality this involves, since, in company with Hugh McColl, he explains expressions like $A = 0$, $A + B = 1$ etc.—whose sense, on the Boolean conception, is self-explanatory when taken in conjunction with the stipulations of the first part—all over again without referring back. But in this way the last weak link between the two parts is also snapped, and the signs 0, 1, = receive yet a third meaning in addition to their Boolean and arithmetical ones. According to Boole 0 means the extension of a concept under which nothing falls, as for example the extension of the concept 'whole number whose square is 2'. By 1, Boole understands the extension of his *universe of discourse*. These meanings hold for the first as much as the second part. If one now ruptures this connection, then strictly speaking 0 has no longer an independent meaning in the second part; combined with the identity sign it means a denial expressed as a judgement, while '= 1' designates an affirmation, which I express by the judgement-stroke. Then, besides this, the identity sign still has an independent meaning in formulae like $A = B$. But that even Boole on his approach does not establish an organic connection between the two parts can be seen from the fact that he does not use the equations of the first part as constituents of equations of the second part, and, if you hold strictly to their meanings, cannot so use them. For in the first part $A = B$ is a judgement, whereas if it were made a constituent of an equation of the second part, as say in

$$(A = B)\, C = D$$

---

* This is not meant to imply that concept formation takes up a great deal of space in their presentations. Rather, that their logics are essentially doctrines of inference, in which the formation of concepts is presupposed as something that has already been completed.

** The relation of identity has greater content and so is less extensive and general than that of subordination.

$A = B$ would mean the class of time instants at which the content of the judgement '$A = B$' was to be affirmed. On the other hand, if, to avoid this, you do not resort to the expedient of the idea of a class of time instants, then you get in return the double sense of the 0, the 1 etc. in the same formula, which would then, to say the least, become unperspicuous.

As opposed to this, I start out from judgements and their contents, and not from concepts. The precisely defined hypothetical relation between contents of possible judgement has a similar significance for the foundation of my concept-script to that which identity of extensions has for Boolean logic. I only allow the formation of concepts to proceed from judgements. If, that is, you imagine the 2 in the content of possible judgement

$$2^4 = 16$$

to be replaceable by something else, by (-2) or by 3 say, which may be indicated by putting an x in place of the 2:

$$x^4 = 16,$$

the content of possible judgement is thus split into a constant and a variable part. The former, regarded in its own right but holding a place open for the latter, gives the concept '4th root of 16'.*

We may now express

$$2^4 = 16$$

by the sentences '2 is a fourth root of 16' or 'the individual 2 falls under the concept "4th root of 16"' or 'belongs to the class of 4th roots of 16'. But we

---

* The reader may be surprised I don't put this in the form

$$2 = \sqrt[4]{16}.$$

The reason is that $\sqrt[4]{16}$ may not in the same context mean now this, now that, 4th root of 16. Otherwise you could form the inference

$$2 = \sqrt[4]{16}$$
$$\underline{-2 = \sqrt[4]{16}}$$
$$2 = -2.$$

By using $\sqrt[4]{16}$ on one side of an identity sign, you have laid it down that $\sqrt[4]{16}$ is to mean a particular 4th root of 16, just as the letter a too must be given the same meaning throughout a given context. If it is in fact stipulated that $\sqrt[4]{16}$ is to mean the positive real root then $-2 = \sqrt[4]{16}$ is false and $2 = \sqrt[4]{16}$ is not to be read:

'2 is a 4th root of 16',   but
'2 is *the* positive real root of 16'.

We can see from this that the root sign cannot properly be used to help express that an individual falls under the concept of a root.

may also just as well say '4 is a logarithm of 16 to the base 2'. Here the 4 is being treated as replaceable and so we get the concept 'logarithm of 16 to the base 2':

$$2^x = 16.$$

The x indicates here the place to be occupied by the sign for the individual falling under the concept. We may now also regard the 16 in $x^4 = 16$ as replaceable in its turn, which we may represent, say, by $x^4 = y$. In this way we arrive at the concept of a relation, namely the relation of a number to its 4th power. And so instead of putting a judgement together out of an individual as subject* and an already previously formed concept as predicate, we do the opposite and arrive at a concept by splitting up the content of possible judgement.** Of course, if the expression of the content of possible judgement is to be analysable in this way, it must already be itself articulated. We may infer from this that at least the properties and relations which are not further analysable must have their own simple designations. But it doesn't follow from this that the ideas of these properties and relations are formed apart from objects: on the contrary they arise simultaneously with the first judgement in which they are ascribed to things. Hence in the concept-script their designations never occur on their own, but always in combinations which express contents of possible judgement. I could compare this with the behaviour of the atom: we suppose an atom never to be found on its own, but only combined with others, moving out of one combination only in order to enter immediately into another.*** A sign for a property never appears without a thing to which it might belong being at least indicated, a designation of a relation never without indication of the things which might stand in it.

In contrast with Boole, I now reduce his *primary propositions* to the *secondary* ones. I construe the subordination of the concept 'square root of

---

* The cases where the subject is not an individual are completely different from these and are here left out of consideration.

** A great deal of tedious discussion about negative concepts such as 'not-triangle' will, as I hope, be rendered redundant by the conception of the relation of judgement and concept outlined here. In such a case one simply doesn't have anything complete, but only the predicate of a judgement which as yet lacks a subject. The difficulties arise when people treat such a fragment as something whole.

In this connection, I find it extraordinary that some linguists have recently viewed a '*Satzwort*' (sentence-word), a word expressing a whole judgement, as the primitive form of speech and ascribe no independent existence to the roots, as mere abstractions. I note this from the *göttingschen gelehrten Anzeigen* 6 April 1881: *A. H. Sayce, Introduction to the Science of Language* 1880 by A. Fick.

*** As I have since seen, *Wundt* makes a similar use of this image in his *Logik*.

4' to the concept '4th root of 16' as meaning: if something is a square root of 4 it is a 4th root of 16:

$$\vdash\begin{array}{l} x^4 = 16 \\ x^2 = 4. \end{array}$$

I believe that in this way I have set up a simple and appropriate organic relation between Boole's two parts. Moreover, on this view we do justice to the distinction between concept and individual, which is completely obliterated in Boole. Taken strictly, his letters never mean individuals but always extensions of concepts. That is, we must distinguish between concept and thing, even when only one thing falls under a concept. The concept 'planet whose distance from the sun lies between that of Venus and that of Mars' is still something different from the individual object the Earth, even though it alone falls under the concept. Otherwise you couldn't form concepts with different contents whose extensions were all limited to this one thing, the Earth. In the case of a concept it is always possible to ask whether something, and if so what, falls under it, questions which are senseless in the case of an individual. We must likewise distinguish the case of one concept being subordinate to another from that of a thing falling under a concept although the same form of words is used for both. The examples given above

$$\vdash\begin{array}{l} x^4 = 16 \\ x^2 = 4 \end{array} \qquad \text{and} \qquad \vdash\!\!-2^4 = 16$$

show the distinction in the concept-script. The generality in the judgement

$$\vdash\begin{array}{l} x^4 = 16 \\ x^2 = 4 \end{array}$$

'All square roots of 4 are 4th roots of 16' is expressed by means of the letter x, in that the judgement is put forward as holding no matter what one understands by x. I stipulated that roman letters used in the expression of judgements should always have this sense.

Let us now look at the case where the content of such a general affirmative judgement occurs as part of a compound judgement, say as the antecedent of an hypothetical judgement; e.g.:

If every square root of 4 is a 4th root of m, then m must be 16.

The expression

$$\vdash\begin{array}{l} m = 16 \\ x^4 = m \\ x^2 = 4 \end{array}$$

does not correspond to the sentence, and is even false, which is why the judgement stroke has been left off the left-hand end of the uppermost horizontal stroke; for we may substitute numbers for x and m which falsify this content. Thus if we take m to be 17, then the consequent $m = 16$ would become $17 = 16$ and so would be false. Of course that doesn't yet necessarily make the whole

$$\left[\begin{array}{l} 17 = 16 \\ x^4 = 17 \\ x^2 = 4 \end{array}\right.$$

false; for if the antecedent

$$\left[\begin{array}{l} x^4 = 17 \\ x^2 = 4 \end{array}\right.$$

were also false, the whole would be true despite the falsity of the consequent.*

But we may take a value for x, 3 say, which satisfies the condition

$$\left[\begin{array}{l} x^4 = 17 \\ x^2 = 4 \end{array}\right.$$

for

$$\left[\begin{array}{l} 3^4 = 17 \\ 3^2 = 4 \end{array}\right.$$

is true, since not only $3^4 = 17$ but also $3^2 = 4$ is false. Thus if we give m the value 17 and x the value 3, the antecedent

$$\left[\begin{array}{l} x^4 = m \\ x^2 = 4 \end{array}\right.$$

is satisfied but the consequent

$$m = 16$$

is false. Thus

$$\left[\begin{array}{l} m = 16 \\ x^4 = m \\ x^2 = 4 \end{array}\right.$$

is not true for all values of x and m, which is what would be asserted by prefacing the formula with the judgement-stroke. But the sentence

'If every square root of 4 is a 4th root of m, then m must be 16'

says something different. You could also express its content as follows:

'If, whatever you understand by x it holds that $x^4 = m$ must be true if $x^2 = 4$, then $m = 16$'.

We can see: the generality to be expressed by means of the x must not govern the whole

$$\left[\begin{array}{l} m = 16 \\ x^4 = m \\ x^2 = 4 \end{array}\right.$$

---

*Cf. Footnote above p. 10ff. and *Begriffsschrift* § 5, where the latter admittedly contains the mistake pointed out by Schröder in his review. This however had no effect on what followed.

but must be restricted to

$$\left\lfloor \begin{array}{l} x^4 = m \\ x^2 = 4 \end{array} \right.$$

I designate this by supplying the content-stroke with a concavity in which I put a gothic letter which also replaces the x:

$$-\!\!\!\bigcup_{\mathfrak{a}}\!\!\left\lfloor \begin{array}{l} \mathfrak{a}^4 = m \\ \mathfrak{a}^2 = 4. \end{array} \right.$$

I thus restrict the scope of the generality designated by the gothic letter to the content, into whose content stroke the concavity has been introduced (§11 of the *Begriffsschrift*).* So our judgement is given the following expression:

$$\vdash\!\!\!\!\begin{array}{l} \rule[0.5ex]{1em}{0.4pt}m = 16 \\ \bigcup_{\mathfrak{a}}\!\!\left\lfloor \begin{array}{l} \mathfrak{a}^4 = m \\ \mathfrak{a}^2 = 4. \end{array} \right. \end{array}$$

By means of this notation, I am now also able to express particular and existential judgements. I render the sentence 'Some 4th roots of 16 are square roots of 4' thus:

$$\vdash\!\!\bigcup_{\mathfrak{a}}\!\!\left\lfloor \begin{array}{l} \mathfrak{a}^2 = 4 \\ \mathfrak{a}^4 = 16. \end{array} \right.$$

For

$$-\!\!\!\bigcup_{\mathfrak{a}}\!\!\left\lfloor \begin{array}{l} \mathfrak{a}^2 = 4 \\ \mathfrak{a}^4 = 16 \end{array} \right.$$

means the content of possible judgement

'If anything is a 4th root of 16, it is not a square root of 4', or 'No 4th roots of 16 are square roots of 4'.

We now designate this content as a false generalization by prefacing it with a negation-stroke, and present the result as an assertion by means of the judgement-stroke. Analogously

$$\vdash\!\!\bigcup_{\mathfrak{a}}\!\! \mathfrak{a}^2 = 4 \text{ means:}$$

'There is at least one square root of 4'.

This is the negation of the generalization of the negation of the equation

$$\mathfrak{a}^2 = 4.$$

We can now also easily show the link between particular and existential judgements. For in

$$\vdash\!\!\bigcup_{\mathfrak{a}}\!\!\left\lfloor \begin{array}{l} \mathfrak{a}^2 = 4 \\ \mathfrak{a}^4 = 16 \end{array} \right.$$

---

* In discussing my monograph, E. Schröder made the proposal that the designation of generality be introduced into Boolean logic by the use of gothic letters. However that is inadequate, since the scope over which the generality is supposed to extend is still left open. The drawback that a second negation sign is needed is connected with this.

we may insert two negation-strokes in immediate succession, which thus cancel each other out

$$\vdash\!\!\smile^{\mathfrak{a}}\!\!\pitchfork\!\!\pitchfork\!\!\top\!\begin{array}{l} a^2 = 4 \\ a^4 = 16 \end{array}$$

and think of this as concatenated as indicated here:

$$\mathbf{I}\!\!\top\!\!\smile^{\mathfrak{a}}\!\!\top \quad \top\!\top\!\begin{array}{l} a^2 = 4 \\ a^4 = 16 \end{array}$$

just as you may analyse

$$\vdash\!\!\smile^{\mathfrak{a}}\!\!\top\, a^2 = 4 \quad \text{into}$$

$$\mathbf{I}\!\!\top\!\!\smile^{\mathfrak{a}}\!\!\top\, a^2 = 4.$$

Thus the only distinction between

$$\vdash\!\!\smile^{\mathfrak{a}}\!\!\pitchfork\!\!\pitchfork\!\!\top\!\begin{array}{l} a^2 = 4 \\ a^4 = 16 \end{array} \qquad \text{and} \qquad \vdash\!\!\smile^{\mathfrak{a}}\!\!\top\, a^2 = 4$$

is that

$$\top\!\top\!\begin{array}{l} a^2 = 4 \\ a^4 = 16 \end{array}$$

takes the place of $a^2 = 4$. But according to § 7 of the *Begriffsschrift*,* this means that a is a square root of 4 *and* a 4th root of 16. So just as you can translate

$$\vdash\!\!\smile^{\mathfrak{a}}\!\!\top\, a^2 = 4 \quad \text{as}$$

'There is at least one square root of 4', you may express

$$\vdash\!\!\smile^{\mathfrak{a}}\!\!\pitchfork\!\!\pitchfork\!\!\top\!\begin{array}{l} a^2 = 4 \\ a^4 = 16 \end{array} \qquad \text{or} \qquad \vdash\!\!\smile^{\mathfrak{a}}\!\!\top\!\begin{array}{l} a^2 = 4 \\ a^4 = 16 \end{array}$$

by the sentence

'There is at least one number which is both a square root of 4 and a 4th root of 16'. But this is equivalent to the expression:

'At least one 4th root of 16 is a square root of 4.'

I have now shown that the difference in extent of the domains governed by Boolean logic and by my concept-script, extraneous as it might at first sight appear, is in fact as closely as possible bound up with their original construction. A few examples may now serve to illustrate how the construction of the concept-script enables it when combined with the signs of arithmetic to achieve the more far-reaching goals it set itself.

(1) There are at least two different square roots of 4. The sentence '$a = b$ follows from $a^2 = 4$ and $b^2 = 4$' is denied in its generality.

$$\vdash\!\!\smile^{\mathfrak{a}}\!\!\smile^{\mathfrak{b}}\!\!\top\!\begin{array}{l} a = b \\ a^2 = 4 \\ b^2 = 4 \end{array}$$

---

* See also above, footnote on p. 10ff.

(2) there is at most one number whose double is 4

$$\left[\!\!\left[\begin{array}{l} a = b \\ 2a = 4 \\ 2b = 4 \end{array}\right.\right.$$

(3) 4 is a positive whole number (including 0). That is, 4 belongs to the series beginning with 0, in which the immediate successor of any member is obtained by adding 1.*

$$\vdash\!\!-\frac{\gamma}{\beta}\,(0_\gamma + 1 = 4_\beta)$$

(4) 12 is a multiple of 4; that is, 12 follows 0 in the arithmetical progression with difference 4.** Two numbers with opposed signs are here not counted as multiples of one another, and 0 only counted as a multiple of itself.

$$\vdash\!\!-\frac{\gamma}{\beta}\,(0_\gamma + 4 = 12_\beta)$$

(5) 12 is a common multiple of 4 and 6; that is, 12 is a multiple of 4, *and*** 12 is a multiple of 6.

$$\left[\!\!\left[\begin{array}{l} \frac{\gamma}{\beta}\,(0_\gamma + 4 = 12_\beta) \\[2mm] \frac{\gamma}{\beta}\,(0_\gamma + 6 = 12_\beta) \end{array}\right.\right.$$

(6) 4 is a common (aliquot) factor of 12 and 20.

$$\left[\!\!\left[\begin{array}{l} \frac{\gamma}{\beta}\,(0_\gamma + 4 = 12_\beta) \\[2mm] \frac{\gamma}{\beta}\,(0_\gamma + 4 = 20_\beta) \end{array}\right.\right.$$

(7) The multiple of a multiple of a number is a multiple of that number.

$$\left[\!\!\left[\begin{array}{l} \frac{\gamma}{\beta}\,(0_\gamma + a = c_\beta) \\[2mm] \frac{\gamma}{\beta}\,(0_\gamma + a = b_\beta) \\[2mm] \frac{\gamma}{\beta}\,(0_\gamma + b) = c_\beta) \end{array}\right.\right.$$

(8) A and B are congruent modulo M. Here A, B and M need not be whole numbers; nothing further than their addibility is presupposed. This

---

* Cf. *Begriffsschrift* § 29, where in the gloss on formula (99) for $\frac{\gamma}{\beta}f(x_\gamma, z_\beta)$ one should read $\frac{\gamma}{\beta}f(x_\gamma, z_\beta)$.

** *Begriffsschrift* § 26.

*** See footnote above, p. 10ff.

way of speaking would be inconvenient for ordinary use, but it is only meant to have application when it is necessary to go back to the concept.

$$\vdash \frac{\gamma}{\beta}\, (A_\gamma + M = B_\beta)$$

$$\vdash \frac{\gamma}{\beta}\, (B_\gamma + M = A_\beta)$$

(9) 13 is prime. Here 1 is counted as a prime number, 0 not. More explicitly: 13 is a positive non-zero whole number $\left(\frac{\gamma}{\beta}\,(0_\gamma + 1 = 13_\beta)\right)$, and* whatever positive number $\mathfrak{b}$ may be which is greater than $1\left(\frac{\gamma}{\beta}(1_\gamma + 1 = \mathfrak{b}_\beta)\right)$ and different from $13\,(\!-\!\!\top\!\!-\mathfrak{b} = 13)$, 13 cannot be a multiple of $\mathfrak{b}$ $\left(\!-\!\top\!\frac{\gamma}{\beta}(0_\gamma + \mathfrak{b} = 13_\beta)\right)$.

$$
\begin{array}{l}
\vdash\!\!-\!\!\underset{\mathfrak{b}}{\cup}\!\!-\!\!\top\!\!-\!\!\top\frac{\gamma}{\beta}\,(0_\gamma + \mathfrak{b} = 13_\beta) \\[4pt]
\qquad\quad\vdash\frac{\gamma}{\beta}\,(1_\gamma + 1 = \mathfrak{b}_\beta) \\[4pt]
\qquad\quad\vdash\mathfrak{b} = 13 \\[4pt]
\qquad\qquad\vdash\frac{\gamma}{\beta}\,(0_\gamma + 1 = 13_\beta)
\end{array}
$$

(10) A and B are positive non-zero whole numbers that are co-prime. Here 1 is treated as prime to every number.

$$
\begin{array}{l}
\vdash\!\!-\!\!\underset{\mathfrak{b}}{\cup}\!\!-\!\!\top\!\!-\!\!\top\frac{\gamma}{\beta}\,(0_\gamma + \mathfrak{b} = A_\beta) \\[4pt]
\qquad\quad\vdash\frac{\gamma}{\beta}\,(0_\gamma + \mathfrak{b} = B_\beta) \\[4pt]
\qquad\quad\vdash\frac{\gamma}{\beta}\,(1_\gamma + 1 = \mathfrak{b}_\beta) \\[4pt]
\qquad\quad\vdash\frac{\gamma}{\beta}\,(0_\gamma + 1 = A_\beta) \\[4pt]
\qquad\qquad\vdash\frac{\gamma}{\beta}\,(0_\gamma + 1 = B_\beta)
\end{array}
$$

(11) A is a positive non-zero rational number; that is, *there is** at least one positive non-zero whole number which is a multiple of A.

$$
\begin{array}{l}
\vdash\!\!-\!\!\underset{\mathfrak{n}}{\cup}\!\!-\!\!\top\frac{\gamma}{\beta}\,(0_\gamma + A = \mathfrak{n}_\beta) \\[4pt]
\qquad\quad\vdash\frac{\gamma}{\beta}\,(0_\gamma + 1 = \mathfrak{n}_\beta)
\end{array}
$$

---

* See footnote above, p. 10ff.
** See above p. 14 and *Begriffsschrift* § 12.

(12) A is the least common multiple of B and Γ. More explicitly: every common multiple of B and Γ is greater than or equal to A, and* A is a common multiple of B and Γ.

$$\frac{\gamma}{\beta}(0_\gamma + B = A_\beta)$$
$$\frac{\gamma}{\beta}(0_\gamma + \Gamma = A_\beta)$$
$$A \leq \alpha$$
$$\frac{\gamma}{\beta}(0_\gamma + B = \alpha_\beta)$$
$$\frac{\gamma}{\beta}(0_\gamma + \Gamma = \alpha_\beta)$$

In neither this nor the preceding examples is the concept of a product presupposed.

(13) The real function $\Phi(x)$ is continuous at $x = A$; that is, given any positive non-zero number $\mathfrak{n}$, *there is*** a positive non-zero $\mathfrak{g}$ such that any number $\mathfrak{d}$ lying between $+\mathfrak{g}$ and $-\mathfrak{g}$ satisfies the inequality $-\mathfrak{n} \leq \Phi(A + \mathfrak{d}) - \Phi(A) \leq \mathfrak{n}$

$$-\mathfrak{n} \leq \Phi(A + \mathfrak{d}) - \Phi(A) \leq \mathfrak{n}$$
$$-\mathfrak{g} \leq \mathfrak{d} \leq \mathfrak{g}$$
$$\mathfrak{g} > 0$$
$$\mathfrak{n} > 0$$

I have assumed here that the signs $<$, $>$, $\leq$ mark the expressions they stand between as real numbers.

(14) The real function $\Phi(x)$ of a real variable x is continuous throughout the interval from A to B.

$$-\mathfrak{n} \leq \Phi(\mathfrak{c} + \mathfrak{d}) - \Phi(\mathfrak{c}) \leq \mathfrak{n}$$
$$-\mathfrak{g} \leq \mathfrak{d} \leq \mathfrak{g}$$
$$A \leq \mathfrak{c} + \mathfrak{d} \leq B$$
$$\mathfrak{g} > 0$$
$$\mathfrak{n} > 0$$
$$A \leq \mathfrak{c} \leq B$$

If in this case the formula seems longwinded by comparison with the verbal expression, you must always bear in mind that it gives the definition of a concept which the latter only names. Even so, a count of the number of individual signs needed for the two may well not turn out unfavourably for the formula.

---

* See footnote p. 10ff.
** See above p. 14 and *Begriffsschrift* § 12.

(15) $\Phi(x,y)$ is a real function of x and y continuous at $x = A, y = B$.

$$\begin{aligned}
&-\mathfrak{n} \leq \Phi(A + \mathfrak{d}, B + \mathfrak{e}) - \Phi(A, B) \leq \mathfrak{n}\\
&-\mathfrak{g} \leq \mathfrak{d} \leq \mathfrak{g}\\
&-\mathfrak{g} \leq \mathfrak{e} \leq \mathfrak{g}\\
&\mathfrak{g} > 0\\
&\mathfrak{n} > 0
\end{aligned}$$

(16) A is the limit of the Φ-series beginning with B (Cf. *Begriffsschrift* §§ 9, 10, 26, 29).

$$\begin{aligned}
&A + \mathfrak{n} \geq \mathfrak{a} \geq A - \mathfrak{n}\\
&\underset{\beta}{\overset{\gamma}{-}}\Phi(\mathfrak{d}_\gamma, \mathfrak{a}_\beta)\\
&\underset{\beta}{\overset{\gamma}{-}}\Phi(B_\gamma, \mathfrak{d}_\beta)\\
&\mathfrak{n} > 0
\end{aligned}$$

E.g. 1 is the limit approached by members of the series beginning with 0, in which the successor (y) of each member (x) is derived by the rule $1/3 + 2/3\, x = y$

$$\begin{aligned}
&1 + \mathfrak{n} \geq \mathfrak{a} \geq 1 - \mathfrak{n}\\
&\underset{\beta}{\overset{\gamma}{-}}\left(\frac{1}{3} + \frac{2}{3}\mathfrak{d}_\gamma = \mathfrak{a}_\beta\right)\\
&\underset{\beta}{\overset{\gamma}{-}}\left(\frac{1}{3} + \frac{2}{3}0_\gamma = \mathfrak{d}_\beta\right)\\
&\mathfrak{n} > 0
\end{aligned}$$

This is the series: $0,\ 1/3,\ 1/3 + 2/9,\ 1/3 + 2/9 + 4/27, \ldots$

(17) A is the limit approached by the value of the real function $\Phi(x)$ as the argument approaches B from above.

$$\begin{aligned}
&\mathfrak{n} \geq \Phi(B + \mathfrak{a}) - A \geq -\mathfrak{n}\\
&\mathfrak{d} > \mathfrak{a} > 0\\
&\mathfrak{d} > 0\\
&\mathfrak{n} > 0
\end{aligned}$$

(18) A is the limit approached by the value of the real function $\Phi(x)$ as x tends through real values towards plus infinity.

$$\begin{aligned}
&-\mathfrak{n} \leq \Phi(\mathfrak{d}) - A \leq \mathfrak{n}\\
&\mathfrak{d} > \mathfrak{g}\\
&\mathfrak{g} > 0\\
&\mathfrak{n} > 0
\end{aligned}$$

(19) A is the least upper bound of the numbers falling under the concept X; that is, every number with the property X is less than or equal to A

$$\left(-\!\!\!\smile\!\!\!\underset{\ \ \ }{\overset{\mathfrak{d}}{\mathsf{T}}}\!\!\begin{array}{c}A \geq \mathfrak{d}\\ X(\mathfrak{d})\end{array}\right)\!\Big) and^* \text{ for every positive non-zero } \mathfrak{n} \text{ there is}^{**} \text{ a number with}$$

the property X greater than $A - \mathfrak{n}$

$$\underset{\ \ \ }{\overset{\mathfrak{n}}{\mathsf{TT}}}\!\!\smile\!\!\underset{\ \ \ }{\overset{\mathfrak{d}}{\mathsf{T}}}\!\!\begin{array}{l}\!\!\!\!\!\begin{array}{l}A - \mathfrak{n} < \mathfrak{d}\\ X(\mathfrak{d})\end{array}\\ \!\!\!\!\!\mathfrak{n} > 0\\ \smile\!\!\begin{array}{l}A \geq \mathfrak{d}\\ X(\mathfrak{d})\end{array}\end{array}$$

Here the $\mathfrak{d}$ in $\left(\mathsf{T}\!\!\begin{array}{l}A - \mathfrak{n} < \mathfrak{d}\\ X(\mathfrak{d})\end{array}\right)$ has nothing to do with the $\mathfrak{d}$ in $\left(\mathsf{T}\!\!\begin{array}{l}A \geq \mathfrak{d}\\ X(\mathfrak{d})\end{array}\right)$

so that you could replace the second $\mathfrak{d}$ by a different gothic letter. Use is made here of the generalized concept of a function explained in §§ 9 and 10 of the *Begriffsschrift*. According to that, you can render $X(\varDelta):\varDelta$ has the property X, or falls under the concept X.

X might e.g. be the property of being a multiple of $\varGamma$ less than B. Then

$$\left(\mathsf{TT}\!\!\underset{\beta}{\overset{\gamma}{\ }}\!\!\begin{array}{l}(0_\gamma + \varGamma = \mathfrak{d}_\beta)\\ \mathfrak{d} < B\end{array}\right)$$

takes the place of $X(\mathfrak{d})$ and we have: A is the least upper-bound of multiples of X that are less than B.

$$\underset{\ \ \ }{\overset{\mathfrak{n}}{\mathsf{TT}}}\!\!\smile\!\!\underset{\ \ \ }{\overset{\mathfrak{d}}{\mathsf{T}}}\!\!\begin{array}{l}A - \mathfrak{n} < \mathfrak{d}\\ \mathsf{TT}\!\underset{\beta}{\overset{\gamma}{\ }}\!\begin{array}{l}(0_\gamma + \varGamma = \mathfrak{d}_\beta)\\ \mathfrak{d} < B\end{array}\\ \mathfrak{n} > 0\\ \smile\!\!\begin{array}{l}A \geq \mathfrak{d}\\ \mathsf{TT}\!\underset{\beta}{\overset{\gamma}{\ }}\!\begin{array}{l}(0 + \varGamma = \mathfrak{d}_\beta)\\ \mathfrak{d} < B\end{array}\end{array}\end{array}$$

(20) Given an arbitrary positive non-zero number ($\mathfrak{d}$), we may find a positive non-zero number ($\mathfrak{n}$) such that if it is greater than the absolute value of the real number $\mathfrak{c}$, and if $\mathfrak{r}$ lies in the interval $[A,B]$, the absolute value of the real function $\varPhi(\mathfrak{r}, \mathfrak{c})$ is less than $\mathfrak{d}$.

$$\smile\!\!\underset{\ \ \ }{\overset{\mathfrak{d}}{\mathsf{T}}}\!\!\underset{\ \ \ }{\overset{\mathfrak{n}}{\mathsf{TT}}}\!\!\smile\!\!\underset{\ \ \ }{\overset{\mathfrak{c}}{\mathsf{T}}}\!\!\underset{\ \ \ }{\overset{\mathfrak{r}}{\mathsf{T}}}\!\!\begin{array}{l}-\mathfrak{d} < \varPhi(\mathfrak{r}, \mathfrak{c}) < \mathfrak{d}\\ A \leq \mathfrak{r} \leq B\\ -\mathfrak{n} < \mathfrak{c} < \mathfrak{n}\\ \mathfrak{n} > 0\\ \mathfrak{d} > 0\end{array}$$

---

* See note on p. 10ff.
** See above p. 14.

(21) Given an arbitrary positive non-zero number (ᣔ), we may find for every value of ᴦ within the interval $[A,B]$ a positive non-zero number such that if the absolute value of ᴄ is smaller than it, the absolute value of the real function $\Phi(ᴦ, ᴄ)$ is less than ᣔ.

$$\begin{array}{l} -ᣔ < \Phi(ᴦ, ᴄ) < ᣔ \\ -ꞑ < ᴄ < ꞑ \\ ꞑ > 0 \\ ᣔ > 0 \\ A \leq ᴦ \leq B \end{array}$$

If I stress that the Boolean formula-language cannot match this, it is only in order to point out the more far-reaching goals of my concept-script. The formulae just given would be of slight value if particular signs had to be invented for each one of them. But this is so far from being the case that on the contrary nothing is invented in setting up a single one of them. A few new signs suffice to present a wide variety of mathematical relations which it has hitherto only been possible to express in words. This of itself justifies their introduction, since the formulae are much briefer and more perspicuous than the equivalent definitions of the concepts in words. Too great a horror of new signs, leading to the old ones being made to carry more meanings than they can bear, is far more damaging than an over-fertile delight in invention, since anything superfluous soon disappears of its own accord, leaving what is of value behind. But the usefulness of such formulae only fully emerges when they are used in working out inferences, and we can only fully appreciate their value in this regard with practice. A longer connected passage would really be demanded to give at least something approaching an idea of this. Nevertheless the following example I have chosen may tempt people to experiment with the concept-script. It is of little significance which topic I choose, since the inference is always of the same sort and is always governed by the same few laws, whether one is working in the elementary or the advanced regions of the science. But in the latter case more would probably be needed by way of preparation.

If I often refer to my *Begriffsschrift* in what follows, I will nevertheless try as far as possible to make myself understood without recourse to it. This of course obliges me to accompany formulae that really ought to speak for themselves with continual prose glosses.

I wish to prove the theorem that the sum of two multiples of a number is in its turn a multiple of that number. Here, as above, I count a number as a multiple of itself; nought or a number with opposed sign do not count as multiples. The numbers whose multiples are to be considered are subject to no conditions other than that the following addition theorems:

$$\vdash \quad (n + b) + a = n + (b + a) \tag{1}$$

$$\vdash \quad n = n + 0 \tag{2}$$

hold for them. Not only are we not presupposing any multiplication theorem, we are not even to assume the concept of multiplication. Of the theorems of pure logic we principally require that introduced as (84) on p. 65 of the *Begriffsschrift*, which we may first reproduce as it stands. We may express it in words as follows: if the property F is hereditary in the f-series, then if x has the property F and precedes y in the f-series, then y has the property F.

$$
\begin{array}{l}
F(y) \\
\dfrac{\gamma}{\beta} f(x_\gamma, y_\beta) \\
F(x) \\
\delta \Big(\begin{array}{l} F(\alpha) \\ \,\,| \\ \alpha \big\backslash f(\delta,\alpha) \end{array}
\end{array}
$$

How 'f-series and 'hereditary' are to be understood will become clear from their application.* I now regard it as superfluous to introduce the combination of signs

$$
\left(\begin{array}{l} \delta \Big(\begin{array}{l} F(\alpha) \\ | \\ \alpha \big\backslash f(\delta,\alpha) \end{array} \end{array} \right)
$$

and will once more replace it by the original expression

$$
\left(\begin{array}{l} {}^{\mathfrak{d}}\quad{}^{\mathfrak{a}} \,\, F(\mathfrak{a}) \\ \qquad\quad f(\mathfrak{d},\mathfrak{a}) \\ \qquad\quad F(\mathfrak{d}) \end{array} \right)
$$

used to define it in § 24 of the *Begriffsschrift*. Our formula now assumes the form:

$$
\begin{array}{l}
F(y) \\
\dfrac{\gamma}{\beta} f(x_\gamma, y_\beta) \\
F(x) \\
{}^{\mathfrak{d}}\quad{}^{\mathfrak{a}} \,\, F(\mathfrak{a}) \\
\qquad\quad f(\mathfrak{d},\mathfrak{a}) \\
\qquad\quad F(\mathfrak{d})
\end{array}
\tag{3}
$$

In addition we need the formula (4) which is introduced as (96) on p. 71 of the *Begriffsschrift*. It means: if y follows x in the f-series, then every result of applying the operation f to y follows x in the f series:

$$
\begin{array}{l}
\dfrac{\gamma}{\beta} f(x_\gamma, z_\beta) \\
f(y, z) \\
\dfrac{\gamma}{\beta} f(x_\gamma, y_\beta)
\end{array}
\tag{4}
$$

---

* See also §§ 24 and 26 of the *Begriffsschrift*.

In the preface of my *Begriffsschrift* I already said that the restriction to a single rule of inference which I there laid down was to be dropped in later developments. This is achieved by converting what was expressed as a judgement in a formula into a rule of inference. I do this with formulae (52) and (53) of the *Begriffsschrift*, whose content I render by the rule: in any judgement you may replace one symbol by another, if you add as a condition the equation between the two. We now make use of (3), taking the formula $\frac{\gamma}{\beta}(0_\gamma + a = (n + x)_\beta)$ for the function $F(x)$, and the formula $x + a = y$ for $f(x,y)$. What we referred to above as 'the property F' is now the property of a number yielding a multiple of a when added to n; the f-series is now an arithmetical progression with difference a. I substitute 0 for x. (3) then becomes (5):

$$
\begin{array}{l}
\dfrac{\gamma}{\beta}(0_\gamma + a = (n + y)_\beta) \\[4pt]
\dfrac{\gamma}{\beta}(0_\gamma + a = y_\beta) \\[4pt]
\dfrac{\gamma}{\beta}(0_\gamma + a = (n + 0)_\beta) \\[4pt]
\dfrac{\gamma}{\beta}(0_\gamma + a = (n + \mathfrak{a})_\beta) \\[4pt]
\mathfrak{b} + a = \mathfrak{a} \\[4pt]
\dfrac{\gamma}{\beta}(0_\gamma + a = (n + \mathfrak{b})_\beta)
\end{array}
\tag{5}
$$

We must first rid this of the bottom-most condition

$$
\left(
\begin{array}{l}
\dfrac{\gamma}{\beta}(0_\gamma + a = (n + \mathfrak{a})_\beta) \\[4pt]
\mathfrak{b} + a = \mathfrak{a} \\[4pt]
\dfrac{\gamma}{\beta}(0_\gamma + a = (n + \mathfrak{b})_\beta)
\end{array}
\right)
$$

which states that the property of yielding a multiple of a when added to n is hereditary in our arithmetical progression; i.e. if one member of this series has this property its successor has it too. As above, we substitute $x + a = y$ for $f(x,y)$, 0 for x, $(n + b)$ for y and $(n + m)$ for z in (4), giving us (6):

$$
\begin{array}{l}
\dfrac{\gamma}{\beta}(0_\gamma + a = (n + m)_\beta) \\[4pt]
(n + b) + a = n + m \\[4pt]
\dfrac{\gamma}{\beta}(0_\gamma + a = (n + b)_\beta)
\end{array}
\tag{6}
$$

We apply to this the rule established above by substituting $(b + a)$ for m in the second line, and at the same time adding the condition $b + a = m$. This gives us (7).

$$\frac{\gamma}{\beta}\,(0_\gamma\,a = (n+m)_\beta)$$
$$(n+b)+a = n+(b+a)$$
$$b+a = m$$
$$\frac{\gamma}{\beta}\,(0_\gamma + a = (n+b)_\beta) \tag{7}$$

From which together with (1) there follows (8)

$$\frac{\gamma}{\beta}\,(0_\gamma + a = (n + \overset{.}{m})_\beta)$$
$$b+a = m$$
$$\frac{\gamma}{\beta}\,(0_\gamma + a = (n+b)_\beta) \tag{8}$$

Here we may now introduce gothic letters, $\mathfrak{b}$ and $\mathfrak{a}$ in place of the roman letters b and m* and obtain (9):

$$\frac{\gamma}{\beta}\,(0_\gamma + a = (n+\mathfrak{a})_\beta)$$
$$\mathfrak{b}+a = \mathfrak{a}$$
$$\frac{\gamma}{\beta}\,(0_\gamma + a = (n+\mathfrak{b})_\beta) \tag{9}$$

In this, the scope of the generality designated by b (or $\mathfrak{b}$) remains as before the whole judgement, whereas the scope of the generality designated by m (or $\mathfrak{a}$) does not include the condition $\frac{\gamma}{\beta}\,(0_\gamma + a = (n+b)_\beta)$, which is possible since it does not contain m. (9) asserts the inheritance already mentioned.

Hence from (5) and (9) we may infer (10):

$$\frac{\gamma}{\beta}\,(0_\gamma + a = (n+y)_\beta)$$
$$\frac{\gamma}{\beta}\,(0_\gamma + a = y_\beta)$$
$$\frac{\gamma}{\beta}\,(0_\gamma + a = (n+0)_\beta) \tag{10}$$

We once more apply our rule to this by substituting n for $n+0$ and adding the condition $n = n+0$.

$$\frac{\gamma}{\beta}\,(0_\gamma + a = (n+y)_\beta)$$
$$\frac{\gamma}{\beta}\,(0_\gamma + a = y_\beta)$$
$$\frac{\gamma}{\beta}\,(0_\gamma + a = n_\beta)$$
$$n = n+0 \tag{11}$$

---

* *Begriffsschrift* § 11, pp. 21 and 22.

But we may immediately drop this condition again because of (2). This gives us (12), the theorem to be proved:

$$
\begin{array}{l}
\vdash \; \frac{\gamma}{\beta}\,(0_\gamma + a = (n + y)_\beta) \\[2mm]
\quad \frac{\gamma}{\beta}\,(0_\gamma + a = y_\beta) \\[2mm]
\quad \frac{\gamma}{\beta}\,(0_\gamma + a = n_\beta)
\end{array}
\tag{12}
$$

Continuing in a similar way you may also easily derive the theorem that the multiple of the multiple of a number is a multiple of that number. For this, you only require the addition theorem $\vdash n + 0 = n$ and formula (78) of the *Begriffsschrift*. Since nothing fundamentally new would emerge in the process, I will not carry out the derivation, but instead will repeat the preceding computation as it appears when no words are interpolated, and complete familiarity with the concept-script is assumed. The numbers on the right name the formulae, those on the left refer back to earlier ones. The different sorts of line drawn between the individual judgements are to indicate the mode of inference. The formulae (5) and (11) are left to be derived by the reader, which is a simple problem. The formula (3) here represents a form of mathematical induction. It follows from §§ 24 and 26 of my *Begriffsschrift* that this mode of inference is not, as one might suppose, one peculiar to mathematics, but rests on general laws of logic.

4

$$
\begin{array}{l}
\vdash \; \frac{\gamma}{\beta}\,(0_\gamma + a = (n + m)_\beta) \\[2mm]
\quad (n + b) + a = n + m \\[2mm]
\quad \frac{\gamma}{\beta}\,(0_\gamma + a = (n + b)_\beta)
\end{array}
\tag{6}
$$

$$
\begin{array}{l}
\vdash \; \frac{\gamma}{\beta}\,(0_\gamma + a = (n + m)_\beta) \\[2mm]
\quad (n + b) + a = n + (b + a) \\[2mm]
\quad b + a = m \\[2mm]
\quad \frac{\gamma}{\beta}\,(0_\gamma + a = (n + b)_\beta)
\end{array}
\tag{7}
$$

(1)[::]

$$
\begin{array}{l}
\vdash \; \frac{\gamma}{\beta}\,(0_\gamma + a = (n + m)_\beta) \\[2mm]
\quad b + a = m \\[2mm]
\quad \frac{\gamma}{\beta}\,(0_\gamma + a = (n + b)_\beta)
\end{array}
\tag{8}
$$

$$\frac{\gamma}{\beta}\,(0_\gamma + a = (n + a)_\beta)$$
$$\mathfrak{d} + a = a$$
$$\frac{\gamma}{\beta}\,(0_\gamma + a = (n + \mathfrak{d})_\beta) \qquad (9)$$

(5): ────────────────────────

$$\frac{\gamma}{\beta}\,(0_\gamma + a = (n + y)_\beta)$$
$$\frac{\gamma}{\beta}\,(0_\gamma + a = y_\beta)$$
$$\frac{\gamma}{\beta}\,(0_\gamma + a = (n + 0)_\beta) \qquad (10)$$

(2):: ════════════════════════

$$\frac{\gamma}{\beta}\,(0_\gamma + a = (n + y)_\beta)$$
$$\frac{\gamma}{\beta}\,(0_\gamma + a = y_\beta)$$
$$\frac{\gamma}{\beta}\,(0_\gamma + a = n_\beta) \qquad (12)$$

You may be inclined to regard such a derivation as longwinded in comparison with other proofs unless you consider the demands which this proof satisfies and which are to be made of those other proofs if there is to be any point in the comparison. These demands are as follows:

(1) One may not stop at theorems less simple than those used above. If e.g. someone wished to use multiplication theorems here, he would first have to prove them from our two addition theorems.

(2) One may not appeal to intuition as a means of proof;* for it is a law of scientific economy to use no more devices than necessary.

(3) One must take care there are no gaps in the chain of inference. This would e.g. be violated even by the fact that only an example of a theorem was strictly speaking proved and its generalization left to the reader.

Precision and rigour are the prime aims of the concept-script; brevity will only be sought after if it can be achieved without jeopardizing those aims.

I now return once more to the examples mentioned earlier, so as to point out the sort of concept formation that is to be seen in those accounts. The fourth example gives us the concept of a multiple of 4, if we imagine the 12 in $\frac{\gamma}{\beta}\,(0_\gamma + 4 = 12_\beta)$ as replaceable by something else; the concept of the

────────────

* Whereas it is permissible to use intuition as a helpful expedient in pinning down an idea.

relation of a number of its multiple if we imagine the 4 as also replaceable; and the concept of a factor of 12 if we imagine the 4 alone as replaceable. The 8th example gives us the concept of the congruence of two numbers with respect to a modulus, the 13th that of the continuity of a function at a point etc. All these concepts have been developed in science and have proved their fruitfulness. For this reason what we may discover in them has a far higher claim on our attention than anything that our everyday trains of thought might offer. For fruitfulness is the acid test of concepts, and scientific workshops the true field of study for logic. Now it is worth noting in all this, that in practically none of these examples is there first cited the genus or class to which the things falling under the concept belong and then the characteristic mark of the concept, as when you define 'homo' as '*animal rationale*'. Leibniz has already noted that here we may also conversely construe '*rationale*' as genus and '*animal*' as species. In fact, by this definition '*homo*' is to be whatever is '*animal*' as well as being '*rationale*'.* If the circle *A* represents the extension of the concept '*animal*' and *B* that of '*rationale*', then the region common to the two circles corresponds to the extension of the concept '*homo*'. And it is all one whether I think of that as having been formed from the circle *A* by its intersection with *B* or vice versa. This construction corresponds to logical multiplication. Boole would express this, say, in the form $C = AB$, where *C* means the extension of the concept '*homo*'. You may also form concepts by logical addition. We have an example

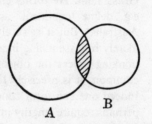

of this if we define the concept 'capital offence' as murder or the attempted murder of the Kaiser or of the ruler of one's own *Land* or of a German prince in his own *Land*. The area *A* signifies the extension of the concept 'murder', the area *B* that of the concept 'attempted murder of the Kaiser or of the ruler of one's own *Land* or of a German prince in his own *Land*'. Then the whole area of the two circles, whether they have a region in common or not, will represent the extension of the concept 'capital offence'. If we look at what we have in the diagrams, we notice that in both cases the boundary of the concept, whether it is one formed by logical multiplication or addition is

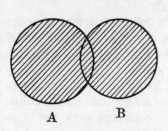

---

* Wundt in his *Logik* I, p. 224 does not concede this, but his own geometrical representation on p. 252 refutes him. One must always hold fast to the fact that a difference is only logically significant if it has an effect on possible inferences.

made up of parts of the boundaries of the concepts already given. This holds for any concept formation that can be represented by the Boolean notation. This feature of the diagrams is naturally an expression of something inherent in the situation itself, but which is hard to express without recourse to imagery. In this sort of concept formation, one must, then, assume as given a system of concepts, or speaking metaphorically, a network of lines. These really already contain the new concepts: all one has to do is to use the lines that are already there to demarcate complete surface areas in a new way. It is the fact that attention is principally given to this sort of formation of new concepts from old ones, while other more fruitful ones are neglected which surely is responsible for the impression one easily gets in logic that for all our to-ing and fro-ing we never really leave the same spot. Obviously, the more finely the original network of lines is drawn, the greater the possible set of new concepts. We might now fancy we could obtain all possible concepts if we took as our system of given concepts that of the individual objects (or, more precisely, a system of concepts under each of which only one object falls). This is in fact the course adopted by R. Grassmann. He forms classes or concepts by logical addition. He would e.g. define 'continent' as 'Europe or Asia [or Africa] or America or Australia'. But it is surely a highly arbitrary procedure to form concepts merely by assembling individuals, and one devoid of significance for actual thinking unless the objects are held together by having characteristics in common. It is precisely these which constitute the essence of the concept. Indeed one can form concepts under which no object falls, where it might perhaps require lengthy investigation to discover that this was so. Moreover a concept, such as that of number, can apply to infinitely many individuals. Such a concept would never be attained by logical addition. Nor finally may we presuppose that the individuals are given *in toto*, since some, such as e.g. the numbers,* are only yielded by thought.

If we compare what we have here with the definitions contained in our examples, of the continuity of a function and of a limit, and again that of following a series which I gave in § 26 of my *Begriffsschrift*, we see that there's no question there of using the boundary lines of concepts we already have to form the boundaries of the new ones. Rather, totally new boundary lines are drawn by such definitions—and these are the scientifically fruitful ones. Here too, we use old concepts to construct new ones, but in so doing we combine the old ones together in a variety of ways by means of the signs for generality, negation and the conditional.

I believe almost all errors made in inference to have their roots in the imperfection of the concepts. Boole presupposes logically perfect concepts as ready to hand, and hence the most difficult part of the task as having been

---

* That is to say, the number 3 is not to be regarded as a concept, since the question that falls under it is nonsense. Whereas tripleness—the property of being composed of three things—is a concept.

already discharged; he can then draw his inferences from the given assumptions by a mechanical process of computation. Stanley Jevons has in fact invented a machine to do this. But if we have perfect concepts whose content we do not need to refer back to, we can easily guard ourselves from error, even without computation. This is why Boolean logic disappoints the hopes which, in the light of all that has been achieved by using symbolism in mathematics, we might entertain of it; and not because those achievements are linked to the concept of magnitude. That is a view which has surely only arisen as a result of an over-hasty generalization from past experience. Boolean formula-language only represents a part of our thinking; our thinking as a whole can never be coped with by a machine or replaced by purely mechanical activity. It is true that the syllogism can be cast in the form of a computation, albeit one which cannot be performed without thinking. Still the fact that it follows a few fixed and perspicuous forms gives it a high degree of certainty. But we can only derive any real benefit from doing this, if the content is not just indicated but is constructed out of its constituents by means of the same logical signs as are used in the computation. In that case, the computation must quickly bring to light any flaw in the concept formations. But neither does this form any part of Boole's original plan, nor can his formula-language be subsequently adapted for this purpose. For even if its form made it better suited to reproduce a content than it is, the lack of a representation of generality corresponding to mine would make a true concept formation—one that didn't use already existing boundary lines—impossible. It was certainly also this defect which hindered Leibniz from proceeding further.

Now that I have spelled out the ways in which my concept-script goes beyond Boolean logic, and the consequences this brings in its wake, I will continue with my comparison, confining my attention to the domain common to the two formal languages. In this I can ignore Boole's first part.

In my case contents of possible judgements A and B are connected by the conditional stroke as in $\overset{\displaystyle -A}{\underset{\displaystyle B}{\llcorner}}$, in Boole's by equations, addition and multiplication. Of the four possibilities

$$\begin{array}{ll} \text{I} & A \text{ and } B \\ \text{II} & A \text{ and not } B \\ \text{III} & \text{not } A \text{ and } B \\ \text{IV} & \text{not } A \text{ and not } B, \end{array}$$

my $\overset{\displaystyle -A}{\underset{\displaystyle B}{\llcorner}}$ denies the third, Boole's identity sign the middle two; for Boole himself the addition sign denies the first and the last, for Leibniz and Stanley Jevons only the last; and finally the multiplication sign affirms the first possibility, and so denies the other three. The first thing one notices is that Boole uses a greater number of signs. Indeed I too have an identity sign, but I use it between contents of possible judgement almost exclusively to stipulate the sense of a new designation. Furthermore I now no longer regard it as a primitive sign but would define it by means of others. In that case there would be one sign of mine to three of Boole's. I follow the basic principle of introducing as few primitives as possible, not from any aversion to new signs—in that case, I would, like Boole, have endowed old ones with new meanings—but because it makes it difficult to survey the state of a science if the same thing is dressed up in different garbs. That seems to me the only reasonable ground for resisting new designations. This does not prevent the subsequent introduction of a simple sign for a very complicated combination of signs that occurs frequently. But then you don't lay down as primitive the sentences which hold for such signs, you derive them from their meanings. The more primitive signs you introduce, the more axioms you need. But it is a basic principle of science to reduce the number of axioms to the fewest possible. Indeed the essence of explanation lies precisely in the fact that a wide, possibly unsurveyable, manifold is governed by one or a few sentences. The value of an explanation can be directly measured by this condensation and simplification: it is zero if the number of assumptions is as great as the number of facts to be explained. Now, to arrive at the fewest possible primitive signs, I must choose those with the simplest possible meanings, just as in chemistry the only hope of decreasing the number of elements is further analysis. But the simpler a content is, the less it says. For instance, my conditional stroke, which only denies the third of the four cases, says less than the Boolean identity sign which denies the second as well. The multiplication sign says even more, because it denies the fourth possibility as well, eliminating all choice. Only the addition sign, like my conditional stroke, excludes only one case, if you adopt Stanley Jevons' improvement,* and it only is an improvement because it diminishes the content of the sign. Of course, in some cases, the result is more cumbersome formulae. The exclusive 'a or b', which Boole can simply express by $a + b$, has to be written by Schröder in the form $ab_1 + a_1 b$. But this only concerns particular cases. In general it is always the sign with the simplest content which is the most widely applicable and leads to the clearest way of putting things. A content which is a component part of another, as that of my conditional stroke is of Boole's identity sign (if we simply ignore the idea of the class of time instants), as that of the inclusive 'or' is of the exclusive, will probably occur in several other contexts beside this one; indeed it will probably occur more often in other contexts. Even if two contents of possible judgement do in fact stand in the exclusive 'or' relation, in many inferences what matters is that one of the two contents holds; for others it's only essential that they don't both hold; finally there will be a few inferences, but probably the smallest number, in which both facts are needed. And this still doesn't take any account of the fact that for the most part contents of possible judgement only stand in one of the two relations

---

* See note above on p. 10 [**].

anyway. Boole's identity sign does the work of two of my conditional strokes: $\dfrac{\ulcorner A}{\llcorner B}$ and $\dfrac{\ulcorner B}{\llcorner A}$. Here, as above, it is true that in many cases use will only be made of $\dfrac{\ulcorner A}{\llcorner B}$ or only of $\dfrac{\ulcorner B}{\llcorner A}$, in a few use will be made of both, and the fact is that the combination of precisely these two assumptions may not occur appreciably more frequently than any others. It might be held that we have to choose primitive signs with a simple content if only because we cannot express a content by means of signs with more content. But in fact it isn't impossible; it is only that a frequent construction will then be expressed by a more complex formula than one that is relatively uncommon. E.g. Boole for his part has to use a more cumbersome expression for Schroder's $a + b$, the inclusive '*a* or *b*'. But the exclusive 'or' perhaps only occurs once for every ten occurrences of the inclusive. So in chemistry everyone will regard it as more appropriate to represent the elements hydrogen and oxygen by single letters H and O, and to form OH from them, than to designate the hydroxyl complex OH by a single letter, while using a combination of signs to designate hydrogen as de-oxidized hydroxyl.

Now to obtain a sign joining two contents of possible judgement whose meaning was as simple as possible, I had four choices open, all from this point of view equally justified: I could have adopted as the meaning of such a sign the denial of any one of the four cases mentioned above. But it sufficed to choose one, since the four cases can be converted into one another by replacing A and B by their denials. To use a chemical metaphor, they are only allotropes of the same element. I chose the denial of the third case, because of the ease with which it can be used in inference, and because its content has a close affinity with the important relation of ground and consequent.

The fundamental principle of reducing the number of primitive laws as far as possible wouldn't be fully satisfied without a demonstration that the few left are also sufficient. It is this consideration which determined the form of the second and third sections of my book. Here too it would be wrong to suppose that a direct comparison with Boole's work is possible. In his case there is nothing remarkable in the attempt to manage everything with the fewest possible primitive laws. His only object is to find a brief and practical way to solve his problems. I sought as far as possible to translate into formulae everything that could also be expressed verbally as a rule of inference, so as not to make use of the same thing in different forms. Because modes of inference must be expressed verbally, I only used a single one by giving as formulae what could otherwise have also been introduced as modes of inference. This admittedly gave rise to a longwindedness which might appear pedantic. Not that it would not have been a simple matter for me to give the transitions a briefer form, as I have done in the examples given here and already indicated in the preface to my book. But it wasn't my intention to provide a sample of how to carry out such derivations in a brief and practical way: it was to show that I can manage throughout with my basic laws. Of course the fact that I managed with them in several cases could not render this more than probable. But it wasn't a matter of indifference which example I chose for my demonstration. So as not perhaps to overlook precisely those transformations which are of value in scientific use, I chose the step by step derivation of a sentence which, it seems to me, is indispensable to arithmetic, although it is one that commands little attention, being regarded as self-evident. The sentence in question is the following:

If a series is formed by first applying a many-one operation to an object (which need not belong to arithmetic), and then applying it successively to its own results, and if in this series two objects follow one and the same object, then the first follows the second in the series, or vice versa, or the two objects are identical.

I proved this sentence from the definitions of the concepts of following in a series, and of many-oneness by means of my primitive laws. In the process I derived the sentence that if in a series one member follows a second, and the second a third, then the first follows the third. Apart from a few formulae introduced to cater for Aristotelian modes of inference, I only assumed such as appeared necessary for the proof in question.

These were the principles which guided me in setting up my axioms and in the choice and derivation of other sentences. It was a matter of complete indifference to me whether a formula seemed interesting or to say nothing. That my sentences have enough content, in so far as you can talk of the content of sentences of pure logic at all, follows from the fact that they were adequate for the task. Sentences that were indispensable links in a chain of inference had to be assumed even if they contained superfluous conditions. We have a similar situation in Boolean computation. If there you multiply an equation through by a letter, you introduce into it something which is superfluous for its validity, and so reduce its content, just as when you add an unnecessary condition to a judgement. But there are times when such a diminution in content, far from being a loss, is a necessary point of transition in the development.

In accordance with my guiding principles, I also had to assume formulae which merely express the different ways in which you may alter the order of a number of conditions. Instead of giving a general rule that conditions may be ordered at random, I only introduced a much weaker axiom that two conditions may be interchanged, and then derived from this the permissibility of other transpositions. We have something similar in Boolean computation where it is a matter of changing the order of factors or summands. Schröder lays down the commutative and associative laws of multiplication and addition as axioms in his '*Operationskreise des Logik-kalkuls*', but doesn't derive from it for the case of more than three factors or summands that the order and grouping is arbitrary. But such proofs would be necessary, if you wished to prove in Boole's formal logic, as far as this is possible, the sentences derived by me, with an equally complete chain of inference. This wouldn't be afforded by 'mental multiplying out'. You also need the sentence that you may interchange two sides of an equation, and that equals may always be substituted for equals. Schröder does not include these among his thirteen axioms, although there is no justification for leaving them out, even if you regard them as self-evident truths of logic. And so he really uses fifteen axioms. In my *Begriffsschrift* I laid down nine axioms, to which we must add the rules set out in words, than in essentials are determined by the modes of designation adopted. They are as follows:

(1) What follows the content-stroke must be a content of possible judgement (p. 2).
(2) The rule of inference.
(3) Different gothic letters are to be chosen when one occurs within the scope of another* (p. 21).
(4) A rule for replacing roman letters by gothic (p. 21).
(5) A rule for exporting a condition outside the scope of a gothic letter (p. 21).

We may ignore here what I have to say about the use of Greek small letters, since it lies outside the domain within which we may compare the concept-script and Boole's formula-language. So with 14 primitive sentences I command a somewhat wider domain than does Schröder with 15. But I have since seen that the two basic laws for identity are completely dispensable, and that we may reduce the three basic laws for negation to two. After this simplification I need only 11 basic sentences. I see in this the success of my endeavour to have simple primitive constituents and proofs free from gaps. And so I replace the logical forms which in prose proliferate indefinitely by a few. This seems to me essential if our trains of thought are to be relied on; for only what is finite and determinate can be taken in at once, and the fewer the number of primitive sentences, the more perfect a mastery can we have of them.

Since, then, Boolean computations cannot be compared with the derivations I gave in the *Begriffsschrift*, it may not be out of place to introduce here an example where there can be a comparison. It would not be surprising and I could happily concede the point, if Boolean logic were better suited than my concept-script to solve the kind of problems it was specifically designed for, or for which it was specifically invented. But maybe not even this is the case. Since the question involved is for me one of slight importance, I will confine myself to using the concept-script to solve a problem that has been treated by Boole,** then by Schröder,*** and then Wundt,**** while very briefly indicating how it differs from Boole's method.

---

* Strictly, this rule is implicit in the first.
** *Op. cit.* pp. 146 f.
*** *Der Operationskreis des Logikkalkuls*, pp. 25 f.
**** *Logik* I, p. 356.

In Schröder's formulation, the problem is as follows. Suppose we observe a class of phenomena (natural kinds or artefacts, e.g. substances) and arrive at the following general results:

(α) If the characteristics or properties A and C are simultaneously absent from any of the phenomena, the property E is found together with either the property B or the property D but not both.

(β) Wherever A and D are found together in the absence of E, B and C are either both present or both absent.

(γ) Wherever A is found together with B or E or both, either C or D is to be found but not both. And conversely wherever one of C, D is found without the other, then A is to be found together with B or E or both.

We now have to find:

(1) What in general can be inferred about B, C and D from the presence of A,

(2) Whether any relations whatever hold between the presence or absence of B, C and D independently of the presence or absence of the remaining properties,

(3) What follows for A, C and D from the presence of B,

(4) What follows for A, C and D considered in themselves.

In the solution I use the corresponding Greek capitals so that e.g. *A* means the circumstance that the property A is to be found in the object under consideration.

I first translate the individual data.

(α) The denial of *A* and *Γ* has a consequence the affirmation of *E* (1).

$$\vdash\!\!\begin{array}{l}\llcorner E\\ \llcorner_\top A\\ \llcorner_\top \Gamma\end{array}\qquad(1)$$

The denial of *A* and *Γ* has as a consequence the affirmation of one of the two *B* or *Δ* (2);

$$\vdash\!\!\begin{array}{l}\llcorner B\\ \llcorner_\top \Delta\\ \llcorner_\top A\\ \llcorner_\top \Gamma\end{array}\qquad(2)$$

but it is impossible to have *B* and *Δ* together with the denial of *A* and *Γ* (3).

$$\vdash\!\!\begin{array}{l}\llcorner B\\ \llcorner \Delta\\ \llcorner_\top A\\ \llcorner_\top \Gamma\end{array}\qquad(3)$$

(β) If *A* and *Δ* are both to be affirmed and *E* denied, *B* and *Γ* are either both to be affirmed or both denied; that is, if *B* is affirmed, *Γ* is also to be affirmed (4);

$$\vdash\!\!\begin{array}{l}\llcorner \Gamma\\ \llcorner B\\ \llcorner A\\ \llcorner \Delta\\ \llcorner_\top E\end{array}\qquad(4)$$

but if *B* is denied, *Γ* is also to be denied (5).

(5)

(*γ*) I begin by breaking this down.

(*γ*₁) If *A* and *B* are affirmed, *Γ* or *Δ* is to be affirmed
(6) but not both (7).

(6)

(7)

(*γ*₂) The same result holds if *A* and *E* are affirmed:
(8) and (9).

(8)

(9)

(*γ*₃) If *Γ* is affirmed and *Δ* denied, *A* is to be affirmed
(10). Since *Γ* is already a condition one of the
two is also to be affirmed, for at least *Γ* is.[1]

(10)

---

[1] *γ*₃ and *γ*₄ are evidently faulty: no single interpretation will make them consistent either with the problem or for that matter internally. They do not even as they stand make clear sense. The most likely hypothesis to explain Frege's mistakes here is that while working at the problem, he sometimes approached it as it stands in the text, and sometimes following Schröder's version which contained a misprint of 'C' for 'E' in the last clause of (*γ*). E.g. the prose of *γ*₃ tallies with the Schröder misprinted version, but *γ*₄ is a hybrid of the two readings. The resulting formulae are

wrong in the sense that (10) needs supplementing by (10)′ and (12)

replacing by (12)′. (11) is written here, but not subsequently, by Frege in

the form which we have followed the German editors in emending as above.

There is a further slip in that Frege here writes his (12) with *A* for the *Δ*, where we have similarly corrected it. Luckily, despite this morass of confusion it has no effect on the solution of the problem: e.g. Frege makes no further use of his defective (12) and as far as we can see the formulae omitted by Frege would contribute nothing to the resolution of this problem. He does indeed get the problem right, although the correctness of his solution is put in jeopardy by the fact that he does not of course show that (10)′ and (12)′ yield nothing further of relevance to the questions asked. It does not seem worth exploring this minor and irritating matter further. (trans.)

(γ_4) If Γ is denied and Δ affirmed, A is to be affirmed
(11) and one of the two B or E is also to be
affirmed. Here that can only be B (12).

$$\begin{array}{l} \rule{0pt}{0pt} \\ \end{array} \quad \begin{array}{l} A \\ \top\ \Gamma \\ \Delta \end{array} \qquad (11)$$

$$\begin{array}{l} B \\ \top\ E \\ \Delta \end{array} \qquad (12)$$

These are the data. The first question is already answered in part by (6)
and (7). The remaining data yield no answers to this question, either because,
as in (2) or (3) they do not contain the affirmation of A but its denial as a
condition, or, as in (10), (11), (12), do not contain A as a condition at all,
or because, as in (4), (5), (8), (9) they contain E as well as A, B, Γ, Δ. The
question arises whether E could perhaps be eliminated from some of these
last. This can be done if E is a consequence in one judgement, as it is in (1),
and a condition in another as it is in (9). We then write (9) unaltered as
far as the condition E and replace this by the two conditions on which E
depends in (1). This yields (13). This judgement
is satisfied no matter what the meanings of A, Γ
and Δ, first because $\top\ \Gamma$ appears as a condition
of $\top\ \Gamma$ itself, and secondly because two of the
conditions, A and $\top\ A$, are contradictory. For
you obtain a truth by putting an arbitrary content
of possible judgement as the consequence of two

$$\begin{array}{l} \Gamma \\ \Delta \\ A \\ A \\ \top\ \Gamma \end{array} \qquad (13)$$

contradictory conditions.* Thus (13) gives no information about the contents A, Γ and Δ. We may proceed with (1) and (8) as with (1) and (9).
But we only have to glance at the formula to convince ourselves that we do
not get any information by doing this either, since the resulting formula
once again contains two contradictory conditions. Whereas in (8) and (9)
the affirmation of E occurs as a condition in both judgements, it cannot
be eliminated, but where its affirmation is a condition in one and its denial
in the other, as in (8) and (4) it may. That is, you can transform a judgement
with something denied as a condition by presenting the affirmation of the
condition denied as a consequence and making the denial of the original
consequence a condition.** So (4) and (5) may be transformed into

(14) and (15). Each of these two
judgements can now be combined with either of the judgements (8) and (9) in order to
eliminate E. We need only
glance at the formulae to

$$\begin{array}{l} E \\ \top\ \Gamma \\ B \\ A \\ \Delta \end{array} \qquad (14) \qquad\qquad \begin{array}{l} E \\ \top\ \Gamma \\ B \\ A \\ \Delta \end{array} \qquad (15)$$

---

* *Begriffsschrift* Formula (36), p. 45.
** *Begriffsschrift Formulae* (33) and (34), pp. 44 f.

convince ourselves that, as above, the results to be obtained from (8) and (14), (8) and (15), and (9) and (14) do not tell us anything which doesn't hold independently of the contents. But from (9) and (15) we obtain the formula opposite. Here the antecedents that occur twice over, A and Δ, can be assimilated. The two Γ can also be assimilated by first, as before making B the consequence and Γ the condition and now dropping one of the Γs (16). This is the third answer to the first question and the judgements (6), (7) and (16) contain everything that is to

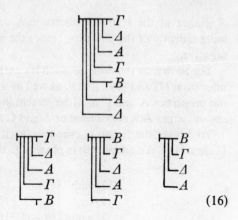

$$(16)$$

be obtained from the data in answer to the first question. At most, it might still be possible to give the results in a different form by eliminating a letter—B, say. (6) and (16) yield no result of value. (7) and (16) give us the formula alongside; which gives us (17) when simplified as above. This tells us that when the property A is present, the properties C and D exclude one another. (6) then shows that one of the two properties C and D is present when, besides A, B is also present.

$$(17)$$

I move on to the second question. To decide whether any relations hold between B, Γ and Δ independently of A and E, we must eliminate the latter from the data and see whether the results contain anything other than logical platitudes. Instead of the data containing E we may straight off use the formula (16) we have already discovered. We have accordingly to eliminate A from (2), (3), (6), (7), (10), (11) and (16). We begin by transforming (2) and (3) into (18) and (19).

$$(18) \qquad (19)$$

We may now combine

(6) with (10) or (7) with (10) or (16) with (10) or
(6) with (11) or (7) with (11) or (16) with (11) or

(6) with (17) or (7) with (17) or (16) with (17) or
(6) with (18) or (7) with (18) or (16) with (18).

A glance at the formulae shows that these pairs yield results that hold independently of the contents. Hence the second question is to be answered negatively.

The answer to the third question is contained in (6), (7) and (19). We may infer from (7) and (19), that if, as well as B, the property D is present, one of the properties A and C must be present, but not both. (6) shows that if D is absent, either A is also absent or A and C are both present.

To answer the fourth question we need to eliminate *B* from (2), (3), (6), (7) and (16). We adopt (19) in place of (3). Of the possible combinations

(2) with (6),	(16) with (6),
(2) with (7),	(16) with (7),
(2) with (19),	(16) with (19)

only the last but one is of any use, and has already been used to give us (17). So the answer to the fourth question is that the properties A, C and D cannot all be present at once, and that as (10) and (11) show, the presence of one of the properties C and D without the other implies the presence of A.

This solution requires practically no theoretical preparation at all. I have accompanied the account with every rule required for solving the problem, and this may have created the impression of a greater length than the true one. So I will now collate the data and computation in brief and in a surveyable form:

Data

Computation

$$
\begin{array}{lll}
4 \quad
\begin{array}{l}
\vdash \Gamma \\
\;\vdash B \\
\;\vdash A \\
\;\vdash \Delta \\
\;\top E
\end{array}
&
[5] \quad
\begin{array}{l}
\vdash \Gamma \\
\;\vdash B \\
\;\vdash A \\
\;\vdash \Delta \\
\;\top E
\end{array}
&
3 \quad
\begin{array}{l}
\vdash B \\
\;\vdash \Delta \\
\;\top A \\
\;\top \Gamma
\end{array}
\\[2em]
\times & (9): \; \cdot\!-\!\cdot\!-\!\cdot\!-\!\cdot & \times
\\[1em]
\begin{array}{l}
\vdash E \\
\;\top \Gamma \\
\;\vdash B \\
\;\vdash A \\
\;\vdash \Delta \quad (14)
\end{array}
&
\begin{array}{l}
\vdash \Gamma \\
\;\vdash B \\
\;\vdash A \\
\;\vdash \Delta \quad (16')
\end{array}
&
\begin{array}{l}
\vdash A \\
\;\vdash B \\
\;\vdash \Delta \\
\;\top \Gamma \quad (19)
\end{array}
\\[2em]
&
(7): \; \cdot\!-\!\cdot\!-\!\cdot\!-\!\cdot &
\\
&
\begin{array}{l}
\vdash \Gamma \\
\;\vdash \Delta \\
\;\vdash A \quad (17)
\end{array}
&
\end{array}
$$

Here the $\times$ between two formulae indicates the transition spelt out above. The sign $\cdot\!-\!\cdot\!-\!\cdot$ that stands between (5) and (16′) and between (16′) and (17) indicates a rule that abbreviates the other route followed above. It runs as follows:

If two judgements (e.g. (5) and (9)) have a common consequence ($\top\Gamma$), and one has a condition contradicting a condition of the other (E and $\top E$), we may form a new judgement (16′), by attaching to the common consequence ($\top\Gamma$), the conditions of the two original judgements ((5) and (9)) minus the contradictory ones (E and $\top E$), but in which conditions common to both judgements are only written once (A and Δ).

(16′) isn't essentially different from (16).

The answer to the first question is contained in (6) and (17);
The answer to the third question is contained in (6), (7) and (19);
The answer to the fourth question is contained in (10), (11) and (17);
The answer to the second question is in the negative.

Whereas the dominant procedure in Boole is the unification of different judgements into a single expression, I analyse the data into simple judgements, which are then in part already answers to the questions. I then select from the simple judgements those lending themselves to the eliminations needed, and so arrive at the rest of the answers. These will then only contain what we wanted to find out.

I believe that I have in this way shown that if in fact science were to require the solution of such problems, the concept-script can cope with them without any difficulty. But we see too that, in all this, its real power, which resides in the designation of generality, the concept of a function, in the possibility of putting more complicated expressions in the positions here occupied by simple letters, in no way comes into its own.

We may finally add a remark about the externals of my concept-script.

Schröder reproaches me for deviating from the normal way of writing from left to right in writing from above downwards. In fact I am in complete accord with usual practice; for in an arithmetical derivation too we put the individual equations in succession one beneath the other. But every equation is a content of possible judgement, or a judgement, as is every inequality, congruence etc. Now what I set beneath one another are also contents of possible judgement, or judgements. It is only when the simple contents of possible judgement are indicated by single letters that we have this appearance of something odd. As soon as they are spelt out, as they almost always are in actual use, each one is extended in a line from left to right, and they are severally written one beneath another. We thus make use of the advantage that a formal language, laid out in two dimensions on the written page, has over spoken language, which unfolds in the one dimension of time. Boole does not need to take up a line for each single content of possible judgement, because he has no thought of presenting them at greater length than by a single letter. This has the consequence that it would be extremely difficult to grasp what was going on, if one wished subsequently to introduce whole formulae in place of these single letters.

I believe in this essay I have shown:

(1) My concept-script has a more far-reaching aim than Boolean logic, in that it strives to make it possible to present a content when combined with arithmetical and geometrical signs.

(2) Disregarding content, within the domain of pure logic it also, thanks to the notation for generality, commands a somewhat wider domain than Boole's formula-language.

(3) It avoids the division in Boolean logic into two parts (primary and secondary propositions) by construing judgements as prior to concept formation.

(4) It is in a position to represent the formations of the concepts actually needed in science, in contrast to the relatively sterile multiplicative and additive combinations we find in Boole.

(5) It needs fewer primitive signs for logical relations and hence fewer primitive laws.

(6) It can be used to solve the sort of problems Boole tackles, and even do so with fewer preliminary rules for computation. This is the point to which I attach least importance, since such problems will seldom, if ever, occur in science.

Boole's logical Formula-language and my Concept-script[1]

[1882]

Since this journal[2] has already devoted some attention to the Boolean presentation of logical laws by means of equations, I hope that a comparison of it with another way of designating logical relations, proposed by me,* will not be unwelcome. First, however, I would like to stress that the aim of my concept-script is different from that of Boolean logic. I wanted to supplement the formula-language of mathematics with signs for logical relations so as to create a concept-script which would make it possible to dispense with words in the course of a proof, and thus ensure the highest degree of rigour whilst at the same time making the proofs as brief as possible. For this purpose the signs I introduced had to be such as were suitable for combining of themselves with those ordinarily employed in mathematics. The Boolean signs (in part stemming from Leibniz) are completely unsuited to this, which is scarcely to be wondered at when you consider their purpose; they are merely meant to present the logical form with no regard whatever for the content. I think it is necessary to preface my remarks in this way to guard against the false impression that one could validly compare the two scripts in every respect.

It is only the second part of Boolean logic—the part dealing with *secondary propositions*—that I wish to investigate here, leaving open the possibility of my taking the comparison further on another occasion. By *secondary propositions* Boole understands hypothetical, disjunctive, and in general such judgements as state a relation between contents of possible judgement, as opposed to the *primary propositions*, in which concepts are set in relation to one another. I make a distinction between judgement and content of possible judgement, reserving the first word for cases where such a content is put forward as true.

If, therefore, it is a question of setting two contents of possible judgement

---

* *Begriffsschrift*, Halle a.S. 1879.

---

[1] In all probability this essay contains the content of a manuscript returned to Frege by R. Avenarius with the letter of 20/4/1882. Avenarius there cites the title as 'Boole's logical formula-language' and rejects the manuscript for the *Vierteljahrsschrift für wissenschaftliche Philosophie* (ed.).
[2] *Vierteljahrsschrift für wissenschaftliche Philosophie.*

A and *B* in relation, we have to hold before our minds the following cases:

$$A \text{ and } B,$$
$$A \text{ and not } B,$$
$$\text{not } A \text{ and } B,$$
$$\text{not } A \text{ and not } B.$$

These cases can for their part be either affirmed or denied. Now Boole has the equals sign

$$A = B,$$

the addition sign

$$A + B,$$

the multiplication sign

$$A \cdot B,$$

and subtraction sign

$$A - B.$$

We may here disregard logical division as less important.

The equals sign for Boole affirms the denial of the two middle cases, so that the cases left open are '*A* and *B*' and 'not *A* and not *B*'. In '*A* = 1' and '*B* = 0' the assertoric force of the identity sign stands out unalloyed. The first equation puts *A* forward as true, the second *B* as false. For Boole '*A* + *B*' means the denial of the first and the last cases, leaving open the two middle ones. You can translate it as '*A* or *B*', where 'or' is to be understood in the exclusive sense. Leibniz and some of Boole's followers, such as S. Jevons and E. Schröder, have kept the meaning of the inclusive 'or' for the + sign. In that case only the last of the four cases is denied by '*A* + *B*'. '*A*·*B*' means the first case, '*A* and *B*'. The denial of a content of possible judgement is expressed by Boole by means of '1 − *A*', and by others in other ways. To this is added the above-mentioned '*A* = 0' for the case where the denial is expressed as a judgement. Some people have a further sign for inequality, which also includes a denial. What strikes one in all this is the superfluity of signs. This, in its turn, entails a superfluity of primitive rules for computation. The reason for this lies doubtless in the desire to force on logic signs borrowed from an alien discipline, instead of taking one's departure from logic itself and its own requirements.

I have followed another path, by giving to each primitive sign as simple a meaning as possible. If, given two designations, one says all that is meant by the other, but not conversely, I call the meaning of the second simpler than that of the first because it has less content. If we now apply this yardstick we see that the simplest relation of two contents of possible judgement results from denying one of the four cases

A and B,

A and not B,

not A and B,

not A and not B,

for the denial of two of these cases says more than that of one on its own, and the denial of three even more: it is tantamount to the affirmation of the fourth case. None of the Boolean signs meets the requirement that the meaning is the simplest possible. It is only met by the + sign in the sense adopted E. Schröder,* of the inclusive 'or'. The advantage of the latter makes itself immediately felt in the greater adaptability of the formulae when compared with Boole's. I don't understand how W. Schlötel** can find anything slovenly in this. This objection would only be justified if the meaning, once adopted, were not adhered to in what followed. Whether a special sign is adopted for the inclusive 'or' or not is merely a question of convenience. Now the exclusive 'A or B' contains two things:

1. That one of the two obtains
2. That they don't both obtain.

Since these two don't always go together, since rather, by the laws of probability, their combination is rarer than either on its own, it is more convenient for the individual cases which occur more frequently to have signs of their own that it is for their combination, which is relatively uncommon. And even when A and B do stand in the exclusive 'or' relation, almost invariably only one of the two will come into consideration in a given inference: either that A and B are not both false, or that they are not both true. For the rarer exclusive 'A or B', Boole has the simple designation '$A + B$', for the commoner inclusive 'A or B', the complex expression '$A + B(1 - A)$'. In the case of Schröder the converse is true: he renders the former by '$AB_1 + A_1B$', the latter by '$A + B$'. The suffix 1 here means a denial, so that A_1 means the denial of A.

The Boolean '$A = B$' contains three things:

1. that A doesn't obtain without B,
2. that B doesn't obtain without A;
3. the judgement that this is so.

Here too the combination is given the honour of a simple designation, while the constituent elements have to be content with complex expressions.

As the affirmation of the first case, Boole's logical product '$A \cdot B$' means the denial of the last three of our cases, and so is very rich in content. However this designation is more convenient than the others, since we obtain a simple content by mere denial of such a product.

If one wishes to avoid the defect in the Boolean signs we have just

---

* *Der Operationskreis des Logikkalkuls.* Leipzig 1877.
** *Vierteljahrsschrift für wissenschaftl. Philos.* I, p. 456.

emphasized, one must introduce a special designation for the denial of one of the four cases set out above. It is enough for this purpose to select a single one of those cases for by using a negation sign one can obtain from each of the four cases any other. If, for instance, we put Γ for the denial of A those four cases then run:

not Γ and B,

not Γ and not B,

Γ and B,

Γ and not B;

that is the first case has assumed the form of the third, the second that of the fourth, and conversely the third that of the first, the fourth that of the second. If now it is possible to manage with one single sign which denies one of the four cases, we ought to do so, for the fewer primitive signs one introduces, the fewer primitive laws one needs, and the easier it will be to master the formulae.

Now, I have chosen the third case 'not A and B' as the one whose denial receives a special sign:

$$\vdash\!\!\begin{array}{l}A\\B\end{array}$$

To form the denials of the remaining cases, I make use of the negation-stroke, a small vertical stroke attached beneath one of the horizontal strokes. So

$$\vdash\!\!\begin{array}{l}A\\B\end{array}$$

means the denial of 'not not A and B', i.e. of 'A and B',

$$\vdash\!\!\begin{array}{l}A\\B\end{array}$$

the denial of the case 'A and not B',

$$\vdash\!\!\begin{array}{l}A\\B\end{array}$$

the denial of the case 'not A and not B'.

If the cases are to be affirmed, instead of denied, this is done by means of a negation-stroke attached to the left hand end of the uppermost horizontal stroke. Accordingly

$$\vdash\!\!\begin{array}{l}A\\B\end{array}$$

means 'not A and B',

$$\vdash\!\!\begin{array}{l}A\\B\end{array}$$

'A and B',

$$\text{⌐⌐}\begin{array}{l} A \\ B \end{array}$$

'A and not B', and finally

$$\text{⌐⌐}\begin{array}{l} A \\ B \end{array}$$

'not A and not B'. It is easy to see that you can translate

$$\text{⌐}\begin{array}{l} A \\ B \end{array}$$

by 'A or B' in the inclusive sense, and

$$\text{⌐⌐}\begin{array}{l} A \\ B \end{array}$$

by 'neither A nor B'.

Nothing is yet asserted, no judgement is made, by all these designations; only a new content of possible judgement is formed from given ones. Now in order to put a content forward as true, I make use of a small vertical stroke, the judgement stroke, as in

$$\vdash\!\!-3^2 = 9$$

whereby the truth of the equation is asserted, whereas in $-\!\!-3^2 = 9$ no judgement has been made. Hence since the judgement stroke is lacking, we can even write down $-\!\!-3^2 = 4$ without saying anything untrue. If we include the negation-stroke, we can add the judgement stroke too without falling into error

$$\vdash\!\!\top 3^2 = 4$$

means: 3^2 is not equal to 4

By

$$\vdash\!\!\sqsubset\begin{array}{l} 1^2 = 4 \\ 1 + 3 = 5 \end{array}$$

the fact that the case that 1^2 is not equal to 4 and that $1 + 3 = 5$ does not obtain is asserted; and this rightly, since $1 + 3$ simply is not equal to 5. Likewise it is correct to put the judgement stroke in

$$\vdash\!\!\sqsubset\begin{array}{l} 2^2 = 4 \\ 2 + 3 = 5 \end{array}$$

because the case that 2^2 is not equal to 4 and $2 + 3 = 5$, does not obtain; for, of course $2^2 = 4$. Similarly

$$\vdash\!\!\sqsubset\begin{array}{l} (-2)^2 = 4 \\ -2 + 3 = 5 \end{array}$$

is right for two reasons: because $(-2)^2 = 4$, and because $-2 + 3$ does not equal 5. Whatever number you may put in the place of the 1 in

$$\vdash \begin{array}{l} 1^2 = 4 \\ 1 + 3 = 5 \end{array}$$

the content is always correct. To express this general assertion, I use a roman letter:

$$\vdash \begin{array}{l} x^2 = 4 \\ x + 3 = 5 \end{array}$$

You can also render this: if $x + 3 = 5$, then $x^2 = 4$. And so we have here a hypothetical judgement. And the outstanding importance of this judgement has persuaded me to give the sign

$$\vdash \begin{array}{l} A \\ B \end{array}$$

precisely the meaning of the denial of the case 'not A and B'. Of course this alone doesn't yet give us a genuine hypothetical judgement: that arises only when A and B have in common an indefinite component which makes the situation described general.

I believe I have now adequately shown, that, as is proper, I divide the different tasks with which Boole burdens the one sign among several signs, without thereby increasing the total number of signs. The signs which I have also introduced elsewhere may be ignored in this context, since I am restricting myself to what corresponds to Boole's *secondary propositions*. As against his addition, subtraction, multiplication and equals signs, and his 0 and 1, we have:

1. The horizontal 'content-stroke',
2. The negation-stroke,
3. The vertical stroke that combines two content-strokes, 'the conditional-stroke',
4. The vertical judgement-stroke.

Here, I haven't counted Boole's division sign and other numbers besides 0 and 1, since these are easier to dispense with.

[Dialogue with Pünjer on Existence][1]

[Before 1884]

[I. *The Dialogue*]

1. *Pünjer:* 'Something does not have the characteristic of flying, but does
fall under the concept "bird"': does this have the same meaning
as 'Among what *is*, is something that does not have the
characteristic of flying, but does fall under the concept "bird"'?
2. *Frege:* What does *is* mean?
3. *P.* It means *can be experienced* (by us).
4. *F.* Is it not pleonastic to say of something that it can be
experienced?
5. *P.* No, since by manipulating at will the ideas derived from
experience, we are able to form ideas to which nothing that can
be experienced corresponds.
6. *F.* Is it *A* or the idea of *A* that is the real, as opposed to the
grammatical, subject in the sentence '*A* is something that can
be experienced'.
7. *P.* *A*.
8. *F.* 'The statement "*A* cannot be experienced" is the negation of the
statement "*A* can be experienced"'. Is that correct?
9. *P.* Yes, if by '*A* cannot be experienced' is understood: the sentence
'*A* can be experienced' is false.
10. *P.* The statement '*A* cannot be experienced' is not possible.
Therefore the question is nonsensical. Neither does it make
sense to deny that a thing can be experienced.
11. *F.* In that case it seems to me pleonastic to say of something that
it can be experienced.
12. *P.* 'There are men' means 'To the concept *man* there corresponds
something that can be experienced'. Or 'One of the things that

---

[1] Frege's partner in the dialogue is the protestant theologian Bernard Pünjer
(1850–1885), who held a chair at Jena from 1880. Both the parenthetical remark at
84 and the style of Pünjer's contributions leave no doubt that what we have in I is
the record of a dialogue which actually took place. According to comments on the
copies that have been preserved, the manuscript to II was found in an envelope
together with the transcript of the dialogue.
Frege's own more rigorous treatment of the theme in the *Grundlagen* (§ 53)
provides a clue for dating the two manuscripts. In any case the date of Pünjer's
death sets an upper limit to the time of composition (ed.).

can be experienced falls under the concept *man*. 'There are no centaurs' means 'To the idea or concept *centaur* there corresponds nothing that can be experienced'.

13. *F.*   Here the negation goes with the 'corresponds'.

14. *P.*   Yes. Or none of the things which can be experienced fall under the concept *centaur*.

15. *F.*   To say of a thing that it can be experienced is not to characterize it in any way.

16. *P.*   No. That is the difference between this statement and the others.

17. *F.*   It still seems to me therefore as if it is pleonastic to say of something that it can be experienced, because by saying this we learn nothing new about the subject. You just explained 'There are' and why such judgements are not pleonastic, but you did not explain why the judgement 'This can be experienced' is not pleonastic.

18. *P.*   'This can be experienced' means 'The idea of the "this" is not an hallucination, it is not something which originates from myself alone; but the idea has been formed as a result of the ego's being affected by the this'.

19. *F.*   So you distinguish two kinds of ideas?

20. *P.*   Yes; there are two kinds of idea: those that originate from the ego alone, and those that are formed through something affecting the ego. In order to distinguish these I say: the objects of ideas of the latter kind can be experienced; to ideas of the former kind there do not correspond any objects that can be experienced.

21. *F.*   It seems to me then as if the real subject on your way of thinking is the idea. Do you not admit that in every substantive statement the real subject is assigned to a class and is thereby distinguished from other things that do not belong to that class?

22. *P.*   I admit that; but a statement of existence is not a substantive one. I do not admit it if by 'substantive' is understood 'not self-evident', 'not containing a purely logical law'.

23. *F.*   When you say 'There are men' and 'There are no centaurs' you are also making a classification. But you are not classifying things, which in one case are not there at all, and in the other case are not being assigned to one of two classes, but you are classifying the concepts 'man' and 'centaur' by assigning one to the class of concepts under which something falls, and excluding the other from this class. This is why I hold that in these sentences the concepts are the real subjects. If you say 'This can be experienced', where this has the sense 'This idea of mine is not something originating from myself alone', then you

are classifying the idea. You are assigning it to one of the two kinds that you distinguished earlier. This is why I maintain that it is here the idea that is the real subject. Another way of putting the same thing is to say: The idea has the property that something corresponds to it.

24. *P.*   At this point the question arises of what negation is. Negation is possible only when something has already been posited. Hence if we say 'Centaurs do not exist', this is possible only because we first think of them as being outside ourselves. We have a twofold ground for denying existence: 1. a logical contradiction, 2. outside the concept or idea in experience.[1] So properly speaking the real subject is neither the concept nor the idea.

25. *F.*   In saying this you are only citing the ground on which we base a judgement about existence. One can also derive a judgement like 'There are square roots of 4' from the concept of the square root of 4.

26. *P.*   'There are square roots of 4' does not mean 'there is something that can be experienced which falls under the concept square root of 4', if we understand by what can be experienced something self-subsistent, something existing in its own right. Numbers exist only in something. Hence this judgement is essentially different from the judgement 'there are men'. I shall never say '4 exists'. And equally I shall not say 'a square root of 4 exists'. Here the 'there is' is used in a different sense. It means: it is a property of 4 that it can result from multiplying a number by itself, that one can find a number which yields 4 when multiplied by itself. We can only make the judgement after we have formed the proposition $2^2 = 4$ (or $(-2)^2 = 4$). This is what it has in common with the other existential judgements such as 'there are men'.

27. *F.*   It was earlier objected to me with the example 'there are square roots of 4' that this is an existential judgement. Now you seem not to count it as such, because you do not want to say 'A square root of 4 exists'.

28. *P.*   'There are square roots of 4' is an existential judgement.

---

29. *F.*   (on 18) The proposition 'The idea of the this has been formed as a result of the ego's being affected by the this' is self-evident, if it is possible without absurdity to formulate its content at all; for we cannot use the expression 'The idea of this' before we have made the judgement 'Something corresponds to this idea of mine' or 'This idea of mine has been formed as a result of

---

[1] These are the words as they occur in the manuscript (ed.).

something affecting the ego'. Only then can we assign the name 'this' to what has done the affecting, to what corresponds to my idea.

30. *P.*   'The idea of the this has been formed as a result of the ego's being affected by the this' is only another way of saying 'To this idea of mine there corresponds something that can be experienced'.

31. *F.*   I understand your remark (20) in the following way: If you want to say that *B* is an idea that does not originate from the ego alone, but is formed through something affecting the ego, then you use the words 'The object of *B* can be experienced'. The two sentences are synonymous. Is that right?

32. *P.*   Instead of '*B* is an idea that etc.' I should say 'The idea *B* is etc.', assuming straight off that *B* is an idea.

33. *F.*   I grant that it is not self-evident and pleonastic to say 'The idea *B* does not originate from the ego alone, but is formed through something affecting the ego'; for not every idea is formed through something affecting the ego; at least the point is a debatable one. The negation of this sentence would be 'The idea *B* is not formed through something affecting the ego' if we assume that *B* is an idea. In that case the negation has a perfectly good sense and hence it is not pleonastic and self-evident to utter the sentence 'The idea *B* is formed through something affecting the ego' or the sentence 'The object of *B* can be experienced', which you maintain to have the same meaning. But if these sentences have the same meaning, then in the judgement 'The negation of the sentence "The idea *B* is formed through something affecting the ego" has a good sense' we may replace 'The idea *B* is formed through something affecting the ego' by 'The object of *B* can be experienced'. We then obtain the judgement: The negation of the sentence 'The object of *B* can be experienced' has a good sense. This contradicts your earlier position.

34. *P.*   There is no contradiction in calling the negation of the statement 'The object of the idea *B* can be experienced' legitimate, but the negation of the statement 'The object *B* can be experienced' illegitimate.

35. *F.*   If I understand you rightly, the contradiction is resolved as follows: In the expression 'The object of the idea' the word 'object' is used in a different sense from in 'The object *A* can be experienced'.

36. *P.*   No. The word 'object' has the same meaning, but 'object of an idea' means something different from 'object'.

37. *F.*   Does adding 'of an idea' merely serve to restrict the sense?

38. *P.*   'Object' by itself means object that is not merely object of an

idea, but of experience. The contrast to draw should really be that between object of an idea and object of experience.

---

39. *P.*   (referring to 26 & 27) Number cannot be experienced in the same sense as Paul.

40. *F.*   So you distinguish two senses of 'can be experienced'?

41. *P.*   No. Number can be experienced in the same general sense. The concept of that which can be experienced is in both cases the same; it is the same whether I say number, thing or colour can be experienced.

42. *F.*   You do not always understand by 'can be experienced' something that can be experienced on its own?

43. *P.*   What cannot be experienced on its own can still be experienced, as e.g. a colour, which can only be experienced in something.

44. *F.*   You said (26) that you would not say '4 exists'. Are you here using 'exist' in the same sense as 'capable of being experienced'?

45. *P.*   Yes, I take it back that I would not say '4 exists', 'a square root of 4 exists'.

46. *F.*   The difference between the judgements 'There are men' and 'There are square roots of 4' does not lie in the 'there are' but in the difference between the concepts 'man' and 'square root of 4'. We understand by a man something that exists in its own right, but we do not understand this by a square root of 4.

47. *P.*   I agree with that.

48. *F.*   Is the sentence '*A* can be experienced' right, if *A* is taken to be an idea?

49. *P.*   Yes. An idea can be experienced.

50. *F.*   Is there an idea of an idea?

51. *P.*   There are ideas of ideas.

52. *F.*   You once referred to an idea as a fluctuating image, a series of inner perceptions. What are the inner perceptions out of which the idea of the idea *A* is formed?

53. *P.*   They are the particular mental acts performed in having the idea *A*.

54. *F.*   Do 'act of forming an idea' and 'idea' mean the same?

55. *P.*   Yes.

56. *F.*   So we are wrong to distinguish the act of forming an idea from an idea.

57. *P.*   Yes.

58. *F.*   From your remarks (18) and (20) it follows that 'This can be experienced' has the same meaning as 'To this idea of mine there corresponds something that can be experienced'. Here 'can be experienced' is defined in terms of itself.

59. *P.*   But it isn't meant to be a definition. I still maintain that the expression 'The idea of the this' can always be used.

60. *F.*   Has every idea an object?

61. *P.*   Yes. Every idea has of necessity an object. 'object of an idea' is the same as 'content of an idea'.

62. *F.*   Is the content of the idea *A* the same as *A*?

63. *P.*   No. What is represented in the idea is the fluctuating image. To be exact, it should be distinguished from the idea. What is represented does not include the mental act.

64. *F.*   Is the object of an idea different from what is represented in it?

65. *P.*   Yes.

66. *F.*   If you see a *Fata morgana* or have an hallucination, what then is the object of your idea?[1] (no reply).

---

67. *F.*   Do you admit that the negation of the sentence 'The object of *B* can be experienced' has a good sense?

68. *P.*   Yes.

69. *F.*   Do you admit that one can give the name *A* to the object of the idea *B*?

70. *P.*   Yes.

71. *F.*   Then you admit that the negation of the sentence '*A* can be experienced' has a good sense.

72. *P.*   Yes. But in your question (8) *A* was understood not as an object of an idea, but as an object of experience.

73. *F.*   I didn't say of *A* that it was meant to be an object of an idea or an object of experience; I left the matter quite open. That is why I understood your answer (10) more generally that you now seem to understand it. However, since I had used the expression 'idea of *A*' in (6), the suggestion was rather that *A* be understood as an object of an idea.

74. *P.*   But surely *A* was there expressly understood to be an object of experience.

75. *F.*   I don't see that. Perhaps we can take things further by asking: Do you admit that there are objects of ideas, where these ideas have not been caused by something affecting the ego?

---

[1] This part of the dialogue—from 52 onwards—is particularly obscure. Because there are clear Kantian overtones in the use here of '*Vorstellung*' ('idea') and '*Anschauung*' ('inner perception'), it might be thought better to have translated the former by 'representation' and the latter by 'intuition'. It is, however, doubtful whether the use of overt Kantian terminology would have made things any clearer. Fortunately, we do not need to understand Pünjer at this point in order to follow the objections that Frege later brings against him (trans.).

76.	*P.*	Yes.
77.	*F.*	Do you admit that objects of ideas which have not been caused by something affecting the ego do not exist?
78.	*P.*	Yes.
79.	*F.*	Then it follows that there are objects of ideas—ideas which have not been caused by something affecting the ego—which do not exist. Now if you are using the word 'exists' in the same sense as the expression 'there is', then you have at the same time both asserted and denied the same predicate of the same subject. The inference is valid; for the concept 'objects of ideas which have not been caused by something affecting the ego' is exactly the same in both premises, and is exactly the same as it is in the conclusion. Do you grant this?
80.	*P.*	Yes. But the word 'there is' is wrongly used in this context.
81.	*F.*	Then put in its place another expression that will express the matter better.
82.	*P.*	We can't: any other expression would again fail to say what is meant to be expressed.
83.	*F.*	So in your opinion we have here a contradiction in the nature of things—one to which reason is necessarily captive; for we cannot get rid of it by merely changing the mode of expression.
84.	*P.*	Before we deny the existence of anything whatever, we have to represent it as existing in order to go on to deny existence of it. But I don't think that we shall get any further along these lines. How do you explain 'there are men'?
		(What follows this is left out, because we went round in a circle, coming back again to the question:)
85.	*P.*	How do you explain 'There are living beings'?
86.	*F.*	As follows: the statement that A, no matter what I take A to be, does not fall under the concept 'living being' is false.
87.	*P.*	What are we supposed to have in mind by A?
88.	*F.*	The meaning I assign to A is not meant to be subject to any restriction at all. If I am meant to say anything about it, it can only be something self-evident, such as $A = A$.
89.	*P.*	The mistake rests on the fact that you continue to think of A as a thing that has being, with the consequence that you are simply presupposing the 'there is'.
90.	*F.*	A is not subject to the restriction that it is something that has being, unless we understand by has being something that goes without saying, in which case the restriction is no restriction.
91.	*P.*	What is 'going without saying'?
92.	*F.*	I say a statement goes without saying if it does nothing to qualify the thing it is made about.
93.	*P.*	You only recognize statements that are made about something?
94.	*F.*	'There are statements which are not made about anything'

would mean 'There are judgements in which there is no distinguishing subject and predicate'.

95. *P.*   What do you understand by a thing of which a statement can be made?

96. *F.*   What can be made into the subject of a judgement.

[97.] *F.*   'Some men are Germans' means the same as 'There are German men'. As from 'Sachse is a man' there follows 'There are men' so from 'Sachse is a man' and 'Sachse is a German' there follows 'Some men are German' or 'there are German men'.

[98.] *P.*   'Some men are Germans' does not mean the same as 'There are German men'. 'There are men' cannot be inferred from 'Sachse is a man' alone; you need the further sentence 'Sachse exists' as well.

[99. *F.*]   My reply to this would be: If 'Sachse exists' is supposed to mean 'The word "Sachse" is not an empty sound, but designates something', then it is true that the condition 'Sachse exists' must be satisfied. But this is not a new premise, but the presupposition of all our words—a presupposition which goes without saying. The rules of logic always presuppose that the words we use are not empty, that our sentences express judgements, that one is not playing a mere game with words. Once 'Sachse is a man' expresses an actual judgement, the word 'Sachse' must designate something, and in that case I do not need a further premise in order to infer 'There are men' from it. The premise 'Sachse exists' is redundant, if it is to mean something different from the above-mentioned presupposition of all our thinking. Can you furnish an example where a sentence of the form '*A* is a *B*' has a sense and is true—*A* being the name of an individual—whilst 'there are *B*'s' is false? 'Some men are Germans' can also be expressed 'A part of mankind falls under the concept "a German".' But by part here we are to understand a non-empty part, a part containing individuals. If this were not the case, there would be no men who are Germans, so we should say 'No man is a German'; this, however, is the contradictory opposite of 'Some men are Germans'. Hence from 'Some men are Germans' we can infer conversely 'there are German men'. 'Some men are Germans' can also be . . .[1]

---

[1] The manuscript breaks off at this point (ed.).

[II. *Frege's concluding comments*]

Formulation of the dispute:

We considered the sentences 'This table exists' and 'There are tables'. The question arose whether the word 'exists' in the first sentence has essentially the same content as does the 'there are' in the second.

You did not dispute, I think, that these sentences are not only distinguished by their subjects' being different, but that the predicates also differ in a certain respect; but in spite of this you maintained that the meaning is essentially the same. Can you now tell me just what, according to you, they have in common and where the difference lies?

We need to come to an understanding about how a particular affirmative judgement with 'some' is to be understood. I believe the way it is to be generally understood in logic is brought out by adding the gloss 'at least one—possibly all'. Then 'Some men are negroes' would mean 'Some—possibly all—but at least one man is a negro'.

If we are agreed on this, then a particular affirmative judgement such as 'Some men are negroes' can be converted into 'Some negroes are men'. The resistance one naturally has to this is based on the fact that one involuntarily adds in thought 'but some negroes are not men'. This thought is excluded by our rider 'possibly all'.

Now you wanted to construe the expression 'Men exist' as having the same meaning as 'Something existing is a man'. The trouble with the latter is that, grammatically, it is not existence but being a man which occurs as predicate. But it is existence that is really meant to be asserted. Now we can adopt a grammatical form which brings this out by converting and saying 'Some men exist', taking this in the sense of 'Some—possibly all—but at least one man exists'. It will then follow that this means the same as 'Men exist'.

Now I have understood throughout that on your view you take the difference in meaning of 'exist' in 'Leo Sachse exists' and 'Men exist' to be of the same kind as the difference in meaning of 'is a German' in 'Leo Sachse is a German' and 'Some men are German', so that 'exists' is related to 'exist' in the first two sentences as, in the last two, 'is a German' is related to 'are German'. I have deliberately made the subjects 'Leo Sachse' and 'some men' the same in both cases to create the impression that they do parallel one another. I believe the only reason we omit the 'some' in the sentence 'men exist' is to forestall the objection 'not all?'

Now you marshalled your argument, I believe, as follows.

First of all you wanted me to admit that 'There are men' means the same as 'Among that which has being is some man' or 'A part of what has being is a man', or 'Something that has being is a man'. As expressions with the same meaning as 'has being' you also used 'can be experienced', 'existing', 'that whose idea has been caused by something affecting the ego'. These variants, I believe, make no essential difference. With them some secondary difficulties may crop up or disappear. The main difficulty remains the same and so does the general outline of the plan of attack. I now had further to be brought to admit that the verb 'to be' ('to exist') is used in the same sense as in the sentence 'Leo Sachse *is*' or 'exists'.[1] With that you seemed to have won the day.

Now I can readily grant that the expression 'there are men' means the same as 'Something existing is a man'—only, however, on condition that 'exists' predicates something self-evident, so that it really has no content. The same goes for the other expressions which you use in place of 'exist'.

But if the proposition 'Leo Sachse is' is self-evident then the 'is' cannot have the same content as the 'there are' of 'There are men', for the latter does not say something self-evident. Now if you express what is said by 'There are men' by 'Men exist' or 'Among that which has being is some man', that the content of the statement cannot lie in the 'exist' or 'has being' etc. And this is the πρῶτον ψεῦδος by which you could not help but be forced into making contradictory judgements—the error of thinking that the content of what is predicated in 'Some men exist' or 'Something existing is a man' or 'Men exist' is contained in the word 'exist'. This is not the case; this word only contains the form of a predicate as does the copula 'is' in the sentence 'The sky is blue'. Like the 'it' in 'it is raining', the 'exist' in 'Men exist' is to be understood as a mere auxiliary. As language, feeling at a loss for a grammatical *subject*, invented 'it', so here, feeling at a loss for a grammatical *predicate*, it has invented 'exist'.

I shall use the fact that instead of 'exists' one can also say 'is identical with itself' to show that the content of what is predicated does not lie in the word 'exists'. 'There are men' means the same as 'Some men are identical with themselves' or 'Something identical with itself is a man'. Neither in '*A* is identical with itself' nor in '*A* exists' does one learn anything new about *A*. Neither statement can be denied. In either you can put what you like for *A*, and it still remains true. They do not assign *A* to one of two classes in order to mark it off from some *B* which does not belong to that class. The point in saying '*A* is identical with itself' can only be to express the logical law of identity; the point cannot be to impart any further knowledge about *A*. Just as it could be maintained that 'exist' means the same in 'This table exists' and 'Tables exist', so we can say that the predicate 'identical with itself' has the same sense in 'This table is identical with itself' and 'Tables are identical with themselves'. But in that case we have also to acknowledge that the judgements 'This table exists' and 'This table is identical with itself' are completely self-evident, and that consequently in these judgements no real

---

[1] If the reader is to follow the argument at this point, he should bear in mind that in German the expression 'there are', as in Frege's example 'There are men', is *not* rendered by a form of the verb 'to be' ('*sein*') but by '*es gibt*' which comes from '*geben*', meaning 'to give'. The corresponding English expression 'there is' is likewise so rendered (trans.).

content is being predicated of this table. Just as we call statements such as 'Men exist' existential judgements, thinking the content of what is predicated to lie in the word 'exist', so we might call the statement 'Some men are identical with themselves' an identity judgement, and 'There are men' would be an identity judgement. In general, in any attempt to prove that the content of what is predicated in 'There are men' was located in the 'exist' of 'Men exist', we could, without any falsification, switch 'are identical with themselves' throughout for 'exist'. I shall seek to show this.

But if the content of what is predicated in the judgement 'Men exist' does not lie in the 'exist', where then does it lie? I answer: in the form of the particular judgement. Every particular judgement is an existential judgement that can be converted into the 'there is' form. E.g. 'Some bodies are light' is the same as 'There are light bodies'. 'Some birds cannot fly' is the same as 'There are birds that cannot fly', and so on. It is more difficult to do the opposite and convert a judgement with 'there is' into a particular judgement. Out of context the word 'some' has no sense; it is an auxiliary like 'all', 'each', 'none' and so on, which, in the context of a sentence, has a logical function to perform. This function consists in putting two concepts into a certain logical relationship. In 'Some men are negroes' the concepts 'man' and 'negro' are put into this relationship. So we always need two concepts if we want to form a particular judgement. Now of course the sentence 'There are flying fish' can easily be converted into 'Some fish can fly', because we have two concepts 'fish' and 'being able to fly'. It becomes more difficult if we try to put 'There are men' into the form of a particular judgement. If we define man = rational living being, we may say 'Some living beings are rational' and, assuming the definition to be correct, this means the same as 'There are men'.

This recourse is only open to us when the concept can be analysed into two characteristic marks. There is another method closely connected with this one. E.g. if we have to convert 'There are negroes', we may say that negro = negro that is a man, because the concept 'negro' is subordinate to the concept 'man'. Here again we have two concepts and may say 'Some men are negroes' or 'Some negroes are men'. But this works only in the particular case of the concept 'negro'. For 'There are birches' we should have to select a different superordinate concept, such as 'tree'. If one wants to do the thing quite generally, one needs to look for a concept superordinate to all concepts. Such a concept, if one wishes to give it that name, can no longer have any content at all since its extension will be unlimited; for any content can only consist in a certain delimitation of the extension. As such a concept we might select that of 'being identical with itself', since we said that 'There are men' is the same as 'There are men identical with themselves' or 'Something identical with itself is a man'.

Language has availed itself of a different resource. The copula, i.e. the mere form of a predicate without content, was excellently suited for forming a concept without content. In the sentence 'The sky is blue' the predicate is 'is blue', but strictly the content of the predicate lies in the word 'blue'. Leave this out and what remains—'The sky is'—is a predicate without content. In this way we form a quasi-concept—'being'—without content, since its extension is unlimited. This makes it possible to say: men = men that have being; 'There are men' is the same as 'Some men are' or 'Something that has being is a man'. Thus here the real content of what is predicated does not lie in 'has being' but in the form of the particular judgement. Faced with an impasse, language has simply created the word 'being' in order to enable the form of the particular judgement to be employed. When philosophers speak of 'absolute being', that is really an apotheosis of the copula.

But it is easy to see now how this came about. People felt that the sentence 'There is a centre of mass of the earth' is not self-evident, and that consequently there is a content to what is predicated. And it is now readily intelligible why, when they employed the form 'A centre of mass of the earth exists', people believed this content to reside in the word 'exist'. In this way a content was packed into the word 'exist', without anyone's being able to specify in what this content really consists.

It may now be shown how Pünjer, as a result of the $\pi\rho\tilde{\omega}\tau\sigma\nu\ \psi\epsilon\tilde{\upsilon}\sigma\varsigma$ of seeing in the 'exist' the content of what is predicated in 'Men exist', was bound to be driven into making contradictory assertions. I was easily able to convince him that the denial of '*A* can be experienced' is impossible where can be experienced = is = exists. He had also to concede that to say of a thing that it can be experienced does not characterize that thing in any way. On the other hand, however, he wanted to salvage a content for a statement saying of something that it can be experienced. Something was surely meant to be said in the sentence 'This table can be experienced', 'This table exists'; it was surely meant to state something that was not pleonastic or self-evident. So he was forced into the contradiction of taking the denial of 'This table can be experienced' as something that was not pleonastic and self-evident.[1] He had to deprive the expression 'can be experienced' of all content without making it devoid of content. Pünjer wanted to convey the content of the judgement 'This can be experienced' by 'The idea of the this is not an hallucination, it is not something which originates from myself alone, but the idea has been formed as a result of the ego's being affected by the this'. To this I had to object that one only has the right to form the expressions 'idea of the this', 'the ego's being affected by the this', after having made the judgement 'something corresponds to this idea of mine'. If nothing corresponds to this idea of mine, then the expression 'idea of the this' has no sense and thus the sentence as a whole has no sense. Pünjer then altered his account, though without conceding that it was incorrect: 'The object of the idea *B* can be experienced' means 'The idea *B* has been formed through something affecting the ego'. I was now able to infer from this that the negation of the sentence 'The object of the idea *B* can be experienced' has a

---

[1] *sic* (trans.).

good sense. But Pünjer had said earlier that the negation of the sentence '*A* can be experienced' is impossible. We now have to qualify this somewhat and say: If *A* is an object of experience, then the negation of 'A can be experienced' is impossible, but if *A* is object of an idea, then the negation of that sentence is possible. We see how this example confirms that it is impossible to assign to the predicate 'can be experienced' a sense that is not self-evident whilst making the general claim that it has no sense to deny of a thing that it can be experienced. At the same time we see that the concept of what can be experienced acquires a content only through its extension being delimited in some way. In fact all objects are divided into two classes: objects of experience and objects of ideas. The latter do not all fall under the concept 'what can be experienced'. From this it can be further inferred that not every concept is subordinate to the concept of what can be experienced—for the concept 'object of an idea' is not. And from this it follows that the concept of what can be experienced is not generally suited for the purpose of expressing a judgement with 'there is' in the form of a particular judgement. In order to justify the expression 'object of an idea' as being generally applicable, Pünjer had to maintain that every idea has an object, that there are ideas of objects which have not been formed through something affecting the ego. If we apply to this his definition of sentences with 'there is', a contradiction must emerge. In fact, according to this definition, the judgement 'there are objects of ideas that have not been formed through something affecting the ego' is synonymous with 'Among what can be experienced is something that falls under the concept "object of an idea that has not been formed through something affecting the ego"'. But now according to Pünjer's account, objects of ideas not formed by virtue of something affecting the ego cannot be experienced. So we arrive at the statement 'Among what can be experienced is something that cannot be experienced'.

We may also put it like this: from the two premisses

1. There are objects of ideas that are not formed through something affecting the ego;

2. Objects of ideas that are not formed through something affecting the ego cannot be experienced;

there follows the conclusion:

There are objects of ideas—which objects cannot be experienced. This is a contradiction once it is allowed that the same kind of existence is expressed by 'there is' as is meant to be conveyed by 'can be experienced'.

In general one can lay down the following:

If you want to assign a content to the verb 'to be', so that the sentence '*A* is' is not pleonastic and self-evident, you will have to allow circumstances under which the negation of '*A* is' is possible; that is to say, that there are subjects of which being must be denied. But in that case the concept 'being' will no longer be suitable for providing a general explanation of 'there are' under which 'there are *B*'s' means the same as 'something that has being falls under the concept *B*'; for if we apply this explanation to 'There are subjects of which being must be denied', then we get 'Something that has being falls under the concept of not-being' or 'Something that has being is not'. There is no way of getting over this once a content of some kind—it doesn't matter what it is—is agreed to the concept of being. If the explanation of 'there are *B*s' as meaning the same as 'Something that has being is *B*' is to work, we just have to understand by being something that goes entirely without saying.

For this reason the contradiction still remains if we say '*A* exists' means 'The idea of the *A* has been caused by something affecting the ego'. However, still other difficulties crop up here, only some of which I want to mention.

When Leverrier put to himself the question whether there were planets beyond the orbit of Uranus, he was not asking whether his idea of a planet beyond the orbit of Uranus had been caused, or might have been caused, by something affecting the ego. When there is a dispute over whether there is a God, the dispute is not over whether our idea of a God has been caused, or may be caused, by something affecting the ego. Many who believe that there is a God will dispute that their idea of Him has been caused by God's immediately affecting their ego, for it can only be a question here of something affecting them immediately. However, this is only by the way. The upshot is as follows:

We can say that the meanings of the word 'exist' in the sentences 'Leo Sachse exists' and 'Some men exist' display no more difference than does the meanings of 'is a German' in the sentences 'Leo Sachse is a German' and 'Some men are Germans'. But then the sentence 'Some men exist' or 'Something existing is a man' only means the same as 'There are men' if the concept 'existing thing' is superordinate to the concept man. So if such forms of expression are to have the same meaning in general, the concept 'existing thing' must be superordinate to every concept. This is only possible if the word 'exist' means something that goes entirely without saying, and if therefore nothing at all is predicated in the sentence 'Leo Sachse exists', and if in the sentence 'Some men exist' the content of what is predicated does not lie in the word 'exist'. The existence expressed by 'there is' is not contained in the word 'exist' but in the form of the particular judgement. 'Some men are Germans' is just as good an existential judgement as 'Some men exist'. But once the word 'exist' is given a content, which is predicated of an individual thing, this content can be made into the characteristic mark of a concept—a concept under which there falls the individual thing of which existence is being predicated. E.g. if one divides everything into two classes

1. What is in my mind, ideas, feelings etc.
   and
2. What is outside myself,

and says of the latter that it exists, then one can construe existence as a characteristic mark of the concept 'centaur', although there are no centaurs. I would not acknowledge anything as a centaur that was not outside my mind; this means that I shall not call mere ideas or feelings centaurs.

The existence expressed by 'there is' cannot be a characteristic mark of a concept whose property it is, just because it is a property of it. In the sentence 'There are men' we seem to be speaking of individuals that fall under the concept 'man', whereas it is only the concept 'man' we are talking about. The content of the word 'exist' cannot well be taken as the characteristic mark of a concept, because 'exists', as it is used in the sentence 'Men exist', has no content.

We can see from all this how easily we can be led by language to see things in the wrong perspective, and what value it must therefore have for philosophy to free ourselves from the dominion of language. If one makes the attempt to construct a system of signs on quite other foundations and with quite other means, as I have tried to do in creating my concept-script, we shall have, so to speak, our very noses rubbed into the false analogies in language.

[Draft towards a Review of Cantor's *Gesammelte Abhandlungen zur Lehre vom Transfiniten*][1]

[1890–1892]

Since these papers have been published in this journal, my concern will be less to expound than to critically evaluate their contents.

Their aim is to gain acceptance for the actual infinite. This is achieved in part negatively by refuting attempted disproofs, and in part positively by demonstrating its existence. Some of the considerations advanced belong more to theology or the philosophy of religion, some more to mathematics or logic. I may here be allowed to confine myself to an evaluation of the latter, which are closer to my interests and which of themselves provide a wealth of material for discussion.

On the whole the objections to the infinite seem to me well and truly met. These objections arise because properties are ascribed to the infinite which do not belong to it: either properties of the finite are carried over as a matter of course to the infinite (p. 3), or a property that only belongs to the absolute infinite is extended indiscriminately to the infinite in general. It is a merit of these papers to have brought out this distinction within the infinite so forcibly (part equal to whole). All this relates only to the genuine, the 'actual' infinite. The opposition against acknowledging the actual infinite which mathematicians display is to be traced back in part to their confounding this with the potential infinite—an opposition which, properly speaking, holds only against construing the potential infinite as if it were the actual infinite. So, many mathematicians and philosophers only acknowledge the potential infinite. Cantor now succeeds in showing that this infinite

---

[1] In the *Zeitschrift für Philosophie und philosophische Kritik* Cantor had published the following articles on the theory of the transfinite: *Über die verschiedenen Standpunkte in Bezug auf das actuale Unendlichkeit* (Vol 88 (1886) pp. 224–233), *Mitteilungen zur Lehre vom Transfiniten* (Vol. 91 (1887), pp. 81–125, 252–270 and Vol. 92. (1888), pp. 240–265). In 1890 they were published together in a volume: *Zur Lehre vom Transfiniten. Gesammelte Abhandlungen aus der Zeitschrift für Philosophie und philosophische Kritik. Erste Abteilung.* They are also to be found in G. Cantor, *Gesammelte Abhandlungen mathematischen und philosophischen Inhalts*, ed. E. Zermelo (Berlin 1932). Frege reviewed the 1890 collection in the *Zeitschrift für Philosophie und philosophische Kritik*. See Vol. 100 (1892), pp. 269–272. Except for some small alterations, the first part of the piece from the *Nachlaß* agrees with the first paragraph of this review. The agreement extends to the end of the sentence 'Cantor is less felicitous when he comes to giving definitions', but from then on the review diverges completely from what is printed here (ed.).

presupposes the actual infinite, that the 'receding limit' must have an infinite path, if it really is to recede ever and ever further (footnote to p. 30).[1]

Cantor is less felicitous when he comes to giving definitions.

We may begin here by making a general observation. When negroes from the heart of Africa see a telescope or pocket watch for the first time, they are inclined to credit these things with the most astounding magical properties. Many mathematicians react to philosophical expressions in a similar manner. I am thinking in particular here of the following: 'define' (Brahma), 'reflect' (Vishnu), 'abstract' (Shiva). The names of the Indian gods in brackets are meant to indicate the kind of magical effects the expressions are supposed to have. If, for instance, you find that some property of a thing bothers you, you abstract from it. But if you want to call a halt to this process of destruction so that properties you want to see retained should not be obliterated in the process, you reflect upon these properties. If, finally, you feel sorely the lack of certain properties in the thing, you bestow them on it by definition. In your possession of these miraculous powers you are not far removed from the Almighty. The significance this would have is practically beyond measure. Think of how these powers could be put to use in the classroom: a teacher has a good-natured but lazy and stupid pupil. He will then abstract from the laziness and stupidity, reflecting all the while on the good-naturedness. Then by means of a definition he will confer on him the properties of keenness and intelligence. Of course so far people have confined themselves to mathematics. The following dialogue may serve as an illustration:

Mathematician: The sign $\sqrt{-1}$ has the property of yielding -1 when squared.

Layman: This pattern of printer's ink on paper? I can't see any trace of this property. Perhaps it has been discovered with the aid of a microscope or by some chemical means?

Mathematician: It can't be arrived at by *any* process of sense perception. And of course it isn't produced by the mere printer's ink either; a magic incantation, called a definition, has first to be pronounced over it.

Layman: Ah, now I understand. You expressed yourself badly. You mean that a definition is used to stipulate that this pattern is a sign for something with those properties.

Mathematician: Not at all! It is a sign, but it doesn't designate or mean anything. It itself has these properties, precisely in virtue of the definition.

Layman: What extraordinary people you mathematicians are, and no mistake! You don't bother at all about the properties a thing actually has, but imagine that in their stead you can bestow a property on it by a definition—a property that the thing in its innocence doesn't dream of—and

---

[1] The concept of a '*wandelnde Grenze*' or '*wandelbare Grenze*' [receding, changing limit] was introduced by Herbart (ed.).

now you investigate the property and believe in that way you can accomplish the most extraordinary things!

This illustrates the might of the mathematical Brahma. In Cantor it is Shiva and Vishnu who receive the greater honour. Faced with a cage of mice, mathematicians react differently when the number [*Anzahl*] of them is in question. Some—and Biermann seems to be one of them—include in the number the mice just as they are, down to the last hair; others—and I may surely count Cantor amongst them—find it out of place that hairs should form part of the number and so abstract from them. They find in mice a whole host of other things besides which are out of place in number and are unworthy to be included in it. Nothing simpler: one abstracts from the whole lot. Indeed when you get down to it everything in the mice is out of place: the beadiness of their eyes no less than the length of their tails and the sharpness of their teeth. So one abstracts from the nature of the mice (p. 12, p. 23, p. 56). But from their nature as what is not said; so one abstracts presumably from all their properties, even from those in virtue of which we call them mice, even from those in virtue of which we call them animals, three-dimensional beings—properties which distinguish them, for instance, from the number 2.

Cantor demands even more: to arrive at cardinal numbers, we are required to abstract from the order in which they are given. What is to be understood by this? Well, if at a certain moment we compare the positions of the mice, we see that of any two one is further to the north than the other, or that both are the same distance to the north. The same applies to east and west and above and below. But this is not all: if we compare the mice in respect of their ages, we find likewise that of any two one is older than the other or that both have the same age. We can go on and compare them in respect of their length, both with and without their tails, in respect of the pitch of their squeaks, their weight, their muscular strength, and in many other respects besides. All these relations generate an order. We shall surely not go astray if we take it that this is what Cantor calls the order in which things are given. So we are meant to abstract from this order too. Now surely many people will say 'But we have already abstracted from their being in space; so *ipso facto* we have already abstracted from north and south, from the difference in their lengths. We have already abstracted from the ages of the animals, and so *ipso facto* from one's being older than another. So why does special mention have also to be made of order?'

Well, Cantor also defines what he calls an ordinal type; and in order to arrive at this, we have, so he tells us, to stop short of abstracting from the order in which the things are given. So presumably this will be possible too, though only with Vishnu's help. We can hardly dispense with this in other cases too. For the moment let us stay with the cardinal numbers.

So let us get a number of men together and ask them to exert themselves to the utmost in abstracting from the nature of the pencil and the order in which its elements are given. After we have allowed them sufficient time for this difficult task, we ask the first 'What general concept (p. 56) have you arrived at?' Non-mathematician that he is, he answers 'Pure Being'. The second thinks rather 'Pure nothingness', the third—I suspect a pupil of Cantor's—'The cardinal number one'. A fourth is perhaps left with the woeful feeling that everything has evaporated, a fifth—surely a pupil of Cantor's—hears an inner voice whispering that graphite and wood, the constituents of the pencil, are 'constitutive elements', and so he arrives at the general concept called the cardinal number two. Now why shouldn't one man come out with the answer and another with another? Whether in fact Cantor's definitions have the sharpness and precision their author boasts of is accordingly doubtful to me. But perhaps we got such varying replies because it was a pencil we carried out our experiment with. It may be said 'But a pencil isn't a set'. Why not? Well then, let us look at the moon. 'The moon is not a set either!' What a pity! The cardinal number one would be only too happy to come into existence at any place and at any time, and the moon seemed the very thing to assist at the birth. Well then, let us take a heap of sand. Oh dear, there's someone already trying to separate the grains. 'You are surely not going to try and count them all! That is strictly forbidden! You have to arrive at the number by a single act of abstraction' (footnote to p. 15). 'But in order to be able to abstract from the nature of a grain of sand, I must surely first have looked at it, grasped it, come to know it!' 'That's quite unnecessary. What would happen to the infinite cardinals in that case? By the time you had looked at the last grain, you would be bound to have forgotten the first ones. I must emphasize once more that you are meant to arrive at the number by a single act of abstraction. Of course for that you need the help of supernatural powers. Surely you don't imagine you can bring it off by ordinary abstraction. When you look at books, some in quarto, some in octavo, some thick, some thin, some in Gothic type and some in Roman and you abstract from these properties which distinguish them, and thus arrive at, say, the concept "book", this, when you come down to it, is no great feat. Allow me to clarify for you the difference between ordinary abstraction and the higher, supernatural, kind.

With ordinary abstraction we start out by comparing objects a, b, c, and find that they agree in many properties but differ in others. We abstract from the latter and arrive at a concept Φ under which a and b and c all fall. Now this concept has neither the properties abstracted from nor those common to a, b and c. The concept "book", for instance, no more consists of printed sheets—although the individual books we started by comparing do consist of such—than the concept "female mammal" bears young or suckles them with milk secreted from its glands; for it has no glands. Things are quite different with supernatural abstraction. Here we have, for instance, a heap of sand ...[1]

---

[1] At this point the manuscript breaks off (ed.).

On the Concept of Number[1]

[1891/92]

[A Criticism of Biermann]

In my *Grundlagen* (§ 68) I called the concept F equal in number to the concept G if it is possible to correlate one-to-one the objects falling under F with those falling under G and then gave the following definition:

> The number[2] belonging to the concept F is the extension of the concept 'equal in number to the concept F'.

The following discussion will show that this definition gives the right results when applied, by deriving the basic properties of the numbers from it. But first we need to clarify a few points and meet some objections. The way the word number is used outside mathematics does not reveal the sense of the word with the clarity that is indispensable for scientific purposes. Things are, so to speak, dragged into the number, lock, stock and barrel; people imagine a number of trees as something rather like a group or row of trees, so that the trees themselves belong to the number. On this view, the number of peas on the table would not only be changed, say, if I filed something off one of them or if I took away one and put another in its place; it would also be changed if I simply shuffled the peas about; for a change in spatial relations means that the whole is changed, as a heap of sand is changed if someone spreads it out without adding or taking away a grain of sand. If we ask what the number 2 is, likely enough the answer will be 'two things'. Now put an apple and a pear in front of someone who has given this answer and say 'Here you have your number 2'. Perhaps he will begin to hesitate at this point, but he will be even more unsure if we ask him to multiply this number 2 by the number 1 which we could give him, say, in the shape of a

---

[1] According to notes on the transcripts on which this edition is based, both the following papers were found, unseparated, in a folder under the heading: 'On the Concept of Number'. They were probably written in the years 1891/92 since the section beginning on p. 87 is a preliminary draft of Frege's article *Über Begriff und Gegenstand*, published in 1892. The section dealing with Biermann may have been written earlier. This is indicated by the use of the word '*Inhalt*' (p. 85) where Frege's later practice would require '*Bedeutung*' (ed.).

[2] Here and in the first five sentences of the paragraph following the word translated 'number' is '*Anzahl*', which strictly means 'natural number'. Throughout most of the rest of the paper Frege uses '*Zahl*', which has the same broad application as our 'number' (trans.).

strawberry. It would, indeed, be very pleasant if we could conjure up a five-pound note by multiplying a cork by a nail. All this is pure childishness, of course, and that we have to bother with such things is a sufficient indictment of the times we live in. Yet even mathematicians will stoop to giving such definitions as:*

> '*The concept of number may be defined as the idea of a plurality composed of things of the same kind*. When we use the term "one" for each of the elements of the same kind, *counting the elements or units* of the set consists in assigning the new terms two, three, etc., to one and one—and one, etc. Number is the idea of the groups of elements designated by these terms.'

Expressions such as 'things of the same kind', 'elements', 'one', 'unit' are all jostled together here, as though the third section of my *Grundlagen* had never been written. Do these expressions have the same meaning, or not? If they do, why this plethora of terms? If they don't, what is the difference between them?** At any rate, we may at least assume that 'elements' is intended to mean the same as 'things of the same kind' and 'group' the same as 'plurality'. Strange what importance is so often attached to a mere change in expression when presenting these rudiments. It seems almost as though the expressions 'one' and 'element of our group' are intended to have the same meaning, and yet the replacement of the latter by the former is stressed as an important step. Why does counting the elements or units of a set not consist in assigning new terms to element and element—and element? Or is that what it actually does? Let us assume, to clarify matters, that there is a lion standing beside a lioness lying on the ground and together they form a picturesque group of things of the same kind; both animals do, of course, belong to the species *felis leo*. At first we have nothing more than just this group. But now comes the highly significant act of designating both the lion and the lioness by the term one; then follows the no less significant act of assigning the new term two to one and one (and thus, indubitably, to our group); and we are very happy to have acquired the number two at this juncture. For surely what we need most of all is to have the terms and words; once we have them we can say: 'Number is the idea of groups of elements designated by these terms.' Accordingly, in our case the number two would presumably be the idea of the group of lions. We might still ask what the word 'one' actually means in that case. Does it designate a number? According to Biermann's notion, one would then be a group of elements. Now we have just used the term one to designate the lioness. Since the lioness is not an idea we must presumably accept the idea of the lioness

---

* Otto Biermann, *Theorie der analytischen Funktionen* [Leipzig 1887] § 1.

** I'll wager Biermann did not know this himself at the time and still does not know.

as the meaning of the word 'one'. The lioness is made up of molecules, after all, and so may well be seen as a group.

Perhaps Biermann also takes the word 'group' in such a way that a single thing is also a group, no matter whether it is composite or not, although the contrary is indicated by the fact that Biermann speaks of element*s*, things of the same kind, and stresses the way a number is *composed*.

Admittedly, we also used one to designate the lion, and this could give us pause should we find the idea [image][1] of the lion different from that of the lioness; on the other hand, the idea [image] we have can be so blurred that the idea [image] of the lion merges with that of the lioness. Hence, just as two is the idea [image] of our group of lions, one would be an idea [image] though a pretty blurred one, of a lion. What degree of vagueness we would have to assume admittedly remains uncertain. As a second example, let us take the Laocoön group, the well-known Greek sculpture found in 1506. We might well doubt whether in this case the components may be assumed to be of the same kind.

Biermann does not state to what extent the similarity he requires allows scope for differences. If the coincidence were exact, should we ever get beyond the number one? Presumably, then, a certain degree of latitude must be allowed. We also speak of two cats even if they are not the same colour, or two coins even if one is made of gold and the other of nickel. No doubt we shall always be able to discover some sort of similarity, even if it consists in nothing more than each of the elements having the property of being like itself in every respect. What then is the point of this condition of being of the same kind, when either it is always fulfilled, or we never know when it is fulfilled? Biermann does not know himself. He is onto something, but doesn't know what. He could have found out the answer from my *Grundlagen*, just as he could have learnt a great deal more that he does not know, but he must have thought in his heart of hearts: *metaphysica sunt, non leguntur.*

Let us return to the Laocoön group. Since the whole thing is made of marble and since, moreover, the parts of the group represent living beings, presumably there is nothing to prevent us from regarding the elements as being sufficiently alike. So what we do first—and this is very significant indeed—is to designate Laocoön, or more precisely his marble image, and each of his sons, and the serpent as well, by the term one. Then we again assign terms to one and one—and one ... All right, what actually is one in this case? The idea [image] of a living being sculpted in marble which is so blurred we are not able to distinguish whether what is represented is the figure of a snake or a human being, an older or a younger man? That seems

---

[1] The difficult word '*Vorstellung*' we have rendered throughout as 'idea', sometimes enclosing the word 'image' in brackets afterwards where this sense seems more appropriate. Owing to the influence of Kant, the term was of course frequently used in German philosophical writings of Frege's time. The standard English translation of '*Vorstellung*' as it occurs in Kant is 'representation' (trans.).

a trifle implausible. In that case, 'one' would presumably have to have a different meaning from what it had in the previous example. Or must the idea [image] be taken to be so blurred that it is quite impossible to say what it is an idea of? Is there only one one? Or are there many ones? Could we say in the latter case 'Laocoön is a one' or 'The idea of Laocoön is a one'? Or can Biermann give us an example of something that is a one? What does it mean when someone says: this or that is a one? And if there are several ones, we must still be able to express the fact that something belongs to the species one. The phrase 'by designating each of the elements of the same kind by one' may lead someone to suppose that one is a title like 'Sir', for instance. We have the privilege of conferring this title, and everything and everyone receiving it is simply a one as a result. Then we could never go wrong in calling something one, just as a reigning monarch can never go wrong when he bestows a title on someone. Of course, this title 'One' would be pretty worthless; you cannot imagine it amounting to anything much. At the same time, conferring this title would be a source of revenue for us, in so far as it is through this that we come into possession of the numbers. If there were only one one, if, that is, 'one' were a proper name, what would 'one and one' mean? Clearly, one again; for what can 'Charlemagne and Charlemagne' mean, if not Charlemagne? Then there must be several ones after all, and our earlier conjecture that one is a vague idea is possibly false.

At this stage the most obvious thing seems to be to regard 'one' as a title. We have conferred this title on Laocoön, his sons and the serpent, and we now assign a new term to the Laocoön group. Very well, but which? We must not imagine for *one* moment that there is no need for a new term, since we could simply call our group the Laocoön group. That would clearly not be the right term to assign to it. Biermann knows best what term we need to use here. Perhaps he would fix on the term 'four'. Others would perhaps prefer 'one'; but why should the same thing not have different titles?

Now Biermann says 'Number is the idea of the groups of elements designated by those terms'. Fine! We designate the group itself—so here the Laocoön group—by the term 'four' or 'one' or by both; but the number is not the group itself which we designate by the number word, it is the idea of it. Is the idea of the Laocoön group the number one or the number four or what number? Why not one and four at the same time, as the whim takes us? But we must have made a mistake! The whole group consists of molecules of calcium carbonate. Here we have elements of our group that are of the same kind. Possibly it would have been better if we had designated each of these molecules by the term one. Well, we go ahead and do this and so are able to designate the Laocoön group by a new term. The number is now the idea of the group designated by this term (our old Laocoön group over again). It is only at this point that we begin to see how subtle the term 'idea' is. To be sure, the Laocoön group is the same; but now we have a different idea of it. That is why we now have a different number. If our idea of a plurality composed of things of the same kind, e.g. a heap of sand, changes, the number changes as well; for the number is simply the idea of the heap of sand. If, for instance, we spread the heap of sand out, the idea of the heap of sand when spread out is clearly a different idea from that of the original heap. These ideas are numbers and they are different; this means that they are different numbers. To arrive at this result there is no need to add or take away a grain of sand.

Let us assume a child and a painter are looking at a group, consisting of an apple, a pear and a nut. Following Biermann's instructions they may both have reached the point of designating this group by the new term three. Suppose now a cloth be spread over this plurality composed of things of the same kind; what ideas of them are left behind in the minds of the observers? Evidently quite different ones. In the case of the child ideas of taste will predominate, in the case of the painter ideas of the colours and how they shade off, of the shadows and outlines, etc., so that the two of them, if Biermann's definition were correct, would have quite different numbers, that is, different ideas of the group of elements designated by the word three. But I suppose Biermann would say that all this is psychology, that these considerations have nothing to do with arithmetic. Just so! But how did we get here? *Via* the term 'idea' which Biermann uses and which simply *does* belong to psychology. Any attempt to exclude psychological considerations from mathematics has my full approval. But let us do the job properly. Away with the word idea! To be sure, we must then dispense with such interesting psychological propositions as 'Through number we possess the idea of a plurality or set of similar things'.[1] The full implications of this proposition can only be realized when it is applied to examples; thus we possess the idea of a heap of sand through the idea of a heap of sand; we possess the idea of the constellation of Orion through the idea of the constellation of Orion; we possess the idea of the Laocoön group through the idea of the Laocoön group. But let us not make an issue of whether arithmetic is the proper place for this psychological truth. Let us rather rejoice over truths wherever we find them. And let us look to see whether Biermann's book does not yield yet more meat for psychology. Sure enough! We learn something about the composition of ideas:

'*Two numbers formed from an indeterminate basic element e or the abstract unit 1 ...*', etc.[2]

If only we knew what an 'indeterminate basic element' is! Perhaps we shall glean it by comparing this with a later passage:

'*We construct a number containing all the elements of two numbers a and b formed from the same basic element.*'[3]

---

[1] Cf. Biermann, p. 1.

[2] *Ibid.*

[3] *Ibid.*

Thus we have, say, two heaps of peas,* and we make a single heap with them. What is the basic element the heap is made up of? A pea? A single pea? Which pea? An indeterminate pea. I confess that I have not yet seen an indeterminate pea, but I can well imagine that Biermann has the concept pea in mind; or would it be an idea of a pea? I trust I do Biermann no injustice if I assume that he has never broached this question. Though we cannot, to be sure, say that a heap of peas is composed of an indeterminate pea, or of the concept pea, or of an idea of a pea, we can say that it is composed of peas, i.e. of objects falling under the concept pea. Therefore, in view of the fact that Biermann's terminology is somewhat imprecise, we may assume that his phrase 'number formed from an indeterminate basic element' is intended to mean: 'number whose components fall under one concept' and that is only another term for something that has already given us food for thought—elements of the same kind; evidently, Biermann is fond of presenting us with the same thing in different guises so that we do not find it too easy to achieve clarity. But we are forgetting, and perhaps Biermann is, too, that it is not the heap of peas that is a number, but the idea of the heap. The number, i.e. the idea, is not, however, made up of peas. What is an element of a number? After what has just been said everyone must think: an element of the group whose idea is the number. Let us consider Biermann's formulation once more: 'We construct a number containing all the elements of two numbers *a* and *b* formed from the same basic element.' That is to say: we form the idea of a group, which idea contains all the elements of two numbers. In our example we had to take the peas as the elements of the numbers. Thus we formed a leguminous idea which may possibly be of some use as a nitrogenous food. But I think it would be better if we left aside the question of forming this idea: the feat is beyond us. By element of a number should we perhaps understand: idea of a component of the group whose idea is the number? The elements of the number in our example would then not be the peas, but the ideas of the peas. True, Biermann had previously spoken only of elements of the group whose idea is the number; but that may well have slipped his mind, which would be only human after all; or possibly he wants to catch a superficial critic off his

---

* No doubt Biermann is thinking 'How vulgar to talk about peas, apples and the like when we are supposedly dealing with scientific issues. It sounds for all the world like someone talking to little children!' Well, I am indeed trying to show that we are only left with puerilities once we go to the core of his argument and strip off the semblance of learning he is able to create by using terms like 'element', 'group', 'idea', 'assign', and so on. There is no better place to hide the most childish confusions than in the most learned-sounding terms. That is why the cruder the examples we use to throw light on these terms, the more pitifully apparent it becomes how utterly obscure they are. Biermann's account is able to retain its aura of learning only because he forbears applying it to particular cases. It would be out of place to be too serious here.

guard, for such a reader might well be beguiled by the use of the same word 'element' into thinking that we are still dealing here with elements of the group. We may surely allow that the idea of a heap of peas contains ideas of peas. At all events it will contain, in addition, the idea of a certain proximity which we indicate, of course, by the word 'heap'. True, Biermann nowhere says that the idea we are to form should contain only the elements of the numbers *a* and *b*; if we took him at his word, we could go on adding as many ideas as we liked not containing elements of the numbers *a* and *b*; but that would hardly measure up to his view. But is there any need at all for a new heap or an idea of it?* We simply form an idea containing the ideas of the two original heaps, that is, the idea of a group of the two heaps whose ideas are the numbers *a* and *b*. Unfortunately, this idea would also contain an element that does not occur in *a* and *b*—an idea of the spatial relationship of the two heaps—and here, of course, we may choose any one of many such relationships. Or are the two numbers *a* and *b*, which are ideas after all, supposed to merge into one idea, in keeping with the psychological principle of the fusing of likes, much as, say, the ideas [images] of two similar faces merge together? Unfortunately, the result would turn out somewhat blurred.** Yet I hear Biermann crying out in despair 'This eternal psychologizing! If only I had not used the word "idea"! I did not mean it as seriously as all that!' But Biermann also says things like 'we become aware', 'we arrive at the concept of a set', 'we abstract'. And this is already quite enough to lead us off into psychological irrelevancies. 'We' is not an object of mathematics at all, just as little as our ideas are. Truths in mathematics are eternal and not dependent on whether we are alive or dead or become aware of them.

I can well imagine that Biermann has used the word 'idea' in much the same way as we use 'Esteemed Sir' and 'Honoured Sir', to make what he says sound weightier and more impressive without actually changing its sense. There is more than one circle of society in which people do not feel fully clothed if they lack a title. And likewise it is possible that a certain modesty—which, incidentally, redounds to his credit—has prevented Biermann from taking the peas with all their adventitious little wrinkles and introducing them into mathematics without dressing them up. For my part, I am more for things in their raw and natural state and prefer the following to Biermann's formulation: Number is a plurality composed of things of the same kind, or numbers are groups of elements. I concede that this sounds somewhat less impressive; the first formulation, in particular, has a touch of

---

* That [i.e. that we need an idea of a new heap] would even be wrong, for the ideas of proximity which are elements of the ideas of the original heaps of peas would be quite missing from the idea of a new heap of peas. Yet the idea we are to form is supposed to contain *all* the elements of the numbers *a* and *b*.

** As we know, this process may be emulated by photographic means.

tautology about it and might make you suspect the hand of a girl at a finishing school; but that is the very reason I prefer it. And if the word 'idea' is really intended to serve as nothing more than an ornament, I shall be able to adopt my formulation without departing in essentials from what Biermann thinks. Granted, the statement that the Laocoön group may bear the title one as well as the title four now sadly reduces to nothing. But this is offset by the fact that from this point on mathematics really has something to get its teeth into.

As is well known, this discipline is concerned with numbers. Now heaps of peas, of sand, and other heaps are numbers; herds of sheep, of cows and of other animals are numbers, too. Consequently, all these heaps and herds are objects of mathematics. Indeed, we may perhaps say that mathematics is concerned with all possible things; a window is one, a house with many windows is one, the country in which there are many houses is one.* Now if every such one is a number, then the window is a number, etc. No doubt Biermann will say 'Just so! Mathematics is concerned with all possible things in respect of what is number about them.' The striking thing, however, is that herds of sheep are seldom mentioned in this discipline. I believe they do not even appear in Biermann's book at all. Does my memory deceive me, or have I really only read about herds of sheep—if I have read about them at all in mathematical books—in the sets of examples given to illustrate the application of mathematical propositions? But I am probably putting words into Biermann's mouth that he has never thought of uttering. Number is not something *attaching to* the herds; the herds themselves just as they are, skin and bone and dirt, are numbers. It looks as though I have got confused here with J. S. Mill's view according to which a number is a property of an aggregate—that is, the way an aggregate is put together. I must confess that there were times, as I was struggling through Biermann's obscurities, when this view seemed to me full of insight. But it appears that light is now beginning to penetrate these regions of darkness. Let us take Biermann's formula: 'Two numbers formed from an indeterminate basic element or the abstract unit 1 are equal, when to each element of the one there belongs an element of the other'[1] and apply it e.g. to herds of sheep. How clear everything now becomes! Two herds of sheep are equal when to each sheep of one herd there belongs a sheep of the other. Admittedly, when a sheep A belongs to a sheep B is something we are not told. Let us turn to the difficult question of whether it is conceivable that a herd of sheep is equal

---

* '*Omnia una sunt*', a Latinist would say, if not deterred by his feeling for the language, which would here be confirmed by the nature of things as well. Apparently, Biermann has not yet got round to asking himself what underlies this phenomenon of language; for he can say 'units' as though it were the same thing.

---

[1] Biermann, p. 1.

to a constellation of stars. The one thing we do at least know is that both are numbers. The only question we still have to settle is whether they are formed from the same basic element.* I believe we have already worked out what Biermann means: when he says that a number is formed from an indeterminate basic element, he means that a number is formed from objects falling under one concept, and the 'indeterminate basic element' then corresponds to the concept. In this case we can point to such a concept: heavy, inert body. Both the sheep and the stars fall under this concept. There can, therefore, presumably be no doubt that the herd of sheep and the constellation are formed from 'the same indeterminate basic element'. Now it is surely conceivable that every star in the constellation belongs to a sheep in the herd, and so it is also conceivable that a herd of sheep should be equal to a constellation. We must not say here that they may of course be equal in respect of the number of solid inert bodies out of which they are made up; for the herd of sheep is itself one of the numbers and the constellation itself is the other. We have already established that according to Biermann number is not a property in respect of which the herd is interchangeable with the constellation. True, we may say, this beetle and the bark of this tree are equal[1] so far as their colour is concerned; but here neither the beetle nor the bark are a colour; moreover we do not have two colours, but one and the same. So according to Biermann this case is quite different from that of the numbers; for even if the phrase 'idea of a group' were to mean something quite different from the group itself, it still would not mean a property of the group. And even if, quite contrary to normal usage, Biermann were to use the term 'idea' in such a way that the idea of a group was a property of it, the proposition 'a number is the idea of a group' would amount to the same as 'a number is the number of a group': that is to say, a number is that property of a group which we call idea or number.

We still need to emphasize that according to Biermann's definition the word 'equal' does *not* mean complete coincidence: a number may be equal to another without being the same; a herd of sheep may be equal to a constellation without being the constellation itself. The question now arises what the number words mean: the most obvious answer would be that the number word 'two', for example, designates one (and only one) number, so that we may say: two is a number, three is a number, and so on. Two and three would be related to the concept of number in the same way as, say, Archimedes, Euclid and Diophantus are related to the concept of mathematician. If we say this, however, we should certainly get into difficulties. Let us again imagine a group consisting of a lion standing and a

---

* It is not clear from Biermann's wording whether or not this condition must be fulfilled; what we have is only: 'from a', and not 'from the same'. To be on the safe side, we will assume that it must.

---

[1] Here English idiom requires 'alike' rather than 'equal', but in German the same word—'*gleich*'—does duty for both (trans.).

lioness lying on the ground. This group is a number. Let us assign to it the number word 'two' as its proper name. Then in future we shall mean our group of lions when we say 'two'. Let us now think of the Goethe–Schiller memorial in Weimar. We surely cannot give the Goethe–Schiller group the same name as the group of lions. To do this could lead to some singularly unfortunate mistakes in identity! We do not seem able to manage with the number words alone. But Biermann has a simple way of getting round this difficulty; as we call Homer, Virgil and Goethe poets, so we might with equal justification call both the Goethe–Schiller group and the group of lions two. If we call something two, that shows we want to allocate it to a certain species: we want to say that it has a certain property or properties. In just the same way by calling someone a poet I acknowledge he has certain properties characteristic of being a poet,* or by calling a thing blue I attribute a certain property to it or assign it to some species or other. Likewise by calling a group three I would be saying that it has a certain property. As we call the properties green, blue, yellow colours, so we could call two and three numbers. But wait! Here we are again on the same false track as before. We cannot repeat often enough: number is a group or plurality composed of things of the same kind; therefore numbers are the subjects of the properties expressed by the number words. We are no more justified in asserting that two is a number than we are in counting green as a coloured object instead of a colour. Thus we are now able to say: two, three, four, etc., are properties of groups with constituents of the same kind, which groups or sets are called numbers. A somewhat more elevated way of putting the same thing is to say: two, three, four, etc., are properties of ideas of groups with constituents of the same kind, and these ideas are called numbers. The most remarkable thing for the layman, for me myself and perhaps even for Biermann in all this, and the most astonishing, is that the number words do not designate numbers but properties of numbers. The equation $2 = 1 + 1$ is generally considered to be true. Biermann's definition of $a = b$ is not applicable here, since it relates to numbers, i.e. groups, whereas for us the sign '2' on the left does not mean a number here but a property of a number. Let us see whether we fare any better with the plus sign. Biermann says: 'We construct a number containing all the elements of two numbers a and b formed from the same basic element' ... 'The resultant number we designate by $a + b$...'[1]

We do not learn from this what $2 + 3$ and $2 + 1$ mean, for 1, 2 and 3 are not numbers at all. But perhaps we learn something else which merits our attention. As we have seen, the constellation Orion is a number, the belt in this constellation is likewise a number and, moreover, a different one. If we understand Biermann correctly, both numbers are formed from 'the same

---

* We need not ask here whether one or more than one property is involved in the word 'two'.

---

[1] Biermann, p. 1.

basic element', for the elements of the belt are also the elements of Orion.
Let us then form a number containing all the elements of Orion and of its
belt. What could be simpler! We do not even have to bother constructing
this number: it is already there. The constellation of Orion is itself this
number. So let us designate Orion by a and its belt by b; then we have $a + b$
$= a$, whilst at the same time we have remained happily in accord with
Biermann's definitions of the plus sign and the equals sign. But that's enough
of pretending to be more stupid than we are! After all, Biermann is writing
for people already familiar with these matters who will read the right thing
into his words even when they are false or devoid of sense!* After all, the
words are there so that the reader may understand what is meant, despite
them. We have to bear in mind the condition that no element may be
common to both numbers. It follows that no number may ever be added to
itself: presumably we should have to say that $a + a$ is devoid of sense; yet a
little further on Biermann's text reads: $a + a + a \ldots$ (b-times). Let us see
how that comes about. Biermann says: 'If we substitute the number a for
each of the elements of a number b we obtain the sum $a + a + a \ldots$ (b-times),
which we designate in short by $a \times b$ or ab.'[1] The sense of this definition is
not easy to grasp; let us take an example to clarify what is at stake: let b be
the Goethe–Schiller group in the square in front of the theatre in Weimar,
which according to Biermann is indubitably a number. Let a be the constellation of Orion. Now let us first of all substitute Orion for the figure of Goethe.
It is no easy thing that Biermann is asking of us; his arithmetic would seem
to be designed for gods. For him personally all this is child's play; we shall
witness still greater feats. For the figure of Schiller let us now
substitute—well, what? Why, Orion, too!** And what do we get then?

Orion + Orion + Orion (Goethe–Schiller–group times).

Who would have thought it! A little later Biermann says: 'In $a + a + \ldots + a$
(b-times) we may pick one out of each group of a elements and their
combination yields b'. If Biermann had not said it, I would not have believed

---

* It would have been more to the purpose, in my view, if § 1 had been
left unwritten. That would have spared the author a certain amount of effort,
if only a modicum, and reduce the cost of printing, without imposing any
further labour upon the reader.
** This seems a difficult thing to conceive of, let alone to carry out in
practice. But we can see what is involved if we take one of the commercial
photographs of the said memorial and with a penknife cut out the piece with
the figure of Goethe on it, and do the same with the figure of Schiller. We
then cut two pieces of cardboard with exactly the same outlines as the pieces
removed and draw the constellation of Orion on each of them. Finally, we
place these pieces of cardboard in the holes made in the photograph: Seeing
is believing!

---

[1] Biermann, p. 3.

it. What is a group of *a* elements? For *a* is itself a group! And in our example it just is the constellation of Orion. What is a group of Orion-elements? And here there is even more than one! Has the word 'Orion' suddenly become an adjective? In the Chinese language there is indeed no distinction between a substantive and adjective. Has this usage been smuggled in here? Is an Orion-element an Orionic element, a star of the constellation of stars? What groups of these stars are we talking about here? Well, no matter! Presumably, what is meant by an Orion-element is a star. So if we combine certain stars, what do we get then? The Goethe–Schiller group in Wiemar! It is possibly not quite clear to everyone how this comes about. Perhaps we may be able to throw further light on the matter by taking into consideration a few words in Biermann's account which we have so far skipped over. For Biermann talks about the 'abstract unit 1', from which a number may be formed. To go by the definite article, there is only one abstract unit and this is designated by '1'. Units have been mentioned before: 'counting the elements or units'. According to this, 'unit' should mean the same as 'element'. In that case, 'the abstract unit' should mean: the abstract element. Admittedly, this has not got us any further. The meaning of the word 'element' surely seems abstract enough already. From what are we to abstract further? What is the relationship of the meanings of the words 'unit', 'one' and the 'abstract unit'? Biermann's way of putting it seems to imply that there are many units, and perhaps many ones as well, but only the one abstract unit 1. But isn't it very foolish of us to ask so many questions? The same might happen to us as happened to the schoolboy who asked his teacher in religious instruction to explain something further and was told 'But that is just the divine mystery in all its profundity!' Obscurity often has the greatest effect. If we established precisely what we understand by words like 'number', 'unit', 'one', 'the abstract unit 1', 'element', 'indeterminate basic element', we should forfeit the possibility of using a word now in one sense now in another, and as an end result the whole force of Biermann's account would be dissipated. Let us rather rejoice that we at last appear to have found, in the 'abstract unit 1', something that I have long been looking out for—one of those numbers with which mathematics is concerned; for when you come down to it, the heaps of sand and peas, the Goethe–Schiller statue and the Laocoön group did, after all, look somewhat incongruous in a discussion of arithmetic. Let us also hope that in the course of Biermann's account the abstract 2 and the abstract 3 will delight us by turning up just as unexpectedly as 1 has done. We might be somewhat at a loss, if we had not experienced so many extraordinary things already, to image how it is possible to *form* something out of the unique 'abstract unit 1'; or is perhaps 1 not the only component? We already met a similar case when a number had to be formed from the 'indeterminate basic element'. We attempted to explain this by a sort of miracle, but this explanation hardly seems to suit the present case; for what would here be the concept corresponding to the concept pea in our earlier example, and what objects, e.g., would fall under this concept? But we are asking too many questions again. I suppose it would be unwise to expect an answer from Biermann; for we have probably carried his thought much further than he did himself, expending, as he did, so little thought on § 1, possibly to avoid becoming entangled in the dreaded profundities of metaphysics; yet all that is needed is a pinch of logic. True, the way things have now fallen out, there is nothing in § 1 to warm the heart of the logician or mathematician.* In this paragraph, and in some of the later ones, we might well find further material to improve our minds. For instance, is it not touching to see with what ingenuousness the word 'number'[1] is introduced in § 2, p. 10: 'Two numerical magnitudes of the new kind are equal when they can be transformed in such a way that both contain the same elements with the same number in each'? It should, of course, have been stated with what meaning 'number' is being used here. That was the problem to be solved! Biermann probably imagines that he has solved it, when he has, on the contrary, done all he could to dodge this crucial point. He has shown the most consummate skill in missing the very point that is at stake. But let us put all that aside now. I find it nauseating to have to clean out the same old stable over and over again, solely in order that others may join Biermann in writing even more paragraphs like his § 1. I can well understand someone despairing of ever giving an accurate definition of number or even thinking that such a definition would be unfruitful and pointless and so beginning his book with a few principles concerning number, whilst simply assuming that everyone will know in any given case how to distinguish a number (natural number) from anything else and will recognize these principles as true without proof. But what I find difficult to understand is that anyone should recognize it to be necessary or at any rate useful to discuss the concept of number and then conduct this discussion so superficially and without availing himself of what has already been achieved in this field, with the result that he skirts the issue and does not even notice that he has done so. This is a procedure which deserves academic recognition, even if it does make one or two things seem axiomatic which could be proved if probed more deeply. What we do in such a case is to leave certain questions to look after themselves and simply take up the argument at a later stage. If someone proceeds in the way Biermann does, he merely deludes himself,

---

* It is proof of the obstacles we have to contend with in order to make any common progress that writers of our day, including even historians of philosophy like K. Fischer (cf. my *Grundlagen*, p. III), behave just as if the human race, as far as these questions are concerned, had been asleep until now and had only just awoken from its slumber, and this after thinkers of acknowledged stature like Spinoza long ago conveyed illuminating thoughts about number. But who would think of consulting Spinoza about such childishly simple matters!

---

[1] Here again we have '*Anzahl*', the word for natural number (trans.).

and possibly his readers as well, into thinking he has achieved something when he has uttered a few incomprehensible and barren phrases. This is just window-dressing and downright unscientific. Either certain questions should be left aside altogether, or we should really go deeply into them and not just make a parade of doing so.*

I cannot repeat the substance of my *Grundlagen* here. It is bad enough that I have been obliged to expend so many extra words on issues that have been essentially resolved.** Here we can do no more than make the following brief remarks: there is only one number called 0, there is only one number called 1, only one number called 2, and so on. There are various designations for any one number. It is the same number which is designated by '1 + 1' and '2'. Nothing can be asserted of 2 which cannot also be asserted of 1 + 1; where there appears to be an exception, the explanation is that the signs '2' and '1 + 1' are being discussed and not their content. It is inevitable that various signs should be used for the same thing, since there are different possible ways of arriving at it, and then we first have to ascertain that it really is the same thing we have reached.*** $2 = 1 + 1$ does

---

* Biermann may find my attack has become too personal when I take the liberty of surmising what he has been thinking, and on occasion surmising that he has not been thinking at all. Of course, I shall be more than willing to acknowledge my conjectures mistaken if Biermann will communicate what he was actually thinking. It would be a source of special pleasure to me if his thoughts should turn out to have more sense in them that I suspected. Of course, I could have saved myself the effort of trying to penetrate the workings of his mind by simply adhering to the text of his argument. I could then have briefly shown the mistakes in his logic. But this way of proceeding might easily have prompted a charge of unfairness. Someone might then have said, for instance: he sticks to the letter of the argument, which admittedly, is not quite happy in places; he pontificates on matters of style and makes no attempt at all to deal with the thoughts themselves. I did not just want to show that there are faults of expression; I wanted to show that the thought itself is sometimes incorrect and sometimes impossible to locate. I found myself in the same position as a judge who sometimes has to have recourse to the legislator's intentions when the text of the law proves inadequate: in such a case you could not get by without making conjectures.

** Biermann ought really to apologise to me for having put me to so much trouble simply because he has made so little effort himself.

*** It is wrong when a distinction is made in school or textbooks between $\sqrt{a^2}$ and $\sqrt{(-a)^2}$. We have to decide once and for all which of the numbers whose square is b we want to understand by $\sqrt{b}$. To designate first one, then another, by '$\sqrt{b}$' is reprehensible. Each sign may have only one meaning so that we run no risk of drawing wrong conclusions. We should not talk about the different ways in which a number comes into being. Numbers do not come into being, they are eternal. There is not a 4 resulting from 2^2, and another resulting from $(-2)^2$; '4', '2^2', '$(-2)^2$', are simply different signs for the same thing and their differences simply indicate the different ways in which it is possible for us to arrive at the same thing.

not mean that the contents of '2' and '1 + 1' agree in one respect, though they are otherwise different; for what is the special property in which they are supposed to be alike? Is it in respect of number? But two is a number through and through and nothing else but a number. This agreement with respect to number is therefore the same here as complete coincidence, identity. What a wilderness of numbers there would be if we were to regard 2, 1 + 1, 3 − 1, etc., all as different numbers which agree only in one property. The chaos would be even greater if we were to recognize many noughts, ones, twos, and so on. Every whole number would have infinitely many factors, every equation infinitely many solutions, even if all these were equal to one another. In that event we should, of course, be compelled by the nature of the case to regard all these solutions that are equal to one another as one and the same solution. Thus the equals sign in arithmetic expresses complete coincidence, identity.

Numerical signs, whether they are simple or built up by using arithmetical signs, are proper names of numbers. Therefore, we cannot use the names of numbers either with the indefinite article, e.g. this is a one, or in the plural—many twos. The plus sign does not mean the same as 'and'. In the sentences '3 and 5 are odd', '3 and 5 are factors of 15 other than 1' we cannot substitute '2 and 6' or '8' for '3 and 5'. On the other hand, '2 + 6' or '8' are always substitutable for '3 + 5'. It is therefore incorrect to say '1 and 1 is 2' instead of 'the sum of 1 and 1 is 2'. It is wrong to say 'number is just so many ones'; and if we say 'units' for 'ones', if anything we magnify the error by confusing units with one, even though verbally there is a gain in smoothness. Our feeling for language warns us against the form 'ones' for good reason. If we say 'units' instead, we merely get round the prohibition.

[*A criticism of Kerry*][1]

On Concept and Object

In a series of articles in this Quarterly on intuition and its psychical elaboration, Benno Kerry has several times referred to my *Grundlagen der Arithmetik* and other works of mine, sometimes agreeing and sometimes disagreeing with me. I cannot but be pleased at this, and I think the best way I can show my appreciation is to take up the discussion of the points he contests. This seems to me all the more necessary, because his opposition is at least partly based on a misunderstanding, which might be

---

[1] Until his death in 1889 Benno Kerry was *Privatdozent* in Philosophy at the University of Strasburg.

The dispute with Kerry relates to Kerry's eight articles *Über Anschauung und ihre psychische Verarbeitung* in the *Vierteljahrsschrift für wissenschaftliche Philosophie*: ⌒ (1885), pp. 433–493, 10 (1886), pp. 419–467, 11 (1887), pp. 53–116, 11 (1887), pp. 249–307, 13 (1889), pp. 71–124, 13 (1889), pp. 392–419, 14 (1890), pp. 317–353, 15 (1891), pp. 127–167. In the second and fourth articles Kerry had gone into Frege's views in particular detail.—The piece for the *Nachlaß* is obviously a preliminary draft of the article *Über Begriff und Gegenstand*, which appeared in 1892. The latter is printed on the left with the original pagination, with the corresponding passages of the piece from the *Nachlaß* on the right (ed.).

Translators' note: For the article *Über Begriff und Gegenstand* we have taken over the translation by Peter Geach published in *Translations from the Philosophical Writings of Gottlob Frege*, ed. Geach and Black, pp. 42–55 (Blackwell 1960), both because we are largely in agreement with it and because it has been so widely read and quoted from. Where the wording of the draft agrees with that of the published article, we have relied heavily on the Geach translation, though we have departed from it in several places, mainly in order to remain consistent with the renderings we have adopted elsewhere of certain terms—here notably '*bedeuten*' and '*Bedeutung*'. Again such a departure has been necessary in places where the agreement in wording extends only to part of a sentence.

We have chosen not to adhere to the format of the German text in presenting the draft *as if both* it *and* the criticism of Biermann were about the concept of number. The fact that they were both found, unseparated, in a folder under the heading 'On the Concept of Number' seems to us no good reason for the German editors' lay-out.

We should like to express our grateful thanks to Professor P. T. Geach for permitting us to make use of his translation in this way.

shared by others, of what I say about the concept; and because, even apart from this special occasion, the matter is important and difficult enough for a more thorough treatment than seemed to me suitable in my *Grundlagen*.

The word 'concept' is used in various ways; its sense is sometimes psychological, sometimes logical, and sometimes perhaps a confused mixture of both. Since this licence exists, it is natural to restrict it by requiring that when once a usage is adopted it shall be maintained. What I decided was to keep strictly to a purely logical use; the question whether this or that use is more appropriate is one that I should like to leave on one side, as of minor importance. Agreement about the mode of expression will easily be reached when once it is recognized that there is something that deserves a special term.

It seems to me that Kerry's misunderstanding results from his unintentionally confusing his own usage of the word 'concept' with mine. This readily gives rise to contradictions, for which my usage is not to blame.

[193] Kerry contests what he calls my definition of 'concept'. I would remark, in the first place, that my

I turn now to consider, as briefly as possible, the objections which B. Kerry* has brought against my definitions.

He begins by contesting what he calls my definition of a concept, and there is no doubt that here he is

---

* *Über Anschauung und ihre psychische Verarbeitung* in *der Vierteljahrschrift für wissenschaftliche Philosophie*, Volume XI, No. 3, pp. 249 ff.

explanation is not meant as a proper definition. One cannot require that everything shall be defined, any more than one can require that a chemist shall decompose every substance. What is simple cannot be decomposed, and what is logically simple cannot have a proper definition. Now something logically simple is no more given us at the outset than most of the chemical elements are; it is reached only by means of scientific work. If something has been discovered that is simple, or at least must count as simple for the time being, we shall have to coin a term for it, since language will not originally contain an expression that exactly answers. On the introduction of a name for something logically simple, a definition is not possible; there is nothing for it but to lead the reader or hearer, by means of hints, to understand the words as is intended.

Kerry wants to make out that the distinction between concept and object is not absolute. 'In a previous passage,' he says, 'I have myself expressed the opinion that the relation between the content of the concept and the concept-object is, in a certain respect, a peculiar and irreducible one; but this was in no way bound up with the view that the properties of being a concept and of being an object are mutually ex-

touching on a crucial point, perhaps the most important one in the whole issue. The first thing to say is that my explanation is not meant as a proper definition. One cannot define everything, any more than one can decompose every chemical substance. To do either presupposes that we are dealing with something composite. In many cases one has to be satisfied with leading the reader, by means of hints, to understand the word as it is intended.

The difference of opinion concerns the distinction between concept* and object. Kerry would like to make out that it is not absolute. 'In a previous passage,' he says, 'we have ourselves expressed the opinion that the relation between the concept-content and the concept-object is, in a certain respect, a peculiar and irreducible one; but this was in no way bound up with the view that the properties of being an

---

*In my paper *Funktion und Begriff* (Jena 1891) I called a concept a function whose value is always a truth-value, and this could be taken as a definition. But in that case the difficulty which, as I am trying to show, arises for the concept, arises for the function too.

clusive. The latter view no more follows from the former than it would follow, if, e.g., the relation of father and son were one that could not be further reduced, that a man could not be at once a father and a son (though of course not, e.g., father of the man whose son he was).'

Let us fasten on this simile. If there were, or had been beings that were fathers but could not be sons, such beings would obviously be quite different in kind from all men who are sons. Now it is something like this that happens here. The concept (as I understand the word) is predicative.*

On the other hand, a name of an object, a proper name, is quite incapable of being used as a grammatical predicate. This admittedly needs elucidation, otherwise it might appear false. Surely one can just as well assert of a thing that it is Alexander the Great, or is the number four, or is the planet Venus, as that it is green or is a mammal? [194]. If anybody thinks this, he is not distinguishing the usages of the word 'is'. In the last two examples it serves as a copula, as a mere verbal sign of predication. (In this sense the

object and being a concept are mutually exclusive. The latter view no more follows from the former than it would follow if, say, the relation of father and son were one that could not be further reduced, that a man could not be at once a father and a son (though of course not e.g. father of the man whose son he was).'[1]

Let me fasten on this simile. If there were, or had been, beings that were fathers, though they were so constituted by nature that they could not be sons, such beings would be obviously quite different in kind from all men who are sons. Now something like this happens here.

The concept—as I understand the word—is predicative even in cases where we speak of a subject-concept. For instance, the sentence 'All mammals are warm-blooded' says the same as 'Whatever is a mammal is warm-blooded'. On the other hand, a name of an object—a proper name—is quite incapable of being used as a grammatical predicate. This may strike one as false if one does not distinguish between a proper name's occurring as only part of a predicate, which is certainly possible, and its being itself the whole predicate, which is not possible. One can assert of a thing that it is green or is a mammal; but one cannot in the same way assert of a thing that it is Alexander the Great, or is the number four, or is Venus.

---

* It is, in fact, the reference of a grammatical predicate.

---

[1] *Vjschr. f. wissensch. Philosophie* 11 (1887), p. 272 (ed.).

German word *ist* can sometimes be replaced by the mere personal suffix: cf. *dies Blatt ist grün* and *dies Blatt grünt.*) We are here saying that something falls under a concept, and the grammatical predicate stands for this concept. In the first three examples, on the other hand, 'is' is used like the 'equals' sign in arithmetic, to express an equation.*

In order to see this, it is of course necessary to distinguish the two uses of the word 'is'. For in the first cases it serves as a copula, as a mere auxiliary indicating that we have a statement, and is sometimes then replaceable by the mere verb ending: e.g. '*dieses Blatt ist grün*' ['this grass is green'], '*dieses Blatt grünt*' [*lit.* 'this grass greens']. Here one is saying that something falls under a concept. The grammatical predicate means this concept. In the second cases, the word 'is' is used like the equals sign in arithmetic, to express an equation.* Let us consider the following example: in the sentence 'That is Saturn' we have two proper names for the same object. For the word 'that', together with an appropriate pointing gesture, must here be construed as a proper name (in the logical sense) i.e. as a sign for an object. I am not here asserting the meaning of the word 'Saturn' of the object I am pointing to; if that were so, I should be asserting an object of itself, which would be nonsensical—one just cannot assert an object of

---

* I use the word 'equal' and the symbol '=' in the sense 'the same as', 'no other than', 'identical with'. Cf. E. Schroeder, *Vorlesungen ueber die Algebra der Logik* (Leipzig 1890), Vol. 1, § 1. Schroeder must however be criticized for not distinguishing two fundamentally different relations; the relation of an object to a concept it falls under, and the subordination of one concept to another. His remarks on the *Vollwurzel* are likewise open to objection. Schroeder's symbol ≠ does not simply take the place of the copula.

---

* I use the word 'equal' and the sign '=' in the sense 'the same as', 'not different from'. Cf. E. Schröder, *Vorlesungen über die Algebra der Logik* (Leipzig 1890), Vol. 1, § 1, especially p. 127 & p. 128. Schröder, however, is to be criticized for not here distinguishing two fundamentally different relations; the relation of an object to a concept it falls under, and the subordination of one concept to another. His discussion of the *Vollwurzel* is likewise open to objection.

In the sentence 'The morning star is Venus', we have two proper names, 'morning star' and 'Venus', for the same object. In the sentence 'the morning star is a planet' we have a proper name, 'the morning star', and a concept-word, 'planet'. So far as language goes, no more has happened than that 'Venus' has been replaced by 'a planet'; but really the relation has become wholly different. An equation is reversible; an object's falling under a concept is an irreversible relation. In the sentence 'the morning star is Venus', 'is' is obviously not the mere copula; its content is an essential part of the predicate, so that the word 'Venus' does not constitute the whole of the predicate.* One might say instead: 'the morning star is no other than Venus'; what was previously implicit in the single word 'is' is here set forth in four separate words, and

something—. The 'is' is not the mere copula, but is to be compared with a word like 'grünt', in which the verb ending by itself takes the place of the copula, whilst the stem gives the actual content.* The content of the predicate is not comprised in the word 'Saturn' alone; an essential part of it is contained in the word 'is', or at least has to be added in thought. As the logical predicate we may take, say: no other than Saturn. It is this which is predicated here and not just Saturn. *Saturn* is an object, *no other than Saturn* is a concept.

---

* Cf. my *Grundlagen*, § 66, footnote.

* Cf. my *Grundlagen*, § 57.

in 'is no other than' the word 'is' now really is the mere copula. What is predicated here is thus not *Venus* but *no other than Venus*. These words stand for a concept; admittedly only one object falls under this, but such a concept must still always be distinguished from the object.* We have here a word 'Venus' that can never be a proper predicate [195] although it can form part of a predicate. The reference** of this word is *thus* something that can never occur as a concept, but only as an object. Kerry, too, would probably not wish to dispute that there is something of this kind. But this would mean admitting a distinction, which it is very important recognize, between what can occur only as an object, and everything else. And this distinction would not be effaced even if it were true, as Kerry thinks it is, that there are concepts that can also be objects.

There are, indeed, cases that seem to support his view. I myself have indicated (in *Grundlagen*, § 53, *ad fin.*) that a concept may fall under a higher concept—which, however, must not be confused with one concept's being subordinate to another. Kerry does not appeal to this; instead, he gives the following example: 'the concept "horse" is a concept easily attained', and thinks that the concept 'horse' is an object, in fact one of the objects that fall under the concept 'concept easily at-

Thus, as we see, we have here the case of something making its appearance only as an object, never as a concept, and Kerry himself surely does not wish to dispute that this is possible either. But this means admitting a distinction, which it is of fundamental importance to recognize, between what, by its very nature, can occur only as an object, and everything else. And this distinction would not be effaced even if it were true, as Kerry thinks it is, that there are concepts that can also be objects. Now there are in fact cases which seem to support this view. I myself have pointed out (*Grundlagen*, § 53 to the end) that a concept may fall under a higher concept which, however, is not to be confused with one concept's being subordinate to another. Kerry does not appeal to this; instead, he gives the following example: 'the concept "horse" is a concept easily attained', and thinks that the concept 'horse' is an object, in fact one of the objects that fall under the concept

---

* Cf. my *Grundlagen*, § 51.

** Cf. my paper, 'On Sense and Reference' (*Ueber Sinn und Bedeutung*), shortly to appear in the *Zeitschrift für Phil. und phil. Kritik*.

tained'. Quite so; the three words 'the concept "horse"' do designate an object, but on that very account they do not designate a concept, as I am using the word. This is in full accord with the criterion I gave— that the singular definite article always indicates an object, whereas the indefinite article accompanies a concept word.*

Kerry holds that no logical rules can be based on linguistic distinctions; but my own way of doing this is something that nobody can avoid who lays down such rules at all; for we cannot come to an understanding with one another apart from language, and so in the end we must always rely on other people's understanding words, inflexions, and sentence-construction in essentially the same way as ourselves. As I said before, I was not trying to give a definition, but only hints; and to this end I appealed to the general feeling for the German language. It is here very much to my advantage that there is such good accord between the linguistic distinction and the real one. As regards the indefinite article there are probably no exceptions to our rule at all for us to remark, apart from obsolete formulas like *Ein edler Rath* ['Councillor']. The matter is not so simple for the definite article, especially [196] in the plural; but then my criterion does not relate to this case. In the singular, so far as I can see, the matter is doubtful only when a singular takes the place of a plural, as in the sentence 'the Turk besieged

'concept easily attained'. Quite so; the three words 'the concept "horse"' do designate an object, but for that very reason they do not designate a concept in the sense in which I am using the word. This is in full accord with the criterion I gave—that the singular definite article always indicates an object, whereas the indefinite article accompanies a concept-word.* Now it is true that Kerry holds that no logical prescriptions can be based on linguistic distinctions; but proceeding as I do, this is something that nobody can possibly avoid who lays down such prescriptions; for you cannot make yourself understood apart from language, and so in the end you must always rely on the reader or hearer's understanding words, inflexions and sentence-construction as you do yourself. As was said, I was not trying to give a definition, but only hints; and to this end I appealed to the general feeling for the German language; for my criterion relates directly only to the German language. It is here very much to my advantage that the linguistic distinction accords so well with the real one. As regards the indefinite article there are, I should say, no exceptions to our rule at all to remark, apart from the archaic form '*Ein edler Rat*' [Councillor], which here and there is still in official use. If the article in the plural can be replaced by 'all' and the meaning is that the statement is to hold of each individual member of the class, then we have a concept-

---

* *Grundlagen*, § 51; 66, footnote; § 68, footnote on p. 80.

* My *Grundlagen*, § 51; § 66, footnote; § 68, footnote on p. 80.

Vienna', 'the horse is a four-legged animal'. These cases are so easily recognizable as special ones that the value of our rule is hardly impaired by their occurrence. It is clear that in the first sentence 'the Turk' is the proper name of a people. The second sentence is probably best regarded as expressing a universal judgement, say 'all horses are four-legged animals' or 'all properly constituted horses are four-legged animals'; these will be discussed later.*

word (e.g. *die Pferde sind pflanzen-fressende Tiere*).[1] On the other hand, the phrase 'the Romans' in the sentence 'The Romans conquered Gaul' is to be regarded as a proper name, for here we are not saying of each Roman that he has conquered Gaul; we are speaking of the Roman people, which is to be regarded logically as an object. There are also cases in which the singular is used in the sense of the plural—e.g. 'The horse is a herbivorous animal'. This case is so easily recognizable as an exception, that the value of our criterion is hardly impaired by it. (If the grammatical subject is a concept word, the sentence can be transformed into one in which the subject occurs predicatively with the indefinite article—e.g. 'If something is a horse, then it is a herbivorous animal'. The fuller account given in the *Grundlagen* makes it clear, I think, what I have in mind.)

---

* Nowadays people seem inclined to exaggerate the scope of the statement that different linguistic expressions are never completely equivalent, that a word can never be exactly translated into another language. One might perhaps go even further, and say that the same word is never taken in quite the same way even by men who share a language. I will not enquire as to the measure of truth in these statements; I would only emphasize that nevertheless different expressions quite often have something in common, which I call the sense, or in the special case

---

[1] In the German sentence the word '*die*' is the plural form of the definite article. The natural English translation would be 'Horses are herbivorous animals' (trans.).

Kerry calls my criterion unsuitable; for surely, he says, in the sentence 'the concept that I am now talking about is an individual concept' the name composed of the first eight words stands for a concept; but he is not taking the word 'concept' in my sense, and it is not in what I have laid down that the contradiction lies. But nobody can require that my mode of expression shall agree with Kerry's.

It must indeed be recognized that we are here confronted by an awkwardness of language, which I admit cannot be avoided, if we say that the concept *horse* is not a concept,* whereas e.g., the [197]

Therefore when Kerry says that my criterion does not meet the case, claiming that in the sentence 'The concept that I am now talking about is an individual concept' the name composed of the first eight words surely means a concept, the contradiction does not lie in what I have laid down; it obtains between the sense I attach to the word 'concept' and that adopted by Kerry. But nobody can require that my stipulations shall be in accord with Kerry's mode of expression, but only that they be consistent in themselves. True, we cannot fail to recognize that we are here confronted by an awkwardness of language, which I admit is unavoidable, if we assert 'the concept *horse* is not a concept',* whereas, e.g. the city of Berlin is a city, and the volcano

of sentences, the thought. In other words, we must not fail to recognize that the same sense, the same thought, may be variously expressed; thus the difference does not here concern the sense, but only the apprehension, shading, or colouring of the thought, and is irrelevant for logic. It is possible for one sentence to give no more and no less information than another; and, for all the multiplicity of languages, mankind has a common stock of thoughts. If all transformation of the expression were forbidden on the plea that this would alter the content as well, logic would simply be crippled; for the task of logic can hardly be performed without trying to recognize the thought in its manifold guises. Moreover, all definitions would then have to be rejected as false.

---

* A similar thing happens when we say as regards the sentence 'this

---

* A similar thing happens when we say 'In the sentence "this rose is red", the grammatical predicate "red" belongs to the subject "this rose"'. Here the four words 'the grammatical predicate "red"' are not a grammatical predicate, but a subject. By the very act of explicitly calling it a grammatical predicate in this way, we deprive it of this property.

city of Berlin is a city, and the volcano Vesuvius is a volcano. Language is here in a predicament that justifies the departure from custom. The peculiarity of our case is indicated by Kerry himself, by means of the quotation-marks around 'horse'; I use italics to the same end. There was no reason to mark out the words 'Berlin' and 'Vesuvius' in a similar way. In logical discussions one quite often needs to assert something about a concept, and to express this in the form usual for such assertions—viz. to make what is asserted of the concept into the content of the grammatical predicate. Consequently, one would expect that the reference of the grammatical subject would be the concept; but the concept as such cannot play this part, in view of its predicative nature; it must first be converted into an object,* or, speaking more precisely, represented by an object. We designate this object by prefixing the words 'the concept'; e.g.

'The concept *man* is not empty'.

Here the first three words are to be regarded as a proper name,** which can no more be used predicatively than 'Berlin' or 'Vesuvius'. When we

Vesuvius is a volcano. Language is here in a predicament that justifies the departure from what we normally say. The peculiarity of our case is indicated by Kerry himself by means of the quotation-marks around 'horse'. (We have used italics here to the same end.) There was no reason to mark out the words 'Berlin' and 'Vesuvius' in a similar way above. In logical discussions one quite often needs to assert something about a concept,* and to express this in the grammatical form usual for such statements, so that what is asserted becomes the content of the grammatical predicate. Consequently, one would expect the concept to be the content of the grammatical subject; but the concept as such cannot play this part, in view of its predicative nature; it must first be converted into an object, or, speaking more precisely: an object that is connected with it in accordance with a rule must be substituted for it, and it is this object we designate by an expression of the form 'the concept *x*'. (Cf. p. X of my *Grundlagen*.)

---

rose is red': The grammatical predicate 'is red' belongs to the subject 'this rose'. Here the words 'The grammatical predicate "is red"' are not a grammatical predicate but a subject. By the very act of explicitly calling it a predicate, we deprive it of this property.

* Cf. my *Grundlagen*, p. X.
** I call anything a proper name if it is a sign for an object.

---

* When we say 'All men are mortal', we do not assert mortality of the concept *man*, but we subordinate the concept *mortal* to the latter concept. [This is obviously a slip on Frege's part; what he means of course is that we subordinate the concept *man* to the concept *mortal* (trans.).]

say 'Jesus falls under the concept *man*', then, setting aside the copula, the predicate is:

'someone falling under the concept *man*'

and this means the same as:

'a man'.

But the phrase

'the concept *man*'

is only part of this predicate.

Somebody might urge, as against the predicative nature of the concept, that nevertheless we speak of a subject-concept. But even in such cases, e.g. in the sentence

'all mammals have red blood'

we cannot fail to recognize the predicative nature* of the concept; for we can say instead:

[198] 'whatever is a mammal
          has red blood'

or:

'if anything is a mammal,
then it has red blood'.

So the phrase 'the concept *horse*' must be regarded as a proper name, which can no more be used pre-

---

* What I call here the predicative nature of the concept is just a special case of the need of supplementation, the 'unsaturatedness', that I gave as the essential feature of a function in my work *Function und Begriff* (Jena, 1891). It was there scarcely possible to avoid the expression 'the function $f(x)$', although there too the difficulty arose that what this expression stands for is not a function.

dicatively than can, say, 'Berlin' or 'Vesuvius'. If we say that Bucephalus falls under the concept *horse*, then the predicate here is clearly 'falling under the concept *horse*', and this has the same meaning as 'a horse'. But the phrase 'the concept *horse*' is only part of this predicate.

When I wrote my *Grundlagen der Arithmetik*, I had not yet made the distinction between sense and reference;* and so, under the expression 'a possible content of judgement, I was combining what I now designate by the distinctive words 'thought' and 'truth-value'. Consequently, I no longer entirely approve of the explanation I then gave (*op. cit.* p. 77), as regards its wording; my view is, however, still essentially the same.

When I wrote my *Grundlagen*, I had not yet made the distinction between sense and meaning;* and so, under the expression 'content of possible judgement', I was combining what I now distinguish by the words 'thought' and 'truth-value'. For this reason I no longer hold my choice of expressions in the second footnote to p. 77 to be quite suitable, although in the main my view remains the same: a concept is essentially predicative in nature,** whilst the very opposite is true of an object, so that a proper name (sign or name of an object) can never contain the whole predicate.

---

* Cf. my essay 'On Sense and Reference' in the *Zeitschrift für Phil. und phil. Kritik.*

---

* Cf. my paper *Über Sinn und Bedeutung* in the *Zeitschrift für Phil. und Phil. Kritik.*

** What I have here called the predicative nature of a concept is just a special case of the need for supplementation or the unsaturatedness that I gave as being essential to a function in my paper *Funktion und Begriff.* It was there scarely possible to avoid the expression 'the function $f(x)$', although in that case too the difficulty arose that the meaning of the words 'the function $f(x)$' is not a function.

We may say in brief, taking 'subject' and 'predicate' in the linguistic sense: A concept is the reference of a predicate; an object is something that can never be the whole reference of a predicate, but

[Continued on p. 105]

We may say in brief: a concept is what can be predicated. An object is what cannot be predicated, though something can be predicated of it.*

---

* In his second article (p. 424) Kerry says 'By the number 4 we understand the result of additively combining 3 and 1. The concept-object answering to the concept given here is the individual number 4, a quite definite number in the natural number series. This object obviously bears just the marks named in its concept, and no other besides—provided we refrain, as we surely must, from counting as *propria* of the object the infinitely many relations in which it stands to all other individual numbers: "the" 4 is likewise the result of additively combining 3 and 1.'

We must assume from this that Kerry calls the content of the words 'the result of additively combining 3 and 1' a concept. I would agree with him if there was no definite article before 'result'. I think he will claim the content of the quoted words, without the definite article, to be a concept too, so that in this respect there will be complete agreement between us. Now how, according to Kerry, would the concept which answers first to the whole phrase be distinguished from that which answers, secondly, to this phrase with the definite article omitted? The definite article does not add a new characteristic mark. What it *does* do is to indicate:

1. That there is such a result.
2. That there is only one such.

From what I have said in my *Grundlagen*, from § 45 up to and

[Footnote* to p. 100 continued]
including § 53, there can be no doubt that no further characteristic marks are ascribed to our concept in these two sentences, but that properties are asserted of it. Incidentally, I am sorry that Kerry is at such pains to blur afresh the distinction I wisely drew between the uses of the words 'property' and 'characteristic mark'—a distinction that alone makes it possible to achieve complete clarity concerning the fallacy in the ontological proof of the existence of God. Therefore the sentence 'There is a result of additively combining 3 and 1' no more ascribes a further characteristic mark to the concept *result of additively combining 3 and 1* than the existence, which is asserted in the sentence 'There is a God', is a characteristic mark of the concept *God*. What is here said of existence holds also for oneness. So we might well arrive at Kerry's view that the words 'the result of additively combining 3 and 1' mean the same concept as the words 'result of additively combining 3 and 1'; for how else are concepts to be distinguished if not by their characteristic marks or the way in which they are formed? The distinction between the two expressions would then be similar to that between 'Berlin' and 'the city of Berlin'. These both designate the same object. It is just that the latter happens in addition to remind us of certain properties. However it soon becomes clear that our two expressions do not mean the same, as we should have to suppose they did if we wished to construe them as designations of concepts; unless one wished to maintain that there was a further way of distinguishing concepts other than through their

[Footnote* to p. 100 continued]

characteristic marks and mode of formation. When Kerry says 'By the number 4 we understand the result of additively combining 3 and 1', this is obviously meant to be a definition. A definition is always a logical identity. The sentence 'The number 4 is nothing other than the result of additively combining 3 and 1' would have the same sense. Thus this sentence does not claim to assert that the number 4 falls under the concept *result of additively combining 3 and 1*, as does 'The number 4 is a result of additively combining 3 and 1'. This latter cannot be construed as a logical identity, as a definition, because it leaves it open whether there may not be something else which is also a result of this operation, and because it has a sense only if it has previously been established what the words 'the number 4' designate. This can only be fixed by a logical identity to the effect that the same thing is to be understood by the words 'the number 4', whose sense we know because the meanings of its parts and of the grammatical forms employed are known to us. It is, accordingly, clear that the definite article makes an essential contribution to the sense of our sentence and that the position here is consequently quite different from what it is in the case of 'The capital of the German Empire is the city of Berlin', where if you leave out 'the city of' you are only suppressing a qualification which is incidental to the sense. Thus I see no alternative but to deny that the words 'the result of additively combining 3 and 1' mean a concept, if one refuses to allow the possibility that concepts should be distinct from one another even through their characteristic marks

[Footnote* to p. 100 continued]

and mode of formation are the same. This alternative would be open to Kerry.

In fact Kerry seems to countenance this possibility when he says on pp. 456 ff.[1] that the concept of a concept can contain the same characteristic marks as the concept itself. But there is no doubt that here again a property is being confused with a characteristic mark. I do not believe that anything of value is to be learned by taking this route or that logicians will have any inclination to tread the same path. On the contrary, it seems far and away more appropriate to regard the replacement of the indefinite by the definite article as signifying the transition from a concept to an object falling under it, where the case holds that there is only one such object. So I do not go along with Kerry's saying that the object is like the concept in having as characteristic marks those of the concept; I say instead that the object has the characteristic marks of the concept as properties. And here we have the distinction. For the relation of a characteristic mark to a concept is different from that of property to an object (cf. *Grundlagen*, § 53).

Another consideration shows that the words 'the result of additively combining 3 and 1' designate an object. We have already seen that the first sentence of the passage from Kerry quoted above is to be construed as a definition and thus as a logical identity. Now at the end we have: '"the" 4 is likewise the result of additively combining 3 and 1'. The author's view is that the role of

---

[1] *Vjschr. f. wissensch. Philosophie* 10 (1886) (ed.).

[Footnote* to p. 100 continued]

the grammatical subject is to designate the concept-object and presumably the definite article is enclosed in quotation marks to mark this object off from the concept. Obviously this last sentence has the sense of a logical identity too: ' "the" 4 is nothing other than the result of additively combining 3 and 1'.

The view that this sentence is meant to express that an object falls under the concept *result of* etc. is immediately ruled out by the occurrence of the definite article before 'result'. Otherwise the indefinite article would have been used or the article would have to have been omitted. Now if the left-hand side of this identity is an object, the right-hand side must be an object too. Further, the right-hand side of the first identity is at the same time the right-hand side of the second: hence the two expressions to the left must designate the same thing: the number 4 is nothing other than 'the' 4. I can see no significance in the use of quotation marks here. In my view the reason for the sorry state of affairs we find in Kerry, where the distinctions between concept and object, characteristic mark and property, are effaced is that logical and psychological questions and viewpoints are scrambled together, which greatly detracts from the value of his articles. He will speak now of a concept, then of the idea of a concept, now of an object, then of the idea of it, without its even being wholly clear whether it is the one or the other that is in question, whether we are engaged in a logical or psychological inquiry. Now it is no particular cause for wonder if we can find no way of distinguishing between the idea of a concept and

can be the reference of a subject. It must here be remarked that the words 'all', 'any', 'no', 'some', are prefixed to concept-words. In universal and particular affirmative and negative sentences, we are expressing relations between concepts; we use these words to indicate the special kind of relation. They are thus, logically speaking, not to be more closely associated with the concept-words that follow them, but are to be related to the sentence as a whole. It is easy to see this in the case of negation. If in the sentence

'all mammals are land-dwellers'

the phrase 'all mammals' expressed the logical subject of the predicate *are land-dwellers*, then in order to negate the whole sentence we should

that of an object. Perhaps they are often even difficult to hold apart. But here Kerry has simply succumbed to a widespread sickness. Indeed would not Locke's empiricism and Berkeley's idealism, and so much that is tied up with these philosophies, have been impossible if people had distinguished adequately between thinking in the narrower sense and ideation, between the parts of a content (concepts, objects, relations) and the ideas we have? Even if with us men thinking does not take place without ideas, still the content of a judgement is something objective, the same for everybody, and as far as it is concerned it is neither here nor there what ideas men have when they grasp it. In any case these are subjective and will differ from one person to another. What is here being said of the content as a whole applies also to the parts which we can distinguish within it.

have to negate the predicate: 'are not land-dwellers'. Instead, we must put the 'not' in front of 'all'; from which it follows that 'all' logically belongs with the predicate. On the other hand, we do negate the sentence 'The concept *mammal* is subordinate to the concept *land-dweller*' by negating the predicate: 'is not subordinate to the concept *land-dweller*'.

If we keep it in mind that in my way of speaking expressions like 'the concept *F*' designate not concepts but objects, most of [199] Kerry's objections already collapse. If he thinks (cf. p. 281) that I have identified concept and extension of concept, he is mistaken; I merely expressed ny view that in the expression 'the number that applies to the concept *F* is the extension of the concept *like-numbered to the concept F*' the words 'extension of the concept' could be replaced by 'concept'. Notice carefully that here the word 'concept' is combined with the definite article. Besides, this was only an incidental remark; I did not base anything upon it.

Thus Kerry does not succeed in filling the gap between concept and object. Someone might attempt, however, to make use of my own statements in this sense. I have said that to assign a number involves an

So if we hold on to the fact that the words 'the concept *F*' designate not a concept but an object, most of Kerry's objections don't begin to stand up. If he thinks (p. 281) that I have identified concept and extension of a concept, this is simply not the case. I merely expressed my view that in the expression 'the number belonging to the concept *F* is the extension of the concept *like-numbered to the concept F*', the words 'extension of the concept' could be replaced by the word 'concept'. N.B. the word 'concept' is here combined with the definite article. Besides this was only an incidental remark; I based nothing on it in order not to have to grapple with the misgivings to which it might give rise. So Kerry's opposition to it has no bearing at all on the real core of my position.*

Thus Kerry in his account does not succeed in filling the gap between concept and object. Someone might attempt, however, to make use of my own statements in this sense. For example, I have said (*Grund-*

---

* The question whether one should simply put 'the concept' for 'the extension of the concept' is in my view one of expediency.

assertion about a concept;* I speak of properties asserted of a concept, and I allow that a concept may fall under a higher one.** I have called existence a property of a concept. How I mean this is best made clear by an example. In the sentence 'there is at least one square root of 4', we have an assertion, not about (say) the definite number 2, nor about −2, but about a concept, *square root of 4*; viz. that it is not empty. But if I express the same thought thus: 'The concept *square root of 4* is realized', then the first six words form the proper name of an object, and it is about this object that something is asserted. But notice carefully that what is asserted here is not the same thing as was asserted about the concept. This will be surprising only to somebody who fails to see that a thought can be split up in many ways, so that now one thing, now another, appears as subject or predicate. The thought itself does not yet determine what is to be regarded as the subject. If we say 'the subject of this judgement', we do not designate anything definite unless at the same time we indicate a definite kind of analysis; as a rule, we do this in connexion with a definite wording. But we must never forget that different sentences may express the same thought. For example, the thought we are considering could also be taken as an assertion about the number 4:

'The number 4 has the property that there is something of which it is the square.'

lagen, § 46) that a statement of number contains an assertion about a concept; I speak of properties asserted of a concept, and I allow that a concept may fall under a higher one (*Grundlagen*, § 53). I have called existence a property of a concept. How I mean this is best made clear by an example.

In the sentence 'There is at least one square root of 4', we have an assertion not about, say, the particular number 2, nor about −2, but about a concept, *square root of 4*; viz. that it is not empty but is realized. But if I express the same thought thus: 'The concept *square root of 4* is realized', then the first six words form the proper name of an object. In general a content can be analysed in a number of ways and language seeks to provide for this by having at its disposal different expressions for the same content. The distinction between the active and passive form, for example, enables us to present different parts of the content as the subject. This is why it is almost invariably a mistake to put the definite article before the word 'subject' in such expressions as 'the subject of the judgement', 'the subject of the content of a possible judgement'; for no part of the content can be picked out in advance as the subject. Even the expressions 'singular content of possible judgement', 'particular content of possible judgement' are not quite accurate in that they ascribe to the content itself an attribute which, strictly speaking, belongs to it only under a certain form—a certain way

Language has means of presenting now one, now another, part of the [200] thought as the subject; one of the most familiar is the distinction of active and passive forms. It is thus not impossible that one way of analysing a given thought should make it appear as a singular judgement; another, as a particular judgement; and a third, as a universal judgement. It need not then surprise us that the same sentence may be conceived as an assertion about a concept and also as an assertion about an object; only we must observe that what is asserted is different. In the sentence 'there is at least one square root of 4' it is impossible to replace the words 'square root of 4' by 'the concept *square root of 4*; i.e. the assertion that suits the concept does not suit the object. Although our sentence does not present the concept as a subject, it asserts something about it; it can be regarded as expressing the fact that a concept falls under a higher one.* But this does not in any way efface the distinction between object and concept. We see to begin with that in the sentence 'there is at least one square root of 4' the predicative nature of the concept is not belied; we could say 'there is something that has the property of giving the result 4 when multiplied by itself.' Hence what is here asserted about a concept can never be asserted about an object; for a

of analysing it into subject and predicate.

It is conceivable that the same content should appear in one form as singular, in another as particular. It need not then surprise us that we can discern in the same content an assertion about a concept and also an assertion about an object. We must only take note that what is asserted of the one is different from what is asserted of the other. In the sentence 'There is at least one square root of 4' it is impossible to replace the words 'square root of 4' by 'the concept *square root of 4*'; i.e. the assertion that suits the concept does not suit the object. All the same something is asserted of a concept in our sentence. We can even say that our concept is presented as falling under a higher one*—one whose sole characteristic mark is *is realized*, understanding this word in the sense in which we are using it in the present context. But this does not in any way efface the distinction between concept and object. We see to begin with that in the expression 'There is at least one square root of 4', 'square root of 4' is being used predicatively: 'there is something that is a square root of 4'. In place of this we could say 'there is something that has the property of giving the result 4 when multiplied by itself'. Hence what is here asser-

---

* In my *Grundlagen* I called such a concept a second-order concept; in my work *Function und Begriff* I called it a second-level concept, as I shall do here.

* In my *Grundlagen* I called such a concept a second order concept; in my *Funktion und Begriff* I called it a second level concept, as I shall do here.

proper name can never be a predicative expression, though it can be part of one. I do not want to say it is false to assert about an object what is here asserted about a concept; I want to say it is impossible, senseless, to do so.

The sentence 'there is Julius Caesar' is neither true nor false but senseless; the sentence 'there is a man whose name is Julius Caesar' has a sense, but here again we have a concept, as the indefinite article shows. We get the same thing in the sentence 'there is only one Vienna'. We must not let ourselves be deceived because language often uses the same word now as a proper name, now as a concept-word; in our example, the numeral indicates that we have the latter; 'Vienna' is here a concept-word, like 'metropolis'. Using it in this sense, we may say: 'Trieste is no Vienna'. If, on the other hand, we substitute [201] 'Julius Caesar' for the proper name formed by the first six words of the sentence 'the concept *square root of 4* is realized', we get a sentence that has a sense but is false; for the assertion that something is realized (as the word is being taken here) can be truly made only about a quite special kind of objects, viz. such as can be designated by proper names of the form 'the concept *F*'. Thus the words 'the concept *square root of 4*' have an

ted of a concept can never be asserted of an object. This is not to say that it is false to do this, but impossible: a sentence which tried to express such a thing would be absolutely devoid of sense; for it has no sense to use the name of an object predicatively. We have seen that even where the form of a sentence makes it look as if this is being done, the truth is that the object forms only part of what is asserted, since 'nothing other than' has to be added in thought. A sentence such as 'There is at least Julius Caesar' is senseless, although the sentence 'There is at least one man whose name is "Julius Caesar"' has a sense; but here again we have a concept, as the 'one' shows.

If, on the other hand, we substitute the proper name 'Julius Caesar' for the proper name formed by the first six words of the sentence 'The concept *square root of 4* is realized', we get a sentence that has a sense but is false; for the assertion that something is realized, as the word is meant here, is one we can only truly make of such objects as stand in a quite special relation to a concept. Thus the words 'the concept *square root of 4*' have an essentially different behaviour, as essentially different behaviour, as regards possible substitutions, from the words 'square root of 4' in our original sentence; i.e. the reference of the two phrases is essentially different.

What has been shown here in one example holds good generally; the behaviour of the concept is essentially predicative, even where something is being asserted about it; consequently it can be replaced there only by another concept, never by an object. Thus the assertion that is made about a concept does not suit an object. Second-level concepts, which concepts fall under, are essentially different from first-level concepts, which objects fall under.

The relation of an object to a first-level concept that it falls under is different from the (admittedly similar) relation of a first-level to a second-level concept. (To do justice at once to the distinction and to the similarity, we might perhaps say: An object falls *under* a first-level concept; a concept falls *within* a second-level concept.) The distinction of concept and object thus still holds, with all its sharpness.

regards possible substitutions, from the words 'square root of 4' in our original sentence; i.e. the meanings of the two properties are different, though related.

What has been shown here in one example holds good generally: the behaviour of the concept is essentially predicative even when something is being asserted of it; consequently it can be replaced there only by another concept, never by an object; i.e. the assertion that is made about a concept does not fit an object at all. Moreover a concept (of second level) under which a concept falls is essentially different from a concept (of first level) under which objects fall.

In the sentence 'There is at least one square root of 4' we assert that the first level concept *square root of 4* falls under a concept of second level, whereas in the sentence 'The concept *square root of* 4 is realized' we assert that the object *the concept square root of 4* falls under the first level concept *concept that is realized*. We do indeed have the same thought in the two concepts, [*sic.*] but this, being analysed differently, is construed in a different way.

The relation of an object to a concept that it falls under is different from the admittedly similar relation of a concept to a concept (of second level). From now on we shall give parallel expression to the similarity and the difference by saying than an object falls *under* a concept, and a concept falls *within* a concept (of second level); for, strictly speaking, we have been making a mistake in using the same words to cover both cases. From this we can see that the distinction between object and concept still holds in all its sharpness.

Connected with this is another distinction, namely that between property and characteristic mark. I have already explained this in § 53 of my *Grundlagen* and at the time I thought I had made it sufficiently clear. Since, however, Kerry makes no use of it and falls into error as a result, I can only assume, alas, that he has not understood me; this time I will try to be more successful.

With this there hangs together what I have said (*Grundlagen*, § 53) about my usage of the words 'property' and 'mark'; Kerry's discussion gives me occasion to revert once more to this.

The words serve to signify relations, in sentences like 'Φ is a property of Γ' and 'Φ is a mark of Ω'. In my way of speaking a thing can at once be a property and a mark but not of the same thing.

The words 'property' and 'characteristic mark' serve to designate relations such that something can at the same time be a property of Γ and a characteristic mark of Δ. We express ourselves more precisely if we use the words 'characteristic mark' *only* in the phrase 'characteristic mark of a concept'. If a thing is a property of an object, then it is a characteristic mark of a first level concept. We may also speak of properties of a first level concept, and these will then be characteristic marks of second level concepts. I will call the concepts under which an object falls its properties.

I call the concepts under which an object falls its properties; thus 'to be Φ is a property of Γ' is just another way of saying: 'Γ falls under the concept of a Φ'. If the object Γ has the properties Φ, X, and Ψ, I may combine them into Ω; so that it is the same thing if I say that Γ has the [202] property Ω, or, that Γ has the properties Φ, X, and Ψ. I then call Φ, X, and Ψ marks of the concept Ω, and, at the same time, properties of Γ. It is clear that the relations of Φ to Γ and to Ω are quite different, and that conse-

If the object Γ has the properties Φ, X and Ψ, I may combine them into Ω; so that it is the same thing if I say that Γ has the property Ω, or, that Γ has the property Φ and Γ has the property X and Γ has the property Ψ. I then call Φ, X, and Ψ marks of the concept Ω, and, at the same time, properties of Γ. It is clear that the relations of Φ to Γ and to Ω are

quently different terms are required. *Γ* falls under the concept *Φ*; but *Ω*, which is itself a concept, cannot fall under the first-level concept *Φ*; only to a second-level concept could it stand in a similar relation. *Ω* is, on the other hand, subordinate to *Φ*.

Let us consider an example. Instead of saying:

> '2 is a positive number' and
> '2 is a whole number' and
> '2 is less than 10'.

we may also say

> '2 is a positive whole number less than 10'.

Here

> *to be a positive number,*
> *to be a whole number,*
> *to be less than 10,*

appear as properties of the object 2, and also as marks of the concept

positive whole number less than 10.

This is neither positive, nor a whole number, nor less than 10. It is indeed subordinate to the concept *whole number*, but does not fall under it.

Let us now compare with this what Kerry says in his second article (p. 424). 'By the number 4 we understand the result of additively combining 3 and 1. The concept object here occurring is the numerical individual 4; a quite definite number in the natural number-series. This object obviously bears just the marks that are named in its concept, and no others besides—provided we refrain, as we

quite different; *Γ* falls under the concept *Φ*; but *Ω*, which is itself a concept, cannot fall under the first level concept *Φ*; only to a second level concept could it stand in a similar relation.

surely must, from counting as *propria* of the object its infinitely numerous relations to all other individual numbers; "the" number 4 is likewise the result of additively combining 3 and 1.'

We see at once that my distinction between property and mark is here quite slurred over. Kerry distinguishes here between the number 4 and 'the' number 4. I must confess that this distinction is incomprehensible to me. The number 4 is to be a concept; 'the' number 4 is to be a concept-object, and none other than the numerical individual 4. It needs no proof that what we have here [203] is not my distinction between concept and object. It almost looks as though what was floating (though very obscurely) before Kerry's mind were my distinction between the sense and the reference of the words 'the number 4'.* But it is only of the reference of the words that we can say: this is the result of additively combining 3 and 1.

Again, how are we to take the word 'is' in the sentences 'the number 4 is the result of additively combining 3 and 1' and '"the" number 4 is the result of additively combining 3 and 1'? Is it a mere copula, or does it help to express a logical equation? In the first case, 'the' would have to be left out before 'result', and the sentences would go like this:

'The number 4 is a result of additively combining 3 and 1';

---

* Cf. my essay 'On Sense and Reference' (cited above).

'"The" number 4 is a result of additively combining 3 and 1."

In that case, the objects that Kerry designates by

'the number 4' and '"the" number 4'

would both fall under the concept

result of additively combining 3 and 1.

And then the only question would be what difference there was between these objects. (I am here using the words 'object' and 'concept' in my accustomed way.) I should express as follows what Kerry is apparently trying to say:

'The number 4 has those properties, and those alone, which are marks of the concept: *result of additively combining 3 and 1.*'

I should then express as follows the sense of the first of our two sentences:

'To be a number 4 is the same as being a result of additive combination of 3 and 1.'

In that case, what I conjectured just now to have been Kerry's intention could also be put thus:

'The number 4 has those properties, and those alone, which are marks of the concept *a number 4.*'

[204] (We need not here decide whether this is true.) The inverted commas around the definite article in the words '"the" number 4' could in that case be omitted.

But in these attempted interpretations we have assumed that in at least one of the two sentences the definite articles in front of 'result' and 'number 4' were inserted only by an oversight. It we take the words as they stand, we can only regard them as having the sense of a logical equation, like:

'The number 4 is none other than the result of additively combining 3 and 1.'

The definite article in front of 'result' is here logically justified only if it is known (i) that there is such a result; (ii) that there is not more than one. In that case, the phrase designates an object, and is to be regarded as a proper name. If both of our sentences were to be regarded as logical equations, then, since their right sides are identical, it would follow from them that the number 4 is 'the' number 4, or, if you prefer, that the number 4 is no other than 'the' number 4; and so Kerry's distinction would have been proved untenable. However, it is not my present task to point out contradictions in his exposition; his way of taking the words 'object' and 'concept' is not properly my concern here. I am only trying to set my own usage of these words in a clearer light, and incidentally show that in any case it differs from his, whether that is consistent or not.

I do not at all dispute Kerry's right to use the words 'concept' and 'object' in his own way, if only he would respect my equal right, and admit that with my use of terms I have got hold of a distinction of the highest importance. I admit that there is a quite peculiar obstacle in the way of an understanding with my reader. By a kind of necessity of language, my expressions, taken literally, sometimes miss my thought; I mention an object, when what I intend is a concept. I fully realize that in such cases I was relying upon a reader who would be ready to meet me half-way—who does not begrudge a pinch of salt.

Somebody may think that this is an artificially created difficulty; that there is no need at all to take account of such an unmanageable thing as what I call a concept; that one might, like Kerry, regard an object's falling under a concept as a relation, in which the same thing could occur now as object, now as concept. [205] The words 'object' and 'concept' would then serve only to indicate the different positions in the relation. This may be done; but anybody who thinks the difficulty is avoided this way is very much mistaken; it is only shifted. For not all the parts of a thought can be complete; at least one must be 'unsaturated', or predicative; otherwise they would not hold together. For example, the sense of the phrase 'the number 2' does not hold together with that of the expression 'the concept *prime number*' without a link. We apply such a link in the sentence 'the number 2 falls under the concept *prime number*'; it is contained in the words 'falls under', which need to be completed in two ways—by a subject and an accusative; and only because their sense is thus 'unsaturated' are they capable of serving as a link. Only when they have been supplemented in this twofold respect do we get a complete sense, a thought. I say that such words or phrases stand for a relation. We now get the same difficulty for the relation that we were trying to avoid for the concept. For the words 'the relation of an object to the concept it falls under' designate not a relation but an object; and the three proper names 'the number 2', 'the concept *prime number*', 'the relation of an object to a concept it falls under', hold aloof from one another just as much as the first two do by themselves; however we put them together, we get no sentence. It is thus easy for us to see that the difficulty arising from the 'unsaturatedness' of one part of the thought can indeed be shifted, but not avoided. 'Complete' and 'unsaturated' are of course only figures of speech; but all that I wish or am able to do here is to give hints.

It may make it easier to come to an understanding if the reader compares my work *Function und Begriff*. For over the question what it is that is called a function in Analysis, we come up against the same obstacle; and on thorough investigation it will be found that the obstacle is essential, and founded on the nature of our language; that we cannot avoid a certain inappropriateness of linguistic expression; and that there is nothing for it but to realize this and always take it into account.

[Comments on Sense and Meaning]¹

[1892–1895]

In an article (*Über Sinn und Bedeutung*) I distinguished between sense and meaning in the first instance only for the case of proper names (or, if one prefers, singular terms). The same distinction can also be drawn for concept-words. Now it is easy to become unclear about this by confounding the division into concepts and objects with the distinction between sense and meaning, so that we run together sense and concept on the one hand and meaning and object on the other. To every concept-word or proper name, there corresponds as a rule a sense and a meaning, as I use these words. Of course in fiction words only have a sense, but in science and wherever we are concerned about truth, we are not prepared to rest content with the sense, we also attach a meaning to proper names and concept-words; and if through some oversight, say, we fail to do this, then we are making a mistake that can easily vitiate our thinking. The meaning of a proper name is the object it designates or names. A concept-word means a concept, if the word is used as is appropriate for logic. I may clarify this by drawing attention to a fact that seems to weigh heavily on the side of extensionalist as against intensionalist logicians: namely, that in any sentence we can substitute *salva veritate* one concept-word for another if they have the same extension, so that it is also the case that in relation to inference, and where the laws of logic are concerned, that concepts differ only in so far as their extensions are different. The fundamental logical relation is that of an object's falling under a concept: all relations between concepts can be reduced to this. If an object falls under a concept, it falls under all concepts with the same extension, and this implies what we said above. Therefore just as proper names can replace one another *salva veritate*, so too can concept-words, if their extension is the same. Of course the thought will alter when such replacements are made, but this is the sense of the sentence, not its meaning.* The meaning, which is the truth-value, remains the same. For this reason we might easily come to propose the extension of a concept as the

---

* Cf. my article *Über Sinn und Bedeutung*.

---

¹ These comments were not composed before 1892, the year in which the article *Über Sinn und Bedeutung* appeared. They are part of a bundle of papers entitled 'Schrödersche Logik', which existed in a complete form prior to the destruction of the *Nachlaß*. The first part of these constituted a draft of Frege's article *Kritische Beleuchtung einiges Punkte in E. Schröder's Vorlesungen über die Algebra der Logik* (ed.).

meaning of a concept-word; to do this, however, would be to overlook the fact that the extensions of concepts are objects and not concepts (Cf. my essay *Funktion und Begriff*). Nevertheless there is a kernel of truth in this position. In order to bring it out, I need to advert to what I said in my monograph on *Funktion und Begriff*. On the view expressed there a concept is a function of one argument, whose value is always a truth-value. Here I am borrowing the term 'function' from Analysis and, whilst retaining what is essential to it, using it in a somewhat extended meaning, a procedure for which the history of Analysis itself affords a precedent. The name of a function is accompanied by empty places (at least one) where the argument is to go; this is usually indicated by the letter '*x*' which fills the empty places in question. But the argument is not to be counted as belonging to the function, and so the letter '*x*' is not to be counted as belonging to the name of the function either. Consequently one can always speak of the name of a function as having empty places, since what fills them does not, strictly speaking, belong to them. Accordingly I call the function itself unsaturated, or in need of supplementation, because its name has first to be completed with the sign of an argument if we are to obtain a meaning that is complete in itself. I call such a meaning an object and, in this case, the value of the function for the argument that effects the supplementing or saturating. In the cases we first encounter the argument is itself an object, and it is to these that we shall mainly confine ourselves here. Now with a concept we have the special case that the value is always a truth-value. That is to say, if we complete the name of a concept with a proper name, we obtain a sentence whose sense is a thought; and this sentence has a truth value as its meaning. To acknowledge this meaning as that of the True (as the True) is to judge that the object which is taken as the argument falls under the concept. What in the case of a function is called unsaturatedness, we may, in the case of a concept, call its predicative nature.* This comes out even in the cases in which we speak of a subject-concept ('All equilateral triangles are equiangular' means 'If anything is an equilateral triangle, then it is an equiangular triangle').

Such being the essence of a concept, there is now a great obstacle in the way of expressing ourselves correctly and making ourselves understood. If I want to speak of a concept, language, with an almost irresistible force, compels me to use an inappropriate expression which obscures—I might almost say falsifies—the thought. One would assume, on the basis of its analogy with other expressions, that if I say 'the concept *equilateral triangle*' I am designating a concept, just as I am of course naming a planet if I say 'the planet Nepture'. But this is not the case; for we do not have anything with a predicative nature. Hence the meaning of the expression 'the

---

* The words 'unsaturated' and 'predicative' seem more suited to the sense than the meaning; still there must be something on the part of the meaning which corresponds to this, and I know of no better words. Cf. Wundt's *Logik*.

concept *equilateral triangle*' (if there is one in this case) is an object. We cannot avoid words like 'the concept', but where we use them we must always bear their inappropriateness in mind.* From what we have said it follows that objects and concepts are fundamentally different and cannot stand in for one another. And the same goes for the corresponding words or signs. Proper names cannot really be used as predicates. Where they might seem to be, we find on looking more closely that the sense is such that they only form part of the predicate: concepts cannot stand in the same relations as objects. It would not be false, but impossible to think of them as doing so. Hence, the words 'relation of a subject to a predicate' designate two quite different relations, according as the subject is an object or is itself a concept. Therefore it would be best to banish the words 'subject' and 'predicate' from logic entirely, since they lead us again and again to confound two quite different relations: that of an object's falling under a concept and that of one concept being subordinated to another. The words 'all' and 'some', which go with the grammatical subject, belong in sense with the grammatical predicate, as we see if we go over to the negative (not all, *nonnulli*). From this alone it immediately follows that the predicate in these cases is different from that which is asserted of an object. And in the same way the relation of equality, by which I understand complete coincidence, identity, can only be thought of as holding for objects, not concepts. If we say 'The meaning of the word "conic section" is the same as that of the concept-word "curve of the second degree"' or 'The concept *conic section* coincides with the concept *curve of the second degree*', the words 'meaning of the concept-word "conic section"' are the name of an object, not of a concept; for their nature is not predicative, they are not unsaturated, they cannot be used with the indefinite article. The same goes for the words 'the concept *conic section*'. But although the relation of equality can only be thought of as holding for objects, there is an analogous relation for concepts. Since this is a relation between concepts I call it a second level relation, whereas the former relation I call a first level relation. We say that an object a is equal to an object b (in the sense of completely coinciding with it) if a falls under every concept under which b falls, and conversely. We obtain something corresponding to this for concepts if we switch the roles of concept and object. We could then say that the relation we had in mind above holds between the concept Φ and the concept X, if every object that falls under Φ also falls under X, and conversely. Of course in saying this we have again been unable to avoid using the expressions 'the concept Φ', 'the concept X', which again obscures the real sense. So for the reader who is not frightened of the concept-script I will add the following: The unsaturatedness of a concept (of first level) is represented in the concept-script by leaving at least one empty place in its designation where the name of the object which we are saying falls under the concept is to go. This place or places always has to be filled

---

* I shall deal with this difficulty.

in some way or other. Besides being filled by a proper name it can also be filled by a sign which only indicates an object. We can see from this that the sign of equality, or one analogous to it, can never be flanked by the designation of a concept alone, but in addition to the concept an object must also be designated or indicated as well. Even if we only indicate concepts schematically by a function-letter, we must see to it that we give expression to their unsaturatedness by an accompanying empty place as in $\Phi(\ )$ and $X(\ )$. In other words, we may only use the letters (Φ, X), which are meant to indicate or designate concepts, as function-letters, i.e. in such a way that they are accompanied by a place for the argument (the space between the following brackets). This being so, we may not write $\Phi = X$, because here the letters Φ and X do not occur as function-letters. But nor may we write $\Phi(\ ) = X(\ )$, because the argument-places have to be filled. But when they are filled, it is not the functions (concepts) themselves that are put equal to one another: in addition to the function-letter there will be something else on either side of the equality sign, something not belonging to the function.

These letters cannot be replaced by letters that are not used as function-letters: there must always be an argument-place to receive the 'a'. The idea might occur to one simply to write $\Phi = X$. This may seem all right so long as we are indicating concepts schematically, but a mode of designation that is really adequate must provide for all cases. Let us take an example which I have already used in my paper on *Funktion und Begriff*.

For every argument the function $x^2 = 1$ has the same (truth-) value as the function $(x + 1)^2 = 2(x + 1)$ i.e. every object falling under the concept *less by 1 than a number whose square is equal to its double* falls under the concept *square root of 1* and conversely. If we expressed this thought in the way that we gave above,[1] we should have

$$(a^2 = 1) \overset{a}{\underset{\cap}{=}} ((a + 1)^2 = 2(a + 1))$$

What we have here is that second level relation which corresponds to, but should not be confused with, equality (complete coincidence) between objects. If we write it $\overset{a}{\underset{\cap}{\rule{0pt}{1em}}}{\vdash}(a^2 = 1) = ((a + 1)^2 = 2(a + 1))$, we have expressed what is essentially the same thought, construed as an equation between values of functions that holds generally. We have here the same second level relation; we have in addition the sign of equality, but this does not suffice on its own to designate this relation: it has to be used in combination with the sign for generality: in the first line we have a general statement but not an equation. In $\dot{\varepsilon}(\varepsilon^2 = 1) = \dot{a}((a + 1)^2 = 2(a + 1))$ we do have an equation, but not between concepts (which is impossible) but between objects, namely extensions of concepts.

Now we have seen that the relation of equality between objects cannot be

---

[1] It may be that the notation used in the following formula, which Frege has *not* explained above, was introduced in the lost first part of the manuscript (see footnote to p. 118) (ed.).

conceived as holding between concepts too, but that there is a corresponding relation for concepts. It follows that the word 'the same' that is used to designate the former relation between objects cannot properly be used to designate the latter relation as well. If we try to use it to do this, the only recourse we really have is to say 'the concept Φ is the same as the concept X' and in saying this we have of course named a relation between objects,* where what is intended is a relation between concepts. We have the same case if we say 'the meaning of the concept-word A is the same as that of the concept word B'. Indeed we should really outlaw the expression 'the meaning of the concept-word A', because the definite article before 'meaning' points to an object and belies the predicative nature of a concept. It would be better to confine ourselves to saying 'what the concept word A means', for this at any rate is to be used predicatively: 'Jesus is, what the concept word "man" means' in the sense of 'Jesus is a man'.

Now if we bear all this in mind, we shall be well able to assert 'what two concept-words mean is the same if and only if the extensions of the corresponding concepts coincide' without being led astray by the improper use of the word 'the same'. And with this statement we have, I believe, made an important concession to the extensionalist logicians. They are right when they show by their preference for the extension, as against the intension, of a concept that they regard the meaning and not the sense of words as the essential thing for logic. The intensionalist logicians are only too happy not to go beyond the sense; for what they call the intension, if it is not an idea, is nothing other than the sense. They forget that logic is not concerned with how thoughts, regardless of truth-value, follow from thoughts, that the step from thought to truth-value—more generally, the step from sense to meaning—has to be taken. They forget that the laws of logic are first and foremost laws in the realm of meanings and only relate indirectly to sense. If it is a question of the truth of something—and truth is the goal of logic—we also have to inquire after meanings; we have to throw aside proper names that do not designate or name an object, though they may have a sense; we have to throw aside concept-words that do not have a meaning. These are not such as, say, contain a contradiction—for there is nothing at all wrong in a concept's being empty—but such as have vague boundaries. It must be determinate for every object whether it falls under a concept or not; a concept word which does not meet this requirement on its meaning is meaningless. E.g. the word '$\mu\tilde{\omega}\lambda\upsilon$' (Homer, *Odyssey* X, 305) belongs to this class, although it is true that certain characteristic marks are supplied. For this reason the context cited need not lack a sense, any more than other contexts in which the name 'Nausicaa', which probably does not mean or name anything, occurs. But it behaves as if it names a girl, and it is thus assured of a sense. And for fiction the sense is enough. The thought, though it is devoid of meaning, of truth-value, is enough, but not for science.

---

* These objects have the names 'the concept Φ' and 'the concept X'.

In my *Grundlagen* and the paper *Über formale Theorien der Arithmetik* I showed that for certain proofs it is far from being a matter of indifference whether a combination of signs—e.g. $\sqrt{-1}$—has a meaning* or not, that, on the contrary, the whole cogency of the proof stands or falls with this. The meaning is thus shown at every point to be the essential thing for science. Therefore even if we concede to the intensionalist logicians that it is the concept as opposed to the extension that is the fundamental thing, this does not mean that it is to be taken as the sense of a concept-word: it is its meaning, and the extensionalist logicians come closer to the truth in so far as they are presenting—in the extension—a meaning as the essential thing. Though this meaning is certainly not the concept itself, it is still very closely connected with it.

Husserl takes Schröder[1] to task for the unclarity in his discussion of the words '*unsinnig*' [without sense], '*einsinnig*' [having one sense], and '*mehrsinnig*' [having more than one sense], '*undeutig*' [without meaning], '*eindeutig*' [having one meaning], '*mehrdeutig*' [having more than one meaning] (pp. 48 ff. and 69),[2] and unclarity indeed there is, but even the distinctions Husserl draws are inadequate. It was hardly to be expected that Schröder's use of the particles '*sinnig*' and '*deutig*' would not differ from my own; still less can I take issue with him over this, since when his work appeared nothing had been published by me in this connection. For him this distinction is connected with that between common names and proper names, and the unclarity springs from a faulty conception of the distinction between concept and object. According to him there is nothing amiss with common names that are *mehrdeutig*, they are this when more than one

---

* It is true that I had not then settled upon my present use of the words 'sense' and 'meaning', so that sometimes I said 'sense' where I should now say 'meaning'.

---

[1] In what follows Frege is referring to the review of Schröder's *Vorlesungen über die Algebra der Logik* (*Exakte Logik*) I (Leipzig 1890), which Husserl had written for the *Gottingischen Gelehrten Anzeigen* (pp. 243–278, April 1891) (ed.).

[2] In the place referred to by Frege Schröder fixes on the adjectives ending in '*deutig*' as terms for the sizes of extensions of concepts. *Schröder* speaks generally of names and calls proper names '*eindeutig*', common names like 'my hand' '*zweideutig*' [having two meanings], common names in general '*mehrdeutig*' or '*vieldeutig*' [having many meanings]. The corresponding formations with '*sinnig*' are employed by Schröder to distinguish terms whose use is precisely fixed ('*einsinnig*' or 'univocal'), from terms with multiple meanings ('*doppelsinnig*' [having a double sense], '*mehrsinnig*' or 'equivocal') and from formations without sense ('*unsinnig*'; 'round square' in *Schröder*'s example). With Husserl Frege chiefly criticizes Schröder for calling a name like 'round square' '*undeutig*' when for this label to apply the name is surely already presupposed as being significant as such, so that it cannot at the same time be designated as '*unsinnig*' (ed.).

object falls under the corresponding concept.* On this view it would be possible for a common name to be *undeutig* too, like 'the round square', without its being defective. Schröder, however, calls it *unsinnig* as well and is thus untrue to his own way of speaking; for according to this the 'round square' would have to be called *einsinnig*, and Husserl was right when he called it a univocal common name; for 'univocal' and 'equivocal' correspond to Schröder's '*einsinnig*' and '*mehrsinnig*'. Husserl says (p. 250) 'Obviously he confuses two quite different questions here, namely (1) whether a name has a *Bedeutung* (a '*Sinn*'); and (2) whether there does or does not exist an object corresponding to the name'. This distinction is inadequate. The word 'common name' leads to the mistaken assumption that a common name is related to objects in essentially the same way as is a proper name, the difference being only that the latter names just one thing whilst the former is usually applicable to more than one. But this is false, and that is why I prefer 'concept-word' to 'common name'. A proper name must at least have a sense (as I use the word); otherwise it would be an empty sequence of sounds and it would be wrong to call it a name. But if it is to have a use in science we must require that it have a meaning too, that it designates or names an object. Thus it is *via* a sense, and only *via* a sense that a proper name is related to an object.[1]

A concept-word must have a sense too and if it is to have a use in science, a meaning; but this consists neither of one object nor of a plurality of objects: it is a concept. Now in the case of a concept it can of course again be asked whether one object falls under it, or more than one or none. But this relates directly to the concept and nothing else. So a concept-word can be absolutely impeccable, logically speaking, without there being an object to which it is related through its sense and meaning (the concept itself). As we see, this relation to an object is more indirect and inessential, so that there seems little point in dividing concept-words up according as no object falls under the corresponding concepts or one object or more than one.

---

* If, as Husserl says in the first footnote to p. 252, a distributive name is one 'whose *Bedeutung* is such that it designates any one of a plurality of things', then a concept-word (common name) is at any rate not a distributive name.

---

[1] Since Schröder and Husserl did not distinguish, in the way Frege did, between the *Sinn* and *Bedeutung* of an expression, we have thought it best in this paragraph to preserve the actual German where these terms or (more commonly) their cognates with '*sinnig*' and '*deutig*' occur in quotation from these authors, or where Frege himself uses the latter in alluding to their views. We have given what help we could to the reader by providing renderings in square brackets; he should only remember not to attribute to the words 'sense' and 'meaning', as they occur in these renderings, the significance they have in the main body of the text, where they are of course used to render Frege's '*Sinn*' and '*Bedeutung*' (trans.).

Logic must demand not only of proper names but of concept-words as well that the step from the word to the sense and from the sense to the meaning be determinate beyond any doubt. Otherwise we should not be entitled to speak of a meaning at all. Of course this holds for all signs and combinations of signs with the same function as proper names or concept-words.

Logic[1]

[1897]

[128] The word 'true' specifies the goal. Logic is concerned with the predicate 'true' in a special way. The word 'true' characterizes logic. True cannot be defined; we cannot say: an idea is true if it agrees with reality.

[129] True primitive and simple. This feature of our predicate is to be brought out by comparing it with others. Predicating it is always included in predicating anything whatever. To locate the domain of application of the predicate 'true'. Not applicable to what is material. It is most frequently ascribed to sentences—but only to assertoric sentences. Not, however, to sentences as series of sounds.

[129] Translation.

[130] We do not need to consider mock assertions in logic.

[131] The sense of a sentence is called a thought. The predicate 'true' applies to thoughts. Does it also apply to ideas? Even where an idea is called true, it is really a thought to which this predicate is ascribed. A thought is not an idea and is not composed of ideas. Thoughts and ideas are fundamentally different. By associating ideas we never arrive at anything that could be true.

[131f.] The proper means of expression for a thought is a sentence. On the other hand, a sentence is hardly an appropriate vehicle for conveying ideas. By contrast, pictures and musical compositions are unsuited for expressing thoughts. The predicate 'true' compared with 'beautiful'. The latter admits of degree, not the former. What is beautiful is beautiful only for him who experiences it as such. There is no disputing tastes. What is true is true in itself; nothing is beautiful in itself. The assumption of a normal human being always underlies objective judgements of beauty. However, what is normal?

[132f.] The objective sense of 'beautiful' can only be based on the subjective sense. Nor is it of any use to replace the assumption of a normal human being by that of an ideal one. A work of art is a structure of ideas within us. Each of us has his own. Aesthetic judgements don't contradict one another. Anyone who asserts that it ·is only our recognizing a thing as true that makes it so, would, by so doing, contradict the content of his own assertion. In reality he could assert

---

[1] The date mentioned on p. 147 and the quotation on p. 158 make it probable that this essay was composed in 1897 (ed.).

nothing. Every opinion would then be unjustified; there would be no science. Properly speaking, there would be nothing that is true. The independence of being recognized by us is integral to the sense of the word 'true'. Nor do thoughts have to be thought by us in order to be true. Laws of nature are discovered (not invented).

[133f.] Thoughts are independent of our thinking. A thought does not belong specially to the person who thinks it, as an idea does to the person who has it: whoever thinks it encounters it in the same way, as the same thought. Otherwise two people would never attach the same thought to the same sentence. A contradiction between the assertions of different people would be impossible. A dispute about the truth of something would be futile. There would be no common ground to fight on. As each man makes a judgement about his poem, if the judgement is an aesthetic one, so each man would make a judgement about his thought, if the thought were related to a sentence as the auditory ideas of the spoken sounds are related to the sound waves. If a thought were something mental, then its truth could only consist in a relation to something external, and that this relation obtained would be a thought into the truth of which we could inquire.

[134f.] Treadmill. A thought is something impersonal. Writing on a wall. Objection: what of a sentence like 'I am cold'? The spoken word often needs to be supplemented. The word 'I' does not always designate the same person. A sentence containing 'I' can be càst into a more appropriate form. Interjections are different. The words 'now' and 'here' analogous to 'I'. Identity of the speaker essential where a subjective judgement of taste is concerned.

[135] Objection: my use of the word 'thought' is out of the ordinary.

[136] Footnote. Dedekind's way of using it agrees with mine.

[137] Thoughts are not generated by, but grasped by, thinking.

[137f.] A thought not something spatial, material. Only in a special sense is it something actual.

[138] False thoughts are also independent of the speaker. The predicate 'true' is predicated in predicating anything. In an assertoric sentence the expression of a thought and the recognition of its truth usually go hand in hand. This does not have to be so. An assertoric sentence does not always contain an assertion. Grasping a thought usually precedes the recognition of truth. Judging, asserting.

[139f.] A sentence is also meant to have an effect on the imagination and feelings. It is able to do this because it consists of heard sounds. Onomatopoeia. Words also have an effect on the imagination through the sense they have. But ideas and sense must not be confused. A word by itself does not determine an idea. Different ideas answer to the same word. Words furnish hints to the imagination.

[140] The means available to the poet. 'Dog' and 'cur' can be substituted

for one another without altering the thought. What distinguishes
them is of the nature of an interjection. Criterion. To distinguish
thoughts that are expressed from those that are merely evoked in us.
A sad tone of voice, 'ah', 'unfortunately'.

[141] Changes in language give rise to borderline cases.[1]

Introduction

The predicate *true*, thoughts, consequences for the treatment of logic

When entering upon the study of a science, we need to have some idea, if
only a provisional one, of its nature. We want to have in sight a goal to
strive towards; we want some point to aim at that will guide our steps in the
right direction. The word 'true' can be used to indicate such a goal for logic,
just as can 'good' for ethics and 'beautiful' for aesthetics. Of course all the
sciences have truth as their goal, but logic is concerned with the predicate
'true' in a quite special way, namely in a way analogous to that in which
physics has to do with the predicates 'heavy' and 'warm' or chemistry with
the predicates 'acid' and 'alkaline'. There is, however, the difference that
these sciences have to take into account other properties besides these we
have mentioned, and that there is no one property by which their nature is
so completely characterized as logic is by the word 'true'.

Like ethics, logic can also be called a normative science. How must I
think in order to reach the goal, truth? We expect logic to give us the answer
to this question, but we do not demand of it that it should go into what is
peculiar to each branch of knowledge and its subject-matter. On the
contrary, the task we assign logic is only that of saying what holds with the
utmost generality for all thinking, whatever its subject-matter. We must
assume that the rules for our thinking and for our holding something to be
true are prescribed by the laws of truth. The former are given along with the
latter. Consequently we can also say: logic is the science of the most general
laws of truth. The reader may find that he can form no very precise
impression from this description of what is meant. The author's inadequacy
and the awkwardness of language are probably to blame for this. But it is
only a question of giving a rough indication of the goal of logic. What is still
lacking in the account will have to be made good as we go on.

Now it would be futile to employ a definition in order to make it clearer
what is to be understood by 'true'. If, for example, we wished to say 'an idea
is true if it agrees with reality' nothing would have been achieved, since in
order to apply this definition we should have to decide whether some idea or
other did agree with reality. Thus we should have to presuppose the very
thing that is being defined. The same would hold of any definition of the
form '*A* is true if and only if it has such-and-such properties or stands in

---

[1] Frege only took the table of contents as far as p. 141 (ed.).

such-and-such a relation to such-and-such a thing'. In each case in hand it would always come back to the question whether it is true that *A* has such-and-such properties, or stands in such-and-such a relation to such-and-such a thing. Truth is obviously something so primitive and simple that it is not possible to reduce it to anything still simpler. Consequently we have no alternative but to bring out the peculiarity of our predicate by comparing it with others. What, in the first place, distinguishes it from all other predicates is that predicating it is always included in predicating anything whatever.

If I assert that the sum of 2 and 3 is 5, then I thereby assert that it is true that 2 and 3 make 5. So I assert that it is true that my idea of Cologne Cathedral agrees with reality, if I assert that it agrees with reality. Therefore it is really by using the form of an assertoric sentence that we assert truth, and to do this we do not need the word 'true'. Indeed we can say that even where we use the form of expression 'it is true that . . .' the essential thing is really the assertoric form of the sentence.

We now ask: what can the predicate 'true' be applied to? The issue here is to delimit the range of application of the word. Whatever else may be the case, the word cannot be applied to anything that is material. If there is any doubt about this, it could arise only for works of art. But if we speak of truth in connection with these, then we are surely using the word with a different meaning from the one that is meant here. In any case it is only as a work of art that a thing is called true. If a thing had come into existence through the blind play of natural forces, our predicate would be clearly inappropriate. For the same reason we are excluding from consideration the use that is made by, say, an art critic when he calls feelings and experiences true.

No one would deny that our predicate is, for the most part, ascribed to sentences. We are not, however, concerned with sentences expressing wishes, questions, requests and commands, but only with assertoric sentences, sentences that is to say, in which we communicate facts and propound mathematical laws or laws of nature.

Further, it is clear that we do not, properly speaking, ascribe truth to the series of sounds which constitute a sentence, but to its sense; for, on the one hand, the truth of a sentence is preserved when it is correctly translated into another language, and, on the other hand, it is at least conceivable that the same series of sounds should have a true sense in one language and a false sense in another.

We are here including under the word 'sentence' the main clause of a sentence and clauses that are subordinate to it.

In the cases which alone concern logic the sense of an assertoric sentence is either true or false, and then we have what we call a thought proper. But there remains a third case of which at least some mention must be made here.

The sentence 'Scylla has six heads' is not true, but the sentence 'Scylla does not have six heads' is not true either; for it to be true the proper name 'Scylla' would have to designate something. Perhaps we think that the name

'Scylla' does designate something, namely an idea. In that case the first question to ask is 'Whose idea?' We often speak as if one and the same idea occurred to different men, but that is false, at least if the word 'idea' is used in the psychological sense: each man has his own idea. But then an idea does not have heads, and so one cannot cut heads off an idea either. The name 'Scylla' does not therefore designate an idea. Names that fail to fulfil the usual role of a proper name, which is to name something, may be called mock proper names. Although the tale of Willian Tell is a legend and not history and the name 'William Tell' is a mock proper name, we cannot deny it a sense. But the sense of the sentence 'William Tell shot an apple off his son's head' is no more true than is that of the sentence 'William Tell did not shoot an apple off his son's head'. I do not say, however, that this sense is false either, but I characterize it as fictitious. This may elucidate the sense in which I am using the word 'false', which is as little susceptible of a definition proper as is the word 'true'.

If the idealist theory of knowledge is correct then all the sciences would belong to the realm of fiction. Indeed one might try to reinterpret all sentences in such a way that they were about ideas. By doing this, however, their sense would be completely changed and we should obtain quite a different science; this new science would be a branch of psychology.

Instead of speaking of 'fiction', we could speak of 'mock thoughts'. Thus if the sense of an assertoric sentence is not true, it is either false or fictitious, and it will generally be the latter if it contains a mock proper name.* The writer, in common with, for example, the painter, has his eye on appearances. Assertions in fiction are not to be taken seriously: they are only mock assertions. Even the thoughts are not to be taken seriously as in the sciences: they are only mock thoughts. If Schiller's *Don Carlos* were to be regarded as a piece of history, then to a large extent the drama would be false. But a work of fiction is not meant to be taken seriously in this way at all: it's all play. Even the proper names in the drama, though they correspond to names of historical personages, are mock proper names; they are not meant to be taken seriously in the work. We have a similar thing in the case of an historical painting. As a work of art it simply does not claim to give a visual representation of things that actually happened. A picture that was intended to portray some significant moment in history with photographic accuracy would not be a work of art in the higher sense of the word, but would be comparable rather to an anatomical drawing in a scientific work.

The logician does not have to bother with mock thoughts, just as a physicist, who sets out to investigate thunder, will not pay any attention to stage-thunder. When we speak of thoughts in what follows we mean thoughts proper, thoughts that are either true or false.

---

* We have an exception where a mock proper name occurs within a clause in indirect speech.

The sense of an assertoric sentence I call a thought. Examples of thoughts are laws of nature, mathematical laws, historical facts: all these find expression in assertoric sentences. I can now be more precise and say: The predicate 'true' applies to thoughts.

Of course we speak of true ideas[1] as well. By an idea we understand a picture that is called up by the imagination: unlike a perception it does not consist of present impressions, but of the reactivated traces of past impressions or actions. Like any other picture, an idea is not true in itself, but only in relation to something to which it is meant to correspond. If it is said that a picture is meant to represent Cologne Cathedral, fair enough; it can then be asked whether this intention is realized; if there is no reference to an intention to depict something, there can be no question of the truth of a picture. It can be seen from this that the predicate *true* is not really conferred on the idea itself, but on the thought that the idea depicts a certain object. And this thought is not an idea, nor is it made up of ideas in any way. Thoughts are fundamentally different from ideas (in the psychological sense). The idea of a red rose is something different from the thought that this rose is red. Associate ideas or run them together as we may, we shall still finish up with an idea and never with something that could be true. This difference also comes out in the modes we have of communicating. The proper means of expression for a thought is a sentence. But a sentence is hardly an appropriate vehicle for conveying an idea. I have only to remind you how inadequate any description is by comparison with a pictorial representation. Things are not so bad where it is a matter of representing sounds, since we have the resources of onomatopoeia; but onomatopoeia has nothing whatever to do with the expression of thoughts, and whilst in translation the play of sounds is easily lost, the thought must be preserved if we are to speak of a translation at all. Conversely, pictures and musical compositions without accompanying words are hardly suited for expressing thoughts. It is true that we may associate all kinds of thoughts with some work of art or other but there is no necessary connection between the two, and we are not surprised when someone else associates different thoughts with it.

In order to shed a clearer light on the peculiarity of the predicate *true*, let us compare it with the predicate *beautiful*. We can see, to begin with, that what is beautiful admits of degree, but what is true does not. We can think two objects beautiful, and yet think one more beautiful than the other. On the other hand, if two thoughts are true, one is not more true than the other. And here there emerges the essential difference that what is true is true

---

[1] In the German, '*Vorstellungen*'. Throughout this essay the difficult word '*Vorstellung*' has been generally rendered by 'idea'. Admittedly this makes certain passages read unnaturally, but the gist of what Frege is saying should be clear if the reader bears in mind the explanation he gives here of how the term '*Vorstellung*' is being used (trans.).

independently of our recognizing it as such, but what is beautiful is beautiful only for him who experiences it as such. What is beautiful for one person is not necessarily beautiful for another. There is no disputing tastes. Where truth is concerned, there is the possibility of error, but not where beauty is concerned. By the very fact that I consider something beautiful it is beautiful for me. But something does not have to be true because I consider it to be true, and if it is not true in itself, it is not true for me either. Nothing is beautiful in itself: it is only beautiful for some being experiencing it and this is necessarily implicit in any aesthetic judgement. Now it is true that we also make judgements of this kind which seem to lay claim to being objective. Whether we are aware of it or not the assumption of a normal human being always underlies such judgements, and each one of us cannot help but think that he himself is so close to the normal human being that he believes he can speak in his name. What, then, we mean by 'This rose is beautiful' is 'This rose is beautiful for a normal human being'. But what is normal? That depends on the circle of human beings one has in mind. If there is some remote mountain valley where nearly all the people have goitres, then having a goitre will be looked on as normal there, and those who lack such an adornment will be considered ugly. How is a negro from the heart of Africa to be weaned from the view that the narrow nose of the European is ugly, whereas the broad nose of the negro is beautiful? And cannot a negro *qua* negro be just as normal as a white man *qua* white man? Cannot a child be just as normal as a grown-up? The ideas that are awakened in us by the power of association have a great influence on the judgements a man forms of what is beautiful, and these ideas depend upon what he has absorbed in earlier life. But this varies from person to person. And even if we managed to define a normal human being and so 'beautiful' in an objective sense, it would still be only possible to do this on the basis of the subjective sense. Far from having rid ourselves of this, we would have recognized it as the root sense. We could not alter the situation by trying to substitute an ideal human being for a normal one. In the absence of experiences and ideas there would be no instance of anything subjectively beautiful and therefore no instance of anything objectively beautiful either. There is therefore much to be said for the view that the real work of art is a structure of ideas within us and that the external thing—the painting, the statue—is only a means for producing the real work of art in us. On this view, anyone who enjoys a work of art has his own work of art, with the consequence that there is no contradiction whatever between varying aesthetic judgements. Hence: *de gustibus non disputandum.*

If anyone tried to contradict the statement that what is true is true independently of our recognizing it as such, he would by his very assertion contradict what he had asserted; he would be in a similar position to the Cretan who said that all Cretans are liars.

To elaborate: if something were true only for him who held it to be true, there would be no contradiction between the opinions of different people. So to be consistent, any person holding this view would have no right whatever to contradict the opposite view; he would have to espouse the principle: *non disputandum est.* He would not be able to assert anything at all in the normal sense, and even if his utterances had the form of assertions, they would only have the status of interjections—of expressions of mental states or processes, between which and such states or processes in another person there could be no contradiction. And in that case his assertion that something was true only for us and through being recognized by us as such would have this status too. If this view were true, it would be impossible to claim that any of his own opinions was more justified in the eyes of others than the opposite opinion. A view that made such a claim would be unjustified; this would mean, however, that every opinion would be unjustified in the usual sense of the word, and so also those opinions to which we were opposed. There would be no science, no error and no correction of error; properly speaking, there would be nothing true in the normal sense of the word. For this is so closely bound up with that independence of being recognized as true, which we are emphasizing here, that it cannot be separated from it. If anyone seriously and sincerely defended the view we are here attacking, we should have no recourse but to assume that he was attaching a different sense to the word 'true'.

We can go a step further. In order to be true, thoughts—e.g. laws of nature—not only do not need to be recognized by us as true: they do not have to have been thought by us at all. A law of nature is not invented by us, but discovered, and just as a desolate island in the Arctic Ocean was there long before anyone had set eyes on it, so the laws of nature, and likewise those of mathematics, have held good at all times and not just since they were discovered. This shows us that these thoughts, if true, are not only true independently of our recognizing them to be so, but that they are independent of our thinking as such. A thought does not belong specially to the person who thinks it, as does an idea to the person who has it: everyone who grasps it encounters it in the same way, as the same thought. Otherwise two people would never attach the same thought to the same sentence, but each would have his own thought; and if, say, one man put $2 \cdot 2 = 4$ forward as true whilst another denied it, there would be no contradiction, because what was asserted by one would be different from what was rejected by the other. It would be quite impossible for the assertions of different people to contradict one another, for a contradiction occurs only when it is the very same thought that one person is asserting to be true and another to be false. So a dispute about the truth of something would be futile. There would simply be no common ground to fight on; each thought would be enclosed in its own private world and a contradiction between the thoughts of different people would be like a war between ourselves and the inhabitants of Mars. Nor must we say that one person might communicate his thought to another and a conflict would then flare up in the latter's private world. It would be quite impossible for a thought to be so communicated that it should pass out of the private world of one person into that of another. The thought that entered the latter's mind as a result of the communication would be different from the thought in the former's mind; and the slightest alteration can transform a truth into a falsehood. If we wanted to regard a thought as something psychological, as a structure of ideas, without, however, adopting a wholly subjective standpoint, we should have to explain the assertion that $2 + 3 = 5$ on something like the following lines 'It has been observed that with many people certain ideas form themselves in association with the sentence "$2 + 3 = 5$". We call a formation of this kind the sense of the sentence "$2 + 3 = 5$". So far as we have observed hitherto these formations are always true; we may therefore make the provisional statement "Going by the observations made hitherto, the sense of the sentence '$2 + 3 = 5$' is true".' But it is obvious that this explanation would not work at all. And it would leave us where we were, for the sense of the sentence 'It has been observed that with many people certain ideas form themselves etc.' would of course be a formation of ideas too and the whole thing would begin over again. A soup that tastes pleasant to one person, may be nauseous to another. In such a case each person is really making a judgement about his own sensation of taste, and this is different from the other's. The same would hold for thoughts if a thought were related to a sentence in the same kind of way as sensations of taste are related to the chemical stimuli that excite them.

If a thought, like an idea, were something private and mental, then the truth of a thought could surely only consist in a relation to something that was not private or mental. So if we wanted to know whether a thought was true, we should have to ask whether the relation in question obtained and thus whether the thought that this relation obtained was true. And so we should be in the position of a man on a treadmill who makes a step forwards and upwards, but the step he treads on keeps giving way and he falls back to where he was before.

A thought is something impersonal. If we see the sentence '$2 + 3 = 5$' written on a wall, we have no difficulty at all in recognizing the thought expressed by it, and we do not need to know who has written it there in order to understand it.

A sentence like 'I am cold' may seem to be a counter-example to our thesis that a thought is independent of the person thinking it, in so far as it can be true for one person and false for another, and thus not true in itself. The reason for this is that the sentence expresses a different thought in the mouth of one person from what it expresses in the mouth of another. In this case the mere words do not contain the entire sense: we have in addition to take into account who utters it. There are many cases like this in which the spoken word has to be supplemented by the speaker's gesture and expression, and the accompanying circumstances. The word 'I' simply designates a different person in the mouths of different people. It is not necessary that the person who feels cold should himself give utterance to the thought that he feels cold. Another person can do this by using a name to designate the one who feels cold.

In this way a thought can be clothed in a sentence that is more in keeping with its being independent of the person thinking it. The possibility of doing this distinguishes it from a mental state expressed by an interjection. Words like 'here' and 'now' only acquire their full sense through the circumstances in which they are used. If someone says 'it is raining' the time and place of utterance has to be supplied. If such a sentence is written down it often no longer has a complete sense because there is nothing to indicate who uttered it, and where and when. As regards a sentence containing a judgement of taste like 'This rose is beautiful', the identity of the speaker is essential to the sense, even though the word 'I' does not occur in it. So the explanation for all these apparent exceptions is that the same sentence does not always express the same thought, because the words need to be supplemented in order to get a complete sense, and how this is done can vary according to the circumstances.

Whereas ideas (in the psychological sense of the word) have no fixed boundaries, but are constantly changing and, Proteus-like, assume different forms, thoughts always remain the same. It is of the essence of a thought to be non-temporal and non-spatial. In the case of the thought that $3 + 4 = 7$ and the laws of nature there is hardly any need to support this statement. If it should turn out that the law of gravitation ceased to be true from a certain moment onwards, we should conclude that it was not true at all, and put ourselves out to discover a new law: the new one would differ in containing a condition which would be satisfied at one time but not at another. It is the same with place. If it should transpire that the law of gravitation was not valid in the neighbourhood of Sirius, we should search for another law which contained a condition that was satisfied in our solar system but not in the neighbourhood of Sirius. If someone wished to cite, say, 'The total number of inhabitants of the German Empire is 52 000 000', as a counter-example to the timelessness of thoughts, I should reply: This sentence is not a complete expression of a thought at all, since it lacks a time-determination. If we add such a determination, for example, 'at noon on 1 January 1897 by central European time', then the thought is either true, in which case it is always, or better, timelessly, true, or it is false and in that case it is false without qualification. This holds of any particular historical fact: if it is true, it is true independently of the time at which it is judged to be true. It is no objection that a sentence may acquire a different sense in the course of time; for what changes in such a case is of course the language, not the thought. In another language this shift need not take place. It is true of course that we speak of men's thoughts as being liable to change. However it is not the thoughts which are true at one time and false at another: it is only that they are held to be true at one time and false at another.

What if it is objected that I am attaching to the word 'thought' a sense that it does not ordinarily have, and that other people understand by it an

act of thinking, which is obviously private and mental? Well, the important
thing is that I remain true to my way of using it; whether this agrees with the
ordinary use is of less importance. It may well be the case that people
sometimes understand by the word 'thought' an act of thinking—in any
case this is not always so*—and such an act cannot be true.

In logic, as in other sciences, it is open to us to coin technical terms,

---

* Dedekind, in theor. 66 of his book *Was sind und was sollen die Zahlen?*,
uses this word as I do. For he is attempting there to prove that the totality of
things that can be objects of his thinking is infinite. Let s be such an object;
then Dedekind calls $\phi(s)$ the thought that s can be an object of his thinking.
And this thought can now itself be an object of his thinking. Thus $\phi(\phi(s))$ is
the thought that the thought that s can be an object of his thinking can be an
object of his thinking. We can see from this what '$\phi(\phi(\phi(s)))$', '$\phi(\phi(\phi(\phi(s))))$'
and so on, are supposed to mean. It is essential to the proof that the
sentence 's can be an object of Dedekind's thinking' always expresses a
thought when the letter 's' designates such an object. Now if, as Dedekind
wishes to prove, there are infinitely many such objects s, there must also be
infinitely many such thoughts $\phi(s)$. Now presumably we shall not hurt
Dedekind's feelings if we assume that he has not thought infinitely many
thoughts. Equally he should not assume that others have already thought
infinitely many thoughts which could be the objects of his thinking; for this
would be to assume what was to be proved. Now if infinitely many thoughts
have not yet been thought, the infinitely many thoughts $\phi(s)$ must comprise
infinitely many thoughts that are not thought, in which case it cannot be
essential to a thought that it should be thought. And this is precisely what I
am maintaining. If there were only thoughts that are thought, the sign '$\phi(s)$'
would not always have a meaning; to ensure that it did have, it is not
sufficient for 's' to mean something that could be an object of Dedekind's
thinking: it would also have to have been thought by someone in order to be
a possible object of Dedekind's thinking. If this were not the case, then the
sign '$\phi(s)$' would have no meaning for the given s. The sun ($\odot$) can be an
object of Dedekind's thinking; hence the first two members and perhaps a
few successive members of the series '$\odot$, '$\phi(\odot)$', $\phi(\phi(\odot))$' . . . have a meaning.
But as we progressed along the series we would be bound eventually to
reach a member that was meaningless, because the thought which it was
meant to designate had not been thought, and so was not to hand. In that
case '$\phi(s)$' would resemble a power series which did not converge for every
value of the argument. The fact that the series diverged would correspond to
the sign '$\phi(s)$' becoming meaningless. If we assume a power series with
radius of convergence 4 and if we assume, further, that the series has the
value 2 for 1 as argument and the value 5 for 2 as argument, then the
corresponding series of numbers 1, 2, 5 comes to an end at this point and
does not go on to infinity. In the same way the series $\odot$, $\phi(\odot)$, $\phi(\phi(\odot))$, does
not go on to infinity if there are only thoughts that are thought. So the
validity of Dedekind's proofs rests on the assumption that thoughts obtain
independently of our thinking. We can see how this use is one to which the
word 'thought' naturally lends itself.

regardless of whether the words are always used in precisely that way in everyday life. It doesn't matter if the meaning we fix on is not altogether in line with everyday use or doesn't accord with the word's etymology; what does matter is to make it as appropriate a vehicle as possible for use in expressing laws. Provided there is no loss of rigour, the more compendious the formulation of the complete system of laws, the more felicitous is the apparatus of technical terms.

Now we cannot regard thinking as a process which generates thoughts. It would be just as wrong to identify a thought with an act of thinking, so that a thought is related to thinking as a leap is to leaping. This view is in harmony with many of our ways of talking. For do we not say that the same thought is grasped by this person and by that person? And that each person has the same thought over and over again? Now if thoughts only came into existence as a result of thinking or if they were constituted by thinking, then the same thought could come into existence, cease to exist, and then come into existence again, which is absurd. As I do not create a tree by looking at it or cause a pencil to come into existence by taking hold of it, neither do I generate a thought by thinking. And still less does the brain secrete thoughts, as the liver does gall.

The metaphors that underlie the expressions we use when we speak of grasping a thought, of conceiving, laying hold of, seizing, understanding, of *capere, percipere, comprehendere, intelligere*, put the matter in essentially the right perspective. What is grasped, taken hold of, is already there and all we do is take possession of it. Likewise, what we see into or single out from amongst other things is already there and does not come into existence as a result of these activities. Of course all metaphors go lame at some point. We are inclined to regard what is independent of our mental processes as something spatial or material, and the words that we have just listed make it look as if this is what a thought actually is. But this is not where the point of the comparison lies. What is independent of our mental processes, what is objective, does not *have* to be spatial or material or actual. If we were to disregard this we should easily slip into a kind of mythology. To say 'The laws of gravitation, of inertia, of the parallelogram of forces cause the earth to move as it does move', might make it look as if these laws, so to speak, took the earth by the ears and kept it on the path they prescribe. Such a use of the words 'affect', 'cause', would be misleading. On the other hand, it is all right to say that the sun and planets act on one another in accordance with the laws of gravitation.

So even if physical bodies and thoughts resemble one another in being independent of my inner life, we are not entitled to conclude from this that thoughts can be moved as bodies can, or can be smelled or tasted, and it would be invalid to seek somehow to draw from the absurdity of such inference an objection to our views. Although a law of nature obtains quite independently of whether we think of it or not, it does not emit light or sound waves by which our visual or auditory nerves could be affected. But do I not then see that this flower has five petals? We can say this, but if we do, the word 'see' is not being used in the sense of having a mere visual experience: what we mean by it is bound up with thinking and judging. Newton did not discover the law of gravitation because his senses were especially acute.

If we wish to speak of a thought as being actual, we can do so only in the sense that the knowledge that a man has of e.g. a law of nature has an influence on the decisions he makes, which in their turn may affect the course of history. We should then be thinking of the recognition of a law as a case of a law's acting upon us, and it is perhaps possible to do this, just as we can regard, say, the seeing of a flower as the flower's indirectly acting on us.

We can disregard thoughts and we can take possession of them. We might conceive of the latter as a case of our acting on thoughts, which seems to speak against their being timeless. But the thought is not changed in itself by being thus acted on, just as the moon is apparently unaffected whether we take any notice of it or not. So even though it may be possible to speak of thoughts as acting on us, we cannot speak of ourselves as acting on thoughts. We might cite, as an instance of thoughts being subject to change, the fact that they are not always immediately clear. But what is called the clarity of a thought in our sense of this word is really a matter of how thoroughly it has been assimilated or grasped, and is not a property of a thought.

It would be wrong to think that it is only true thoughts that obtained independently of our mental life, and that false ones, on the other hand, belonged, as ideas do, to our inner life. Almost everything that we have said about the predicate *true* holds for the predicate *false* as well. In the strict sense it applies only to thoughts. Where it looks to be predicated of sentences or ideas, still at bottom it is being predicated of thoughts. What is false is false in itself and independently of our opinions. A dispute over the falsity of something is at the same time a dispute over the truth of something. Therefore the thing whose falsity can be a matter for dispute does not belong to some mind or other.

Separating a Thought from its Trappings

In an assertoric sentence two different kinds of thing are usually intimately bound up with one another: the thought expressed and the assertion of its truth. And this is why these are often not clearly distinguished. However, one can express a thought without at the same time putting it forward as true. A scientist who makes a scientific discovery usually begins by grasping just a thought, and then he asks himself whether it is to be recognized as true; it is not until his investigation has turned out in favour of the hypothesis, that he ventures to put it forward as true. We express the same thought in the question 'Is oxygen condensable?' and in the sentence 'Oxygen is condensable', joining it in the one case with a request and in the other with an assertion.

When we inwardly recognize that a thought is true, we are making a judgement: when we communicate this recognition, we are making an assertion.

We can think without making a judgement.

We have seen that the series of sounds that compose a sentence is often not sufficient for the complete expression of a thought. If we wish to bring the essence of a thought into as sharp a focus as possible, we ought not to overlook the fact that the converse case is not uncommon, the case where a sentence does more than express a thought and assert its truth. In many cases a sentence is meant to have an effect on the ideas and feelings of the hearer as well; and the more closely it approximates to the language of poetry, the greater this effect is meant to be. We have indeed stressed the fact that language is but poorly suited for calling up at will an idea in the mind of a hearer with any precision. Who would ever rely on words to evoke as precise a mental picture of an Apollo as can be produced without difficulty by looking at a piece of sculpture? Even so, we do say that the poet paints pictures. And in fact it cannot be denied that the spoken word affects the ideas we have just because it enters consciousness as a complex of auditory sensations. Right from the start we experience the series of sounds themselves, the tone of the voice, the intonation and rhythm with feelings of pleasure or displeasure. These sensations of sound are linked to auditory ideas that resemble them and these latter are linked in turn with further ideas reactivated by them. This is the domain of onomatopoeia. Here we may cite the Homeric verse (Odyssey IX, 71): τριχθά καὶ τετραχθὰ διέσχισεν ἶς ἀνέμοιο.

This is quite independent of the aim of words to express thoughts. Here the sounds are acting only as a sensory stimulus. But because sequences of such sounds are meant to have a sense they act upon the imagination in yet a different way. Anyone who hears the word 'horse' and understands it will probably have straightaway a picture of a horse in his mind. This picture, however, is not to be confused with the sense of the word 'horse'; for the word 'horse' gives no clue to the colour of the horse, or to its carriage when standing still or in motion, or to the side from which it is seen and the like. If different men were able, say, immediately to project onto a canvas the ideas that sprung up in their minds on hearing the word 'horse', then we should be presented with quite different pictures. And even with the same man the word 'horse' does not always conjure up the same idea. Here a great deal depends on the context. We may compare e.g. the sentences 'With what joy he rides his gallant horse' and 'I just saw a horse stumble on the wet asphalt'.

So there can be no question of the same idea always being associated with the word 'horse'. Thus in virtue of its sense such a word will excite a certain idea in us, but by itself it is far from determining this idea completely. Generally speaking the most we are entitled to assume is that the ideas of the speaker and hearer are very roughly in agreement. If several artists produce, independently of one another, illustrations of the same poem, they will diverge considerably from one another in the portrayal they give. Thus the poet does not really depict anything: he only provides the impetus for others to do so, furnishing hints to this end, and leaving it to the hearer to give his words body and shape. And in this connection it is useful to the poet to have at his disposal a number of different words that can be substituted for one another without altering the thought, but which can act in different ways on the feelings and imagination of the hearer. We may think e.g. of the words 'walk', 'stroll', 'saunter'. These means are also used to the same end in everyday language. If we compare the sentences 'This dog howled the whole night' and 'This cur howled the whole night', we find that the thought is the same. The first sentence tells us neither more nor less than does the second. But whilst the word 'dog' is neutral as between having pleasant or unpleasant associations, the word 'cur' certainly has unpleasant rather than pleasant associations and puts us rather in mind of a dog with a somewhat unkempt appearance. Even if it is grossly unfair to the dog to think of it in this way, we cannot say that this makes the second sentence false. True, anyone who utters this sentence speaks pejoratively, but this is not part of the thought expressed. What distinguishes the second sentence from the first is of the nature of an interjection. It might be thought that the second sentence does nevertheless tell us more than the first, namely that the speaker has a poor opinion of the dog. In that case, the word 'cur' would contain an entire thought. We can put this to the test in the following way.

We assume that the first sentence is true and the second sentence is spoken by someone who does not actually feel the contempt which the word 'cur' seems to imply. If the objection were correct, the second sentence would now contain two thoughts, one of which was false; so it would assert something false as a whole, whilst the first sentence would be true. We shall hardly go along with this; rather the use of the word 'cur' does not prevent us from holding that the second sentence is true as well. For we have to make a distinction between the thoughts that are expressed and those which the speaker leads others to take as true although he does not express them. If a commander conceals his weakness from the enemy by making his troops keep changing their uniforms, he is not telling a lie; for he is not expressing any thoughts, although his actions are calculated to induce thoughts in others. And we find the same thing in the case of speech itself, as when one gives a special tone to the voice or chooses special words. If someone announces the news of a death in a sad tone of voice without actually being sad, the thought expressed is still true even if the sad tone is assumed in order to create a false impression. And we can substitute words like 'ah', and 'unfortunately' for such a tone of voice without altering the thought. Naturally things are different if certain actions are specifically agreed on as a means of communicating something. In language common usage takes the place of such agreements. Of course borderline cases can arise because language changes. Something that was not originally employed as a means of expressing a thought may eventually come to do this because it has constantly been used in cases of the same kind. A thought which to begin with was only suggested by an expression may come to be explicitly asserted by it. And in the period in between different interpretations will be possible. But the distinction itself is not obliterated by such fluctuations in language. In the present context the only essential thing for us is that a different thought does not correspond to every difference in the words used, and that we have a means of deciding what is and what is not part of the thought, even though, with language constantly developing, it may at times be difficult to apply.

The distinction between the active and passive voice belongs here too. The sentences 'M gave document A to N', 'Document A was given by N by M', 'N received document A from M' express exactly the same thought; we learn not a whit more or less from any one of these sentences than we do from the others. Hence it is impossible that one of them should be true whilst another is false. It is the very same thing that is here capable of being true or false. For all this we are not in a position to say that it is a matter of complete indifference which of these sentences we use. As a rule stylistic and aesthetic reasons will give the preference to one of them. If someone asks 'Why has A been arrested?' it would be unnatural to reply 'B has been murdered by him', because it would require a needless switch of the attention from A to B. Although in actual speech it can certainly be very important where the attention is directed and where the stress falls, it is of no concern to logic.

In translating from one language to another it is sometimes necessary to dispense with the original grammatical construction altogether. Nevertheless, this need not affect the thought and it must not do so, if the translation is to be correct. But it is sometimes necessary to sacrifice the feeling and colour of the original.

Again in the two sentences 'Frederick the Great won the battle of Rossbach' and 'It is true that Frederick the Great won the battle of Rossbach', we have, as we said earlier, the same thought in a different verbal form. In affirming the thought in the first sentence we thereby affirm the thought in the second, and conversely. There are not two different acts of judgement, but only one.

(From all this we can see that the grammatical categories of subject and predicate can have no significance for logic.)

The distinction between what is part of the thought expressed in a sentence and what only gets attached to the thought is of the greatest importance for logic. The purity of the object of one's investigation is not of importance only to the chemist. How would the chemist be able to recognize, beyond any doubt, that he has arrived at the same results by different means, if the apparent difference of means could be traced back to impurities in the substances used? There is no doubt that the first and most important discoveries in a science are often a matter of recognizing something as the same again. However self-evident it may seen to us that it is the same sun which went down yesterday and rose today, and however insignificant therefore this discovery may seem to us, it has certainly been one of the most important in astronomy and perhaps the one that really laid the foundations of the science. It was also important to recognize that the morning star is the same as the evening star, that three times five is the same as five times three. It is just as important not to distinguish what is the same as it is to be alive to differences when they don't hit one in the eye. So it is quite wrong to think that one can never make too many distinctions. It does nothing but harm to insist on distinctions where they are not relevant. Thus in general mechanics we shall take care not to speak of the chemical differences between substances and not to state the law of inertia in a special form for, say, each chemical element. We shall only take those differences into account that are essential to the formulation of the laws with which we are actually concerned. Above all, we must not let ourselves be seduced by the presence of extraneous factors into seeing distinctions where there are none.

In logic we must reject all distinctions that are made from a purely psychological point of view. What is referred to as a deepening of logic by psychology is nothing but a falsification of it by psychology.

In human beings it is natural for thinking to be intermingled with having images and feeling. Logic has the task of isolating what is logical, not, to be sure, so that we should think without having images, which is no doubt impossible, but so that we should consciously distinguish the logical from what is attached to it in the way of ideas and feelings. There is a difficulty here in that we think in some language or other and that grammar, which has a significance for language analogous to that which logic has for judgement, is a mixture of the logical and the psychological. If this were not so, all languages would necessarily have the same grammar. It is true that we can express the same thought in different languages; but the psychological trappings, the clothing of the thought, will often be different. This is why the learning of foreign languages is useful for one's logical education. Seeing that the same thought can be worded in different ways, we learn better to distinguish the verbal husk from the kernel with which, in any given language, it appears to be organically bound up. This is how the differences between languages can facilitate our grasp of what is logical. But still the difficulties are not wholly removed in this way, and our logic books still keep dragging in a number of things—subject and predicate, for example—which do not, strictly speaking, belong to logic. For this reason it is useful to be acquainted also with a means of expressing thoughts that is of a radically different nature, such as we have in the formula-language of arithmetic or in my concept-script.

The first and most important task is to set out clearly what the objects to be investigated are. Only if we do this shall we be able to recognize the same as the same: in logic too, such acts of recognition probably constitute the fundamental discoveries. Therefore let us never forget that two different sentences can express the same thought, that we are concerned with only that part of a sentence's content which can be true or false.

Even if there were only a jot more to the thought contained in the passive form than in the active, it would be conceivable that this jot should be false whilst the thought contained in the active form was true, and that we should not be entitled without more ado to go over from the active to the passive form. Likewise if there were only a jot more to the thought contained in the active form than in the passive, we should not be able to go over from the passive form to the active without examining the particular case in hand. But if both transitions can always be made *salva veritate*, then this confirms that what is true here, namely the thought, is not affected by this change of form. This serves as a warning not to attach too much weight to linguistic distinctions, as logicians are prone to: a case in point being the assumption that every thought—or judgement as it is usually called—has a subject and a predicate, so that the subject and predicate of a thought are determined by the thought, as the subject and predicate of a sentence are unambiguously given along with the sentence. If we make this assumption, we only get involved in quite unnecessary difficulties, and, grappling with them to no effect, we only strengthen the impression that the science of logic is really quite superfluous.

We shall have no truck with the expressions 'subject' and 'predicate', of which logicians are so fond, especially since they not only make it more difficult for us to recognize the same as the same, but also conceal distinctions that are there. Instead of following grammar blindly, the logician ought rather to see his task as that of freeing us from the fetters of language. For however true it is that thinking, at least in its higher forms, was only made possible by means of language, we have nevertheless to take great care not to become dependent on language; for very many of the mistakes that occur in reasoning have their source in the logical imperfections of language. Of course if we see the task of logic to be that of describing how men actually think, then we shall naturally have to accord great importance to language. But then the name logic is being used for what is really only a branch of psychology. This is as if one imagined that one was doing astronomy when one was developing a psycho-physical theory of how one sees through a telescope. In the former case the things that are the proper concern of logic do not come into view any more than in the latter case do the problems of astronomy. Psychological treatments of logic arise from the mistaken belief that a thought (a judgement as it is usually called) is something psychological like an idea. This view leads necessarily to an idealist theory of knowledge; for if it is correct, then the parts that we distinguish in a thought, such as subject and predicate, must belong as much to psychology as do thoughts themselves. Now since every act of cognition is realized in judgements, this means the breakdown of every bridge leading to what is objective. And all our striving to attain to this can be no more than an attempt to draw ourselves up by our own bootstraps. The most we can do is to try to explain how it comes to seem that there is such a thing as what is objective, how we come to assume the existence of something that is not part of our mind without, however, our thereby having any justification for this assumption. Physiological psychology provides us with the most striking case of this slide into idealism because its realistic point of departure stands in such sharp contrast to it. We start out with nerve fibres and ganglion cells and make assumptions about impulses and how they are transmitted, and we seek in this way to make ideation more intelligible, since we can't help regarding processes in the ganglion cells and nerve fibres as more intelligible than the process of ideation. As befits a science worthy of the name, we do not hesitate to take it for granted, when we proceed like this, that ganglion cells and nerve fibres are objective and real. This will probably work perfectly well so long as we confine ourselves to ideation. But we do not stop there: we move on to thinking and judgement as well, and at this point what began as realism suddenly turns into an extreme form of idealism; in this way realism itself cuts off the branch on which it is sitting. Now everything is dissolved into ideas and as a result the earlier explanations themselves become illusory. Anatomy and physiology turn into fictions. The whole physio-anatomical foundation of nerve fibres, ganglion cells, stimuli, impulses and transmission of impulses disintegrates. And what are we left with? Ideas of nerve fibres, ideas of ganglion cells, ideas of stimuli and so on. And what did we start off with the intention of explaining! The having of ideas! Well, can one say of these explanations that there is any truth or reason in them at all? Standing by a river one often sees eddies in the water. Now would it not be absurd to claim that such an eddy of water was sound or true? And even if the dance of the atoms and molecules in my brain was a thousand times more spirited and frenzied than the dance of gnats on a summer evening, would it not be just as absurd to assert that it was sound or true? And if the explanations above were gyrations of this sort, could we say they were true? And is it any different in the end if these explanations are congeries of ideas? And the phantasms that pass before the mind of the typhus victim in a constant procession, as one picture gives way to another, are they true? They are no more true than they are false; they are simply processes, as an eddy in water is a process. And if we are to speak of a right, it can only be the right of things to happen as they do happen. One phantasm contradicts another no more than one eddy in water contradicts another.

If the visual idea of a rose is associated with the idea of a delicate scent and to these are added the auditory ideas of the words 'rose' and 'scent', as well as the motor ideas associated with uttering these words, and if we go on and on heaping associations upon associations until the most complex and elaborate idea is formed, what purpose does it serve? Do we really think we should have a thought as a result? The result would no more be a thought than an automaton, however cunningly contrived, is a living being. Put something together out of parts that are inanimate and you still have something inanimate. Combine ideas and you still have an idea and the most varied and elaborate associations can make no difference. Even if, on top of these, the whole is imbued with feelings and moods, it is all to no avail. The law of gravitation can never come into existence in this way, for this law is quite independent of everything that goes on in my mind and of how my ideas change and fluctuate. But still the grasping of this law is a mental process! Yes, indeed, but it is a process which takes place on the very confines of the mental and which for that reason cannot be completely understood from a purely psychological standpoint. For in grasping the law something comes into view whose nature is no longer mental in the proper sense, namely the thought; and this process is perhaps the most mysterious of all. But just because it is mental in character we do not need to concern ourselves with it in logic. It is enough for us that we can grasp thoughts and recognize them to be true; how this takes place is a question in its own right.* It is surely enough for the chemist too that he can see, smell and taste; it is not his business to investigate how these things take place. It is not immaterial to the success of a scientific investigation that questions which can be treated independently of others are not confounded with them, with the result that we create unnecessary difficulties. That easily leads to our seeing things crossways on. So we shall not trouble ourselves with asking how we actually think or arrive at our convictions. It is not the holding something to be true that concerns us but the laws of truth. We can also think of these as prescriptions for making judgements; we must comply with them in our judgements if we are not to fail of the truth. So if we call them laws of thought or, better, laws of judgement, we must not forget we are concerned here with laws which, like the principles of morals or the laws of the state, prescribe how we are to act, and do not, like the laws of nature, define the actual course of events. Thinking, as it actually takes place, is not always in agreement with the laws of logic any more than men's actual behaviour is in agreement with the moral law. I therefore think it better to avoid the expression 'laws of thought' altogether in logic, because it always misleads us into thinking of laws of thought as laws of nature. If that is what they were we should have to assign them to psychology. We could, with equal justice, think of the laws of geometry and the laws of physics as laws of thought or laws of judgement, namely as prescriptions to which our judgements must conform in a different domain if they are to remain in

---

* I should say that this question is still far from being grasped in all its difficulty. People are usually quite content to smuggle thinking in through a back door in the imagination, so that they don't themselves know how it really got in.

agreement with the truth. Logic, then, is no more the right place for conducting psychological investigations than is geometry or physics. To explain how thinking and judging take place is certainly a feasible undertaking, but it is not a logical one.

Accordingly, the logician does not have to ask what course thinking naturally takes in the human mind. What is natural to one man may well be unnatural to another. The great difference between grammars itself bears witness to this. The logician need fear nothing less than to be reproached with the fact that his statements do not accord with how we think naturally. The normal person with no training in mathematics would find it highly unnatural if he were to have the rudiments of the subject explained to him in terms of the utmost rigour, and for that very reason. A prudent teacher will therefore tend to let rigour go by the board in introducing the subject and will only seek to awaken the need for it bit by bit. Even in the history of mathematics we find that the highest degree of rigour is achieved only towards the end and that consequently it is at the farthest removed from what is natural. Hence to strive to present the process of thinking in its natural form would lead us directly away from logic. If the logician tried to take account of objections on the score that what he said was unnatural, he would be in danger of involving himself in endless disputes over what is natural—disputes which logic is quite incapable of resolving on its own grounds and which, therefore, do not belong to logic. To resolve them we should presumably have to resort to observing primitive peoples.

But above all we should be wary of the view that it is the business of logic to investigate how we actually think and judge when we are in agreement with the laws of truth. If that were so, we should have constantly to have one eye on the one thing and one eye on the other, and continue paying attention to the latter whilst taking a sidelong glance at the former, and in the process we should easily lose sight of a definite goal altogether. We should be seduced into asking questions with no clear meaning and as a result a satisfactory outcome to our investigations would be as good as impossible.

What are often called laws of thought, namely laws in accordance with which judging, at least in normal cases, takes place, can be nothing but laws for holding something to be true, not laws of truth. If a man holds something to be true—and the psychological logicians will surely hold that their own statements at least are true—he thereby acknowledges that there is such a thing as something's being true. But in that case it is surely probable that there will be laws of truth as well, and if there are, these must provide the norm for holding something to be true. And these will be the laws of logic proper. In supplement No. 26 to the 1897 Proceedings of the *Allgemeine Zeitung*, T. Achelis writes in a paper entitled '*Volkerkunde und Philosophie*': 'But we are now clear about this, that the norms which hold in general for thinking and acting cannot be arrived at by the one-sided exercise of pure deductive abstraction alone; what is required is an empiricocritical determination of the objective principles of our psycho-physical organization which are valid at all times for the great consciousness of mankind.'

It is not quite clear whether this is about laws in accordance with which judgements are made or about laws in accordance with which they should be made. It appears to be about both. That is to say, the laws in accordance with which judgements are made are set up as a norm for how judgements are to be made. But why do we need to do this? Don't we automatically judge in accordance with these laws? No! *Not* automatically; normally, yes, but not always! So these are laws which have exceptions, but the exceptions will themselves be governed by further laws. So the laws that we have set up do not comprise all of them. Now what is our justification for isolating a part of the entire corpus of laws and setting it up as a norm? To do that is like wanting to present Kepler's laws of planetary motion as a norm and then being forced, alas, to recognize that the planets in their wilfulness do not behave in strict conformity with them but, like spoilt children, have disturbing effects on one another. Such behaviour would then have to be severely reprimanded.

On this view we shall have to exercise every care not to stray from the path taken by the solid majority. We shall even mistrust the greatest geniuses; for if they were normal, they would be mediocre.

With the psychological conception of logic we lose the distinction between the grounds that justify a conviction and the causes that actually produce it. This means that a justification in the proper sense is not possible; what we have in its place is an account of how the conviction was arrived at, from which it is to be inferred that everything has been caused by psychological factors. This puts a superstition on the same footing as a scientific discovery.

If we think of the laws of logic as psychological, we shall be inclined to raise the question whether they are somehow subject to change. Are they like the grammar of a language which may, of course, change with the passage of time? This is a possibility we really have to face up to if we hold that the laws of logic derive their authority from a source similar to that of the laws of grammar, if they are norms only because we seldom deviate from them, if it is normal to judge in accordance with our laws of logic as it is normal to walk upright. Just as there may have been a time when it was not normal for our ancestors to walk upright, so many modes of thinking might have been normal in the past which are not so now, and in the future something might be normal that is not so at the present time. In a language whose form is not yet fixed there are always points of grammar on which our sense of idiom is unreliable, and a similar thing would have to hold in respect of the laws of logic whenever we were in a period of transition. We might, for instance, be in two minds whether it is correct to judge that every object is identical with itself. If that were so, we should not really be entitled to speak of logical laws, but only of logical rules that specify what is regarded as normal at a particular time. We should not be entitled to express such a rule in a form like 'Every object is identical with itself' for there is here no mention at all of the class of beings for whose judgements the rule is meant to be valid, but we should have to say something like 'At the present time it is normal for men—with the possible exception of certain primitive peoples for whom the matter has not yet been investigated—to judge that every object is identical with itself'. However, once there are laws, even if they are psychological, then, as we have seen, they must always be true, or better, they must be timelessly true if they are true at all. Therefore if we had observed that from a certain time a law ceased to hold, then we should have to say that it was altogether false. What we could do, however, is to try to find a condition that would have to be added to the law. Let us assume that for a certain period of time men make judgements in accordance with the law that every object is identical with itself, but that after this time they cease to do so. Then the cause of this might be that the phosphorus content in the cerebral cortex had changed, and we should then have to say something like 'If the amount of phosphorus present in any part of man's cerebral cortex does not exceed 4%, his judgement will always be in accordance with the law that every object is identical with itself.'

We can at least conceive of psychological laws that refer in this way to the chemical composition of the brain or to its anatomical structure. On the other hand, such a reference would be absurd in the case of logical laws, for these are not concerned with what this or that man holds to be true, but with what is true. Whether a man holds the thought that $2 \cdot 2 = 4$ to be true or to be false may depend on the chemical composition of his brain, but whether this thought is true cannot depend on that. Whether it is true that Julius Caesar was assassinated by Brutus cannot depend upon the structure of Professor Mommsen's brain.

People sometimes raise the question whether the laws of logic can change with time. The laws of truth, like all thoughts, are always true if they are true at all. Nor can they contain a condition which might be satisfied at certain times but not at others, because they are concerned with the truth of thoughts and if these are true, they are true timelessly. So if at one time the truth of some thought follows from the truth of certain others, then it must always follow.

Let us summarize what we have elicited about thoughts (properly so-called).

Unlike ideas, thoughts do not belong to the individual mind (they are not subjective), but are independent of our thinking and confront each one of us in the same way (objectively). They are not the product of thinking, but are only grasped by thinking. In this respect they are like physical bodies. What distinguishes them from physical bodies is that they are non-spatial, and we could perhaps really go as far as to say that they are essentially timeless—at least inasmuch as they are immune from anything that could effect a change in their intrinsic nature. They are like ideas in being non-spatial.

Since thoughts are not mental in nature, it follows that every psychological treatment of logic can only do harm. It is rather the task of this science to purify logic of all that is alien and hence of all that is psychological, and to free thinking from the fetters of language by pointing up the logical imperfections of language. Logic is concerned with the laws of truth, not with the laws of holding something to be true, not with the question of how men think, but with the question of how they must think if they are not to miss the truth.

Negation

A thought proper is either true or false. When we make a judgement about a thought, then we either accept it as true or we reject it as false. The last expression, however, can mislead us by suggesting that a thought which has been rejected ought to be consigned to oblivion as quickly as possible as being no longer of any use. On the contrary, the recognition that a thought is false may be just as fruitful as the recognition that a thought is true. Properly understood, there is no difference at all between the two cases. To hold one thought to be false is to hold a (different) thought to be true—a thought which we call the opposite of the first. In the German language we usually indicate that a thought is false by inserting the word 'not' into the predicate. But the assertion is still conveyed by the indicative form, and has no necessary connection with the word 'not'. The negative form can be retained although the assertion has been dropped. We can speak equally well of 'The thought that Peter did not come to Rome' as of 'The thought that Peter came to Rome'. Thus it is clear that when I assert that Peter did not come to Rome, the act of asserting and judging is no different from when I assert that Peter did come to Rome; the only difference is that we have the opposite thought. So to each thought there corresponds an opposite. Here we have a symmetrical relation: If the first thought is the opposite of the second, then the second is the opposite of the first. To declare false the thought that Peter did not come to Rome is to assert that Peter came to Rome. We could declare it false by inserting a second 'not' and saying 'Peter did (not) not come to Rome' or 'It is not true that Peter did not come to Rome'. And from this it follows that two negatives cancel one another out. If we take the opposite of the opposite of something, we have what we began with.

When it is a question of whether some thought is true, we are poised between opposite thoughts, and the same act which recognizes one of them as true recognizes the other as false. Analogous relations of opposition hold in other cases too, e.g. between what is beautiful and ugly, good and bad, pleasant and unpleasant and positive and negative in mathematics and physics. But these are different from our case in two respects. In the first place there is nothing here which, like nought or a neutrally charged body, occupies a mean between opposites. We can of course say that, in relation to positive and negative numbers, nought is its own opposite, but there is no thought which could count as its own opposite. This is true even of fictions. In the second place we do not have here two classes such that one contains thoughts that are the opposite of those contained in the other, as there is a class of positive and a class of negative numbers. At any rate, I have not yet found any feature that could be used to effect such a division; for the use of the word 'not' in ordinary language is a purely external criterion and an unreliable one at that. We have other signs for negation like 'no', and we often use the prefix 'un' as, for example, in 'unsatisfactory'. Now in view of the fact that 'unsatisfactory' and 'bad' are very close in sense to one another, there would surely appear to be little point in wishing to assign the thoughts contained in 'This work is bad' and 'This work is satisfactory' to the first class and those contained in 'The work is not bad' and 'The work is unsatisfactory' to the second class, and it may well be the case that in some other language the word for 'unsatisfactory' is one in which a negative form is no more to be discerned that it is in 'bad'. We cannot define in what respect the first two thoughts might be supposed to be more closely related than the first and fourth. There is the further fact that negatives can occur elsewhere than in the predicate of a main clause, and that such negatives do not simply cancel each other out: an example would be 'Not all pieces of work are unsatisfactory'. We cannot put for this 'All pieces of work are satisfactory', and nor can we put 'Whoever has worked hard is rewarded, for 'Whoever has not worked hard is not rewarded'. If we compare these with the sentences 'Whoever is rewarded has worked hard', 'Whoever has not worked hard goes away empty-handed', 'Whoever has been idle is not rewarded', '2^4 is not different from 4^2' and '2^4 is the same as 4^2', we shall see that we are tangling with some thorny problems here. What is more it is simply not worth while to try to extricate ourselves, and to expend a great deal of effort on finding answers to them. I at any rate know of no logical law which would take cognizance of a division of thoughts into positive and negative. We shall therefore leave the matter to look after itself until such time as it should become clear to us that such a division is somehow necessary. At which juncture we should naturally expect a criterion to emerge by which the division could be effected.

The prefix 'un', is not always used to negate. There is hardly any difference in sense between 'unhappy' and 'miserable'. Here we have a word which is the opposite of 'happy', and yet is not its negation. For this reason the sentences 'This man is not unhappy' and 'This man is happy' do not have the same sense.

Compound Thoughts

If the jury return a 'Yes' to the question 'Did the accused wilfully set fire to a pile of wood and (wilfully) start a forest fire?' they have simultaneously asserted the two thoughts:

(1) The accused wilfully set fire to a pile of wood,
(2) The accused wilfully started a forest fire.

It is true that our question contains one thought, for it can be answered by making one judgement; but this thought is composed of two thoughts—each of these being capable of being judged on its own—in such a way that by affirming the whole thought I affirm at the same time the component thoughts. Now it might seem that this is really neither here nor there and that the matter is of little importance; but it will become evident that it is closely bound up with very important logical laws. This comes out more clearly as soon as one considers the negation of such a compound thought. When will the jury have to say 'No' to the question above? Obviously the moment they hold but one of the two component thoughts to be false; for example, if they are of the opinion that whilst there is no doubt that the accused wilfully set fire to the pile of wood, he did not intend as a consequence that the forest should catch fire.

The Argument for my stricter Canons of Definition[1]

[1897/98 or shortly afterwards]

Since the necessity for my stricter canons of definition may not yet be sufficiently evident from what I said on the matter in the first part,[2] and since, as it appears, opinion is still greatly divided on this matter, I want to try to argue for my view once again, by drawing a comparison with Peano's mathematical logic. What is at stake here is perhaps the deepest difference between the two concept-scripts. I have drawn attention to certain shortcomings which struck me in the definition of the Peano deduction-sign '⊃', which roughly corresponds to my 'Ɫ'. These shortcomings are certainly due to the fact that, whereas Peano takes a first step in my direction, he doesn't take the second. His definition of the sign '⊃' for the case where it stands between sentences containing no indefinitely indicating letters (*lettres variables*) agrees in essentials with my definition of the sign 'Ɫ'; but for the case where indefinitely indicating letters (*lettres variables*) occur on both sides of the sign '⊃', another definition is given whose relation to the first remains unclear. In my case the combination of condition and consequence is presented as analysed into two components, of which the one is generality, signified by the use of roman letters, while the other is designated by the sign 'Ɫ'. This analysis cannot be clearly discerned in Peano's case because the use of *lettres variables* and the sign '⊃' are both defined simultaneously. In his most recent account, Peano has attempted to remove this shortcoming, but unfortunately, not by following me in taking my

---

[1] The text was presumably composed in 1897/8 or shortly thereafter: right at the beginning Frege mentions having 'drawn attention to certain shortcomings in the definition of the Peano deduction-sign'. This must refer to the article of Frege: *Über die Begriffsschrift des Herrn Peano und meine eigene* that appeared in 1897. Later on Frege talks of Peano's attempts in his most recent account to overcome these shortcomings. From the details of what Frege says, this must refer to the definition of '⊃' in *Formulaire de Mathématiques*' Vol. II, p. 24, which appeared at the end of 1897. (The corresponding definition in *Form.* Vol. I, pp. V/VI, No. 17 is still in the form that Frege criticized in his article) (ed.). It seems to us a natural conjecture that the present article and the next are preliminary drafts of material intended for inclusion in Volume II of the *Grundgesetze*: this both because of the overlap in content between parts of this article and early parts of Volume II and above all because of the way in which *Grundgesetze* Volume I is simply referred to as 'the first part' or 'my first volume' (trans.).

[2] As the editors point out, the reference here is clearly to the first part of the *Grundgesetze* (trans.).

second step, but by retracting the first. He completely abandons the definition of the deduction-sign which agrees in essentials with mine, and now completely excludes this case—the one where '⊃' stands between sentences containing no indefinitely indicating letters. But there surely do occur cases where even in speech the form of a hypothetical sentence ('if . . . then . . .') is used, without the content being general. Let us, however, waive this objection.

As an example, let us take a look now at the Peano sentence

$$\text{'}u, v \ \varepsilon \ \mathrm{K} . f \ \varepsilon \ vfu . \bar{f} \ \varepsilon \ ufv . \supset . \text{num } u = \text{num } v\text{'},$$

which corresponds in essentials to my

$$\text{'}\underset{\begin{array}{l}\rule{0pt}{0pt}\end{array}}{\vphantom{x}}\quad\text{'}$$

Admittedly in my case the two Peano conditions $u, v \ \varepsilon \ \mathrm{K}$ are missing, but this does not make my sentence false. Rather, my signs are so defined, that, without the truth of the claim being put in jeopardy, names of objects other than classes can also be substituted for u and v. In this formula $u, v \ \varepsilon \ \mathrm{K}$ is meant to state that by u and v classes are to be understood. The other two conditions '$f \ \varepsilon \ vfu$' and '$\bar{f} \ \varepsilon \ ufv$' state that f is a function mapping u into v and whose inverse maps v into u. According to Peano these conditions restrict the domain of what is to be understood by the letters. Now this still leaves open a certain leeway for the *meanings** (*significations*) of the letters and that creates generality. Now how is a particular case derived from such a general sentence? Obviously by assigning, subject to the restrictions imposed by the antecedents, particular meanings to the letters in the consequent (the part of the formula to the right of the '⊃'), and so by replacing the letters by signs which have these particular meanings at all times. Here in fact the letter 'f' doesn't occur in the consequent at all. Nevertheless we must still be able to specify such a meaning for this letter too. The antecedents are now dropped, because they have done their job for this case, and because the deduction-sign '⊃' would otherwise stand between sentences that contained no indefinitely indicating letters, which according to the latest version of the Peano concept-script is forbidden. Thus, of the original general sentence there only remains the consequent, which now, however, no longer has any generality.

Let's now look at a sentence which our general sentence may be converted into, by taking as the new consequent the negation of an antecedent, and making the negation of the original consequent into an

---

* By using italics I indicate that I am using this word in the sense of Peano's '*signification*'.

antecedent. This transformation, called by English logicians '*contraposition*', and otherwise known as 'the transition from *modus ponens* to *modus tollens*' is indispensable. The sense is scarcely affected by it, since the sentence gives neither more nor less information after the transformation than before. But since the conditions are not quite the same, the restrictions on the *meanings* of the letters are no longer the same either. If, e.g. I make the negation of the antecedent, 'u is a class', into a consequent ('then u is not a class'), then in conforming with the conditions that v is a class and f maps u into v, and the inverse of $f\,v$ into u, and finally that the cardinality of u is different from the cardinality of v, I can now only give the letter u precisely such *meanings* as were previously excluded. This illustrates how, as a result of legitimate transformations, there is an alteration in the *meanings* that may be assigned to the letters: a fact which hardly makes for greater logical perspicuity.

As against this, my conception is as follows. First, on account of the basic difference between objects and concepts, it is necessary to separate function-letters from object-letters. A sentence completed with a judgement-stroke that contains roman object-letters affirms that its content is true whatever meaningful proper names you may substitute for those letters, provided the same proper name is substituted for one and the same letter throughout the sentence. Since proper names are signs which mean one individual determinate object, another way of putting this is: such a sentence affirms that its content is true, whatever objects be understood by the roman object-letters occurring in it. So here the *meanings* (in Peano's sense) have genuinely unrestricted scope; for that it only includes objects and not functions as well goes without saying, since in view of their fundamental dissimilarity objects and functions cannot be substituted for one another. This is how my conception contrasts with Peano's, for in his case the scope can be more or less restricted, and changes under transformations of the sentence. And so in my case antecedents don't have the function of restricting scope. If I want to derive a particular proposition from such a general sentence—from a sentence whose generality is simply due to the presence of roman letters, I simply put the same proper name for each occurrence in the sentence of the same roman object-letter. In this way the lower limbs (antecedents) stay in place, but can, where appropriate, be detached by certain inferences. This makes it quite unnecessary to look anxiously to see that the leeway allowed by the conditions is not exceeded. In the Peano concept-script the judgements necessary for this are not reflected at all, and so it cannot provide a way of checking them. In my case the designation of generality is quite independent of the hypothetical form of the sentence, and the meaning of the conditional stroke is defined quite independently of generality: and this is the methodologically correct procedure to follow.

It follows from this that certain demands have to be made of the definitions of signs. Let's assume for the sake of simplicity that only one roman letter—an object-letter—occurs in a sentence. It then stands in the argument-place of the designation of a function, which in this case will be a concept. And in the case where the sentence is provided with a judgement-stroke the value of this function must be the True, for every object as argument. And so the designation of this function taken in conjunction with every meaningful proper name which occupies the argument-place must have a meaning. Hence the same must also hold for every function-name which, say, helps form the designation of our function: the proper name formed from this function-name and any proper name whatever in the argument-place must always have a meaning, provided only that this last proper name means something. For the proper name thus formed out of our function-name and this proper name is a part of the proper name of the True that is formed out of the whole function-designation and that very name. But if this part has no meaning, neither can the whole mean anything, and so, in particular, it cannot mean the True. In our example this holds of the function $\mathfrak{P}\xi$. This requirement is not made by Peano and hence is also rarely met, although it is scarcely less necessary for his conception of the hypothetical sentence than for mine. For if, in our example, we take as before 'then u is not a class' as consequent, we must also understand by u something that is not a class, and hence in this case too 'num u' must *mean* something, if it is to be possible to judge whether the condition 'if num u does not coincide with num v' is satisfied, and equally it must also be possible to judge whether a given relation maps u into v or v into u for the case where u is not a class. So the definitions of 'num u' and of mapping ('$f \varepsilon \, vfu$') must be formulated accordingly. Since one cannot know from the outset in which sentences these signs will occur and what restrictions will be thereby placed on the meanings of the letters, the definitions are to be constructed in such a way that a meaning is guaranteed these combinations of signs for every *meaning* of the letters.

We can also argue for this requirement on the ground that the law of the excluded middle must hold. For that implies that every concept must have sharp boundaries, so that it is determined for every object whether it falls under the concept or not. Were this not so, there would be a third case besides just the two cases 'a falls under the concept F' and 'a does not fall under the concept F'—namely, the case where this is undecided. The fallacy known as the 'Sorites' depends on something (e.g. a heap) being treated as a concept which cannot be acknowledged as such by logic because it is not properly circumscribed.

The following consideration also gives the same result. Inference from two premises very often, if not always, depends on a concept being common to both of them. If a fallacy is to be avoided, not only must the sign for the concept be the same, it must also mean the same. It must have a meaning independent of the context and not first come to acquire one in context, which is no doubt what very often happens in speech.

What holds of functions which we have called concepts, that they must have a value for every argument, also holds of the others; for they can be used in the construction of concepts. Thus, e.g.

$$\mathfrak{B}\xi = \mathfrak{B}\grave{\varepsilon}\,(\varepsilon = \mathit{Q})$$

is a concept in the construction of which we use, among others, the function $\mathfrak{B}\xi$. If now for some or other meaningful proper name '$\varDelta$', '$\mathfrak{B}\varDelta$' were meaningless, then

$$'\mathfrak{B}\varDelta = \mathfrak{B}\grave{\varepsilon}\,(\varepsilon = \mathit{Q})'$$

would also be meaningless and so could mean neither the True nor the False; i.e. we should have the case that it would not be determined for the object whether or not it fell under the concept

$$\mathfrak{B}\xi = \mathfrak{B}\grave{\varepsilon}\,(\varepsilon = \mathit{Q})$$

What we have said about object-letters, also holds *mutatis mutandis* for function-letters; a roman function-letter, which is used as a mark of a first level function with one argument, must be replaceable wherever it occurs in sentences by the designation of a first level function with one argument without rendering the whole devoid of meaning. From this it follows that such a letter cannot occur without an argument place: and so Peano's designation '$f\ \varepsilon\ vfu$' must be rejected, because the letter 'f' occurs here without any argument place, so that it e.g. becomes impossible to put in its place the designation of the function $\xi + 1$. If the letter 'ε' in '$f\ \varepsilon\ vfu$' was supposed to occupy the argument place of '$f(\xi)$', you could substitute the designation of the function $\xi + 1$, thus getting

$$'(\varepsilon + 1)\,vfu',$$

but as Peano construes the formula, no such substitution can occur. For the same reason many of Peano's designations in which a function-letter occurs without an argument are to be rejected. They contradict the very essence of a function, its unsaturatedness or need of supplementation. Such designations, which belie the real situation, may indeed seem at first sight convenient, but in the end they always lead into a morass; for at some point or another their inadequacy will become painfully apparent. So here: the letter f is supposed to serve for the designation of generality. But try to move from it to particular cases, and it nearly always breaks down. And indeed a wide variety of designations have been introduced by mathematicians with an eye only on their immediate purpose; but the designations that promise best to survive are those which adapt themselves most readily to diverse requirements and can be applied over the most extensive domain, and this because they fit the subject-matter best. We shall not be able to discover such designations if we are merely concerned to cope with the case in hand and do not pursue our reflections further, but only if we attain the deepest possible insight into the nature of the subject-matter.

Logical Defects in Mathematics[1]

[1898/99 or later, probably not after 1903]

There is little cause for satisfaction with the state in which mathematics finds itself at present, if you have regard not to the outside, to the amount of it, but to the degree of perfection and clarity within. In this respect it leaves almost everything to be desired if you compare it with the ideal you may reasonably propose for this discipline, and when you consider that by its very nature it ought to be better fitted to approach its ideal than is any other discipline. If you ask what constitutes the value of mathematical knowledge, the answer must be: not so much what is known as how it is known, not so much its subject-matter as the degree to which it is intellectually perspicuous and affords insight into its logical interrelations. And it is just this which is lacking. Authors explain the commonest expressions such as 'function', 'variable' and 'equal' in totally different ways and these discrepancies are not just trivial but concern the very heart of the matter. It very often happens that the same word is used by one writer to name a sign, by another a content which he goes on to present as the meaning of that sign. So in the first case a word is understood to mean a material object with physical and chemical properties, such as colour and solubility in hydrochloric acid—while in the second it is understood to mean an object with no such properties. But it isn't only in the case of different authors that we find such discrepancies—ones which affect the very foundations of the subject: not infrequently one and the same author uses a word in a way that conflicts with his own definition. It happens, for instance, that a mathematician so explains the term 'definite integral' that he wants us to understand by it a certain limit of a sum. But the same author isn't deterred in the slightest from using the expression as if he understood it to mean a combination of signs that contains the integral sign as a constituent. So, for instance, Ludwig Scheefer* says '. . . so that, according to the Riemannian definition

---

* [*Allgemeine Untersuchungen über Rectification der Curven,*] *Acta mathematica* V [1884], p. 49.

[1] The editors date this essay between 1898/99 and 1903, largely by the way in which Volume I of the *Grundgesetze* is referred to—the way in which Frege talks of the use of the letter 'ξ' 'in the first volume'. They also mention that some of the material of this essay is developed in the essay *Was ist eine Funktion?* published in 1904. This argument for the dating seems cogent, but we think it possible to go further and say that the way in which *Grundgesetze* Vol. I is referred to is only intelligible if Frege is producing here, as in the case of the preceding article, a draft of material intended for inclusion in Vol. II of the *Grundgesetze* (trans.).

the definite integral $\int_0^{x_+}\sqrt{1 + f'(x)^2}\,dx$ acquires no meaning.' Here the word 'integral' is used in both those senses in the same breath. For if there is talk of the meaning of an integral then all that can be meant is the meaning of a sign, or combination of signs—in fact from the context we can only understand the expression that is here formed with the integral, root and plus signs combined with numerals and letters. But at the same time appeal is made to the Riemannian definition according to which an integral is the limit of a sum, and it would be difficult to understand a limit value in Riemann's sense to mean a sign whose meaning could be asked after. In Riemann we find the following:*

> 'If it** should have the property that however δ and ε may be chosen, it approaches a limit A indefinitely closely as δ becomes indefinitely small, then this value is called $\int_a^b f(x)\,dx$. If it does not have this property $\int_a^b f(x)\,dx$ has no meaning. Even in such a case, however, there have been a number of attempts to attach a meaning to this sign, and among these extensions of the concept of a definite integral *one* is accepted by all mathematicians.'

Here the sign '$\int_a^b f(x)dx$' is nowhere called an integral. Throughout this context I would put this sign in inverted commas to make it clearer that the sign alone is meant, for the definition itself asserts that otherwise a limit value is to be understood by it. Even I wouldn't have found this precaution necessary if experience had not taught me how far one must avoid anything that could in any way encourage the mathematical sickness of our time, of confusing the sign with what is signified. This sickness may well not have been so prevalent when Riemann wrote his article. And so it's easy to understand that he should regard inverted commas as dispensable, since the sense is made clear enough by the use of the phrases 'is called', 'has no meaning', and 'we understand by'. His usage would also correspond to that according to which you do not need to insert inverted commas after the phrase 'is called'. He doesn't seem to have used the expression 'the integral has a meaning'.

The following expressions are found in his writings (5): extension of the validity of the concept 'a function is integrable', 'we may speak of an integral of the function $f(x)$ between a and b', and also (6): 'the possibility of a definite integral'. None of these expressions gives any reason for suspecting Riemann to have been in the grip of the epidemic we have referred to. And so we must not hesitate to assume the opposite. If an astronomer said 'The planet ♃ has a meaning: it means the planet of the solar system with the greatest mass. Whereas the planet ⟨2000⟩ has as yet no meaning, but it could be that it will receive a meaning later', or if he said

---

* *Über die Darstellbarkeit einer Funktion durch eine trigonometrische Reihe.* Werke [ed. by H. Weber, Leipzig 1876]: p. 225.

** That is, the sum.

'The planet ♃ has a certain similarity with the number 4', one would perhaps ask oneself whether he had some kind of brain disorder. But if a mathematician adopts ways of speaking which appear not unworthy of a Dogberry, this happens apparently without any slur on his scientific reputation.

There is a great deal of talk about variables in the mathematical literature. But you may hardly conclude from this that there exists a general agreement about the sense of the word. To my mind it is much more likely that most who use it don't know exactly what sense they attach to it. Whether there is someone who has found a tenable explanation of the word, I don't know. Many do not explain the word at all, which is the most convenient thing to do, but would only be justifiable if there was a general agreement among people about it. At first one might think that you should supply the word 'number' and understand by 'variable number' a number with different properties at different times, so that e.g. at one time it was prime, at another a square. But that would obviously be quite beside the point, if only because it is doubtful whether there are any variable numbers in this sense at all. Here you might think of the fact that a number, e.g. 15 000, at one time was the number of inhabitants of Jena, at another not, and that we could construe this altered relation to the concept *inhabitant of Jena* as an alteration in the number 15 000. However it wouldn't be the possibility of this alteration which we need in Analysis. The expression 'the number of inhabitants of Jena varies' isn't strictly correct. One does not mean by it that the same number assumes different properties, but that in the course of time ever new numbers acquire the status of being the number of inhabitants of Jena. It would be as if you wished to say of countries like England and Holland that the rulers were of variable sex, and as if someone wanted to infer from this that there were people who were now male, now female. The illusion arises from regarding a phrase like 'the King of England' as a proper name. But it isn't, and only becomes one if you supplement it with a time reference. In the same way, phrases like 'the number of inhabitants of Jena', 'the number of known moons of Jupiter' cannot be construed as proper names of numbers. But once supplemented, the proper name designates a quite definite number, for which there can no longer be any talk of a variation that is of any use to Analysis. Fine, you say, but that is still only an altered and, I will admit, improved way of talking: instead of saying 'a number varies', we must say 'in the course of time ever new numbers assume a certain status'; still that surely doesn't make any material difference. To me, however, the way of speaking doesn't appear to be so unimportant; a wrong idiom can easily lead to real confusion. And the distinction isn't all that slight either. Variation always presupposes something permanent that varies. To say of a man that he has grown older is to presuppose something permanent—which is designated by the proper name of the man—so that, despite the variation, you are acknowledging it is the same man. Otherwise you would have to say 'a younger man has vanished and an older one appeared'. Without such a permanent we have nothing of which we can say that it has varied. If there are no variable numbers, one may not use proper names that designate them. In that case it is quite wrong to say 'the variable x'. What we then have is surely no mere difference of idiom. So it is not clear straight off what you ought to say instead in Analysis.

The scale of the changes required makes them none too easy to comprehend. Add to this the fact that it is only in kinematics that time comes into consideration, whereas variables also enter into other branches of mathematics. It is completely out of place to introduce time there. But a variation that isn't a variation in time isn't one at all in the ordinary sense of the term. It is obviously a question here of a term of art which needs explaining, since the reference to ordinary usage is only misleading. The expression 'variable' gives an image or metaphor which, like most metaphors, at a certain point goes lame. Therefore we shall only be able to use this word without giving rise to objections after we have stipulated more precisely what it is to mean. In one of the most recent textbooks of higher Analysis* we find the following: 'By a real variable, we understand a number that is indeterminate at the outset, and which, depending on the problem in which it occurs, can assume indefinitely many real values.'

This gives rise to a host of questions. The author obviously distinguishes two classes of numbers: the determinate and the indeterminate. We may then ask, say, to which of these classes the primes belong, or whether maybe some primes are determinate numbers and others indeterminate. We may ask further whether in the case of indeterminate numbers we must distinguish between the rational and the irrational, or whether this distinction can only be applied to determinate numbers. How many indeterminate numbers are there? How are they distinguished from one another? Can you add two indeterminate numbers, and if so, how? How do you find the number that is to be regarded as their sum? The same questions arise for adding a determinate number to an indeterminate one. To which class does the sum belong? Or maybe it belongs to a third? Perhaps there is a seminal idea here which we could also find of value outside mathematics. Perhaps we could also divide men, and mathematicians in particular, into the determinate and the indeterminate. What is a value? How does an indeterminate number assume a value? Isn't a value just a number? In which case one number would assume another—or even perhaps itself? But then why does the author use both the words 'value' and 'number', if the same thing is meant? Was it perhaps to hide his misconceptions beneath the charitable cloak of darkness? Incidentally, according to our author, a determinate number can also possess a value—presumably, after it has assumed it—as we learn from the following quotation: 'In contrast with this,

---

* Emanuel Czuber, *Vorlesungen über Differential und Integralrechnung*, Vol. I, Leipzig, Teubner 1898.

we call a number, whether it be determinate or indeterminate, a constant, if by virtue of the problem it possesses a fixed (invariable) value.'

From this we may infer: there are both determinate and indeterminate numbers; not only the latter but also the former can assume values, which they thereupon possess. These values are either fixed and invariable, or variable. What fixed and what variable values are isn't explained, presumably because it is so simple that it needs no explanation. Much more difficult is the distinction between variable numbers and constants. That requires much more complicated definitions—these however offer such great difficulties to the understanding that the author himself has not yet been able to penetrate to the innermost depths of their conceptual content. You might imagine that the indeterminate numbers as such are not susceptible to definition, but the author continues:

'The totality of these values forms a value set, and has the particular name, the *range* or domain of the variable. The variable x counts as having been defined if given any real number it can be determined whether it belongs to the range or not.'

This seems to imply the following: that a variable is defined by its range, so that if you have the same range, you have the same variable. Now it is to be assumed, even if not from his definition, yet on other grounds, that where we have the equation of a curve of the third degree

$$y = x^3$$

the author would speak of a variable x and a variable y, and would give the totality of real numbers as the range of each. So here we would have only one variable, which would however be designated by the two different signs 'x' and 'y'. In § 3 we learn the following:

'If with every value of the real variable x that belongs to its range, is correlated a determinate number y, then y is thereby also in general defined as a variable, and is called a function of the real variable x.'

And so the determinate number y is defined as a number which is at the outset indeterminate, which, depending on the problem in which it occurs, can assume indefinitely many values. So the variation presumably consists in the fact that the number, which at the outset is indeterminate, gradually works its way through to becoming determinate. All the same, it is remarkable that the number y which has become determinate in this way is still a variable and can assume indefinitely many values. Which is the problem in which y occurs? And which the problem in which x occurs? Are they different problems or do we only have one problem? How prudent and well considered here is the restriction 'which belongs to its range'; otherwise it could easily befall the variable x, that it assumed values which, according to the problem in which it occurs, it cannot assume at all. It must be protected from this misfortune.

The use of the letters '*x*' and '*y*' is not above question. Is '*x*' a proper name, designating a variable, and '*y*' the proper name of another—as '3' designates one number and '2' another? Or do these letters only indicate variables? In the first part of this work roman letters have been used without exception to indicate, not to designate, and this is the use that prevails in mathematics. Only a few letters such as '*e*' and the Greek '*π*' are used to designate—as proper names of the base of natural logarithms and of the ratio of the circumference of a circle to its diameter. In the familiar sentence

$$(a + b)\cdot c = a\cdot c + b\cdot c$$

we have the ordinary use of letters to indicate. They serve here to confer generality on the thought. They stand in the place of proper names, but are not such (pronouns). You always obtain a particular case of the general sentence when you substitute the same proper name of a number throughout for the letter *a*, and similarly for *b* and *c*. The sentence now says—and just this is what constitutes its generality—that a true thought is expressed in this way no matter what proper names of numbers may be substituted. So I return to the question: In the sentence 'If with every value of the real variable *x*, which belongs to its range, is correlated a determinate number *y*, then *y* is thereby also in general defined as a variable and is called a function of the real variable *x*' are the letters '*x*' and '*y*' used to designate or indicate? In the first case '*x*' and '*y*' would be proper names of different variables. However that can't be right, since these variables would then have to be made known to us. It would then have had to be said how the variable *x* is given, what properties it has by which you may recognize it and distinguish it from other variables. The same would have had to be said concerning *y*. Since nothing of that sort has been forthcoming, we can hardly assume that the letters are used here to designate. But even if we assume that the letters are used to indicate, we run into difficulties. For in that case the sentence would have to have a sense—a true sense—when we substitute numerical signs for the letters. Let us put '2', say, for '*x*' and '3' for *y*. We then obtain

'If with every value of the real variable 2, which belongs to its range, is correlated a determinate number 3, then 3 is thereby also in general defined as a variable and is called a function of the real variable 2.'

That is completely unintelligible. What, for instance, is a value of 2? You will say the mistake consists in substituting for '*x*' the sign for a determinate number; it would have to be replaced by the sign (proper name) of an indeterminate number. Unluckily, we are not yet acquainted with any indeterminate numbers at all, cannot distinguish one indeterminate number from another and so are not in a position to stipulate proper names for them. You may say 'Surely there are indeterminate numbers and they also can be distinguished and named. For instance, let there be a right-angled co-ordinate system on a plane, including a specification of the unit length for each of the axes. Let *x* then be the abscissa and *y* the ordinate of a point. "*x*" is then the proper name of one indeterminate number and "y" of another; in that case x and y will be indeterminate numbers which can be distinguished from each other, and can be spoken about by using their proper names—simply the letters 'x' and 'y'. And so it will be possible for the variables x and y in the quotation cited to be of this sort.' I reply: give me any point on the plane whatsoever. Then this point will have a quite determinate abscissa and a quite determinate ordinate. So the question of indeterminate numbers simply doesn't arise. It may be objected that we should not take a determinate but an indeterminate point. But then we are back with the same difficulty. I doubt just as much that there are indeterminate points as that there are indeterminate numbers or indeterminate people.

'But the solution of the quadratic equation $x^2 - 4x + 3 = 0$ is surely indeterminate, and so 'x' designates this indeterminate solution and hence an indeterminate number.' I reply: this is neither true nor false, for since there is more than one solution, the definite article in the phrase 'the solution' is a logical error, and the sentence 'The problem contained in that equation permits of more than one solution' expressed correctly what was expressed erroneously above. It's a question of a property of the problem, not of a property of the solution. It is mistaken to say 'the indeterminate solution' or 'the indeterminate number which satisfied the equation': on the other hand we might perhaps call the problem an undetermining one, if this way of speaking were admitted. For this reason the formation '$x = 2 \pm 1$' is to be avoided like the plague. The combination of signs '2 ± 1' has neither sense nor meaning. Still the quadratic equation can be referred to as an example to show that apart from the use of letters to indicate or to designate, we have to assume yet a third. Of course this would be no argument for acknowledging indeterminate numbers. Regarded as a problem, the equation asserts nothing, and so there admittedly can be no question of using the letter x here to indicate—to confer generality on the thought. What we really have here is the designation of a concept, and the challenge to cite objects (in this case numbers) which fall under it. In that case the 'x' is used in the way I used the letter 'ξ' in the first volume:[1] it occupies the argument-places, so that we can recognize them as such. Once you have solved the problem, you may assert the sentence 'If $x = 1$ or $x = 3$, then $x^2 - 4x + 3 = 0$', and here the letter 'x' is once more used to indicate as above, to make the thought general. Whatever numerical sign may be substituted for 'x', we always obtain a true sentence, either because the condition is not fulfilled, in which case it is all one whether the consequent is true or false (for instance if you substitute '2'), or because the condition is fulfilled, in which case the consequent is then also true.

Now how are we to understand the use of the letters 'x' and 'y' in analytic geometry? Of course the equation of a parabola '$y \cdot y - 2x = 0$' isn't meant to assert anything: rather, this equation always occurs as a constituent of

[1] Of the *Grundgesetze* (ed.).

sentences in which something is asserted, and in these sentences these letters *will* be used to indicate; for example 'If x is the abscissa of a point and y the ordinate, and if $y \cdot y - 2x = 0$, then this point lies on a parabola, which ... etc.' Here the co-ordinate system must be presupposed to be already given.

Thus neither do we encounter indeterminate numbers here. There are none such and that there are such is only an illusion created by a defective idiom.

The words 'function' and 'variable' are often used in conjunction with each other. We have in fact just seen how 'the function of the real variable x' has been defined as a variable. As against this Heine* says: 'A *single-valued function* of a variable x means an expression which is uniquely defined for each individual rational or irrational value of x'. We are not in fact told that the letter 'x' occurs in the expression, but this must surely be assumed to be the case. x is called a variable. Whether that means the letter 'x' or what this letter means or indicates is unclear. Nor is it said what a value of x is. The most likely interpretation of Heine's meaning is surely the following: 'A *single valued* function of the letter "x" is a formula (a complex sign) for which it is established what every formula means which is derived from it by substituting for "x" a sign for a rational or irrational number'. Thus on Heine's view it appears that a function is not a number, but a formula, a complex sign. This explanation doesn't appear to agree with Czuber's. It is hardly worth the effort to try to reconcile the two, since, to be sure, Czuber's view is difficult to reconcile with itself. The fact that Heine shows these visible things the honour of bringing them under a concept and laying down a special word—'function'—for it, seems to imply that he regards such physical things as the objects of arithmetical investigation. But then again we have the fact that he uses the word 'define', which can here surely only mean 'stipulate a meaning for a simple or complex sign'. But if signs are taken to have meanings, it is striking that it isn't these meanings, but the signs which are supposed to be the main thing. Why then the meanings, if you don't bother with them but only with the signs? So we see obscurity and disagreement among writers of mathematics, and that where they are explaining words which are some of the most common amongst mathematicians. In point of fact, these questions have already been definitively resolved in our first Volume. I have only raked them up again because I suspect that many will hold my accounts to be extraordinarily difficult to understand, as compared with such accounts as you find in Czuber's lectures or elsewhere, which they will hold to be models of clarity. I have tried to show that this illusion of clarity only lasts as long as you raise none of the questions which those accounts naturally give rise to and so fail to notice that no satisfactory answer is to be found for them.

---

* *Die Elemente der Funktionslehre, Crelle* [*s Journal für die reine und angewandte Mathematik*], Vol. 74 [1872], p. 180.

But this lack of agreement isn't only to be found in the use of expressions from Analysis: it is even to be found in the case of a word like 'equal' and the sign '=', which are used throughout the highest and the lowest branches of mathematics. G. Peano* says that the opinions of writers concerning the identity sign are very diverse, and unfortunately he's quite right. The implications of what he says are enormous. For if you drop equality from arithmetic, there's almost nothing left: and so that claim implies nothing less than that mathematicians have diverse views about the sense of the major part of their theorems. A non-mathematician on hearing this might well clap his hands to his head in amazement, and be completely unable to grasp how such a situation was possible in any science and particularly in mathematics. His amazement would grow if he learnt that this wasn't in the least felt as a major calamity, that most mathematicians believe they have much more important things to do than spend their time splitting hairs in trying to remove this defect. A lot of people may think: if only concern with such questions were not so dreadfully sterile! I would like in return to ask: is mathematics then so calloused by formalism that we no longer bother at all about the sense of our sentences? What use are 100 000 theorems to us, if we ourselves haven't the faintest idea what we mean by them, if the man using a theorem attaches a different sense to it from the man who proved it? How often is the phrase 'power series' used! But what do we understand by it? What is a power? What is a series? People don't even agree about the question whether these things are configurations which men produce with writing implements, possessing physical properties, or whether powers, series and power series are only designated by such configurations, but are themselves non-spatial and invisible. What holds the terms of a series together? That they form a whole, this being just what the series is? Or is it the spatial relation of juxtaposition? You will certainly receive divergent answers to that question. And yet the difference between what is created, spatial, sensible and transitory on the one hand, and what is non-spatial, atemporal, non-sensible on the other, is so huge that it belongs among the greatest which can possibly exist. A science of objects of the one sort must differ far more profoundly from a science of objects of the other sort than, say, astronomy and cryptography. Such questions therefore touch the very heart of arithmetic. And yet this indifference! With the divergence of opinions and modes of expression, anyone using a word such as 'number', 'function' or 'power series' should by rights state what he understands by it. But many would angrily reject the demand that they concern themselves with such tediously academic questions, in the secret fear that they couldn't

---

* *Revue de Mathématiques* (*Rivista di matematica*), Vol. VI, p. 61: 'Del resto le opinioni dei varii Autori, sul concetto di eguaglianza, diversificano assai; ed uno studio di questa questione sarebbe assai utile, specialmente se fatto coll'aiuto di simboli, anziché di parole'.

say anything to the point. Others perhaps would boldy come straight out
with an answer, but only because they were unaware of the hidden pitfalls
and did not feel in the slightest the need to make their own use accord with
their explanations and to test them carefully with that object in mind. What
use to us are explanations when they have no intrinsic connection with a
piece of work, but are only stuck on to the outside like a useless ornament?

On Euclidean Geometry[1]

[1899–1906?]

It seems worthwhile to begin by coming to an understanding about the use of certain expressions. The word 'sentence' ['*Satz*'][2] is used in diverse ways. The one that comes most readily to mind is no doubt the purely linguistic one. It is in this sense that human discourse consists of sentences. However it is not the sentence itself that really concerns us when we speak, but the sense or content which we associate with it and which we wish to communicate. Since the sense itself cannot be perceived by the senses, we have perforce, in order to communicate, to avail ourselves of something that can be perceived. So the sentence and its sense, the perceptible and the imperceptible, belong together. I call the sense of a significant sentence a thought. Thoughts are either true or false. And it is the question whether a thought is true or false that is usually the reason why, in scientific work, we are concerned with thoughts. Now it can happen only too easily that a sign and its content are not clearly differentiated.* This kind of thing happens particularly where the content itself cannot be perceived by the senses, and where, for that reason, the sign is the only thing that we can perceive. Now it is a fact that man is by nature so orientated towards what is external, towards what can be perceived, that what cannot be perceived is often almost completely hidden from him by what can be perceived. The distinction will come very easily to someone who knows several languages, since he will recall that the same sense can be expressed in different languages.

---

* Confusion of numerals and numbers.

---

[1] These pieces form part of the controversy with Hilbert and so cannot be earlier than 1899, the year in which Vol. 1 of the *Grundlagen der Geometrie* was published. Assuming the controversy came essentially to an end with Frege's last paper on the foundations of geometry in 1906, it is very unlikely that the present pieces are later than 1906. However, Frege did, in subsequent unpublished writings, continue to express himself at variance with Hilbert's way of regarding axioms and definitions. See, for instance pp. 247 ff. and pp. 273 f. (ed.).

[2] The German word rendered throughout by 'sentence' is '*Satz*' (plural '*Sätze*') which, as Frege here remarks, is used in diverse ways. The English word does not, unfortunately, have quite the same family of uses as the German word and at certain places, notably where Frege uses compound nouns formed from '*Satz*', the translation is (unavoidably) unintelligible. The insertions in square brackets have therefore been added to enable the reader to follow the drift of Frege's remarks (trans.).

Now I have decided to use the word 'sentence' only to designate what is linguistic—that which has a thought as its sense. Thus I distinguish sentences from thoughts. Now we can understand how easy it is to ascribe to a sentence what belongs, properly speaking, to the thought and how it is that people speak of true sentences instead of true thoughts. They are then calling a sentence true when the sense of the sentence, the thought expressed in it, is true. We should note further that in grammar 'sentence' is often used somewhat differently from how I am using it here, as when one speaks of subordinate clauses [*Nebensätzen*]. In many cases these do not have a complete thought as their sense, but only part of a thought.

It is particularly awkward that in mathematics it has become customary to speak of theorems [*Lehrsätzen*]. This has given the word 'sentence' a chameleon-like quality: whilst we take it to refer to something linguistic, it all of a sudden changes and refers to a thought.

Many readers will have grown so accustomed to the way the word 'sentence' ['*Satz*'] is used in mathematical textbooks that it upsets them to find, in place of the word 'sentence', which they are used to, words like 'thought' or 'truth', to which they are not accustomed. To make it easier to follow I shall put the word 'sentence' ['*Satz*'] in brackets after the word 'thought'.

In the majority of cases what concerns us about a thought is whether it is true. The most appropriate name for a true thought is a truth. A science is a system of truths. A thought, once grasped, keeps pressing us for an answer to the question whether it is true. We declare our recognition of the truth of a thought, or as we may also say, our recognition of a truth, by uttering a sentence with assertoric force. Language is frequently lacking any word or part of a sentence that corresponds to the assertoric force, so that this often can only be felt. Subordinate clauses, which are nothing more than parts of sentences, are often uttered without assertoric force.

Whoever holds Euclidean geometry to be true will ascribe a sense to each of its theorems: he will regard each theorem as expressing a truth. He thereby implies that he recognizes that the concept-words 'point', 'line', 'plane' have a sense. In Euclidean geometry certain truths have traditionally been accorded the status of axioms. No thought that is held to be false can be accepted as an axiom, for an axiom is a truth. Furthermore, it is part of the concept of an axiom that it can be recognized as true independently of other truths.

(Truths can be inferred in accordance with the logical laws of inference.)

If a truth is given, it can be asked from what other truths its truth follows in accordance with the logical laws of inference. When this question has been answered, we can go on to ask of each of the truths that we have thus discovered from what other truths its truth follows in accordance with the logical laws of inference.

On Euclidean Geometry

No man can serve two masters. One cannot serve both truth and untruth. If Euclidean geometry is true, then non-Euclidean geometry is false, and if non-Euclidean geometry is true, then Euclidean geometry is false.

If given a point not lying on a line one and only one line can be drawn through that point parallel to that line then, given any line l and point P not lying on l, a line can be drawn through P parallel to l and any line that passes through P and is parallel to l will coincide with it.

Whoever acknowledges Euclidean geometry to be true must reject non-Euclidean geometry as false, and whoever acknowledges non-Euclidean geometry to be true must reject Euclidean geometry.

People at one time believed they practised a science, which went by the name of alchemy; but when it was discovered that this supposed science was riddled with error, it was banished from among the sciences. Again, people at one time believed they practised a science, which went by the name of astrology. But this too was banished from among the sciences once men had seen through it and discovered that it was unscientific. The question at the present time is whether Euclidean or non-Euclidean geometry should be struck off the role of the sciences and made to line up as a museum piece alongside alchemy and astrology. If one is content to have only phantoms hovering around one, there is no need to take the matter so seriously; but in science we are subject to the necessity of seeking after truth. There it is a case of in or out! Well, is it Euclidean or non-Euclidean geometry that should get the sack? That is the question. Do we dare to treat Euclid's elements, which have exercised unquestioned sway for 2000 years, as we have treated astrology? It is only if we do not dare to do this that we can put Euclid's axioms forward as propositions that are neither false nor doubtful. In that case non-Euclidean geometry will have to be counted amongst the pseudo-sciences, to the study of which we still attach some slight importance, but only as historical curiosities.

[Frege's Notes on Hilbert's '*Grundlagen der Geometrie*']¹

[After 1903]

§ 1

The Elements of Geometry and the five groups of Axioms

Definition: We imagine three different systems of things: we call the things of the *first* system *points* and designate them by *A*, *B*, *C*, . . .; we call the things of the *second* system *lines* and designate them by *a*, *b*, *c* . . .; we call the things of the *third* system *planes* and designate them by *α*, *β*, *γ*, . . .; the points are also called the *elements of linear geometry*, the points and lines the *elements of plane geometry*, and the points, lines and planes, the *elements of spatial geometry* or *of space*.

We imagine the points, lines and planes as standing in certain reciprocal relations, which we designate by words such as '*lie on*', '*between*', '*parallel*', '*congruent*', '*continuous*'; the exact and complete description of these relations is achieved by the *axioms of Geometry*.

. . .

Hilbert
§ 1 (Definition?)
(Pim, Lim, Plim) We.
System.
Relations are described.

---

¹ Frege's notes, which in the manuscript are written out as a continuous series of remarks, probably refer to the 2nd edition of Hilbert's *Grundlagen der Geometrie*. The editors have put alongside Frege's critical notes, which are set out on the right-hand side, the corresponding passages of Hilbert's text. The notes cannot refer to the 1st edition of the *Grundlagen* (1899), since there the theorem 4 criticized by Frege still figures as an axiom and was only proved in 1902 by E. H. Moore. Besides, Frege's last remark evidently refers to the first congruence axiom; but in the first edition § 5 contained the parallels axiom. It is indeed possible that Frege had before him a later edition than the 2nd, but it is hardly probable, if you work on the assumption that Frege wrote down his critique during the period of his first engagement with Hilbert's work, which came to an end in 1906 (the 3rd edition first appeared in 1909) (ed.).

§ 2

The 1st Axiom Group: Axioms of connection

The axioms of this group establish a *connection* between the concepts point, line and plane, defined above and are as follows:

I 1. *Two distinct points A and B always define a line.*

Instead of 'define' we will also use other turns of phrase, such as a '*passes through*' *A* '*and through*' *B*, a '*connects*' *A* '*and*' or '*with*' *B*. If *A* is a point which together with another point defines the line *a*, we also use the phrases: *A* 'lies on' *a*, *A* 'is a point of' *a*, 'There is the point' *A* 'on' *a* etc. If *A* lies on the line *a* and also on the line *b*, we also use the phrase: '*the lines*' *a* 'and' *b* '*have the point A in common*' etc.

§ 2 Concepts defined
(Points)

I 1. Define. Two. Identity denied.
Better:
A lies on *a* (*A* point, *a* line)
If *A* is a point, and *B* is a point, then there is a line on which *A* lies and on which *B* lies etc.
more than one theorem in I 1.

. . .

§ 3

The 2nd Axiom Group: Axioms of ordering

The Axioms of this group define the concept 'between' and make it possible, by using this concept, to order the points of a line, in a plane and in space.

Definition. The points of a line stand in certain relations to one another, for whose description we single out the word '*between*'.

II 1. *If A, B, and C are points of a line and B lies between A and C then B lies between C and A.*

II 2. *If A and C are two points of a line then there is always at least one point B which lies between A and C, and at least one point D such that C lies between A and D.*

II 3. *Given any three points of a line there is always one and only one which lies between the other two.*

Definition. We consider two points *A* and *B* on a line *a*; we call the system of the two points *A* and *B* an *interval* and designate it *AB* or *BA*. The points between *A* and *B* are called points of the interval *AB* or are said to lie *within* the interval *AB*; the points *A* and *B* are called

§ 3 Axioms define concept between

The word 'between' used to describe

Def. System of the two points
Interval

endpoints of the interval *AB*. All other points of
the line *a* are said to lie *outside* the interval *AB*.

. . .

§ 4

Consequences of the axioms of connection and
ordering

From the 1st and 2nd sets of axioms the
following theorems follow:

Theorem 3. Between any two points of a line
there are always infinitely many points.

§ 4 Theorem 3. Between
any two points of a line
there are always in-
finitely many points.
'Infinitely many' is not
explained.
There is no axiom in
whose phrasing 'infi-
nitely many' occurs.

Theorem 4. Given any four points on a line,
they can always be designated by *A*, *B*, *C*, and
D in such a way that the point designated by *B*
lies between *A* and *C*, and also between *A* and
D, and that further the point *C* lies between *A*
and *D* and also between *B* and *D*.

Theorem 4. The letters
and mode of designation
are not part of the con-
tent of the theorem.

Theorem 5. (Generalization of Theorem 4).
Given any finite number of points on a line, they
can always be designated by *A, B, C, D, E, ... K*,
in such a way that the point designated by *B* lies
between *A* on the one side and *C, D, E, ... K* on
the other, that *C* lies between *A* and *B* on the
one side and *D, E, ... K* on the other, and that
D lies between *A, B, C* on the one side and
E ... K on the other etc. In addition to this
mode of designation there is only the converse
mode *K ... E, D, C, B, A* with this feature.

Theorem 5. Dots and
etc. do not belong to the
content of the theorem.
'Finite number'. We
should have to borrow
from arithmetic some
sentence or other con-
taining the expression
'finite number'.

Theorem 6. Any line *a* lying in a plane *α*,
divides the points lying on this plane *α* and not
on *a* into two regions with the following
properties: any point *A* of the one region defines
with any point *B* of the other an interval *AB*
within which lies a point of *a*, whereas any two
points *A* and *A'* of the same region define an
interval *AA'* containing no point of *a*.

Theorem 6. 'Region',
'divide' have not oc-
curred.

. . .

§ 5

The 3rd Axiom Group: Axioms of congruence

III 1. *If A, B are two points of a line a and A' is*
a point of the same or another line a', one can
always find on a given side of the line a' of A'
one and only one point B', *such that the interval*
AB is congruent or equal to the interval A' B',
in signs:

$$AB = A'B'.$$

Every interval is congruent to itself, that is
we always have

$$AB \equiv AB \quad \text{and} \quad AB \equiv BA.$$

§ 5 'One can find'

[17 Key Sentences on Logic]¹

[1906 or earlier]

1. The connections which constitute the essence of thinking are of a different order from associations of ideas.
2. The difference is not a mere matter of the presence of some ancillary thought from which the connections in the former case derive their status.
3. In the case of thinking it is not really ideas that are connected, but things, properties, concepts, relations.
4. A thought always contains something reaching out beyond the particular case so that this is presented to us as falling under something general.
5. In language the distinctive character of a thought finds expression in the copula or personal ending of the verb.
6. A criterion for whether a mode of connection constitutes a thought is that it makes sense to ask whether it is true or untrue. Associations of ideas are neither true nor untrue.
7. What true is, I hold to be indefinable.
8. The expression in language for a thought is a sentence. We also speak in an extended sense of the truth of a sentence.
9. A sentence can be true or untrue only if it is an expression for a thought. The sentence 'Leo Sachse is a man' is the expression of a thought only if 'Leo Sachse' designates something. And so too the sentence 'this table is round' is the expression of a thought only if the words 'this table' are not empty sounds but designate something specific for me.
11. '2 times 2 is 4' is true and will continue to be so even if, as a result of Darwinian evolution, human beings were to come to assert that 2 times 2 is 5. Every truth is eternal and independent of being thought by anyone and of the psychological make-up of anyone thinking it.

---

¹ According to a note of Heinrich Scholz's, the manuscript should be dated around 1906. But it could have formed part of Frege's plans for a text book on logic (cf. pp. 1 ff., 126 ff.) and in that case its date would be much earlier. A further argument for an earlier dating is that, according to notes made by the editors preceding Scholz, the manuscript was found together with the preparatory material for the dialogue with Pünjer (pp. 53 ff. of this volume), where the name 'Leo Sachse' occurs again (ed.).

12. Logic only becomes possible with the conviction that there is a difference between truth and untruth.
13. We justify a judgement either by going back to truths that have been recognized already or without having recourse to other judgements. Only the first case, inference, is the concern of Logic.
14. The theory of concepts and of judgement is only preparatory to the theory of inference.
15. The task of logic is to set up laws according to which a judgement is justified by others, irrespective of whether these are themselves true.
16. Following the laws of logic can guarantee the truth of a judgement only insofar as our original grounds for making it, reside in judgements that are true.
17. No psychological investigation can justify the laws of logic.

On Schoenflies: *Die logischen Paradoxien der Mengenlehre*[1]

[1906]

Plan of critique of Schoenflies etc.

Concept and object,
nomen appelativum, nomen proprium.

Analysis of a sentence, predicative nature of a concept. Function, sharp boundaries, independent of objects, consistency not to be insisted on. Subsumption, subordination. Mutual subordination. Relation. Identity. First and second level relations.

Aggregate, extension of a concept. *Inbegriff*[2] (belong to, include). System, series, set, class.

How applied in criticizing Schoenflies' statements.

Can the extension of a concept fall under a concept, whose extension it is?

It does not need to be all-encompassing.

Russell's contradiction cannot be eliminated in Schoenflies' way. Concepts which coincide in extension, although this extension falls under the one, but not the other.

Remedy from extensions of second level concepts impossible.

Set theory in ruins.

My concept-script in the main not dependent on it. (Contrast with other similar projects.)

---

[1] Frege obviously intended this essay for publication in the *Jahresbericht der deutschen Mathematiker-Vereinigung*. Whether it was rejected by the editor, or, whether because it remained a fragment, it was not submitted by Frege, is not known.—It is dated by Frege's opening remarks (ed.).

[2] As far as we can see, this word does not have a sense in German which fits the context. *Inbegriff* usually means 'essence' or 'embodiment' (as in 'He is the very embodiment of health'). It is for us impossible to determine from these fragmentary notes to what use Frege was putting the term, and we thought it better to leave it untranslated than to put in a probably false conjecture. Frege obviously has in mind the different relation of an object to the extension of a concept under which it falls, and to an aggregate of which it is a part; but further than that we leave for the reader to decide (trans.).

[Discussion]

The article by S, *Über die logischen Paradoxien der Mengenlehre** induces me to make the following remarks, in which I repeat much that I have already discussed previously, since it does not seem to be widely known. I fail to find in S and also in Korselt** the sharp distinction between concept and object.*** In the signs, a proper name (*nomen proprium*) corresponds to an object, a concept-word or concept-sign (*nomen appellativum*) to a concept. A sentence such as 'Two is a prime' can be analysed into two essentially different component parts: into 'two' and 'is a prime'. The former appears complete, the latter in need of supplementation, unsaturated. 'Two'—at least in this sentence—is a proper name, its meaning is an object, which can also be designated with greater prolixity by 'the number two'. The object, too, appears as a complete whole, whereas the predicative part has something unsaturated in its meaning as well. We count the copula 'is' as belonging to this part of the sentence. But there is usually something combined with it which here must be disregarded: assertoric force. We can of course express a thought, without stating it to be true. The thought is strictly the same, whether we merely express it or whether we also put it forward as true. Thus assertoric force, which is often connected with the copula or else with the grammatical predicate, does not belong to the expression of the thought, and so may be disregarded here.

This predicative component part of our sentence which we have described in this way, is also meaningful. We call it a concept-word or *nomen appellativum*, even though it is not customary to include the copula in this. Just as it itself appears unsaturated, there is also something unsaturated in the realm of meanings corresponding to it: we call this a concept. This unsaturatedness of one of the components is necessary, since otherwise the parts do not hold together. Of course two complete wholes can stand in a relation to one another; but then this relation is a third element—and one that is doubly unsaturated! In the case of a concept we can also call the unsaturatedness its predicative nature. But in this connection it is necessary to point out an imprecision forced on us by language, which, if we are not conscious of it, will prevent us from recognizing the heart of the matter: i.e. we can scarcely avoid using such expressions as 'the concept *prime*'. Here there is no trace left of unsaturatedness, of the predicative nature. Rather, the expression is constructed in a way which precisely parallels 'the poet Schiller'. So language brands a concept as an object, since the only way it can fit the designation for a concept into its grammatical structure is as a proper name. But in so doing, strictly speaking it falsifies matters. In the same way, the word 'concept' itself is, taken strictly, already defective, since

---

* The current *Jahresbericht*, Vol. XV, p. 19 (Jan. 1906).
** The current *Jahresbericht*, Vol. XV, p. 215 (March–April 1906).
*** Cf. My essay 'Concept and Object'.

the phrase 'is a concept' requires a proper name as grammatical subject; and so, strictly speaking, it requires something contradictory, since no proper name can designate a concept; or perhaps better still, something nonsensical. It is no objection to say that surely the grammatical predicate 'is rectangular' can be combined with the grammatical subject 'every square', which isn't a proper name; for even the sentence 'every square is rectangular' can only make sense in virtue of the fact that you can assert of an object that it is rectangular, either rightly or wrongly, but in either case significantly. By a proper name I understand the sign of an object, independently of the question whether it be a simple word or sign, or a complex one, provided only that it designates the object determinately.

In the sentence 'Two is a prime' we find a relation designated: that of subsumption. We may also say the object falls under the concept *prime*, but if we do so, we must not forget the imprecision of linguistic expression we have just mentioned. This also creates the impression that the relation of subsumption is a third element supervenient upon the object and the concept. This isn't the case: the unsaturatedness of the concept brings it about that the object, in effecting the saturation, engages immediately with the concept, without need of any special cement. Object and concept are fundamentally made for each other, and in subsumption we have their fundamental union.

We call a concept empty if no object falls under it. The concept-word for an empty concept never yields a true sentence,* no matter what proper name may saturate it, or in other words: no matter what proper name may be attached as a grammatical subject to the concept-word as predicate. A concept under which one and only one object falls must still be distinguished from the latter; its sign is a *nomen appellativum*, not a *nomen proprium*.

With the help of the definite article or demonstrative, language forms proper names out of concept-words. So, for instance, the phrase 'this *A*' on p. 20 of the Schoenflies article is a proper name. If forming a proper name in this way is to be legitimate, the concept whose designation is used in its formation must satisfy two conditions:

1. It may not be empty.
2. Only one object may fall under it.

If the first condition is unsatisfied, there is no object at all to which the proper name would be ascribed. If the second is unsatisfied, there are indeed several such objects, but none of them is determined as the one meant to be designated by the proper name. In science the purpose of a proper name is to designate an object determinately; if this purpose is unfulfilled, the proper name has no justification in science. How things may be in ordinary

---

* For brevity, I here call a sentence expressing a true thought, a true sentence.

language is no concern of ours here. Our first requirement includes the requirement that the concept be consistent.

But this requirement doesn't mean that every concept ought to be consistent, only that a concept must be consistent if you wish to form a proper name from the concept-word together with the definite article or demonstrative. But for this purpose, this requirement doesn't go far enough: the concept is not to be empty, no matter what the reason for its being empty may be.

But if we ask, under what conditions a concept is admissible in science, the first thing to stress is that consistency is not such a condition. The only requirement to be made of a concept is that it should have sharp boundaries; that is, that for every object it holds that it either falls under the concept or does not do so. Essentially this is nothing but the requirement that the principle of non-contradiction should hold. But the admissibility of a concept is entirely independent of the question whether objects fall under it, and if so which, or in other words; whether there be objects, and if so which, of which it can be truly asserted. For, before we can raise such questions, we already need the concept. The requirement that a concept be consistent encounters great difficulties. The only apparent way to show a concept has this property, is to cite an object falling under the concept. But to do that, you already need the concept.

Schoenflies obviously only lays down this requirement as a result of his confounding concepts and objects. It is of course self-evident that an object cannot have inconsistent properties. That the concept of a right-angled equilateral pentagon contains a contradiction does not make it inadmissible. For we can see no reason why a man should not be able to say of an object that it is not a right-angled equilateral pentagon, or why he should not be permitted to say there are no right-angled equilateral pentagons. And before he arrives at such judgements, he must consider the matter, and to do that he requires this concept. It is completely wrongheaded to imagine that every contradiction is immediately recognizable; frequently the contradiction lies deeply buried and is only discovered by a lengthy chain of inference: throughout which you need the concept. The only thing is, given a concept, you may not presuppose without further question that an object falls under it. But someone does that when, by means of a definite article or demonstrative, he forms out of a concept-word a proper name destined for use in science.

Let us now examine Schoenflies' sentences in the light of what we have said so far. Earlier on p. 20 we read,

'1. The *A* has the property *B*, and
2. The *A* does not have the property *B*.'

The definite article before the '*A*' can only be understood in such a way that 'the *A*' is being thought of as a proper name. In logic it must be presupposed that every proper name is meaningful; that is, that it serves its purpose of designating an object. For a sentence containing a meaningless proper name either expresses no thought at all, or it expresses a thought that belongs to myth or fiction. In either case it falls outside the domain governed by the laws of logic. For instance 'the *A*' would be a name that was in this way inadmissible for scientific use if it were formed by means of the definite article from a name of a concept (*nomen appellativum*), under which either no object or more than one fell. The mistake would then not lie in the use of the concept-word in itself, but in forming a proper name from it. Let us now assume 'the *A*' is a meaningful proper name, and look at the concept or logical predicate '*has the property B*'. We must presuppose for this concept that it has sharp boundaries in the sense given above; for only in that case can it be logically recognized as a concept. Then indeed the principle of non-contradiction holds, i.e. that of the two sentences cited always one and only one is right, that is, expresses a true thought; and indeed this holds even if the concept of the predicate is contradictory; for then the second sentence is right, but the first not.

And so the conditions for the validity of the principle of non-contradiction in S's formulation consist in the fact that proper names as well as concept-words satisfy logical requirements. But these do not include the requirement that a concept-word should designate a consistent concept. Since only concepts with sharp boundaries are to be recognized as meaningful by logic, we may also say: proper names and concept-words must be meaningful.

Now if *A* is the concept of a right-angled equilateral pentagon, 'this *A*' is an inadmissible—meaningless—proper name, and nothing whatever can be legitimately inferred either from the sentence 'This *A* has the property *B*' or from 'This *A* does not have the property *B*'; for, strictly, we do not infer from sentences at all, but from thoughts. And only true thoughts are admissible premises of inferences. Also it isn't strictly sentences, it is thoughts which have contradictory counterparts. If you always bear this in mind, that we cannot legitimately infer from sentences, but only from true thoughts, and that proper names and concept-words must be meaningful, then the case of the failure of the principle of non-contradiction or of indirect proof cannot obtain. The failure of the principle of non-contradiction cannot serve as a criterion for the admissibility of a concept; for then you could never avail yourself of indirect proof. We should always have to reckon with its failing. But before we go on to proofs at all, we must have assured ourselves that the proper names and concept-words we employ are admissible. From the failure of indirect proof we can only conclude that we have made a mistake in this respect, which ought not to have occurred at all. Now whether this mistake consists in the use of a meaningless proper name or a meaningless concept-word, cannot be generally answered. At any rate, an inconsistent concept is not to be rejected of itself. Only if someone makes a proper name from the corresponding concept-word by means of the definite article or demonstrative, does he fall into error. But whether it is a mistake of this kind or of another kind which is to blame for the failure of the indirect proof, needs special investigation in each case.

Now Schoenflies states that the concept of the set of all sets which do not contain themselves as elements is not consistent. It must first be remarked that 'the set of all sets which do not contain themselves as elements' is not a concept-word, it is a proper name, and it can only be a question of whether this proper name is meaningful. It is evidently not formed from the nomen appellativum *is a set of all sets which do not contain themselves as elements* with the definite article; for the use of such a predicate has not preceded it: the expression makes its début together with the definite article. And so we have here a different case from the previous one with the phrase 'this *A*'. Hence our proper name requires a special scrutiny. We may distinguish two different ways of using the word 'set', going with two different conceptions, which are probably most plainly identified by the words 'aggregate' and 'extension of a concept'. But frequently these conceptions do not occur in their pure form, but mixed together and this makes for unclarity. The aggregative conception is the first to offer itself, but the requirements of mathematics pull towards the opposite side, and so confusions easily arise.

The word 'aggregate' is connected with 'grex'. An aggregate is something like a herd, a whole whose parts are like one another. But since the agreement is never perfect, and since on the other hand it is surely always possible to find some respect in which the parts do agree, the similarity of the parts is unfitted to serve as a characteristic mark. We can say after all that every object in which we may distinguish parts is an aggregate, for instance the solar system, a heap of sand, a grain of sand, a piece of music, and a corporation. For objects to be recognised as parts of a whole, they have to be held together by relations or interactions of some kind or another. Such relations may be spatial, temporal, physical, psychical, legal, even intervals of pitch. And strictly we ought really to have a different word for 'part' in each of the cases; for obviously a head is a part of a man in a different sense from that in which the man himself is part of a corporation. It not infrequently occurs that parts of an aggregate are themselves aggregates. A grain of sand is part of a heap of sand, a silicic acid molecule part of the grain of sand and also part of the heap of sand. What is part of a part is part of the whole, at least if the word 'part' is taken in essentially the same sense. In this description of an aggregate we perhaps fail to find the precision that is to be expected elsewhere in mathematics. At the same time we have to say that *aggregate* is not really a mathematical concept. But frequently the word '*Menge*' [set] is patently used in the sense which agrees with that given here for aggregate. I need only mention '*Menschenmenge*' [crowd]. But so understood, the word '*Menge*' can surely claim no place in mathematics.

I move on to the extension of a concept. The word itself indicates that we are not here dealing with something spatial and physical, but something logical. By means of our logical faculties we lay hold upon the extension of a concept, by starting out from the concept.

Let the letters 'Φ' and 'Ψ' stand in for concept-words (*nomina appellativa*). Then we designate subordination in sentences of the form 'If something is a Φ, then it is a Ψ'. In sentences of the form 'If something is a Φ, then it is a Ψ

and if something is a Ψ then it is a Φ' we designate mutual subordination, a second level relation, which has strong affinities with the first level relation of equality (identity). The properties of equality, that is, which we express in the sentences '$a = a$', 'if $a = b$, then $b = a$', 'if $a = b$ and $b = c$, then $a = c$', have their analogues for the case of that second level relation. And this compels us almost ineluctably to transform a sentence in which mutual subordination is asserted of concepts into a sentence expressing an equality.

Admittedly, to construe mutual subordination simply as equality is forbidden by the basic difference between first and second level relations. Concepts cannot stand in a first level relation. That wouldn't be false, it would be nonsense. Only in the case of objects can there be any question of equality (identity). And so the said transformation can only occur by concepts being correlated with objects in such a way that concepts which are mutually subordinate are correlated with the same object. It is all, so to speak, moved down a level. The sentence 'Every square root of 1 is a binomial coefficient of the exponent -1 and every binomial coefficient of the exponent -1 is a square root of 1' is thus transformed into the sentence 'The extension of the concept *square root of 1* is equal to (coincides with) the extension of the concept *binomial coefficient of the exponent -1*'.

And so 'the extension of the concept *square root of 1*' is here to be regarded as a proper name, as is indeed indicated by the definite article. By permitting the transformation, you concede that such proper names have meanings. But by what right does such a transformation take place, in which concepts correspond to extensions of concepts, mutual subordination to equality? An actual proof can scarcely be furnished. We will have to assume an unprovable law here. Of course it isn't as self-evident as one would wish for a law of logic. And if it was possible for there to be doubts previously, these doubts have been reinforced by the shock the law has sustained from Russell's paradox.

Yet let us set these doubts on one side for the moment. When we undertake the transformation as above, we acknowledge that there is one and only one object which we designate by the proper name 'the extension of the concept *square root of 1*', and that we also designate the same object by the proper name 'the extension of the concept *binomial coefficient of the exponent of -1*'. Perhaps you suspect that this object is something which we have just called an aggregate; but we will see that an extension of a concept is essentially different from an aggregate.

In the first instance we have in the case of a concept the fundamental case of subsumption, which we express in such a sentence as 'A is a Φ'; where 'A' stands for a proper name, 'Φ' for a concept-word. Now if the extension of the concept Φ, coincides with the extension of the concept Ψ, it follows from 'A is a Φ' that A is a Ψ too. Therefore we then also have a relation of the object A to the extension of the concept Φ, which I will call B. And the fact that this relation holds I will express thus: 'A belongs to B'. And so this is meant to be tantamount to 'A is a Φ, if B is the extension of the concept Φ'.

On superficial reflexion you might compare this relation with that of part to whole; but here we have nothing corresponding to the sentence: What is part of a part, is part of the whole. To be sure, A itself can be the extension of a concept; but if Δ belong to A, and A to B, Δ need not belong to B. In the sentence 'The extension of the concept *prime* is an extension of a concept to which 3 belongs' the phrase 'extension of a concept to which 3 belongs' is to be regarded as a *nomen appellativum.* Now let B be the extension of the concept hereby designated, and A the extension of the concept *prime.* Then A belongs to B and 2 belongs to A; but 2 does not belong to B; for 2 isn't an extension of a concept to which 3 belongs. From this alone it follows that an extension of a concept is at bottom completely different from an aggregate. The aggregate is composed of its parts. Whereas the extension of a concept is not composed of the objects that belong to it. For the case is conceivable that no objects belong to it. The extension of a concept simply has its being in the concept, not in the objects which belong to it; these are not its parts. There cannot be an aggregate which has no parts.

Now of course it can happen that all objects which belong to the extension of a concept are at the same time parts of an aggregate and what is more in such a way that the whole being of the aggregate is completely exhausted by them. In this way it may look as though in such a case the aggregate coincides with the extension of the concept; but it isn't necessary that every part of the aggregate also belongs to the extension of the concept; for it can be that a part of the aggregate, without itself belonging to the extension of the concept, has parts which belong to the extension of the concept, or that a part of the aggregate, without itself belonging to the extension of the concept, is part of an object which belongs to the extension of the concept. So the relation of a part to the aggregate must still always be distinguished from that of an object to the extension of a concept to which it belongs. The extension of the concept is not determined by the aggregate even in this case, where they apparently coincide. A grain of sand is an aggregate. And it can be that the extension of the concept *silicic acid molecule contained in this grain of sand* apparently coincides with the aggregate which we call this grain of sand. But we could just as well let the extension of the concept *atom contained in this grain of sand* coincide with our aggregate. But in that case the two extensions of concepts would coincide, which is impossible. From which it follows that neither of the two extensions of concepts coincides with the aggregate, for if one of them were to do so, then the other could with equal right be said to do so.

What may I regard as the Result of my Work?[1]

[Aug. 1906]

It is almost all tied up with the concept-script. a concept construed as a function. a relation as a function of two arguments. the extension of a concept or class is not the primary thing for me. unsaturatedness both in the case of concepts and functions. the true nature of concept and function recognized.

strictly I should have begun by mentioning the judgement-stroke, the dissociation of assertoric force from the predicate . . .
Hypothetical mode of sentence composition . . .
Generality . . .
Sense and meaning . . .

---

[1] According to a note of the previous editors these jottings bore the date '5.VIII.06'. They are no doubt prefatory to the piece '*Einleitung in die Logik*', which is divided into sections according to the captions given here (ed.).

Introduction to Logic[1]

[August 1906]

Dissociating assertoric force from the predicate

We can express a thought without asserting it. But there is no word or sign in language whose function is simply to assert something. This is why, apparently even in logical works, predicating is confused with judging. As a result one is never quite sure whether what logicians call a judgement is meant to be a thought alone or one accompanied by the judgement that it is true. To go by the word, one would think it meant a thought *accompanied by* a judgement; but often in common usage the word does not include the actual passing of judgement, the recognition of the truth of something. *I use the word 'thought' in roughly the same way as logicians use 'judgement'.* To think is to grasp a thought. Once we have grasped a thought, we can recognize it as true (*make a judgement*) and give expression to our recognition of its truth (*make an assertion*). Assertoric force is to be dissociated from negation too. To each thought there corresponds an opposite, so that rejecting one of them is accepting the other. One can say that to make a judgement is to make a choice between opposites. Rejecting the one and accepting the other is one and the same act. Therefore there is no need of a special name, or special sign, for rejecting a thought. We may speak of the negation of a thought before we have made any distinction of parts within it. To argue whether negation belongs to the whole thought or to the predicative part is every bit as unfruitful as to argue whether a coat clothes a man who is already clothed or whether it belongs together with the rest of his clothing. Since a coat covers a man who is already clothed, it automatically becomes part and parcel with the rest of his apparel. We may, metaphorically speaking, regard the predicative component of a thought as a covering for the subject-component. If further coverings are added, these automatically become one with those already there.

The hypothetical mode of sentence composition

If someone says that in a hypothetical judgement two judgements are set in relation to one another, he is using the word 'judgement' so as not to include the recognition of the truth of anything. For even if the whole compound

---

[1] Parts of these diary notes were later revised by Frege; cf. pp. 197 ff. (ed.).

sentences is uttered with assertoric force, one is still asserting neither the truth of the thought in the antecedent nor that of the thought in the consequent. The recognition of truth extends rather over a thought that is expressed in the whole compound sentence. And on closer examination we find that in many cases the antecedent on its own does not express a thought, and nor does the consequent either (quasi-sentences). What we generally have in these cases is the relation of subordination between concepts. Here it is quite common to conflate two different kinds of things, which I was probably the first to distinguish: the relation I designate by the conditional stroke, and generality. The former corresponds roughly to what logicians intend by 'a relation between judgements'. That is, the sign for the relation (*the conditional stroke*) connects sentences with one another: these are sentences proper, and so each of them expresses a thought.

Now leaving myth and fiction on one side, and considering only those cases in which truth in the scientific sense is in question, we can say that *every thought is either true or false, tertium non datur*. It is nonsense to speak of cases in which a thought is true and cases in which it is false. The same thought cannot be true at one time, false at another. On the contrary, the cases people have in mind in speaking in this way always involve different thoughts, and the reason they believe the thought to be the same is that the form of words is the same; this form of words will then be a quasi-sentence. We do not always adequately distinguish the sign from what it expresses.

If there are two thoughts, only four cases are possible:

1. the first is true, and likewise the second;
2. the first is true, the second false;
3. the first is false, the second true;
4. both are false.

Now if the third of these cases does not hold, then the relation I have designated by the *conditional stroke* obtains. The sentence expressing the first thought is the consequent, the sentence expressing the second the antecedent. It is now almost 28 years since I gave this definition. I believed at the time that I had only to mention it and everyone else would immediately know more about it than I did. And now, after more than a quarter of a century has elapsed, the great majority of mathematicians have no inkling of the matter, and the same goes for the logicians. What pigheadedness! This way academics have of behaving reminds me of nothing so much as that of an ox confronted by a new gate: it gapes, it bellows, it tries to squeeze by sideways, but going through it—that might be dangerous. I can readily believe that it looks strange at first sight, but if it didn't, it would have been discovered long ago. Do we really have to go by our first cursory impression of the matter? Have we no time at all to reflect upon it? No, for what good could come of that! People probably feel the lack of an inner connection between the thoughts: we find it hard to accept that it is only the truth or falsity of the thoughts that is to be taken into account, that their content doesn't really come into it all. This is connected with what I realized about sense and meaning. Well, just let someone try to give an account in which the thought itself plays a bigger role and it will probably turn out that what has been added from the thought is at bottom quite superfluous, and that one has only succeeded in complicating the issue, or that the antecedent and consequent are not sentences proper, neither being such as to express a thought, so that a relation has not been established between two thoughts as one intended, but rather between concepts or relations. Is the relation I designate by the conditional stroke in fact such as can obtain between thoughts? Strictly speaking, no! The most we can say here is that *the sign for this relation* (i.e. the conditional stroke) *connects sentences*. Later the definition will be filled out in such a way as to allow also *names of objects* to be connected by the conditional stroke. At first this will be even harder to swallow. We need first to take a closer look at generality if we are to find it acceptable.

Generality

It is only at this point that the need arises *to analyse a thought into parts* none of which are thoughts. The simplest case is that of splitting a thought into two parts. The parts are different in kind, one being unsaturated, the other saturated (complete). The thoughts we have to consider here are those designated in traditional logic as *singular* judgements. In such a thought something is asserted of an object. The sentence expressing such a thought is composed of a *proper name*—and this corresponds to the *complete* part of the thought—and a *predicative* part, which corresponds to the *unsaturated* part of the thought. We should mention that, strictly speaking, it is not in itself that a thought is singular, but only with respect to a possible way of analysing it. It is possible for the same thought, with respect to a different analysis, to appear as particular (Christ converted some men to his teaching). Proper names designate objects, and a singular thought is about objects. But we can't say that an object is part of a thought as a proper name is part of the corresponding sentence. Mont Blanc with its masses of snow and ice is not part of the thought that Mont Blanc is more than 4000 m. high; all we can say is that to the object there corresponds, in a certain way that has yet to be considered, a part of the thought. By analysing a singular thought we obtain components of the complete and of the unsaturated kind, which of course cannot occur in isolation; but any component of the one kind together with any component of the other kind will form a thought. If we now keep the unsaturated part constant but vary the complete part, we should expect some of the thoughts so formed to be true, and some false. But it can also happen that the whole lot are true. *E.g.* let the unsaturated component be expressed in the words 'is identical with itself'. This is then a particular property of the unsaturated part. We thus obtain a new thought (everything is identical with itself), which compared to the singular thoughts (two is identical with itself, the moon is identical with itself) is general. However the word 'everything', which here takes the place of a proper name ('the moon'), is not itself a proper name, doesn't designate an object, but serves to confer generality of content on the sentence. In logic we can often be too influenced by language and it is in this way that the concept-script is of value: it helps to emancipate us from the forms of language. Instead of saying 'the moon is identical with itself' we can also say 'the moon is identical with the moon' without changing the thought. But in language it is impossible, in making the transition to the general statement, to allow the word 'everything' also to occur in two places. The sentence 'everything is identical with everything' would not have the desired sense. We may, taking a leaf from mathematics, employ a letter and say 'a is identical with a'. This letter then occupies the place (or places) of a proper name, but it is not itself a proper name; it does not have a meaning, but only serves to confer generality of content on a sentence. This use of letters, being simpler and, from a logical point of view, more appropriate, is to be preferred to the means which language provides for this purpose.

If a whole is composed of two sentences connected by 'and', each of which expresses a thought, then the sense of the whole is also to be construed as a thought, for this sense is either true or false; it is true if each component thought is true, and false in every other case—hence when at least one of the two component thoughts is false. If we call the thought of the whole the conjunction of the two component thoughts, then the conjunction too has its opposite thought, as does every thought. Now it is clear what the opposite of a conjunction of the opposite of a thought A with a thought B is. It is what I express by means of the conditional stroke. The sentence expressing thought A is the consequent, that expressing thought B the antecedent. But the whole sentence expressing the opposite of the conjunction of the opposite of A with B may be called the hypothetical sentence whose consequent expresses A and whose antecedent expresses B. The thought expressed by the hypothetical sentence we shall call the hypothetical thought whose consequence is A and whose condition is B. Now if the same proper name occurs in both consequent and antecedent, we may regard the hypothetical thought as singular if we think of it as being analysed into the complete part that corresponds to the proper name and the unsaturated part left over. If we now keep the unsaturated part fixed, and vary the complete part, it may turn out that we always obtain a true thought, no matter what we choose for the complete part. In saying this, we are assuming, as we are throughout this enquiry, that we are operating not in the realm of myth and fiction, but in that of truth (in the scientific sense); consequently every proper name really does achieve its goal of designating an object, and so is not empty. The complete parts of the thoughts that are here in question are of course not themselves the objects designated by the

8.VIII.06

proper names, but are connected with them, and it is essential that there should be such objects if everything is not to fall within the realm of fiction. Otherwise we cannot speak of the truth of thoughts at all. So we are assuming that we have a hypothetical thought—one which can at the same time be construed as a singular thought—from which we, as was said above, always obtain a true thought by keeping the unsaturated part fixed, whatever complete part we saturate it with. In this way we arrive at a general thought, and the singular hypothetical thought from which we started is seen to be a special case of it. For instance:

Thought *A*: that 3 squared is greater than 2.
Thought *B*: that 3 is greater than 2.
Opposite of Thought *A*: that 3 squared is not greater than 2.
Conjunction of the opposite of thought A with thought B: that 3 squared is not greater than 2, and that 3 is greater than 2.
Opposite of the conjunction of the opposite of thought A with thought B: that it is false both that 3 squared is not greater than 2 and that 3 is greater than 2.

This is the hypothetical thought with thought *A* as its consequence and thought *B* as its condition. There is something unnatural about the form of words 'If 3 is greater than 2, then 3 squared is greater than 2' and perhaps even more so about what we get when we replace '3' by '2': 'If 2 is greater than 2, then 2 squared is greater than 2'. But the thought that it is false both that 2 squared is not greater than 2 and that 2 is greater than 2 is a true one. And whatever number we take instead of 3, we always obtain a true thought. But what if we take an object that is not a number? Any sentence obtained from '*a* is greater than 2' by putting the proper name of an object for '*a*' expresses a thought, and this thought is of course false if the object is not a number. It is different with the first sentence, because the expression which results when the proper name of an object is put for '*a*' in '*a* squared' only designates an object in ordinary discourse if this object is a number. The incompleteness of the usual definition of 'squared' is to be blamed for this. This defect can be removed by stipulating that by the square of an object we are to understand the object itself if this object is not a number, but that 'the square of a number' is to be understood in its arithmetical sense. We shall then always obtain from the schema 'that *a* squared is greater than 2' a sentence expressing a false thought if '*a*' is replaced by the name of an object that is not a number. Once this stipulation has been made, we can replace the numeral '3' in our hypothetical by the name of any object whatever, and we shall always obtain a sentence expressing a true thought. The general thought at which we thus arrive is therefore also true. We could express it as follows: 'If something is greater than 2, then its square is greater than 2' or better 'if *a* is greater than 2, then *a* squared is greater than 2'. In this context the construction with 'if' seems the most idiomatic. But now we no longer have two thoughts combined. If we replace '*a*' by the proper name of an object, then the sentence we obtain expresses a thought which is seen to be a particular case of the general thought; in such a particular case we have two thoughts present in the condition and consequence, besides the thought which is present in the whole sentence. We can grasp these in isolation. But we cannot proceed in this way to split up the sentence expressing the general thought without making the parts senseless. For the letter '*a*' is meant to confer generality of content upon the whole sentence, not on its clauses. With '*a* is greater than 2' we no longer have a part expressing a thought: it neither expresses a thought that is true nor one that is false, because '*a*' is neither meant to designate an object as does a proper name, nor to confer generality of content upon this part. It has no function at all in relation to this part: it has no contribution to make to it, as it would have if it conferred a sense on it. The same holds of the other part '*a* squared is greater than 2'. The '*a*' in the one clause refers to the '*a*' in the other, and for this very reason we cannot separate the clauses; for if we did, the contribution that '*a*' is meant to make to the sense of the whole would be utterly destroyed and its function lost. Just so, in Latin a compound sentence whose clauses are introduced by *tot* and *quot* cannot be split up into these clauses without rendering each of them senseless. I call something a *quasi-sentence* if it has the grammatical form of a sentence and yet is not an expression of a thought, although it may be part of a sentence that does express a thought, and thus part of a sentence proper. Hence in the case of a general sentence we cannot draw the distinction we drew earlier between a condition and a consequence. The antecedent and consequent are now quasi-sentences, no longer expressing thoughts. Now we do indeed speak as if the condition were satisfied in some cases and not in others. This makes it clear that what we are here calling the condition is not a thought, for a thought—leaving as always myth and fiction on one side—is only either true or false. There cannot be a case of the same thought being now true, now false. What we have in such a case is simply a quasi-sentence from which sentences proper can be derived, some of which express true thoughts and some false. But then these thoughts are just different. Letters which, like the '*a*' in our example, serve to confer generality of content upon a sentence are, in virtue of this role, essentially different from proper names. I say that a proper name designates (or means) an object; '*a*' indicates an object, it

9.VIII.06   does not have a meaning, it designates or means nothing. In ordinary language words like 'something' and 'it' often take over the role of letters; in some cases even there seems to be nothing at all to take over this role. In this regard, as in others, language is defective. For discerning logical structure it is better to use letters than to rely on the vernacular. Let us now look at the component quasi-sentences of our general sentence. Each of these contains a letter. If we replace these letters by the proper name of an object, we obtain a sentence proper, which is now manifestly composed of this proper name and the remainder. This remainder corresponds to the unsaturated part of the thought and is also part of the quasi-sentence. So each of the component quasi-sentences contains, besides the letter, a constituent which corresponds to the unsaturated part of a thought. These unsaturated parts of a thought are now in turn parts of our general thought, but they need a cement to hold them together; in the same way two complete parts of a thought cannot hold together without a cement. If we express our example of a general thought as follows: 'If a is greater than 2, then a is something whose square is greater than 2', then the words 'is something whose square is greater than 2' and 'is greater than 2' correspond to the two unsaturated parts of a thought that we were speaking about. But the 'is' here must be taken throughout as being devoid of assertoric force. What correspond to the cement are the words 'if' and 'then', the letter 'a' and the occurrence of the word 'is', first immediately after the 'a' and secondly immediately after the 'then'. But, as we know, the truth of the matter is that this particular mode of composition is effected by negating, forming a conjunction, negating again, and generalizing (*sit venia verbo*).

Sense and Meaning

Proper names are meant to designate objects, and we call the object designated by a proper name its meaning. On the other hand, a proper name is a constituent of a sentence, which expresses a thought. Now what has the object got to do with the thought? We have seen from the sentence 'Mont Blanc is over 4000 m high' that it is not part of the thought. Is then the object necessary at all for the sentence to express a thought? People certainly say that Odysseus is not an historical person, and mean by this contradictory expression that the name 'Odysseus' designates nothing, has no meaning. But if we accept this, we do not on that account deny a thought-content to all sentences of the *Odyssey* in which the name 'Odysseus' occurs. Let us just imagine that we have convinced ourselves, contrary to our former opinion, that the name 'Odysseus', as it occurs in the *Odyssey*, does designate a man after all. Would this mean that the sentences containing the name 'Odysseus' expressed different thoughts? I think not. The thoughts would strictly remain the same; they would only be transposed from the realm of fiction to that of truth. So the object designated by a proper name seems to be quite inessential to the thought-content of a sentence which contains it. To the thought-content! For the rest, it goes without saying that it is by no means a matter of indifference to us whether we are operating in the realm of fiction or of truth. But we can immediately infer from what we have just said that something further must be associated with the proper name, something which is different from the object designated and which is essential to the thought of the sentence in which the proper name occurs. I call it the sense of the proper name. As the proper name is part of the sentence, so its sense is part of the thought.

The same point can be approached in other ways. It is not uncommon for the same object to have different proper names; but for all that they are not simply interchangeable. This is only to be explained by the fact that proper names of the same object can have different senses. The sentence 'Mont Blanc is over 4000 m high' does not express the same thought as the sentence 'The highest mountain in Europe is over 4000 m high', although the proper name 'Mont Blanc' designates the same mountain as the expression 'the highest mountain in Europe'. The two sentences 'The Evening Star is the same as the Evening Star' and 'The Morning Star is the same as the Evening Star' differ only by a single name having the same meaning in each. Nevertheless they express different thoughts. So the sense of the proper name 'the Evening Star' must be different from that of the proper name 'the Morning Star'. The upshot is that there is something associated with a proper name, different from its meaning, which can be different as between proper names with the same meaning, and which is essential to the thought-content of the sentence containing it. A sentence proper, in which a proper name occurs, expresses a singular thought, and in this we distinguished a complete part and an unsaturated one. The former corresponds to the proper name, but it is not the meaning of the proper name, but its sense. The unsaturated part of the thought we take to be a sense too: it is the sense of the part of the sentence over and above the proper name. And it is in line with these stipulations to take the thought itself as a sense, namely the sense of the sentence. As the thought is the sense of the whole sentence, so a part of the thought is the sense of part of the sentence. Thus the thought appears the same in kind as the sense of a proper name, but quite different from its meaning.

10.VIII.06   Now the question arises whether to the unsaturated part of the thought, which is to be regarded as the sense of the corresponding part of the sentence, there does not also correspond something which is to be construed as the meaning of this part. As far as the mere thought-content is concerned it is indeed a matter of indifference whether a proper name has a meaning, but in any other regard it is of the greatest importance; at least it is so if we are concerned with the acquisition of knowledge. It is this which determines whether we are in the realm of fiction or truth. Now it is surely unlikely that a proper name should behave so differently from the rest of a singular sentence that it is only in its case that the existence of a meaning should be of importance. If the thought as a whole is to belong to the realm of truth, we must rather assume that something in the realm of meaning must correspond to the rest of the sentence, which has the unsaturated part of the thought for its sense. We may add to this the fact that in this part of the sentence too there may occur proper names, where it does matter that they should have a meaning. If several proper names occur in a sentence, the corresponding thought can be analysed into a complete and unsaturated part in different ways. The sense of each of these proper names can be set up as the complete part over against the rest of the thought as the unsaturated part. We know that even in speech the same thought can be expressed in different ways, by making now this proper name, now that one, the grammatical subject. No doubt we shall say that these different phrasings are not equivalent. This is true. But we must not forget that language does not simply express thoughts; it also imparts a certain tone or colouring to them. And this can be different even where the thought is the same. It is inconceivable that it is only for the proper names that there can be a question of meaning and not for the other parts of the sentence which connect them. If we say 'Jupiter is larger than Mars', what are we talking about? About the heavenly bodies themselves, the meanings of the proper names 'Jupiter' and 'Mars'. We are saying that they stand in a certain relation to one another, and this we do by means of the words 'is larger than'. This relation holds between the meanings of the proper names, and so must itself belong to the realm of meanings. It follows that we have to acknowledge that the part of the sentence 'is larger than Mars' is meaningful, and not merely possessed of a sense. If we split up a sentence into a proper name and the remainder, then this remainder has for its sense an unsaturated part of a thought. But we call its meaning a concept. In doing so we are of course making a mistake, a mistake which language forces upon us. By the very fact of introducing the word 'concept', we countenance the possibility of sentences of the form '*A* is a concept', where *A* is a proper name. We have thereby stamped as an object what—as being completely different in kind—is the precise opposite of an object. For the same reason the definite article at the beginning of 'the meaning of the remaining part of the sentence' is a mistake too. But language forces us into such inaccuracies, and so nothing remains for us but to bear them constantly in mind, if we are not to fall into error and thus blur the sharp distinction between concept and object. We can, metaphorically speaking, call the concept unsaturated too; alternatively we can say that it is predicative in character.

We have considered the case of a compound sentence consisting of a quasi-antecedent and -consequent, where these quasi-sentences contain a letter ('*a*', say). When the letter is subtracted from each of these quasi-sentences the remainder corresponds to an unsaturated part of a thought, and we may now say that such a part of a thought is the sense of the part of a sentence referred to as the remainder. Now such a part also has a meaning, and this we have called a concept. So we have one concept occurring as the meaning of what is left over from the quasi-antecedent, and one concept occurring as the meaning of what is left over from the quasi-consequent. These concepts are here brought into a special connection with one another (we could also say 'relation') and this we call subordination: that is to say, the concept in the quasi-antecedent is made subordinate to the concept in the quasi-consequent. If we regard a singular sentence as composed of a proper name and the remainder, then to a proper name there corresponds an object as its meaning and to the remainder a concept. Here the concept and object present themselves as connected or related in a special way, which we call subsumption. The object is subsumed under the concept. It is clear the subsumption is totally different from subordination.

We have seen that it is true of parts of sentences that they have meanings.

What of a whole sentence, does this have a meaning too? If we are concerned with truth, if we are aiming at knowledge, then we demand of each proper name occurring in a sentence that it should have a meaning. On the other hand, we know that as far as the sense of a sentence, the thought, is concerned, it doesn't matter whether the parts of the sentence have meanings or not. It follows that there must be something associated with a sentence which is different from the thought, something to which it is essential that the parts of the sentence should have meanings. This is to be called the meaning of a sentence. But the only thing to which this is essential is what I call the truth-value—whether the thought is true or false. Thoughts in myth and fiction do not need to have truth-values. A sentence containing a meaningless proper name is neither true nor false; if it expresses a thought at all, then that thought belongs to fiction. In that case the sentence has no meaning. We have two truth-values, the True and the False. If a sentence has a meaning at all, this is either the True or the False. If a sentence can be split up into parts, each of which is meaningful, then the sentence also has a meaning. The True and the False are to be regarded as objects, for both the sentence and its sense, the thought, are complete in character, not unsaturated. If, instead of the True and the False, I had discovered two chemical elements, this would have created a greater stir in the academic world. If we say 'the thought is true', we seem to be ascribing truth to the thought as a property. If that were so, we should have a case of subsumption. The thought as an object would be subsumed under the concept of the true. But here we are misled by language. We don't have the relation of an object to a property, but that of the sense of a sign to its meaning. In fact at bottom the sentence 'it is true that 2 is prime' says no more than the sentence '2 is prime'. If in the first case we express a judgement, this is not because of the word 'true', but because of the assertoric force we give the word 'is'. But we can do that equally well in the second sentence, and an actor on the stage, for example, would be able to utter the first sentence without assertoric force just as easily as the second.*

---

* Remarks on the use of letters in arithmetic (12.VIII.06): people use letters in arithmetic without, as a rule, voicing any opinion on how, for what purpose, or with what justification, they are used, and presumably they are not wholly clear about these matters themselves. Their use in algebra as signs for unknowns (to make it plain what I am referring to, this expression may be allowed here although objections can be brought against it) is not all that different from the use that is standard in arithmetic, despite appearances to the contrary. There is no doubt that, by and large, letters in arithmetic are meant to confer generality of content. But on what? Not, in most cases, on a single sentence or a compound sentence in the grammatical sense, but on a group of apparently self-contained sentences, where it is not always easy to make out where these begin or break off. It is an imperative and essential logical requirement that these apparently self-contained sentences should be combined into a single compound sentence; however, if we comply

A sentence proper is a proper name, and its meaning, if it has one, is a truth value: the True or the False. There are many sentences which can be analysed into a complete part, which is in its turn a proper name, and an unsaturated part, which means a concept. In the same way there are many proper names, whose meanings are not truth values, which can be analysed into a complete part, which is in its turn a proper name, and an unsaturated part. If this latter is to be meaningful, then the result of saturing it with any meaningful proper name whatever must once more be a meaningful proper name. When this happens, we call the meaning of this unsaturated part a function. At this point, however, we need to make a reservation, similar to that we made earlier when the word 'concept' was introduced, about the unavoidable inaccuracy of language. The unsaturated part of a sentence, whose meaning we have called a concept, must have the property of yielding a genuine sentence when saturated by any meaningful proper name; this means that it must yield the proper name of a truth value. This is the requirement that a concept have sharp boundaries. For a given concept, every object must either fall under it or not, *tertium non datur*. From this it follows that a requirement similar to that we have just laid down is to be made of a function. As an example let us start off from the sentence '$3 - 2 > 0$'. We split this up into the proper name '$3 - 2$' and the remainder ' > 0'. We may say this unsaturated part means the concept of a positive number. This concept must have sharp boundaries. Every object must either fall or not fall under this concept. Let us now go further and split the proper name '$3 - 2$' up into the proper name '2' and the unsaturated part '$3 - $ '. Now we may also split the original sentence '$3 - 2 > 0$' up into the proper name '2' and the unsaturated part '$3 - $ > 0'. The meaning of this is the concept of something that yields a positive remainder when subtracted from 3. This concept must have sharp boundaries too. Now if there were a meaningful proper name α such that the unsaturated part '$3 - $ ' did not

---

with these requirements we usually end up with grammatical monstrosities. In the concept-script the judgement-stroke, besides conveying assertoric force, serves to demarcate the scope of the roman letters. In order to be able to narrow the scope over which the generality extends, I make use of gothic letters, and with these the concavity demarcates the scope. Here and there in arithmetic there is also a use of letters which roughly corresponds to that of the gothic letters in my concept-script. But I have found no indication that anyone is aware of this use as a special case. Probably most mathematicians, were they to read this, would have no idea of what I am alluding to. It was not until after some time that I became aware of it myself. We are very dependent on external aids in our thinking, and there is no doubt that the language of everyday life—so far, at least, as a certain area of discourse is concerned—had first to be replaced by a more sophisticated instrument, before certain distinctions could be noticed. But so far the academic world has, for the most part, disdained to master this instrument.

yield a meaningful proper name when saturated by it, then the unsaturated part '3 —   > 0', when saturated by α, would not yield a meaningful proper name either; that is to say, we should not be able to say whether the object designated by α fell under the concept which is the meaning of '3 —   > 0'. We can see from this that the usual definitions of the arithmetical signs are inadequate.

A brief Survey of my logical Doctrines[1]

[1906]

The thought

When I use the word 'sentence' in what follows I do not mean a sentence
that serves to express a wish, a command, or a question, but one that serves
to make an assertion. Although a sentence can be perceived by the senses,
we use it to communicate a content that cannot be perceived by the senses.
We are making a judgement about this content when we accept it as true or
reject it as false. When a sentence is uttered the assertion that it is true
usually goes hand in hand with the communication of the content. But the
hearer does not have to adopt the speaker's stance; not that he has to reject
the content either. He can simply refrain from making a judgement. We may
now think of the content of a sentence as it is viewed by such a hearer.

Now two sentences A and B can stand in such a relation that anyone who
recognizes the content of A as true must thereby also recognize the content
of B as true and, conversely, that anyone who accepts the content of B must
straightway accept that of A. (*Equipollence*). It is here being assumed that
there is no difficulty in grasping the content of A and B. The sentences need
not be equivalent in all respects. For instance, one may have what we may
call a poetic aura, and this may be absent from the other. Such a poetic aura
will belong to the content of the sentence, but not to that which we accept
as true or reject as false. I assume there is nothing in the content of either of
the two equipollent sentences A and B that would have to be immediately
accepted as true by anyone who had grasped it properly. The poetic aura
then, or whatever else distinguishes the content of A from that of B, does not
belong to what is accepted as true; for if this were the case, then it could not
be an immediate consequence of anyone's accepting the content of B that he
should accept that of A. For the assumption is that what distinguishes A and
B is not contained in B at all, nor is it something that anyone must recognize
as true straight off.

So one has to separate off from the content of a sentence the part that
alone can be accepted as true or rejected as false. I call this part the thought

---

[1] In places this piece agrees, even in wording, with the *Einleitung in die Logik* of
August 1906 (pp. 185 ff.). It may well be the case that it constitutes a
revision—probably made shortly afterwards—of part of these diary notes.
According to notes of the previous editors on the transcripts that form the basis of
this edition, the originals of both pieces were found together in the order in which
they have been printed here (ed.).

expressed by the sentence. It is the same in equipollent sentences of the kind given above. It is only with this part of the content that logic is concerned. I call anything else that goes to make up the content of a sentence the colouring of the thought.

Thoughts are not psychological entities and do not consist of ideas in the psychological sense. The thought in Pythagoras's theorem is the same for all men; it confronts everyone in the same way as something objective, whereas each man has his own ideas, sensations, and feelings, which belong only to him. We grasp thoughts but we do not create them.

In myth and fiction thoughts occur that are neither true nor false. Logic has nothing to do with these. In logic it holds good that every thought is either true or false, *tertium non datur*.

Dissociating assertoric force from the predicate

We can grasp a thought without recognizing it as true. To think is to grasp a thought. Once we have grasped a thought, we can recognize it as true—make a judgement—and give expression to this recognition—make an assertion. We need to be able to express a thought without putting it forward as true. In the *Begriffsschrift* I use a special sign to convey assertoric force: the judgement-stroke. The languages known to me lack such a sign, and assertoric force is closely bound up with the indicative mood of the sentence that forms the main clause. Of course in fiction even such sentences are uttered without assertoric force; but logic has nothing to do with fiction. Fiction apart, it seems that it is only in subordinate clauses that we can express thoughts without asserting them. One should not allow oneself to be misled by this peculiarity of language and confuse grasping a thought and making a judgement.

Negation

Assertoric force is to be dissociated from negation too. To each thought there corresponds an opposite, so that rejecting one of them coincides with accepting the other. To make a judgement is to make a choice between opposite thoughts. Accepting one of them and rejecting the other is one act. So there is no need of a special sign for rejecting a thought. We only need a special sign for negation as such.

The hypothetical mode of sentence composition

If we say that in a hypothetical judgement two judgements are put into a relationship with one another, we are using the word 'judgement' so as not to include the recognition of the truth of anything, and thus as I use the word 'thought'. For even if the whole compound sentence is uttered with assertoric force, one is asserting neither the truth of the antecedent nor that of the consequent. What is being judged to be true is rather a thought that is expressed by the whole compound sentence. On a closer examination one finds that in many cases neither the antecedent nor the consequent expresses a thought. In the compound sentence

'If a is greater than 2, then a^2 is greater than 2'

the letter 'a' does not designate an object as does the numeral '2': it only indicates indefinitely. So there is an indefiniteness in both antecedent and consequent, which is why neither of these two clauses expresses a thought. But the whole compound sentence does express a thought, the letter 'a' serving to confer generality of content on the sentence as a whole. It may be remarked that in some of the sentences we utter this indefiniteness is not in evidence at all, or there is but the barest suggestion of it. Nevertheless it is always present when we express a general law. What has the grammatical form of a sentence and yet does not express a thought because it contains something indefinite, I call a quasi-sentence. A sentence proper, on the other hand, expresses a thought. With a general law we are tempted to speak of cases in which the condition is true and of others in which it is false. We must reject this way of speaking. It is only a thought that can be true and a thought is either true or false: it is not true in some cases, false in others. When we should like to distinguish such cases, what we have are quasi-sentences. A sentence proper can be obtained from a quasi-sentence by removing the indefiniteness. Thus from the quasi-sentence '$a > 2$' we obtain as a sentence proper '$1 > 2$', as well as '$2 > 2$' and '$3 > 2$'. Some of the sentences thus obtained may express true, and some false, thoughts. However this is only by the way. We shall treat generality more fully later. To begin with, we shall assume that the antecedent and consequent are sentences proper. The following compound sentence will serve as an example:

'If $\dfrac{17^2 \cdot 19}{2^{11}}$ is greater than 2, then $\left(\dfrac{17^2 \cdot 19}{2^{11}}\right)^2$ is greater than 2'

What is being said here? Each of the two clauses

'$\dfrac{17^2 \cdot 19}{2^{11}}$ is greater than 2'   and   '$\left(\dfrac{17^2 \cdot 19}{2^{11}}\right)^2$ is greater than 2'

expresses a thought which is either true or false. If we call the first thought A and the second B, then four cases are possible:

A is true and B is true,
A is true and B is false,
A is false and B is true,
A is false and B is false.

Obviously it is only the second case that is incompatible with the sentence

$$\text{`If } \frac{17^2 \cdot 19}{2^{11}} \text{ is greater than 2, then } \left(\frac{17^2 \cdot 19}{2^{11}}\right)^2 \text{ is greater than 2'}$$

holding good. So our sentence says that the second case does not obtain; it leaves it open which of the remaining cases holds. This gives us the essence of the hypothetical mode of combining sentences. It is correct to say

'If 3 is greater than 2, then 3^2 is greater than 2'   and
'If 2 is greater than 2, then 2^2 is greater than 2'   and
'If 1 is greater than 2, then 1^2 is greater than 2'.

If these sentences sound strange, a little absurd even, this is due to the fact that in each of these examples one sees at once which of the four cases holds, whereas in the first example one does not. But this difference is quite inessential.

I will call this combination of the thoughts A and B the hypothetical combination of A and B, the first thought being the condition and the second the consequence. If a sentence consists of two sentences combined by 'and' both of which express a thought, then the sense of the whole sentence is to be taken as a thought too, for this sense is either true or false. It is true if each of the constituent thoughts Γ and Δ is true, and false in every other case, and so if at least one of the two constituent thoughts is false. I will call the thought in this whole sentence the conjunction of Γ and Δ. The conjunction of Γ and Δ, in common with every thought, has an opposite.

Now the hypothetical combination of A and B is the opposite of the conjunction of A and the opposite of B. But, conversely, the conjunction of Γ and Δ is the opposite of the hypothetical combination of Γ with the opposite of Δ. By means of negation the hypothetical mode can thus be reduced to conjunction and conjunction to the hypothetical mode. Looked at from a logical standpoint both appear equally primitive. But since the hypothetical mode is more closely connected with drawing inferences, it is best to give it pride of place, and see it as the primitive form, reducing conjunction to it.

Generality

We remarked just now that often in a hypothetical sentence neither the antecedent nor the consequent express thoughts, and that the reason for this is that there is present an indefiniteness, although this does not make the compound sentence as a whole devoid of sense. In the example

'If a is greater than 2, then a^2 is greater than 2'

the letter 'a' gives rise to this indefiniteness and it is due to this letter that the thought of the whole compound sentence is general. This is the usual employment of letters in arithmetic, even if it is not the only one. Of course natural language has means of accomplishing the same thing (e.g. '*tot-quot*' in Latin); but these are less precise. And sentences occur in which we can spot no part at all corresponding to the letter '*a*'. Here we may take the above use of letters in arithmetic as basic. It is not only compound hypothetical sentences that can be general. We may think of the sentence '*a = a*'. In order to make it easier to recognize that the sentence is general, we can add 'no matter what *a* may be'.

If in the sentence

'If *a* is greater than 2, then a^2 is greater than 2'

we substitute for the indefinitely indicating letter '*a*' in turn the numerals '1', '2', '3', each of which designates a particular thing, we obtain the sentences

'If 1 is greater than 2, then 1^2 is greater than 2',
'If 2 is greater than 2, then 2^2 is greater than 2',
'If 3 is greater than 2, then 3^2 is greater than 2'.

The thoughts expressed by these sentences are particular cases of the general thought. Likewise the thoughts '1 = 1', '2 = 2', are particular cases of the general thought expressed in the sentence '*a = a*'.

Here for the first time we have occasion to split up a sentence into parts that are not themselves sentences. Thus in the general sentence we have a part to which congruent parts in the associated particular sentences correspond and a part—in our case it is the letter '*a*'—to which non-congruent parts in the particular sentences—the numerals '1', '2', '3'—correspond. These sentence-parts are different in kind. The part in which the general sentence agrees with the related particular sentences shows gaps at the place where the other part of the sentence, the numeral '1', say, occurs. If we fill these gaps with the letter 'ξ', we obtain in our cases

'If ξ is greater than 2, then ξ^2 is greater than 2',
'$\xi = \xi$'.

We obtain specific sentences from these by filling the gaps with, say, the numerals '1', '2', or '3'. These do not show any gaps but fill the gaps in the first parts so that we get a sentence. If we call the parts of the sentence that show gaps unsaturated and the other parts complete, then we can think of a sentence as arising from saturating a saturated part with a complete part. *The complete part of a sentence I call a proper name, the unsaturated part a concept-name.* To the unsaturated part of the sentence there corresponds an unsaturated part of the thought and to the complete part of the sentence a complete part of the thought, and we can also speak here of saturating the unsaturated part of the thought with a complete part. A thought that is put together in this way is just what traditional logic calls a *singular* judgement. We must notice, however, that one and the same thought can be split up in different ways and so can be seen as put together out of parts in different ways. The word 'singular' does not apply to the thought in itself but only with respect to a particular way of splitting it up. Each of the sentence-parts

'1 is greater than 2' and '1^2 is greater than 2'

can also be seen as put together out of the proper name '1' and an unsaturated part. The corresponding holds for the related thoughts.

Logic in Mathematics[1]

[Spring 1914]

Mathematics has closer ties with logic than does any other discipline; for almost the entire activity of the mathematician consists in drawing inferences. In no other discipline does inference play so large a part, although inferences do occur here and there in other disciplines. Part of the mathematician's activity, besides drawing inferences, is to give definitions. Most disciplines are not concerned with the latter at all; only in jurisprudence is it of some importance, for although its subject-matter is quite different, it is in several respects close to mathematics. Jurisprudence takes its materials from history and psychology and for this reason these must claim to have some share in it. And there is nothing resembling this with mathematics.

Inferring and defining are subject to logical laws. From this it follows that logic is of greater importance to mathematics than to any other science.

If one counts logic as part of philosophy, there will be a specially close bond between mathematics and philosophy, and this is confirmed by the history of these sciences (Plato, Descartes, Leibniz, Newton, Kant).

But are there perhaps modes of inference peculiar to mathematics which, for that very reason, do not belong to logic? Here one may point to the inference by mathematical induction from n to $n + 1$. Well, even a mode of inference peculiar to mathematics must be subject to a law and this law, if it is not logical in nature, will belong to mathematics, and can be ranked with the theorems or axioms of this science. For instance, mathematical induction rests on the law that can be expressed as follows:

If the number 1 has the property Φ and if it holds generally for every positive whole number n that if it has the property Φ then $n + 1$ has the property Φ, then every positive whole number has the property Φ.

If this law can be proved, it will be included amongst the theorems of mathematics; if it cannot, it will be included amongst the axioms. If one draws inferences by mathematical induction, then one is actually making an application of this theorem or axiom; that is, this truth is taken as a premise of an inference. For example: the proof of the proposition $(a + b) + n = a + (b + n)$.

So likewise in other cases one can reduce a mode of inference that is peculiar to mathematics to a general law, if not a law of logic, then one of

---

[1] The dating of the previous editors has been adopted (ed.).

mathematics. And from this law one can then draw consequences in accordance with general logical laws.

Now let us examine somewhat more closely what takes place in mathematics, beginning with *inference*.

We may distinguish two kinds of inferences: inferences from two premises and inferences from one premise.

Now we make advances in mathematics by choosing as the premises of an inference one or two propositions that have already been recognised as true. The conclusion obtained from these is a new truth of mathematics. And this can in turn be used, alone or together with another truth, in drawing further conclusions. It would be possible to call each truth thus obtained a theorem. But usually a truth is only called a theorem when it has not merely been obtained as the result of an inference, but is itself in turn used as a premise in the development of the science, and that not just for one but for a number of inferences. In this way chains of inference are formed connecting truths; and the further the science develops the longer and more numerous become the chains of inference and the greater the diversity of the theorems.

Tracing the
chains of
inference
backwards But one can also trace the chains of inference backwards by asking from what truths each theorem has been inferred. As the diversity of theorems becomes greater as we go forward along the chains of inference, so, as we step backwards, the circle of theorems closes in more and more. Whereas it appears that there is no limit to the number of steps forward we can take, when we go backwards we must eventually come to an end by arriving at truths which cannot themselves be inferred in turn from other truths. Going backwards we come up against the axioms and postulates. We may come up against definitions as well, but we shall take a closer look at that later. If we start from a theorem and trace the chains of inference backwards until we arrive at other theorems or at axioms, postulates or definitions, we discover chains of inference starting from known theorems, axioms, postulates or definitions and terminating with the theorem in question.

Proof The totality of these inference-chains constitutes the *proof* of the theorem. We may say that a proof starts from propositions that are accepted as true and leads *via* chains of inferences to the theorem. But it can also happen that a proof consists only of a single chain of inference. In most cases a proof will proceed *via* truths which are not called theorems for the simple reason that they occur only in this proof, and are not used elsewhere. A proof does not only serve to convince us of the truth of what is proved: it also serves to reveal logical relations between truths. This is why we already find in Euclid proofs of truths that appear to stand in no need of proof because they are obvious without one.

Science demands that we prove whatever is suceptible of proof and that we do not rest until we come up against something unprovable. It must Primitive
truths endeavour to make the circle of unprovable *primitive truths* as small as possible, for the whole of mathematics is contained in these primitive truths as in a kernel. Our only concern is to generate the whole of mathematics from this kernel. The essence of mathematics has to be defined by this kernel of truths, and until we have learnt what these primitive truths are, we cannot be clear about the nature of mathematics. If we assume that we have succeeded in discovering these primitive truths, and that mathematics has been developed from them, then it will appear as a system of truths that are connected with one another by logical inference.

Euclid had an inkling of this idea of a *system*; but he failed to realize it and it almost seems as if at the present time we were further from this goal than ever. We see mathematicians each pursuing his own work on some fragment of the subject, but these fragments do not fit together into a system; indeed the idea of a system seems almost to have been lost. And yet the striving after a system is a justified one. We cannot long remain content with the fragmentation that prevails at present. Order can only be created by a system. But in order to construct a system it is necessary that in any step forward we take we should be aware of the logical inferences involved. The system of mathematics

When an inference is being drawn, we must know what its premises are. We must not allow the premises to be confused with the laws of inference, which are purely logical; otherwise the logical purity of the inferences will be lost and it would not be possible, in the confusion of premises with laws of inference, clearly to distinguish the former. But if we have no clear recognition of what the premises are, we can have no certainty of arriving at the primitive truths, and failing that we cannot construct a system. For this reason we must avoid such expressions as 'a moment's reflection shows that' or 'as we can easily see'. We must put the moment's reflection into words so that we can see what inferences it consists of and what premises it makes use of. In mathematics we must never rest content with the fact that something is obvious or that we are convinced of something, but we must strive to obtain a clear insight into the network of inferences that support our conviction. Only in this way can we discover what the primitive truths are, and only in this way can a system be constructed.

Let us now take a closer look at the axioms, postulates and definitions:

The *axioms* are truths as are the theorems, but they are truths for which no proof can be given in our system, and for which no proof is needed. It follows from this that there are no false axioms, and that we cannot accept a thought as an axiom if we are in doubt about its truth; for it is either false and hence not an axiom, or it *is* true but stands in need of proof and hence is not an axiom. Not every truth for which no proof is required is an axiom, for such a truth might still be proved in our system. Whether a truth is an axiom depends therefore on the system, and it is possible for a truth to be an axiom in one system and not in another. That is to say, it is conceivable that there should be a truth A and a truth B, each of which can be proved from the other in conjunction with truths C, D, E, F, whilst the truths C, D, E, F are not sufficient on their own to prove either A or B. If now C, D, E, F may serve as axioms, then we have the choice of regarding A, C, D, E, F as The axioms

axioms and *B* as a theorem, or *B*, *C*, *D*, *E*, *F* as axioms, and *A* as a theorem. We can see from this that the possibility of one system does not necessarily rule out the possibility of an alternative system, and that we may have a choice between different systems. So it is really only relative to a particular system that one can speak of something as an axiom.

Parenthetical remark on sentence and thought

Here, in passing, I may say something about the expressions '*thought*' and '*sentence*'. I use the word 'sentence' to refer to a sign that is normally complex, whether it is made up of sounds or written signs. Of course this sign must have a sense. Here I am only considering sentences in which we state or assert something. We can translate sentences into another language. The sentence in the other language is different from the original one, for its constituents (component sounds) are different and are put together differently; but if the translation is correct, it will express the same sense and of course it is really the sense that concerns us. The sentence is of value to us because of the sense that we grasp in it, which is recognizably the same in the translation too. I call this sense a thought. What we prove is not a sentence, but a thought. And it is neither here nor there which language is used in giving the proof. It is true that in mathematics we often speak of proofs of a theorem [*Lehrsatz*], understanding by the word 'sentence' ['*Satz*'] what I am calling a thought, or perhaps not distinguishing clearly between the expression in words or signs and the thought expressed.[1] A thought cannot be perceived by the senses, but in the sentence it is represented by what can be heard or seen. For this reason I do not use '*Lehrsatz*' but '*Theorem*', and not '*Grundsatz*' but '*Axiom*', understanding by theorems and axioms true thoughts. This, however, is to imply that a thought is not something subjective, is not the product of any form of mental activity; for the thought that we have in Pythagoras's theorem is the same for everybody, and its truth is quite independent of its being thought by so-and-so or indeed by anyone at all. We are not to regard thinking as the act of producing a thought, but as that of grasping a thought.

Postulates

Postulates seem at first sight to be essentially different from axioms. In Euclid we have the postulate 'Let it be postulated that a straight line may be drawn from any point to any other'.

This is obviously introduced with a view to making constructions. The postulates, so it seems, present the simplest procedures for making every construction, and postulate their possibility. At first we might perhaps think that none of this is of any help in providing proofs, but only for solving problems. But this would be a mistake, for sometimes an auxiliary line is needed for a proof, and sometimes an auxiliary point, an auxiliary number—an auxiliary object of some kind. In the proof of a theorem an auxiliary object is one of which nothing is said in the theorem, but which is

---

[1] The play that Frege is here making on the words '*Lehrsatz*' and '*Satz*' is lost in translation, so we have enclosed them in square brackets after their English equivalents (trans.).

required for the proof, so that this would collapse if there were no such object. And if there is no such object, it seems that we must be able to create one and we need a postulate to ensure that this is possible. But what in actual fact is this drawing a line? It is not, at any rate, a line in the geometrical sense that we are creating when we make a stroke with a pencil. And how in this way are we to connect a point in the interior of Sirius with a point in Rigel? Our postulate cannot refer to any such external procedure. It refers rather to something conceptual. But what is here in question is not a subjective, psychological possibility, but an objective one. Surely the truth of a theorem cannot really depend on something we do, when it holds quite independently of us. So the only way of regarding the matter is that by drawing a straight line we merely become ourselves aware of what obtains independently of us. So the content of our postulate is essentially this, that given any two points there is a straight line connecting them. So a postulate is a truth as is an axiom, its only peculiarity being that it asserts the existence of something with certain properties. From this it follows that there is no real need to distinguish axioms and postulates. A postulate can be regarded as a special case of an axiom.

We come to *definitions*. Definitions proper must be distinguished from *illustrative examples*. In the first stages of any discipline we cannot avoid the use of ordinary words. But these words are, for the most part, not really appropriate for scientific purposes, because they are not precise enough and fluctuate in their use. Science needs technical terms that have precise and fixed meanings, and in order to come to an understanding about these meanings and exclude possible misunderstandings, we give examples illustrating their use. Of course in so doing we have again to use ordinary words, and these may display defects similar to those which the examples are intended to remove. So it seems that we shall then have to do the same thing over again, providing new examples. Theoretically one will never really achieve one's goal in this way. In practice, however, we do manage to come to an understanding about the meanings of words. Of course we have to be able to count on a meeting of minds, on others guessing what we have in mind. But all this precedes the construction of a system and does not belong within a system. In constructing a system it must be assumed that the words have precise meanings and that we know what they are. Hence we can at this point leave illustrative examples out of account and turn our attention to the construction of a system.

In constructing a system the same group of signs, whether they are sounds or combinations of sounds (spoken signs) or written signs, may occur over and over again. This gives us a reason for introducing a simple sign to replace such a group of signs with the stipulation that this simple sign is always to take the place of that group of signs. As a sentence is generally a complex sign, so the thought expressed by it is complex too: in fact it is put together in such a way that parts of the thought correspond to parts of the sentence. So as a general rule when a group of signs occurs in a sentence

Definitions

Illustrative examples

Definition proper

it will have a sense which is part of the thought expressed. Now when a simple sign is thus introduced to replace a group of signs, such a stipulation is a definition. The simple sign thereby acquires a sense which is the same as that of the group of signs. Definitions are not absolutely essential to a system. We could make do with the original group of signs. The introduction of a simple sign adds nothing to the content; it only makes for ease and simplicity of expression. So definition is really only concerned with signs. We shall call the simple sign the *definiendum*, and the complex group of signs which it replaces the *definiens*. The *definiendum* acquires its sense only from the *definiens*. This sense is built up out of the senses of the parts of the *definiens*. When we illustrate the use of a sign, we do not build its sense up out of simpler constituents in this way, but treat it as simple. All we do is to guard against misunderstanding where an expression is ambiguous.

A sign has a meaning once one has been bestowed upon it by definition, and the definition goes over into a sentence asserting an identity. Of course the sentence is really only a tautology and does not add to our knowledge. It contains a truth which is so self-evident that it appears devoid of content, and yet in setting up a system it is apparently used as a premise. I say apparently, for what is thus presented in the form of a conclusion makes no addition to our knowledge; all it does in fact is to effect an alteration of expression, and we might dispense with this if the resultant simplification of expression did not strike us as desirable. In fact it is not possible to prove something new from a definition alone that would be unprovable without it. When something that looks like a definition really makes it possible to prove something which could not be proved before, then it is no mere definition but must conceal something which would have either to be proved as a theorem or accepted as an axiom. Of course it may look as if a definition makes it possible to give a new proof. But here we have to distinguish between a sentence and the thought it expresses. If the *definiens* occurs in a sentence and we replace it by the *definiendum*, this does not affect the thought at all. It is true we get a different sentence if we do this, but we do not get a different thought. Of course we need the definition if, in the proof of this thought, we want it to assume the form of the second sentence. But if the thought can be proved at all, it can also be proved in such a way that it assumes the form of the first sentence, and in that case we have no need of the definition. So if we take the sentence as that which is proved, a definition may be essential, but not if we regard the thought as that which is to be proved.

It appears from this that definition is, after all, quite inessential. In fact considered from a logical point of view it stands out as something wholly inessential and dispensable. Now of course I can see that strong exception will be taken to this. We can imagine someone saying: Surely we are undertaking a logical analysis when we give a definition. You might as well say that it doesn't matter whether I carry out a chemical analysis of a body in order to see what elements it is composed of, as say that it is immaterial whether I carry out a logical analysis of a logical structure in order to find out what its constituents are or leave it unanalysed as if it were simple, when it is in fact complex. It is surely impossible to make out that the activity of defining something is without any significance when we think of the considerable intellectual effort required to furnish a good definition.—There is certainly something right about this, but before I go into it more closely, I want to stress the following point. To be without logical significance is still by no means to be without psychological significance. When we examine what actually goes on in our mind when we are doing intellectual work, we find that it is by no means always the case that a thought is present to our consciousness which is clear in all its parts. For example, when we use the word 'integral', are we always conscious of everything appertaining to its sense? I believe that this is only very seldom the case. Usually just the word is present to our consciousness, allied no doubt with a more or less dim awareness that this word is a sign which has a sense, and that we can, if we wish, call this sense to mind. But we are usually content with the knowledge that we can do this. If we tried to call to mind everything appertaining to the sense of this word, we should make no headway. Our minds are simply not comprehensive enough. We often need to use a sign with which we associate a very complex sense. Such a sign seems, so to speak, a receptacle for the sense, so that we can carry it with us, while being always aware that we can open this receptacle should we have need of what it contains. It follows from this that a thought, as I understand the word, is in no way to be identified with a content of my consciousness. If therefore we need such signs—signs in which, as it were, we conceal a very complex sense as in a receptacle—we also need definitions so that we can cram this sense into the receptacle and also take it out again. So if from a logical point of view definitions are at bottom quite inessential, they are nevertheless of great importance for thinking as this actually takes place in human beings.

An objection was mentioned above which arose from the consideration that it is by means of definitions that we perform logical analyses. In the development of science it can indeed happen that one has used a word, a sign, an expression, over a long period under the impression that its sense is simple until one succeeds in analysing it into simpler logical constituents. By means of such an analysis, we may hope to reduce the number of axioms; for it may not be possible to prove a truth containing a complex constituent so long as that constituent remains unanalysed; but it may be possible, given an analysis, to prove it from truths in which the elements of the analysis occur. This is why it seems that a proof may be possible by means of a definition, if it provides an analysis, which would not be possible without this analysis, and this seems to contradict what we said earlier. Thus what seemed to be an axiom before the analysis can appear as a theorem after the analysis.

But how does one judge whether a logical analysis is correct? We cannot prove it to be so. The most one can be certain of is that as far as the form of words goes we have the same sentence after the analysis as before. But that the thought itself also remains the same is problematic. When we think that we have given a logical analysis of a word or sign that has been in use over a long period, what we have is a complex expression the sense of whose parts is known to us. The sense of the complex expression must be yielded by that of its parts. But does it coincide with the sense of the word with the long established use? I believe that we shall only be able to assert that it does when this is self-evident. And then what we have is an axiom. But that the simple sign that has been in use over a long period coincides in sense with that of the complex expression that we have formed, is just what the definition was meant to stipulate.

We have therefore to distinguish *two quite different cases*:

(1) We construct a sense out of its constituents and introduce an entirely new sign to express this sense. This may be called a 'constructive definition', but we prefer to call it a 'definition' *tout court*.

(2) We have a simple sign with a long established use. We believe that we can give a logical analysis of its sense, obtaining a complex expression which in our opinion has the same sense. We can only allow something as a constituent of a complex expression if it has a sense we recognize. The sense of the complex expression must be yielded by the way in which it is put together. That it agrees with the sense of the long established simple sign is not a matter for arbitrary stipulation, but can only be recognized by an immediate insight. No doubt we speak of a definition in this case too. It might be called an 'analytic definition' to distinguish it from the first case. But it is better to eschew the word 'definition' altogether in this case, because what we should here like to call a definition is really to be regarded as an axiom. In this second case there remains no room for an arbitrary stipulation, because the simple sign already has a sense. Only a sign which as yet has no sense can have a sense arbitrarily assigned to it. So we shall stick to our original way of speaking and call only a constructive definition a definition. According to that a definition is an arbitrary stipulation which confers a sense on a simple sign which previously had none. This sense has, of course, to be expressed by a complex sign whose sense results from the way it is put together.

Now we still have to consider the difficulty we come up against in giving a logical analysis when it is problematic whether this analysis is correct.

Let us assume that *A* is the long-established sign (expression) whose sense we have attempted to analyse logically by constructing a complex expression that gives the analysis. Since we are not certain whether the analysis is successful, we are not prepared to present the complex expression as one which can be replaced by the simple sign *A*. If it is our intention to put forward a definition proper, we are not entitled to choose the sign *A*, which already has a sense, but we must choose a fresh sign *B*, say, which has the sense of the complex expression only in virtue of the definition. The question now is whether *A* and *B* have the same sense. But we can bypass this question altogether if we are constructing a new system from the bottom up; in that case we shall make no further use of the sign A—we shall only use B. We have introduced the sign B to take the place of the complex expression in question by arbitrary fiat and in this way we have conferred a sense on it. This is a definition in the proper sense, namely a constructive definition.

If we have managed in this way to construct a system for mathematics without any need for the sign A, we can leave the matter there; there is no need at all to answer the question concerning the sense in which—whatever it may be—this sign had been used earlier. In this way we court no objections. However it may be felt expedient to use sign A instead of sign B. But if we do this, we must treat it as an entirely new sign which had no sense prior to the definition. We must therefore explain that the sense in which this sign was used before the new system was constructed is no longer of any concern to us, that its sense is to be understood purely from the constructive definition that we have given. In constructing the new system we can take no account, logically speaking, of anything in mathematics that existed prior to the new system. Everything has to be made anew from the ground up. Even anything that we may have accomplished by our analytical activities is to be regarded only as preparatory work which does not itself make any appearance in the new system itself.

Perhaps there still remains a certain unclarity. How is it possible, one may ask, that it should be doubtful whether a simple sign has the same sense as a complex expression if we know not only the sense of the simple sign, but can recognize the sense of the complex one from the way it is put together? The fact is that if we really do have a clear grasp of the sense of the simple sign, then it cannot be doubtful whether it agrees with the sense of the complex expression. If this is open to question although we can clearly recognize the sense of the complex expression from the way it is put together, then the reason must lie in the fact that we do not have a clear grasp of the sense of the simple sign, but that its outlines are confused as if we saw it through a mist. The effect of the logical analysis of which we spoke will then be precisely this—to articulate the sense clearly. Work of this kind is very useful; it does not, however, form part of the construction of the system, but must take place beforehand. Before the work of construction is begun, the building stones have to be carefully prepared so as to be usable; i.e. the words, signs, expressions, which are to be used, must have a clear sense, so far as a sense is not to be conferred on them in the system itself by means of a constructive definition.

We stick then to our original conception: a *definition is an arbitrary stipulation* by which a new sign is introduced to take the place of a complex expression whose sense we know from the way it is put together. A sign which hitherto had no sense acquires the sense of a complex expression by definition.

When we look around us at the writings of mathematicians, we come across many things which look like definitions, and are even called such, without really being definitions. Such definitions are to be compared with those stucco-embellishments on buildings which look as though they supported something whereas in reality they could be removed without the slightest detriment to the building. We can recognize such definitions by the fact that no use is made of them, that no proof ever draws upon them. But if a word or sign which has been introduced by definition is used in a theorem, the only way in which it can make its appearance there is by applying the definition or the identity which follows immediately from it. If such an application is never made, then there must be a mistake somewhere. Of course the application may be tacit. That is why it is so important, if we are to have a clear insight into what is going on, for us to be able to recognize the premises of every inference which occurs in a proof and the law of inference in accordance with which it takes place. So long as proofs are drawn up in conformity with the practice which is everywhere current at the present time, we cannot be certain what is really used in the proof, what it rests on. And so we cannot tell either whether a definition is a mere stucco-definition which serves only as an ornament, and is only included because it is in fact usual to do so, or whether it has a deeper justification. That is why it is so important that proofs should be drawn up in accordance with the requirements we have laid down.

We can characterize another kind of inadmissible definition by a metaphor from algebra. Let us assume that three unknowns x, y, z occur in three equations. Then they can be determined by means of these equations. Strictly speaking, however, they are determined only for the case where there is only one solution. In a similar way the words 'point', 'straight line', 'surface' may occur in several sentences. Let us assume that these words have as yet no sense. It may be required to find a sense for each of these words such that the sentences in question express true thoughts. But have we here provided a means for determining the sense uniquely? At any rate not in general; and in most cases it must remain undecided how many solutions are possible. But if it can be proved that only one solution is possible, then this is given by assigning, *via* a constructive definition, a sense in turn to each of the words that needs defining. But we cannot regard as a definition the system of sentences in each of which there occur several of the expressions that need defining.

A special case of this is where only one sign, which has as yet no sense, occurs in one or more sentences. Let us assume that the other constituents of the sentences are known. The question is now what sense has to be given to this sign for the sentences to have a sense such that the thoughts expressed in them are true. This case is to be compared to that in which the letter x occurs in one or more equations whose other constituents are known, where the problem is: what meaning do we have to give the letter x for the equations to express true thoughts? If there are several equations, this problem will usually be insoluble. It is obvious that in general no number whatsoever is determined in this way. And it is like this with the case in hand. No sense accrues to a sign by the mere fact that it is used in one or more sentences, the other constituents of which are known. In algebra we have the advantage that we can say something about the possible solutions and how many there are—an advantage one does not have in the general case. But a sign must not be ambiguous. Freedom from ambiguity is the most important requirement for a system of signs which is to be used for scientific purposes. One surely needs to know what one is talking about and the statements one is making, what thoughts one is expressing.

Now it is true that there have even been people, who have fancied themselves logicians, who have held that *concept-words* (*nomina appellativa*) are distinguished from proper names by the fact that they are ambiguous. The word 'man', for example, means Plato as well as Socrates and Charlemagne. The word 'number' designates the number 1 as well as the number 2, and so on. Nothing is more wrong-headed. Of course I can use the words 'this man' to designate now this man, now that man. But still on each single occasion I mean them to designate just *one* man. The sentences of our everyday language leave a good deal to guesswork. It is the surrounding circumstances that enable us to make the right guess. The sentence I utter does not always contain everything that is necessary; a great deal has to be supplied by the context, by the gestures I make and the direction of my eyes. But a language that is intended for scientific employment must not leave anything to guesswork. A concept-word combined with the demonstrative pronoun or definite article often has in this way the logical status of a proper name in that it serves to designate a single determinate object. But then it is not the concept-word alone, but the whole consisting of the concept-word together with the demonstrative pronoun and accompanying circumstances which has to be understood as a proper name. We have an actual concept-word when it is not accompanied by the definite article or demonstrative pronoun and is accompanied either by no article or by the indefinite article, or when it is combined with 'all', 'no' and 'some'. We must not think that I mean to assert something about an African chieftain from darkest Africa who is wholly unknown to me, when I say 'All men are mortal'. I am not saying anything about either this man or that man, but I am subordinating the concept man to the concept of what is mortal. In the sentence 'Plato is mortal' we have an instance of *subsumption*, in the sentence 'All men are mortal' one of *subordination*. What is being spoken about here is a concept, not an individual thing. We must not think either that the sense of the sentence 'Cato is mortal' is contained in that of the sentence 'All men are mortal', so that by uttering the latter sentence I should at the same time have expressed the thought contained in the former sentence. The matter is rather as follows. By the sentence 'All men are mortal' I say 'If anything is a man, it is mortal'. By an inference from the general to the particular, I obtain from this the sentence 'If Cato is a man, then Cato is mortal'. Now I still need a second premise, namely 'Cato is a man'. From these two premises I infer 'Cato is mortal'.

Since therefore we need inferences and a second premise, the thought that Cato is mortal is not included in what is expressed by the sentence 'All men are mortal', and so 'man' is not an ambiguous word which amongst its many meanings has that which we designate by the proper name 'Plato'. On the contrary, a concept-word simply serves to designate a concept. And a concept is quite different from an individual. If I say 'Plato is a man', I am not as it were giving Plato a new name—the name 'man'—but I am saying that Plato falls under the *concept man*. Likewise we have two quite different cases when I give the definition '2 + 1 = 3' and when I say '2 + 1 is a prime number'. In the first case I confer on the sign '3', which is so far empty, a sense and a meaning by saying that it is to mean the same as the combination of signs '2 + 1'. In the second case I am subsuming the meaning of '2 + 1' under the concept prime number. I do not give it a new name by doing that. The fact therefore that I subsume different objects under the same concept does not make the concept-word ambiguous. So in the sentences

'2 is a prime number'
'3 is a prime number'
'5 is a prime number'

the word 'prime number' is not somehow ambiguous because 2, 3, 5 are different numbers; for 'prime number' is not a name which is given to these numbers.

It is of the essence of a *concept* to be predicative. If an empty proper name occurs in a sentence, the other parts of which are known, so that the sentence has a sense once a sense is given to that proper name, then, so long as the proper name remains empty, the sentence contains the possibility of a statement, but we do not have an object about which anything is being said. So the sentence 'x is a prime number', does indeed contain the possibility of a statement, but so long as no meaning is given to the letter 'x', we do not have an object about which anything is being said. Another way of putting this would be to say: we have a concept but we have no object subsumed under it. If we take as a further instance the sentence 'x increased by 2 is divisible by 4' then we have a concept again. We can take these two concepts as characteristic marks of a new concept by putting together the sentences 'x is a prime number' and 'x increased by 2 is divisible by 4'. Under this concept there falls only one object—the number 2. But a concept under which only one object falls is still a concept; this does not make the expression for it into a proper name.

Our position is this: we cannot recognize sentences containing an empty sign, the other constituents of which are known, as definitions. But such sentences can have an explanatory role by providing a clue to what is to be understood by the sign or word in question.

I have read that verbal definitions are considered faulty, and it is argued that we should really have no further truck with such definitions. By way of example reference was made to a definition given by me, but it was not said what a verbal definition was.[1] Of course every definition makes use of words or signs. Perhaps what is meant by a verbal definition is one in which the *definiens* contains a word which is a mere word as such, having no sense. Certainly this should not be allowed, but from the fact that the reader attaches no sense to a word it does not follow that the author of the definition has attached no sense to it. The insistence on sense is absolutely justified, and all the more so since many mathematicians seem to prove what are merely sentences without bothering whether they have a sense and what sense it is they have.

How little value is commonly placed on sense and definitions can be seen from the sharply conflicting accounts that mathematicians give of what *number* is. (We are speaking here of the natural numbers.) Weierstrass says 'Number is a series of things of the same kind'. Another says that certain conventional shapes produced by writing, such as 2 and 3, are numbers.[2] A third is of the opinion: if I hear the clock strike three I see nothing in this of what three is. Therefore it cannot be anything visible. If I see three lines, then I hear nothing in this of what three is. Therefore it can be nothing audible either. An axiom is not a visible thing and so if we speak of three axioms, the three here is nothing visible either. Number cannot be anything whatever which can be perceived by the senses.[3]

Obviously each of these attaches a different sense to the word 'number'. So the arithmetics of these three mathematicians must be quite different. A sentence from the first mathematician must have a quite different sense from the equivalent-sounding sentence of the second mathematician. This resembles what it would be like if botanists were not agreed about what they wished to understand by a plant, so that for one botanist a plant was, say, an organically developing structure, for another a human artefact, and for a third something that was not perceptible by the senses at all. Such a situation would certainly not give rise to a common science of botany.

But why should it not be possible to lay it down that by a number is to be meant a series of things of the same kind? Admittedly we can raise objections to such a course. For one thing, it may be thought that the sense of the word 'series' is not firmly enough established. Are we to think in this connection of a spatial ordering, or of a temporal ordering or of a spatio-temporal one perhaps? Further it is not clear what we are to understand by 'of the same kind'. For example, are the notes of a scale of the same kind *qua*

---

[1] Frege is here referring to the article *Über die Stellung der Definition in der Axiomatik* by *A. Schoenfliess* in *Jahresbericht der deutschen Mathematiker-Vereinigung* XX (1911), pp. 222–255 (ed.).

[2] The reference is to the so-called 'formal' theory of arithmetic (arithmetic as a game with signs) held by Frege's contemporaries *E. Heine* and *J. Thomae* (ed.).

[3] The reference is probably to *G. Cantor* (ed.).

notes, or are they of the same kind only if they have the same pitch? But let us assume that explanations were given which cleared these matters up. A train is a series of objects of the same kind which moves along rails on wheels. It may be thought that the engine is nevertheless something of a different kind. Still that makes no essential difference. And so such a number comes steaming here from Berlin. Let us assume that the science of these numbers has been set up. There is no doubt that it must be entirely different from the science in which certain shapes that one makes on a writing surface with a writing instrument are called numbers. Even if the form of words is the same, the thought expressed must be quite different. Now it is striking that the sentences of these fundamentally different sciences, each of which is called arithmetic, are constituted by precisely the same words. And it is even more striking that the practitioners of these sciences have no inkling that their sciences are fundamentally different. They all believe that they are doing arithmetic, and the same arithmetic at that, the same number theory, although what one of them is calling a number has no resemblance at all to what another is calling a number.

How is this possible? One would almost think that mathematicians regard the words used, the form of an expression, as the essential thing, and the thought expressed as quite inessential. Perhaps they think 'The thoughts contained in sentences are really no concern of mathematicians—they are a matter for philosophers; and everything to do with philosophy is of course extremely imprecise, uncertain and essentially unscientific. A mathematician who remains true to his scientific calling will have nothing to do with it. True, it can happen to even the best of them, in a moment of weakness, to let a definition slip, or something which looks like one, but we should not accord any significance to that. It is all one with a man sneezing. Really the only thing that matters is that they should all agree on the words and formulae they use. That is enough for a mathematician who has not been infected by philosophy.'

But is that then a science which proves sentences without knowing what it proves? But is it the case in actual fact that scientists do agree in the words they use? Are not mathematical works written in different languages, and are they not translated into other languages? In which case, of course, we no longer have the same form of words. But there must be something else which is preserved. And what can this be but the sense? So the thought, the sense of a sentence, cannot after all be wholly irrelevant. And does one not feel in the depth of one's being that the thoughts are the essential thing—that it is in fact these alone that we are concerned about?

But how do they come to be treated as irrelevant? How can one possibly imagine that two quite different sciences should really have the same content? Is it only because they are both called arithmetic and both treat of numbers, although what is called a number in the one is quite different from what is called a number in the other? Or is not the explanation rather that we have really to do with the same science; that this man *does* attach the same sense to the word number as that man, only he doesn't manage to get hold of it properly? Perhaps the sense appears to both through such a haze that when they make to get hold of it, they miss it. One of them makes a grasp to the right perhaps and the other to the left, and so although they mean to get hold of the same thing, they fail to do so. How thick the fog must be for this to be possible! But it must surely show up in the proofs that they have not got hold of the same sense. Yes, it could not fail to, if the proofs were drawn up in a logically rigorous way, with no gaps in the chains of inference. But this is just what we shall fail to find. If no use is ever made of a definition, there might as well not be one. However wide it may be of the actual target, no-one will notice. Another mathematician's shot may miscarry on the other side; but since he makes no use of his definition, this too might as well not be there. We can see in this way how definitions, which seem to be utterly irreconcilable, lie peacefully alongside one another like the animals in paradise. If only things were really like that!

Really the question that must surely exercise one is how *multiplication* takes place with Weierstrass's numbers. Next to my window there is a bookcase; on its top shelf there is a series of things of the same kind, a number. This afternoon at approximately 5.15 an express train, which is likewise a number, arrives at Saal station from Berlin. It is a widely held opinion that if one number is multiplied by another, the result is again a number. Accordingly the result of multiplying our series of books by the Berlin express would again have to be a series of things of the same kind. Now how are we to do that? I read in a set of lecture notes which contains a lecture by Weierstrass[1] 'According to the definition a numerical magnitude is formed by the repeated positing of elements of the same kind.' So this, apparently, is meant to be an application of the definition. How does the definition itself go? 'We can imagine a series of things of the same kind if by things of the same kind we understand things which have a complex of determinate characteristics in common. We shall understand by the concept numerical magnitude such a series.'

Mention is made here of numerical magnitude instead of number, but this is immaterial. To begin with, we have an assertion 'We can imagine a series of things of the same kind.' This is a psychological truth, which is really of no concern to us in the present context. But now does it follow from the definition that a numerical magnitude is formed by the repeated positing of elements of the same kind? There is no doubt that on the definition our express is a numerical magnitude, for it is a series of things which have in common a complex of determinate characteristics. Well, is a train formed by the repeated positing of carriages? Do I have to posit repeatedly one and the same carriage? And how do I do that? Or do I have to put one carriage

---

[1] Presumably the lecture notes entitled 'Analytische Funktionen' which are referred to in *Der wissenschaftliche Nachlass von Gottlob Frege*, by *H. Scholz* and *F. Bachmann*. See footnote 2, p. 29 of *Actes du congrès international de philosophie scientifique, Paris 1935* VIII, Paris 1936 (ed.).

next to another? In that case it would be better to say 'A train is formed by putting one carriage next to another.' I do not believe that railwaymen are yet acquainted with this method of forming a train. So I should like to put it in question that a numerical magnitude can thus be formed by the repeated positing of things of the same kind. Certainly nothing can be gathered from the definition about how this is to be done.

The lecture notes go on to say, 'Now the concept "magnitude" can itself be viewed as a unit and posited repeatedly e.g. $b, b, b \ldots$' Who would believe it—one and the same concept can be posited repeatedly! Here b seems to be the sign for the concept magnitude. Is this concept posited repeatedly by writing down the sign for it over and over again? Incidentally there seems to be a mistake here. At least it seems to me as if it is not the concept magnitude, but a particular magnitude that is meant to be repeated. In that case we should presumably have to see b as a sign for this magnitude—for this express train, for example. But what has writing this sign down over and over again got to do with the repeated positing of the express? Or is it perhaps not the express itself, but an idea which I have of it, that we are to take as the numerical magnitude? This would turn the issue into a psychological and subjective one, without its becoming any clearer. Numerical magnitudes would be psychological structures and arithmetic a branch of psychology. But, to return to the point, how do we arrive at *multiplication*? The lecture notes continue 'Now there is a magnitude which contains all these b. If b occurs a-times we designate the sum consisting of a additions of b by $a \times b$.'

This account is open to the objection that the sign 'b' has suddenly turned into a concept-word. At first it was a proper name of a numerical magnitude, of an express train, for instance; now all of a sudden it is a question of all these b. Let us make this plain by an example. We posit, say, the President of the United States repeatedly and thus get a series of President Wilsons, and the proper name we began with turns into a *nomen appellativum*, and each single one of the specimens we obtain by the repeated positing is a President Wilson. So as a result of the repeated positing of President Wilson we have got a series of President Wilsons, and in this series the man President Wilson (now we have a proper name again, as the definite article shows) occurs, and so in this series of President Wilsons *the* man President Wilson occurs more than once.

And this is how we have to think of the matter here. We designate the express which arrives here at approximately 5.15 this afternoon from Berlin by b. b is a numerical magnitude. We posit this numerical magnitude repeatedly, and thus obtain a series of expresses b. We now have a numerical magnitude which contains all these expresses b. Really? This will presumably be an express in turn; but where does it stop? Now the express b occurs more than once in this series. If it occurs a-times, we designate by $a \times b$ the sum consisting of a additions of b. So far not a word has been said about this sum. Probably the numerical magnitude is what contains all the expresses won by positing; and this numerical magnitude is, I suppose, itself a train. Do we now know what $a \times b$ is? a of course is a numerical magnitude too and we were eager to learn how to multiply the express with the series of books on the top of my bookcase by the window. So we want to call this series of books a. But what then are we to understand by a-times? An infernally difficult matter, multiplication of this sort! But according to the lecture notes, we can obtain the numerical magnitude both by positing b a-times and by positing a b-times. So we have a choice. Is it perhaps easier to take the series of books a b-times? It seems just as difficult. Now does the numerical magnitude, which we designate by $a \times b$, actually consist of books or of trains? Who would have thought that multiplying was so difficult! And we expect nine year olds to master it. But just consider the difficulty of positing an express repeatedly. There is nothing wonderful in speed but the aplomb with which numerical magnitudes are made to vanish and what is normally called number to appear in their place is really staggering.

There is yet another way in which number is introduced surreptitiously. We read at § 2 'Since what matters here, however, is not the order of the elements, but only the set of them, it follows that

$$a + b = b + a.'$$

If a numerical magnitude were really a series of things of the same kind, the order of the elements would be relevant; for if you alter the order of the elements, you have a different series. And what is here being called the set of the elements—is not this really what is called the number of the elements? So it is not a question of a series of things of the same kind but of a number, and this shows that a series of similar things and a number are different.

As number proper gets smuggled in here under the guise of a set, in other places it gets smuggled in under the guise of a value. We have seen that in the equation

$$a + b = c$$

a, b, and c are meant to be numerical magnitudes, and we read now 'If we have two equations

$$a + b = c$$
$$a \cdot b = c,$$

then the value of c can be determined by an addition and multiplication if we are given the value of a and b.' Here the value of a numerical magnitude is distinguished from the numerical magnitude itself. And what else can this value be but a number? Now, on Weierstrass's account, is a value really determined by addition? Let us assume that we have a train a and a train b. We uncouple the carriages of b and couple them to a. We thus obtain a train c, and Weierstrass says that it is a result of adding b to a. Here all that has taken place is that a new series c has been formed from a series a and a series b; but there is nothing about how to determine the value of c. It is not that we have fixed what value *c* has—we have constructed *c*. So there is apparent throughout a conflict between the definition Weierstrass gives and the things he goes on to say. What Weierstrass is here calling a value can hardly be anything other that is normally called a number.

We read further in the lecture notes 'A numerical magnitude is determined once we are given the elements and how often each is contained in it'.

Now it is surely the carriages that have to be taken as the elements of a train. Thus a train is determined when we are given its carriages and how often each is contained in it.

One of my university teachers once told of an inventor of a *perpetuum mobile* who exclaimed 'Now I have it; the only thing I lack is a little device which keeps doing this', illustrating the movement with his index finger. This 'how often' strikes me as such a little device which keeps doing this. Does it not in fact conceal the whole difficulty? If we have the little device, then we have a *perpetuum mobile*; and if we can define the words 'how often', we can also define number.

However there is something I have passed over here. We have earlier the statement that the concept of a numerical magnitude has to be extended. 'To this end numerical magnitudes are now to be formed out of different units, whereas the numerical magnitudes considered previously all came from *one* unit'.

Really? Before this we had the statement 'Each single one of the elements which recur in the series is called the unit of the numerical magnitude'.

The unit? 'Each single element is a unit' is all right, but 'each element is *the* unit' is nonsense. If the word 'unit' is meant to have the same meaning as 'element', then we have units if we have elements, but not *the* unit. Several things can indeed be subsumed under one concept: we do this when we call each of them a unit; but we are not entitled to call each of them by the same proper name. And 'the unit' is to be regarded as a proper name, since the form of this expression is such that it designates one determinate object. If we call each of several objects 'the unit', we are making a mistake. It leads to a curious interplay between singular and plural. A numerical magnitude consists of several elements, and yet of only one unit, because each element is the unit. How is this to be imagined? Well, we take a railway wagon, say goods wagon no. 1061 from the Erfurt region. We posit this repeatedly and construct a goods train out of it. The goods train consists of several elements, namely goods wagons, but of only one unit, for each of these goods wagons is the unit—namely, the goods wagon no. 1061 that we began with. This occurs repeatedly. It is true that I have not yet seen a train in which one and the same goods wagon occurs repeatedly, but according to Weierstrass there is no doubt that such a thing must be possible. Thus it is possible for a numerical magnitude or series of things of the same kind to consist of several elements and yet of only one unit.

However let us go back to the sentence 'A numerical magnitude is determined once we are given the elements and how often each is contained in it'.

We have just made every effort to distinguish between element and unit, and now everything is confounded again. The layman will say 'But with a train the question of ordering comes in'. Not at all! We have only a single wagon which occurs repeatedly. In such a case there can be no talk of an ordering. Ordering comes in only when we have different things, not when we have a single thing which occurs repeatedly.

But Weierstrass says 'Numerical magnitudes are now to be formed out of different units'. Because of course there has to be an ordering! And so we get more and more snarled up.

His project being obviously a complete failure, Weierstrass felt himself obliged to bring number proper back in again by the back door. Again and again he comes into conflict with his own statements. If on his definition a is a numerical magnitude, then a-times has no sense. Number proper is dressed up as a set or value or introduced by the phrase 'how often'. In this way we have a curious interplay between singular and plural and correspondingly between proper names and concept-words. If someone who had given the matter no thought were roused from sleep by the question 'What is number?', he would probably come out with an answer not far removed from Weierstrass's. And yet here's a man who, one would have thought, had already reflected on the question.

How, we may then ask, is it possible for so distinguished a mathematician to go so badly astray over this issue? If only he had given it some thought, he could not have failed to get clearer about it. But that is just what he has not done—given it any thought at all. And why not? He obviously believed that none at all was necessary. He was lacking in the first re-quirement—knowledge of his own ignorance. He saw no difficulties at all, everything seemed clear to him, and he didn't notice that he was constantly deluding himself. He did not possess the ideal of a system of mathematics. We do not come across any proofs; no axioms are laid down: we have nothing but assertions which contradict one another. And when on occasion an inference does seem to be drawn from his definition, it is fallacious. If he had but made the attempt to construct a system from the foundation upwards, he could not have failed straightway to see the uselessness of his definition. He had a notion of what number is, but a very hazy one; and working from this he kept on revising and adding to what should really have been inferred from his definition. Thus he asserts that ordering does not come in, and yet ordering is essential for a series. And so he quite fails to see that what he asserted does not flow from his definition, but from his inkling of what number is.

We may add the following. We cannot insist on complete scientific rigour in the classroom because the pupils do not have the intellectual maturity to feel so much as the need for it. It will probably be impossible, in the third or fourth forms, to handle irrational fractions in the way Euclid does—indeed it may scarcely be possible in the fifth form. In all likelihood such matters will, for the most part, be treated very superficially. For didactic reasons difficulties are ironed out, sharp logical edges are rounded off. And no doubt it has to be like that to begin with, but it should not continue so. Later on we should bring up the question of a rigorous deployment of proofs by awakening the need for it and then satisfying it. But it happens all too easily that the teachers, in their efforts to make everything palatable to the pupils, forget this second part of their task altogether. Mathematics can attain its full educational value only if it is pursued with the utmost logical rigour. And if there has to be some slackening of rigour in the early stages, we ought to make up for this later on. If we can only give a thorough logical grounding at the cost of sacrificing some of the material, then we should do this. But such a grounding will often be lacking. In later life people look back on these school topics as something that was mastered a long time ago, which it would not befit a serious thinker to devote any attention to. We are so prone to regarding these things as matters only for the schoolroom, that they seem to be too elementary to be worth reflecting on.

But how, it may be asked, can a man do effective work in a science when he is completely unclear about one of its basic concepts? The concept of a positive integer is indeed fundamental for the whole arithmetical part of mathematics. And any unclarity about this must spread throughout the whole of arithmetic. This is obviously a serious defect and one would imagine that it could not but prevent a man from doing any effective work whatsoever in this science. Surely no arithmetical sentence can have a completely clear sense to someone who is in the dark about what a number is? This question is not an arithmetical one, nor a logical one, but a psychological one. We simply do not have the mental capacity to hold before our minds a very complex logical structure so that it is equally clear to us in every detail. For instance, what man, when he uses the word 'integral' in a proof, ever has clearly before him everything which appertains to the sense of this word! And yet we can still draw correct inferences, even though in doing so there is always a part of the sense in penumbra. Weierstrass has a sound intuition of what number is and working from this he constantly revises and adds to what should really follow from his official definitions. In so doing he involves himself in contradictions and yet arrives at true thoughts, which, one must admit, come into his mind in a purely haphazard way. His sentences express true thoughts, if they are rightly understood. But if one tried to understand them in accordance with his own definitions, one would go astray.

We may look at a few more points in Weierstrass's theory (§ 2): '(...) and defines it by the equation $c = a + b$'. What is being defined here? For neither the plus sign nor the equals sign has occurred previously. A definition must not have the form of an equation in several unknowns. What construction should be placed on the equals sign? The words might lead one to think that '=' and '+' are not to be understood as independent signs at all, each having a sense in its own right, but only that the sentence, as a whole, was meant to say that the series c had arisen in the way described out of the series a and b. This would be perfectly alright in itself; only it does not agree with normal usage; for both '$=$' and '$+$' occur in other combinations. And Weierstrass himself immediately afterwards uses the combinations of signs

$$'b + a = a + b'$$

with the observation that this is an instance of the general law that two things which are not identical may be equal to one another according to a particular definition. And it is true that he has not defined the sign '$=$' as between numerical magnitudes, but the word 'equals'.

Accordingly the word 'equals' does not have the sense of 'the same as'. If we understand the sign '$=$' according to the definition given of the word 'equals', then we must expect that what stands to the left of the sign, as well as what stands to the right, designates a series of things of the same kind. But we still do not know what '$a + b$' is meant to designate. When in the ordinary way we write down '$5 = 3 + 2$' we are not designating a series, a numerical magnitude, by '5' or by '$3 + 2$', as Weierstrass says we are. For what series would it be? What members could it consist of? It is clear that on Weierstrass's definition his numerical magnitudes can be equal to one another without agreeing in every respect; e.g. one might consist of railway wagons, the other of books. Hence a numerical magnitude would not just have one successor, but very many, perhaps infinitely many, all indeed equal to one another, but nevertheless different. But this is a departure from arithmetical usage. What we designate by the numerals are not numerical magnitudes in Weierstrass's sense.

The question now arises whether in arithmetic, according to our usual way of speaking and writing, numbers which are equal to one another may yet be distinguished from one another in any way. Most mathematicians are inclined to say they can; but what they give out as their opinion, though it is quite sincere, does not always agree with what, at rock bottom, their real opinion is. We have seen this from the case of Weierstrass; we had to assume that, contrary to his own words, he had an inkling of the true state of affairs.

Most mathematicians don't express any view at all about the *equals sign*, but rather take its sense for granted. But we cannot without more ado take it as certain that its sense is quite clear to them.

What are we really doing when we write down '$3 + 2$'? Are we presenting a problem for solution? When we write down '$7 - 3$', is it as if we were saying 'look for a number which gives 7 when 3 is added? It might perhaps look to be so, if this combination of signs occurred only on its own. But we also write '$(3 + 2) + 4$'. Are we meant here to add the number 4 to a problem? No, to the number which is the solution to this problem. On the normal reading what comes before the sign '$+$' designates a number. And likewise what occurs to the right of '$+$' designates a number.

It follows that the '(3 + 2)' in '4 + (3 + 2)' must also be regarded as a sign for a number, for that number in fact which is also designated by '5'. So in '3 + 2' and '5' we have signs for the same number. And when we write down '5 = 3 + 2' the meanings of the signs to the left and right of the equals sign don't just agree in such and such properties, or in this or that respect, but agree completely and in every respect. What is designated on the left is the same as what is designated on the right.

But surely the two signs are different; one can see at the first glance that they are different! Here we come up against a disease endemic amongst mathematicians, which I should like to call '*morbus mathematicorum recens*'. Its chief symptom is the incapacity to distinguish between a sign and what it designates. Is it really quite impossible to designate the same thing by different signs? Can the mere fact of a difference in signs be of itself a sufficient ground for assuming that what is designated is also different? What would be the result of taking 2 + 3 to be different from 5? To the question 'Which number follows immediately after 4 in the series of whole numbers?', we should have to answer 'There are infinitely many. Some of them are 5, 1 + 4, 2 + 3, 7 − 2, $(3^2 − 2^2)$.' We should not have a simple series of whole numbers at all, but a chaos. The whole numbers which follow immediately after 4 would not follow immediately after 4 alone, but immediately after 2^2, and $2 \cdot 2$ as well. It is true that these numbers would also be equal to one another, but they would be different nonetheless. Surely we cannot accept this. We hold that the signs '2 + 3', '3 + 2', '1 + 4', '5' do designate the same number. Still an objection may be urged against this, for don't the sentences '5 = 5' and '5 = 2 + 3' have a different content? The former is an immediate consequence of the general principal of identity; but is the latter?

We might say: if we designated the same number by '2 + 3' as by '5' then we should surely have to know that 5 = 2 +3 straightoff, and not need first to work it out. It is clearer if we take the case of larger numbers. It is surely not self-evident that 137 + 469 = 606; on the contrary we only come to see this as the result of first working it out. This sentence says much more than the sentence '606 = 606'; the former increases our knowledge, not so the latter. So the thoughts contained in the two sentences must be different too. Is it possible to designate the same thing by two different names or signs without knowing that it is the same thing one has designated? Of course it is, and this also happens in other contexts. For instance, we have observed a small planet and given it a provisional designation. After a long period of observation we are able to work out the same planet had been observed at an earlier time and had already received a name. Now it can easily happen that the same astronomer has used both names without knowing that they designate the same planet. Again, in exploring a new country, it may happen that two explorers, who have seen the same mountain from different sides, have given it different names, and that it is only subsequently, when they compare maps, that it comes out that they have seen the same mountain and named it differently. It must certainly be conceded therefore that we can name the same object by different names without knowing that it is the same.

On the other hand, one cannot fail to recognize that the thought expressed by '$5 = 2 + 3$' is different from that expressed by the sentence '$5 = 5$', although the difference only consists in the fact that in the second sentence '5', which designates the same number as '$2 + 3$', takes the place of '$2 + 3$'. So the two signs are not equivalent from the point of view of the thought expressed, although they designate the very same number. Hence I say that the signs '5' and '$2 + 3$' do indeed designate the same thing, but do not express the same *sense*. In the same way 'Copernicus' and 'the author of the heliocentric view of the planetary system' designate the same man, but have different senses; for the sentence 'Copernicus is Copernicus' and 'Copernicus is the author of the heliocentric view of the planetary system' do not express the same thought.

It is remarkable what language can achieve. With a few sounds and combinations of sounds it is capable of expressing a huge number of thoughts, and, in particular, thoughts which have not hitherto been grasped or expressed by any man. How can it achieve so much? By virtue of the fact that thoughts have parts out of which they are built up. And these parts, these building blocks, correspond to groups of sounds, out of which the sentence expressing the thought is built up, so that the construction of the sentence out of parts of a sentence corresponds to the construction of a thought out of parts of a thought. And as we take a thought to be the sense of a sentence, so we may call a part of a thought the sense of that part of the sentence which corresponds to it.

Let us now look at the sentence 'Etna is larger than Vesuvius'. A part of a thought corresponds to the word 'Etna', namely the sense of this word. But is the mountain itself with its rocks and lava part of the thought? Obviously not, for one can see Etna, but one cannot see the thought that Etna is higher than Vesuvius. But what are we making a statement about? Obviously about Etna itself. And when we say 'Scylla has 6 heads', what are we making a statement about? In this case, nothing whatsoever; for the word 'Scylla' designates nothing. Nevertheless we can find a thought expressed by the sentence, and concede a sense to the word 'Scylla'. This thought, however, does not belong to the realm of truth and science but to that of myth and fiction. Such a case apart, a proper name must designate something and in a sentence containing a proper name, we are making a statement about that which it designates, about its meaning. But a proper name must have a sense as well, and this will be part of the thought of the sentence in which it occurs. From this we can see that it is possible for two signs to designate the same thing and yet, because they have different senses, not to be interchangeable as far as the thought-content of sentences in which they occur is concerned. But the fact that they are not interchangeable may be the reason why some people have refused to acknowledge that they designate the same number. But we have now seen this reason won't hold water; and we maintain our position that the equals sign in arithmetic is to be construed as a sign of identity.

Moreover we can find confirmation for this in the lecture notes. One of the concerns there is to investigate how the number domain must be extended for subtraction to be always possible. In this connection we read 'In that case $(a - a)$ must also have a meaning: it has the meaning that it leaves unchanged the value of whatever number it is added to.'

Here the value of a numerical magnitude is distinguished from the magnitude itself: this value is meant to be the same after the addition of $(a - a)$ as before. We must now take it that what Weierstrass is calling the value of a numerical magnitude is really a number. The number has therefore remained the same. So we arrive at the view that according to Weierstrass equal numerical magnitudes have the same value. Therefore in making the transition from Weierstrass's numerical magnitudes to their values, we are at the same time making the transition from Weierstrass's equality to identity. If now, as is probable, Weierstrass means by 'value of a numerical magnitude' what is ordinarily called number, then with these numbers we also arrive at identity.

So the situation is as follows. First for Weierstrass the distinction between what he calls a numerical magnitude and a number in arithmetic is blurred. But he still cannot avoid introducing numbers themselves under the guise of values of numerical magnitudes and thus distinguishing between a numerical magnitude and its value; at the same time it incidentally emerges that numerical magnitudes have the same value according as they are, in Weierstrass's terms, equal to one another. But, on close inspection, the equals sign does not occur in arithmetic between names of Weierstrass's numerical magnitudes, but between names of numbers proper, which Weierstrass introduces, albeit covertly, under the name of values of numerical magnitudes.

In this way therefore the conception of number as a series of things of the same kind, as a mass, heap or whole consisting of parts of the same kind, is very closely bound up with the view that the equals sign is not used only as a sign for identity. But then as soon as, by some logical sleight of hand, we get numbers in the sense of arithmetic, as it is inevitable we should, the equals sign is at the same time transmuted into an identity sign. So it is not to be wondered at if there is a constant fluctuation from one conception to another.

We have something analogous in the case of the *plus sign*. This first made its appearance when addition was defined. According to this definition $a + b$ is to designate the numerical magnitude which results by adding one after another all the units of b to the units of a. So the plus sign here occurs between signs of numerical magnitudes. But in the case of multiplication we read 'If one designates the units of b by α and forms

$$\overbrace{\alpha + \alpha + \alpha + \ldots + \alpha}^{b \text{ times}} \ldots,$$

Here the plus sign occurs between signs of units, and by a unit must be understood a member of a series of things of the same kind. So we must assume that it is Weierstrass's view that even a single thing is to be regarded as a series of things of the same kind, as a numerical magnitude, that is, as a series consisting of a single member. So in Weierstrass's sense even a bean is to be regarded as a numerical magnitude. Let us now take a bean and designate it by 'α'. Let us take another bean and designate it by 'β'. If we now put bean β next to bean α, we obtain a new series of things of the same kind, and this Weierstrass will no doubt designate by '$\alpha + \beta$'. If we now take a further bean, designate it by 'γ' and put it next to the numerical magnitude $\alpha + \beta$, consisting of beans α and β we obtain by addition a new numerical magnitude which, following Weierstrass, we designate by '$(\alpha + \beta) + \gamma$'. In this way we shall, according to Weierstrass, be able to form the name of a numerical magnitude from the names of its elements or units by means of the plus sign. But what can '$\alpha + \alpha$' designate on this account? We can of course put bean β next to bean α to form a series of things of the same kind, but how do we manage to put bean α alongside itself? Presumably α will have to be so good as to occur more than once.

Let us now take the planets Jupiter, Saturn, Uranus, and Neptune as an example of a series of things of the same kind. Let us suppose this series to be designated by

'♃ + ♄ + ⛢ + ♆'.

Let us call this numerical magnitude *b*. ♃ is therefore a unit of *b* and so is ♄ and so also is ⛢, and so finally is ♆.

Fortunately none of these units is repeated. Can we now say 'If we designate the units of *b* by "♃" and form

"♃ + ♃ + ♃ + ♃"'?

Does this really designate the same as

'♃ + ♄ + ⛢ + ♆'?

It is not permissible to designate different things by the same sign, for the first thing that we must require of our signs is that they should be unambiguous. Obviously the plus sign cannot be employed here, if one wishes to use it as it is normally used in arithmetic. We do write '1 + 1 + 1 + 1'; but here the first unit-sign means the same as the second, the same as the third, and the same as the fourth. We do not have here different things which form a series, a group or a heap: we just have the number one. It is clear from this that the plus sign cannot correspond to the 'and' of speech. If we say 'Schiller and Goethe are poets', we are not really connecting the proper names by 'and', but the sentences 'Schiller is a poet' and 'Goethe is a poet', which have been telescoped into one. It is different with the sentence 'Siemens and Halske have built the first major telegraph network'.[1] Here we

[1] In Frege's time 'Siemens and Halske' formed the name of a company, now known as 'Siemens A.G.' It seems clear, however, that Frege does not here intend 'Siemens and Halske' to be understood as the name of the company. The example is

don't have a telescoped form of two sentences, but 'Siemens and Halske' designates a compound object about which a statement is being made, and the word 'and' is used to help form the sign for this object. It is only this 'and' which is to be compared with the plus sign. But this comparison also shows at once that the cases 'Siemens and Halske' or 'Earth and Moon' and '1 + 1' are quite different.

Here we see throughout a crude and mathematically unworkable conception in conflict with the only viable one.

The conception of number as a series of things of the same kind, as a group, heap, etc. is very closely connected with the view which takes the sign of equality to designate partial agreement only, and with the view of the plus sign as synonymous with 'and'. But these views collapse at the first serious attempt to use them as a foundation for arithmetic. If we make such an attempt, we are always obliged to smuggle in something which is in conflict with these views. They provide us with examples of what a definition should not be. It is only if we do not go so far as to try and construct a system with the help of these definitions that we can deceive ourselves as to how utterly unworkable they are. And from this we may derive the principle that a definition must prove itself in the construction of a scientific system.

We shall now go into the *definition of concepts* more closely. The simplest case of the occurrence of a concept is that of a sentence whose grammatical subject is a proper name. We may say that in such a sentence an *object* is subsumed under a concept, namely that object of which the grammatical subject is the proper name. The remaining, predicative, part of the sentence means a *concept*. I say therefore: the concept is predicative in character, it is in need of supplementation, just as the predicative part of the sentence always demands a grammatical subject, being manifestly incomplete without it. Because it is thus incomplete, or in need of supplementation, we cannot have the predicative part occurring by itself on one side of a definition, but we have to supplement the predicative part with something which takes the place of the grammatical subject. For this purpose we may take the letter '*a*'. On the right and left sides of the definition we now have an expression which contains the letter '*a*', and we wish to stipulate by its means that both sides of the definition are to have the same sense, no matter what meaningful proper name be put in the place of *a*. We make use of this letter in order to give generality to our stipulation.

Now the simplest case of the definition of a concept is where one concept is combined with another to form a new concept in the following way. We begin by connecting two sentences with 'and'; the compound sentence, like each of its clauses, can be regarded as the expression of a thought—the one we have compounded—just because we can affirm or deny it as a whole. If

---

rather to be compared with 'Bunsen and Kirchhoff laid the foundations of spectrum analysis', which occurs in one of Frege's letters to Russell. See p. 222 of Gottlob Frege *Wissenschaftlicher Briefwechsel* (Felix Meiner 1976) (trans.).

we affirm it, we thereby affirm each of the clauses; if we deny it, we leave it open whether the first or second clause is false or whether both are.

Let us take the case '8 is a perfect cube and 8 is positive'.

In this compound sentence something is asserted of the number 8. We can construe what is present in the sentence over and above the numeral '8' as a sign for a concept, and introduce by definition a new sign for it, as in

$$\left.\begin{array}{c} a \text{ is a cube} \\ \text{and} \\ a \text{ is positive} \end{array}\right\} = a \text{ is a positive cube.}$$

Here the letter 'a' occurs twice on the left. There is no objection to this; but on the right-hand side, where the *definiendum* occurs, the letter 'a' should occur only once. For if 'a' occurred in different places, it would be possible to fill them with different proper names, and thus obtain an undefined expression; but we must make it impossible for an expression to occur which has no sense.

Here we have a concept (that of a positive cube) that is formed by putting together the component concepts (perfect cube and positive). These we call the characteristic marks of this compound concept.

The case where a proper name occurs as the grammatical subject of a sentence, the predicate of which designates a concept, is the simplest language affords, but is not the only possible one. Whenever a proper name occurs in an assertoric sentence, we can regard the remaining part as a concept-sign. A concept-sign always stands in need of completion by a proper name or a sign standing in for a proper name, such as a letter.

The definition of *prime number* will serve as an example. We stipulate

$$\left.\begin{array}{c} \text{If } a \text{ is a multiple of an integer} \\ \text{greater than 1, then } a \text{ is that integer} \\ \text{and} \\ a \text{ is an integer} \\ \text{and} \\ a \text{ is greater that 1} \end{array}\right\} = a \text{ is a prime number.}$$

Here on the left we have the *definiens*, on the right the *definiendum*. We are here saying: No matter what meaningful proper name we put in place of the letter 'a', the expression on the right is always to have the same sense as the expression on the left.

It is an imperative requirement that a concept have *sharp boundaries*. What this means is that it must hold of every object either that it falls under the concept or that it does not. We cannot allow a third case in which it is somehow undecided or indeterminate whether an object falls under the concept.

This yields a requirement for concept-signs. Such a sign, when completed by a proper name, must always result in a sentence. And this sentence must always express a thought which is either true or false. If therefore a new concept-sign is introduced by definition, this requirement has to be satisfied. This happens automatically if the defining side of the definition consists of a properly constructed concept-sign that is completed by a letter which stands in for a proper name and serves to give the necessary generality to the definition. Of course a definition may not be conditional. The stipulation that the *definiendum* is to have in every case the same sense as the *definiens* may not be made to depend on a condition; for then nothing is determined in the case where the condition is not satisfied. The *definiendum* is then without sense. Thus if we replace the indicating letter by the name of an object which fails to satisfy the condition, we shall not have, on the right of the definition, a sentence which expresses a thought that is either true or false, but a senseless combination of signs.

In general, therefore, we must have no truck with conditional definitions. In any case such a definition, if it should be employed, would require a special kind of justification.

We move on to the *definitions of relations*. If two proper names occur in a sentence, the remaining part of the sentence can be regarded as a sign for a relation, as for example in

'3 is greater than 2',

where the numerals '3' and '2' are to be regarded as proper names. When we define a relation we need two indicating signs to stand in for the names of the objects which stand in the relation. For the same reason that we have seen to hold for the definition of concepts each of these letters may occur only once on the side that is defined. Let us take as an example the definition of congruence between numbers.

$$
\left.
\begin{array}{c}
(a - b) \text{ is a multiple of } 7 \\
\text{and} \\
a \text{ is an integer} \\
\text{and} \\
b \text{ is an integer}
\end{array}
\right\} = a \text{ is congruent to } b \text{ modulo } 7.
$$

The purpose of the letters a and b is to make the stipulation general. We say by this that no matter what meaningful proper names are substituted for 'a' and 'b', the expression on the right-hand side is always to have the same sense as the expression on the left. So if e.g. we put '16' for 'a' and 2 for 'b' we get

$$
\left.
\begin{array}{c}
(16 - 2) \text{ is a multiple of } 7 \\
\text{and} \\
16 \text{ is an integer} \\
\text{and} \\
2 \text{ is an integer}
\end{array}
\right\} = 16 \text{ is congruent to } 2 \text{ modulo } 7.
$$

So long as the indefinitely indicating letters are not replaced by proper names, the left-hand side has no sense on its own and neither does the right-hand side. But it is necessary that everything on the left-hand side, apart from the letters, should be understood, so that the left-hand side always has a sense when meaningful proper names are substituted for 'a' and 'b'. From this it follows that the minus sign must not only be defined for the case where it stands between numerals, because otherwise the sentence '$(a - b)$ is a multiple of 7' would not always have a sense when we substitute meaningful proper names for 'a' and 'b'. In that case it would follow that the expression

$$\text{'}a \text{ is congruent to } b \text{ modulo } 7\text{'}$$

would not always have a sense either.

The combination of signs '$(16 - 2)$' is a proper name of a number. Accordingly the sign '$(a - b)$' stands in for a proper name. We obtain a proper name from it by replacing 'a' by a proper name and 'b' likewise. Therefore in the sentence

$$\text{'}(16 - 2) \text{ is a multiple of } 7\text{'}$$

the sign '$(16 - 2)$' has a meaning: it means the number 14. Therefore the sign '$(16 - 2)$' has a sense as well, which is a part of the sense of the above sentence, and this sense is the contribution which the sign '$(16 - 2)$' makes to the expression of the thought. So we may say that the sign '$a - b$' acquires a sense by our replacing each of the two letters by a meaningful proper name. In this respect the sign '$(a - b)$' is on all fours with

$$\text{'}(a - b) \text{ is a multiple of } 7\text{'}$$

By replacing 'a' here by '16' and 'b' by '2' we obtain a sense, namely the sense of the sentence

$$\text{'}(16 - 2) \text{ is a multiple of } 7\text{'}$$

and this sense is a thought. '$(16 - 2)$' has a sense too; but this is not a thought: it is only part of the thought. Still the compound sign '$(a - b)$' and

$$\text{'}(a - b) \text{ is a multiple of } 7\text{'}$$

agree in both acquiring a sense if the letters are replaced by meaningful proper names. The sign '$(a - b)$' at the same time acquires a meaning by such a replacement. If we replace 'a' by '16' and 'b' by '2', this meaning is the number 14. One can now go on to ask whether the sentence

$$\text{'}(16 - 2) \text{ is a multiple of } 7\text{'}$$

has not only a sense, but also a meaning.

Let us take for comparison the sentence 'Etna is higher than Vesuvius'. With this sentence we associate a sense, a thought; we understand it, we can translate it into other languages. In this sentence we have the proper name

'Etna', which makes a contribution to the sense of the whole sentence, to the thought. This contribution is a part of the thought, it is the sense of the word 'Etna'. But we are not making a statement about this sense, but about a mountain, which is not part of the thought. One who holds an idealist theory of knowledge will no doubt say 'That is wrong. Etna is only an idea in your mind.' Anyone who utters the sentence 'Etna is higher than Vesuvius' understands it in the sense that it is meant to assert something about an object that is quite independent of the speaker. Now the idealist may say that it is wrong to hold that the name 'Etna' designates something. If that were so, the speaker, whilst believing himself to be operating in the realm of truth, would be lost in the realm of myth and fiction. But the idealist is not justified in turning the thought round like this, as if the speaker meant to use the name 'Etna' to designate one of his ideas, and communicate something about this. Either the speaker designates what he means to designate by the word 'Etna' or he designates nothing at all by this name, and it is meaningless.

It is therefore essential first, that the name 'Etna' should have a *sense*, for otherwise the sentence would not have a sense, would not express a thought, and secondly, that the name 'Etna' should have a meaning, for otherwise we should be lost in fiction. The latter of course is essential only if we wish to operate in the realm of science. In the case of fiction it does not matter whether the people who occur in it are, as we should say, historical personages. Or speaking more precisely, 'whether the personal proper names occurring in fiction are meaningful'.

Now if we were concerned only with the sense of 'Etna is higher than Vesuvius', we should have no reason for requiring that the name 'Etna' should have a meaning as well; for in order that the sentence have a sense, it is only necessary for the name 'Etna' to have a sense; the meaning contributes nothing to the thought expressed. If therefore we are concerned that the name 'Etna' should designate something, we shall also be concerned with the meaning of the sentence as a whole. That the name should designate something matters to us if and only if we are concerned with truth in the scientific sense. So our sentence will have a meaning when and only when the thought expressed in it is true or false. The meaning of a sentence must be something which remains the same, if one of the parts is replaced by something having the same meaning. We return now to the sentence '$(16 - 2)$ is a multiple of 7'.

The sign '$(16 - 2)$' is a proper name of a number. '$(17 - 3)$' designates the same number, but '$(17 - 3)$' does not have the same sense as '$(16 - 2)$'. Thus the sense of the sentence '$(17 - 3)$ is a multiple of 7' is also different from the sense of the sentence '$(16 - 2)$ is a multiple of 7'; and likewise the sense of the sentence '16 is congruent to 2 modulo 7' is different from the sense of the sentence '17 is congruent to 3 modulo 7'. But the sentence '$(17 - 3)$ is a multiple of 7' must have the same meaning as that of the sentence '(16 − 2) is a multiple of 7'. Now what is not altered by replacing the sign '(16 − 2)' by the sign '(17 − 3)', whose meaning is the same, is what I call the *truth-value*. These sentences are either both true or both false. In our example they are both true, but it is easy to construct a different example in which they are both false. We only need to take the number 3 in place of the number 7.

We say accordingly that sentences have *the same meaning* if they are both true, or if they are both false. On the other hand, they have a *different meaning*, if one is true and the other false. If a sentence is true, I say its meaning is the True. If a sentence is false, I say its meaning is the False. If a sentence is neither true or false, it has no meaning. Nevertheless it may still have a sense, and in such a case I say: it belongs to the realm of fiction.

For brevity I have called a sentence true or false though it would certainly be more correct to say that the thought expressed in the sentence is true or false.

But this, surely, strikes a discordant note. If I say 'the thought that (16 − 2) is a multiple of 7 is true', I am treating *true* as a property of the thought, whereas it has emerged that the thought is the sense and the True the meaning of the sentence. Of course treating truth as a property of sentences or of thoughts is in accordance with linguistic usage. If we say 'The sentence "3 > 2" is true', then the form of words is such that we are saying something about a sentence: we are saying that it has a certain property, a property we designate by the word 'true'. And if we say 'The thought that 3 > 2 is true' the corresponding thing holds of the thought. Still the predicate *true* is quite different from other predicates such as green, salt, rational, for what we mean by the sentence 'The thought that 3 > 2 is true' can be more simply said by the sentence '3 is greater than 2'. Thus we do not need the word 'true' at all to say this. And we can see that really nothing at all is added to the sense by this predicate. In order to put something forward as true, we do not need a special predicate: we only need the assertoric force with which the sentence is uttered.

When we utter an *assertoric sentence*, we do not always utter it with assertoric force. An actor on the stage and poet reading from his works will both give frequent utterance to assertoric sentences, but the circumstances show that their utterances do not have assertoric force. They only act as if they were making assertions. In our definition, too,

$$\left.\begin{array}{c} (a-b) \text{ is a multiple of 7} \\ \text{and} \\ a \text{ is an integer} \\ \text{and} \\ b \text{ is an integer} \end{array}\right\} = a \text{ is congruent to } b \text{ modulo 7}$$

we do not utter the separate parts '(a − b) is a multiple of 7', 'a is an integer', '*b* is an integer', with assertoric force nor do we do so in a case where the letters '*a*' and '*b*' are replaced by proper names. We may even say

$$\left.\begin{array}{c} (16-3) \text{ is a multiple of 7)} \\ \text{and} \\ 16 \text{ is an integer} \\ \text{and} \\ 3 \text{ is an integer} \end{array}\right\} = 16 \text{ is congruent to 3 modulo 7}$$

although some of the clauses are false; for we mean only to put forward the right-hand side of the equation as having the same sense as the left-hand side, without making a judgement about the truth of the clauses.

If a man says something with assertoric force which he knows to be false, then he is lying. This is not so with an actor on the stage, when he says something false. He is not lying, because assertoric force is lacking. And if an actor on the stage says 'it is true that 3 is greater than 2' he is no more making an assertion than if he says '3 is greater then 2'. Whether an assertion is being made, therefore, has nothing at all to do with the word 'true': it is solely a matter of the assertoric force with which the sentence is uttered. So to say of a sentence, or thought, that it is true is really quite different from saying of sea water, for example, that it is salt. In the latter case we add something essential by the predicate, in the former we do not.

Showing, as it does, that truth is not a property of sentences or thoughts, as language might lead one to suppose, this consideration confirms that a thought is related to its truth value as the sense of a sign is to its meaning.

We have seen that '$(a - b)$' and '$(a - b)$ is a multiple of 7' are akin to one another in that both acquire a *sense* and a *meaning* as a result of our putting meaningful proper names for '*a*' and '*b*'. What makes a difference between them is that the sense which '$(a - b)$ acquires in this way is only part of a thought, whereas the sense which '$(a - b)$ is a multiple of 7' acquires in this way is a thought. If we begin by just replacing '*b*' by the proper name '2', we obtain '$(a - 2)$', '$(a - 2)$ is a multiple of 7'. What is present in the second combination of signs over and above the letter '*a*' is the sign of a concept. And we may construe the sentence '$(16 - 2)$ is a multiple of 7' as consisting of the proper name '16' together with this concept-sign, so that in this sentence we are asserting the concept in question of the number 16. What we have is the subsumption of an object under a concept.

We can, in an analogous way, regard what is present in '$a - 2$', apart from the letter '*a*', as a sign. On this view, then, '$16 - 2$' will be composed of the proper name '16' and this sign, which like the concept-sign above, is in need of supplementation. What it designates must be in need of supplementation, just as the concept is. We call it a *function*. The concept-sign, when supplemented by a proper name, yields a proper name. In our case the function-sign, when supplemented by the proper names '2', '3', '4', yields respectively the proper names '$2 - 2$'. '$3 - 2$'. '$4 - 2$'.

The objects

$$2 - 2, 3 - 2, 4 - 2.$$

of which these proper names are the signs, we call the values of our function. Thus

> $2 - 2$ is the value of our function for the argument 2,
> $3 - 2$ is the value of our function for the argument 3,
> $4 - 2$ is the value of our function for the argument 4.

But what we obtain from the sentence

$$\text{'}(a - 2) \text{ is a multiple of 7'}$$

by replacing 'a' by a proper name, is also to be understood as a proper name; for it designates a truth value and such an entity is to be regarded as an object. Thus

$$3 - 2 \text{ is a multiple of 7*}$$

is the False,

$$16 - 2 \text{ is a multiple of 7*}$$

the True. So there is a far-reaching agreement between the cases in which we speak of a function and the cases in which we speak of a concept; and it seems appropriate to understand a concept as a function—namely, a function whose value is always a truth value. So if the concept above is understood as a function, then the False is the value of this function for the argument 3, and the True is the value of the function for the argument 16. What we should otherwise say occurred as a logical subject is here presented as an argument.

It is not possible to give a definition of what a function is, because we have here to do with something simple and unanalysable. It is only possible to hint at what is meant and to make it clearer by relating it to what is known. Instead of a definition we must provide illustrations; here of course we must count on a meeting of minds.

There often seems to be unclarity about what a function is. In this connection the word 'variable' is often used. This makes it look at first as if there were two kinds of number, constant or ordinary numbers and variable numbers. The former, it seems, are designated by the familiar signs for numbers, the latter by the letters 'x', 'y', 'z'. But this cannot be reconciled with the way we proceed in Analysis. When we have the letter 'x' combined with other signs as in

$$\text{'}x - 2\text{'}$$

---

* It is understood that these sentences are here uttered without assertoric force.

Analysis requires that it be possible to substitute different number-signs for this 'x' as in

$$\text{'3}-\text{2', '4}-\text{2', '5}-\text{2', etc.}$$

But here we cannot properly speak of anything altering; for if we say that something alters, the thing which alters must be recognizable as the same throughout the alteration. If a monarch grows older, he alters. But we can only say this because he can be recognized as the same in spite of the alteration. When, on the other hand, a monarch dies and his successor mounts the throne, we cannot say that the former has been transformed into the latter; for the new monarch is just not the same as the old one. Putting '3', '4', '5' in turn for 'x' in '$x-2$' is comparable with this. We do not have here the same thing assuming different properties in the course of time: we have quite different numbers. Now if the letter 'x' designated a variable number, we should have to be able to recognize it again as the same number even though its properties were different. But 4 is not the same number as 3. So there is nothing at all that we could designate by the name 'x'. If it means 3, it does not mean 4, and if it means 4, it does not mean 3. In arithmetic and Analysis letters serve to confer generality of content on sentences. This is no less true when it is concealed by the fact that the greater part of the proof is set out in words. In such a case we must take everything into consideration, and not just what goes on in the arithmetical formulae. We say, for instance, 'Let a designate such-and-such and b such-and-such' and take this to be the point at which we begin our inquiry. But what in fact we have here are antecedents

'if a is such-and-such',
'if b is such-and-such',

and they have to be introduced as such or attached in thought to each of the sentences which follow, and these letters, whose role is merely an indicating one, make the whole general. It is only when, as we say, an unknown is designated by 'x' that we have a somewhat different case. *E.g.* let the question be to solve the equation

$$\text{'}x^2 - 4 = 0\text{'}$$

We obtain the solutions 2 or -2. But even here we may present the equation together with its solution in the form of a general sentence: 'If $x^2 - 4 = 0$, then $x = 2$ or $x = -2$'. We may take this opportunity to point out that the sign '$\pm\sqrt{4}$' is to be rejected out of hand. Here people have not taken sufficient care in using language as a guide. The proper place for the word 'or' is between sentences: 'x is equal to 2 or x is equal to -2'. But we contract the two sentences into 'x is equal to plus 2 or minus 2' and accordingly write '$x = \pm\sqrt{4}$'; however '$\pm\sqrt{4}$' doesn't designate anything at all; it isn't a meaningful sign. What one can say is

'2 is equal to $+\sqrt{4}$ or 2 is equal to $-\sqrt{4}$',

where the assertoric force extends over the whole sentence, the two clauses being uttered without assertoric force. Equally one can say

'-2 is equal to $+\sqrt{4}$ or -2 is equal to $-\sqrt{4}$'

but '2 is equal to $\pm\sqrt{4}$' has no sense.

At this point we may go into the *concept of the square root of 4*. If we think of '$2 \cdot 2 = 4$' as resulting from '$\xi \cdot \xi = 4$' by replacing the letter 'ξ' by the numeral '2', then we are seeing '$2 \cdot 2 = 4$' as composed of the name '2' and a concept-sign, which as such is in need of supplementation, and so we can read '$2 \cdot 2 = 4$' as '2 is a square root of 4'. We can likewise read '$(-2) \cdot (-2) = 4$' as '(-2) is a square root of 4'. But we must not read the equation '$2 = \sqrt{4}$' as '2 is a square root of 4'. For we cannot allow the sign '$\sqrt{4}$' to be equivocal. It is absolutely ruled out that a sign be equivocal or ambiguous. if the sign '$\sqrt{4}$' were equivocal, we should not be able to say whether the sentence '$2 = \sqrt{4}$' were true, and just on this account this combination of signs could not properly be called a sentence at all, because it would be indeterminate which thought it expresses. Signs must be so defined that it is determinate what '$\sqrt{4}$' means, whether it is the number 2 or some other number. We have come to see that the equals sign is a sign for identity. And this is how it has to be understood in '$2 = \sqrt{4}$' too. '$\sqrt{4}$' means an object and '2' means an object. We may adopt the reading '2 is the positive square root of 4'. And so the 'is' is to be understood here as a sign for identity, not as a mere copula.

'$2 = \sqrt{4}$' may not be read as '2 is a square root of 4'; for the 'is' here would be the copula. If I judge '2 is a square root of 4', I am subsuming the object 2 under a concept. This is the case we have whenever the grammatical subject is a proper name, with the predicate consisting of 'is' together with a substantive accompanied by the indefinite article. In such a case the 'is' is always the copula and the substantive a *nomen appellativum*. And then an object is being subsumed under a concept. Identity is something quite different. And yet people sometimes write down an equals sign when what we have is a case of subsumption. The sign '$\sqrt{4}$' is not incomplete in any way, but has the stamp of a proper name. So it is absolutely impossible for it to designate a concept and it cannot be rendered verbally by a *nomen appellativum* with or without an indefinite article. When what stands to the left of an equality sign is a proper name, then what stands to the right must be a proper name as well, or become such once the indicating letters in it are replaced by meaningful signs.

However, let us return from this digression to the matter in hand. Where they do not stand for an unknown, *letters* in arithmetic have the role of conferring generality of content on sentences, not of designating a variable number; for there are no variable numbers. Every alteration takes place in time. The laws of number, however, are timeless and eternal. Time does not enter into arithmetic or Analysis. Time can come in only when it is a matter of applying arithmetic. The number 3 has always been a prime number and will always remain such. How could a change be possible here? It feels incongruous to speak of a variable number and so people prefer to say 'variable magnitude', as if that was a great improvement. Of course an iron rod grows longer when it is heated, and shorter when it cools down—it changes in time. If we measure its length in millimeters, we get now this number, now that. If we now say 'the number which gives the length of this rod at time *t*', we have an expression containing an indefinitely indicating letter '*t*'. If instead of '*t*' we put the proper name of a time instant, it becomes the proper name of a number. This is on all fours with what we have in the case of the expression '$x - 2$'. This likewise becomes a proper name if we put the name of a number for 'x'. In both cases we have a function which may yield different values when saturated by different arguments. Iron rods and time, when you come down to it, are of no account to arithmetic; for this is concerned neither with pebbles, nor with peppermints, nor with railway trains, nor with rows of books, nor with iron rods, nor with time instants. These are things which may come into the applications of mathematics, but they do not have any role in constructing mathematics as a system.

In the light of all this, we can see that there is no place in arithmetic either for variable numbers or for variable magnitudes. 'Magnitude' is either a subterfuge for number, in which case variable magnitudes no more exist than variable numbers, or 'magnitude' is understood in such a way that we can properly speak of variable magnitudes; but in that case they do not belong in arithmetic.

If the letters 'x' and 'y' designated different variables, we should have to be able to say how these are distinguished; but this no one can do. We have only to keep before our mind the fact that we are concerned with pure arithmetic, not with its applications. We may perhaps seek a way out by taking the view that the letters 'x' and 'y' are not signs for what is variable, but are themselves the things that vary. But if we do this, we run foul of the established use of our signs. In the case of the equals sign, for example, it is always presupposed that the simple or complex sign which occurs on the left is either a meaningful proper name, or will become such once the indicating letters in it are replaced by designating signs.

Hence it is impossible to explain what a function is by referring to what is called a variable. *It is rather the case that when we seek to make clear to ourselves what a variable is, we come back again and again to what we have called a function, thus recognizing that variables are not a proper part of the subject-matter of arithmetic.*

(We have seen that a concept can be construed as a special case of a function. We have made it a requirement that concepts have sharp boundaries. There is an analogous requirement for the more general case of a function.)

A great deal of unclarity still prevails over what a function is. In particular, it is easy to confuse a function with the value of a function, as if one wrote

$$fx = f,$$

using the letter on one side to indicate a function, and on the other side to indicate the value of the function. There is admittedly a difficulty which accounts for its being so extremely hard to grasp the true nature of a function. This difficulty lies in the expressions we use. We say 'the function' and 'the concept', expressions which we can hardly avoid but which are inappropriate. The definite article gives these expressions the form of proper names in the logical sense, as if they were meant to designate objects, when this is precisely what they are not meant to do. The very nature of concepts and functions—their unsaturatedness—is thus concealed. Language forces an inappropriate expression on us. This is a situation which, unfortunately, can hardly be avoided, but we can render it harmless by always bearing the inappropriateness of language in mind. At the same time we shall also avoid confusing the value of a function with a function.

Now we sometimes speak of a function when what we have in mind are cases like $(1 + x)^2$. Here '$1 + x$' occurs in the argument-place of the squared function. But '$1 + x$' does not designate a function at all, but only indicates the value of a function indefinitely. If in '$(1 + x)^2$', we put, say, '3' in place of 'x', then we get $(1 + 3)^2$, and here the value of the function $1 + \xi$ for the argument 3 is the argument of the squared function. But this argument is an object, a number. Here a function is compounded out of two functions by taking the value of the first function for a certain argument as an argument of the second function. In this connection we must persist in emphasizing the fundamental difference of object and function. No function-name can stand in a place where an object-name, a proper name, stands and conversely a proper name cannot stand where a function-name stands.

Even where we have a function whose value is the same for every argument, this value must be distinguished from the function. So the function

$$1 + \xi - \xi$$

is different from the number 1 itself. We must not say 'We have $1 + \xi - \xi = 1$ and the equals sign is the identity sign, and so the function $1 + \xi - \xi$ just is the number 1', for when we say 'the function $1 + \xi - \xi$', the letter 'ξ' is not part of the function-sign; for the proper name '$1 + 3 - 3$' is composed of the function-name and the proper name '3', and the letter 'ξ' does not occur in it at all. In the sentence '$1 + a - a = 1$', however, the letter a has the role of conferring generality of content on the sentence, whereas when I say 'the function $1 + \xi - \xi$' the role of the letter 'ξ' is to enable us to recognize the places where the supplementing proper name is to be put. In order to form the differential quotient of a function for the argument 3 we subtract the value of the function for the argument 3 from the value of the function for the argument $(3 + k)$ and divide the difference by k, and so on. For the function $1 + \xi - \xi$ this is represented in the formula

$$\frac{[1 + (3 + k) - (3 + k)] - [1 + 3 - 3]}{k}$$

But in the case of the proper name '1' there are simply no places in which we can first put '3 + k' and then '3'. The prescription can only be carried out where we have a function.

It is a mistake to define the number one by saying 'One is a single thing', because on account of the indefinite article 'a single thing' has to be understood as a concept-word. But in that case the word 'is' is the copula and belongs with the predicate. We then have the object the number one being subsumed under a concept. But that is no definition. A definition always stipulates that a new sign or word is to mean the same as a complex sign we already understand. When the word 'is' is used in a definition, it is to be understood as a sign for identity, not as a copula. If now a proper name occurs to the left of the identity sign, such a sign must occur on the right too; 'a single thing' is, however, a *nomen appellativum*.

As functions of one argument are fundamentally different from objects, so *functions of two arguments* are fundamentally different from functions of one argument.

By supplementing the sign for a function of one argument with a proper name, we obtain a proper name. So e.g. from the function-sign '$\xi - 2$' and the proper name '3' we obtain the new proper name '3 − 2'. The letter 'ξ' in '$\xi - 2$' only serves to keep open the place for the supplementing argument-sign. In the same way, by supplementing the concept-sign '$\xi > 0$' with '1' we obtain '1 > 0' and this is a name of the True.

A function of two arguments is doubly in need of supplementation. In '$\xi - \zeta$' we have a sign for a function of two arguments. The letters 'ξ' and 'ζ' are meant to keep open the places for the argument-signs. The difference between the letters 'ξ' and 'ζ' is to show that a different argument-sign may be put in the two places. By putting the proper name '2' in the ζ-argument place we obtain '$\xi - 2$', which is a function-sign for a function of one argument. In the same way the relation-sign '$\xi > \zeta$' yields the concept-sign '$\xi > 0$'. So as a result of being partly saturated, functions of two arguments yield functions of one argument and relations yield concepts. A further way in which this can happen is through abolishing the difference between the argument-places. If I write '$\xi - \xi$', I indicate, by using the letter 'ξ' in both places, that the same proper name is to be put in both places, and so what I have is the name of a function of only one argument. When I call this the 'name of a function', this is to be taken *cum grano salis*. The proper name which we obtain by supplementing this function with a proper name, e.g. '3 − 3', does not contain the letter 'ξ', although it contains the function-name in question. This 'ξ' is therefore not a constituent of the function-name but only enables us to recognize how the function-sign is combined with the proper name supplementing it. This 'ξ' gives us a pointer for how to use the function-name. We can similarly form a concept-sign from a relation-sign by abolishing the difference between the argument-places. Thus from the relation-sign '$\xi > \zeta$' we obtain the concept-sign '$\xi > \xi$'.

We have seen that the value of one function can occur as the argument of a second function. We may call the former the inner function, the latter the outer function. So from the name of a function of two arguments and a concept-sign we can obtain a relation-sign in which the concept is the outer function. E.g. let '$\xi - \zeta$' be the sign for the function of two arguments and 'ξ is a multiple of 7' the concept-sign. Then '$(\xi - \zeta)$ is a multiple of 7' will be the new relation-sign.

A concept must have sharp boundaries; i.e. it must hold of every object either that it falls under a concept or does not. We may not have a case in which this is indeterminate. From this there follows something corresponding for the case of a relation; for of course by partially saturating a relation we obtain a concept. This must have sharp boundaries. And indeed any concept obtained by partly saturating a relation must have sharp boundaries. This means in other words: Every object must either stand or not stand in the relation to every object. We must exclude a third possibility. If we apply this to the relation $(\xi - \zeta)$ is a multiple of 7, it follows that a meaningful proper name must always result from the complex sign '$\xi - \zeta$' by replacing the letters 'ξ' and 'ζ' by meaningful proper names, and so not only when signs for numbers are inserted. Therefore the minus sign has to be defined in such a way that whatever meaningful proper names are put to the right and left of it, the whole combination of signs always has a meaning. So we arrive at the general requirements:

Every sign for a function of one argument has to be defined in such a way that the result always has a meaning whatever meaningful argument-sign is taken to supplement it.

Every sign for a function of two arguments has to be defined in such a way that the result has a meaning whatever meaningful argument-signs are used to supplement it.

E.g. we could stipulate that the value of the functions $\xi - \zeta$ is always to be the False, if one of the two arguments is not a number, whatever the other argument may be. Of course, we should then also have to know what a number is.

(We can stipulate likewise that the value of the function $\xi > \zeta$ is to be the False, if one of the two arguments is not a real number, whatever the other argument may be.)

But it is precisely on this issue that views have changed. Originally the numbers recognized were the positive integers, then fractions were added, then negative numbers, irrational numbers, and complex numbers. So in the course of time wider and wider concepts came to be associated with the word 'number'. Bound up with this was the fact that the addition sign changed its meaning too. And the same happened with other arithmetical signs. Needless to say, this is a process which logic must condemn and which is all the more dangerous, the less one is aware of the shift taking place. The progress of the history of the sciences runs counter to the demands of logic. We must always distinguish between history and system.

In history we have development; a system is static. Systems can be constructed. But what is once standing must remain, or else the whole system must be dismantled in order that a new one may be constructed. Science only comes to fruition in a system. We shall never be able to do without systems. Only through a system can we achieve complete clarity and order. No science is in such command of its subject-matter as mathematics and can work it up into such a perspicuous form; but perhaps also no science can be so enveloped in obscurity as mathematics, if it fails to construct a system.

As a science develops a certain system may prove no longer to be adequate, not because parts of it are recognized to be false but because we wish, quite rightly, to assemble a large mass of detail under a more comprehensive point of view in order to obtain greater command of the material and a simpler way of formulating things. In such a case we shall be led to introduce more comprehensive, i.e. superordinate, concepts and relations. What now suggests itself is that we should, as people say, extend our concepts. Of course this is an inexact way of speaking, for when you come down to it, we do not alter a concept; what we do rather is to associate a different concept with a concept-word or concept-sign—a concept to which the original concept is subordinate. The sense does not alter, nor does the sign, but the correlation between sign and sense is different. In this way it can happen that sentences which meant the True before the shift, mean the False afterwards. Former proofs lose their cogency. Everything begins to totter. We shall avoid all these disasters if, instead of providing old expressions or signs with new meanings, we introduce wholly new signs for the new concepts we have introduced. But this is not usually what happens; we continue instead to use the same signs. If we have a system with definitions that are of some use and aren't merely there as ornaments, but are taken seriously, this puts a stop to such shifts taking place. We have then an alternative: either to introduce completely new designations for the new concepts, relations, functions which occur, or to abandon the system so as to erect a new one. In fact we have at present no system in arithmetic. All we have are movements in that direction. Definitions are set up, but it doesn't so much as enter the author's head to take them seriously and to hold himself bound by them. So there is nothing to place any check on our associating, quite unwittingly, a different meaning with a sign or word.

We begin by using the addition sign only where it stands between signs for positive integers, and we define how it is to be used for this case, holding ourselves free to complete the definition for other cases later; but this piecemeal mode of definition is inadmissible; for as long as a sign is incompletely defined, it is possible to form signs with it that are to be taken as concept-signs, although they cannot be admitted as such because the concept designated would not have sharp boundaries and so could not be recognized as a concept. An example of such a concept-sign would be '$3 + \xi = 5$'. Now one can show that 2 falls under this concept, since $3 + 2 = 5$.

But whether there are other objects besides this one, and if so which, that fall under the concept would have to be left quite undecided whilst the addition sign remained incompletely defined. Now it will probably not be possible to construct a system without ascending by stages from the simpler to the more difficult cases—much as things have developed historically. But in doing this we do not have to commit the error of retaining the same sign '+' throughout these changes. *E.g.* we may use the sign '⌐' when what is in question is just the addition of positive integers, but define it completely so that the value of the function $\xi \urcorner \zeta$ is determined whatever is taken as the ξ- and the ζ-argument. *E.g.* we may stipulate that the value of this function is to be the False when one of the two arguments is something other than a positive integer.

So *piecemeal definition* and what is referred to as the extension of concepts by stages must be rejected. Definitions must be given once and for all; for whilst the definition of a concept remains incomplete, the concept itself does not have sharp boundaries and cannot be acknowledged as such.

Let us take one more look at the ground we have just covered

A sentence has a sense and we call the sense of an assertoric sentence a thought. A sentence is uttered either with assertoric force or without. It is not enough for science that a sentence should only have a sense; it must have a truth-value too and this we call the meaning of the sentence. If a sentence only has a sense, but no meaning, it belongs to fiction, and not to science.

Language has the power to express, with comparatively few means such a profusion of thoughts that no one could possibly command a view of them all. What makes this possible is that a thought has parts out of which it is constructed and that these parts correspond to parts of sentences, by which they are expressed. The simplest case is that of a thought which consists of a complete part and an unsaturated one. The latter we may also call the predicative part. Each of these parts must equally have a meaning, if the whole sentence is to have a meaning, a truth-value. We call the meaning of the complete part an *object*, that of the part which is in need of supplementation, which is unsaturated or predicative, we call a *concept*. We may call the way in which object and concept are combined in a sentence the *subsumption* of the object under the concept. Objects and concepts are fundamentally different. We call the complete part of a sentence the *proper name* of the object it designates. The part of a sentence that is in need of supplementation we call a *concept-word* or *concept-sign*. It is a necessary requirement for concepts that they have sharp boundaries. Both parts of a sentence, the proper name and the concept-word, may in turn be complex. The proper name may itself consist of a complete part and a part in need of supplementation. The former is again a proper name and designates an object; the latter we call a function-sign. As a result of completing a concept-sign with a proper name we obtain a sentence, whose meaning is a truth-value. As a result of supplementing a function-sign with a proper name we obtain a proper name, whose meaning is an object. We obtain the same perspective on both if we count a concept as a function, namely a function whose value is always a truth-value, and if we count a truth-value as an object. Then a concept is a function whose value is always a truth-value.[1]

But a function-sign may be complex too: it may be composed of a complete part which is again a proper name, and a part that is doubly in need of supplementation—what is a name or sign of a function of two arguments. A function of two arguments whose value is always a truth-value, we call a relation. The requirement that a concept have sharp boundaries corresponds to the more general requirement that the name of a function of one argument, when supplemented with a meaningful proper name, must in turn yield a meaningful proper name. And the same holds *mutatis mutandis* for functions of two arguments.

Let us take a look at something that came still earlier. We realized the necessity of constructing mathematics as a system, which is not to rule out the possibility of there being different systems. It turned out that the foundations of a system are

1. the axioms and
2. the definitions.

The *axioms* of a system serve as premises for the inferences by means of which the system is built up, but they do not figure as inferred truths. Since they are intended as premises, they have to be true. An axiom that is not true is a contradiction in terms. An axiom must not contain any term with which we are unfamiliar.

The *definitions* are something quite different. Their role is to bestow a meaning on a sign or word that hitherto had none. So a definition has to contain a new sign. Once a meaning has been given to this sign by the definition, the definition is transformed into an independent sentence which can be used in the development of the system as a premise for inferences. How are inferences carried out within the system?

Let us assume that we have a sentence of the form 'If A holds, so does B'. If we add to this the further sentence 'A holds', then from both premises we can infer 'B holds'. But for the conclusion to be possible, both premises have to be true. And this is why the axioms also have to be true, if they are to serve as premises. For we can draw no conclusion from something false. But it might perhaps be asked, can we not, all the same, draw consequences from a sentence which may be false, in order to see what we should get if it were true? Yes, in a certain sense this is possible. From the premises

$$\text{If } \Gamma \text{ holds, so does } \Delta$$
$$\text{If } \Delta \text{ holds, so does } E$$

---

[1] This is how the sentence reads in the German. Since it merely repeats the first part of the preceding sentence, the editors suggest that we read 'object' in place of 'truth value', so that the sentence marks a natural inference from the one preceding (trans.).

we can infer

$$\text{If } \Gamma \text{ holds, so does } E$$

From this and the further premise

$$\text{If } E \text{ holds, so does } Z$$

we can infer

$$\text{If } \Gamma \text{ holds, so does } Z.$$

And so we can go on drawing consequences without knowing whether Γ is true or false. But we must notice the difference. In the earlier example the premise 'A holds' dropped out of the conclusion altogether. In this example the condition 'If Γ holds' is retained throughout. We can only detach it when we have seen that it is fulfilled. In the present case 'Γ holds' cannot be regarded as a premise at all: what we have as a premise is

$$\text{If } \Gamma \text{ holds, so does } \varDelta,$$

and thus something of which 'Γ holds' is only a part. Of course this whole premise must be true; but this is possible without the condition being fulfilled, without Γ holding. So, strictly speaking, we simply cannot say that consequences are here being drawn from a thought that is false or doubtful; for this does not occur independently as a premise, but is only part of a premise which as such has indeed to be true, but which can be true without that part of the thought—the part which it contains as a condition—being true.

In *indirect proofs* it looks as if consequences are being drawn from something false. As an example, suppose we have to prove that in a triangle the longer side subtends the greater angle.

To prove:

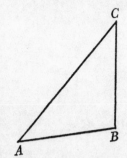

If $\angle B > \angle A$, then $AC > BC$.
We take as given:
  I If $BC > AC$, then $\angle A > \angle B$.
  II If $BC = AC$, then $\angle A = \angle B$.
  III If not $AC > BC$, and if not $BC > AC$, then
      $BC = AC$.
  IV If $\angle A = \angle B$, then not $\angle B > \angle A$.
  V If $\angle A > \angle B$, then not $\angle B > \angle A$.

From II and III there follows:

$$\text{If not } AC > BC \text{ and if not } BC > AC, \text{ then } \angle A = \angle B.$$

From this and IV we have:

$$\text{If not } AC > BC \text{ and if not } BC > AC, \text{ then not } \angle B > \angle A.$$

From I and V:

$$\text{If } BC > AC, \text{ then not } \angle B > \angle A.$$

From the last two sentences there follows:

$$\text{If not } AC > BC, \text{ then not } \angle B > \angle A.$$

And then by contraposition:

$$\text{If } \angle B > \angle A, \text{ then } AC > BC.$$

To simplify matters, I shall assume that we are not speaking of triangles in general, but of a particular triangle. $\angle A$ and $\angle B$ may be understood as numbers, arrived at by measuring the angles by some unit-measure, as e.g. a right-angle. AC and BC may likewise be understood as numbers, arrived at by using some unit-measure for the sides, as e.g. a metre. Then the signs '$\angle A$', '$\angle B$', 'AC', and 'BC' are to be taken as proper names of numbers.

We see that 'not $AC > BC$' does not occur here as a premise, but that it is contained in III as a part—as a condition. So strictly speaking, we cannot say that consequences are being drawn from the false thought (not $AC > BC$). Therefore, we ought not really to say 'suppose that not $AC > BC$', because this makes it look as though 'not $AC > BC$' was meant to serve as a premise for inference, whereas it is only a condition.

We make far too much of the peculiarity of indirect proof *vis-à-vis* direct proof. The truth is that the difference between them is not at all important.

The proof can also be set out in the following way. We now take as given:

I'   If not $\angle A > \angle B$ then not $BC > AC$.
II' If not $\angle A = \angle B$, then not $BC = AC$.
III' If not $BC > AC$ and if not $BC = AC$, then $AC > BC$.
IV' If $\angle B > \angle A$ then not $\angle A = \angle B$.
V'   If $\angle B > \angle A$ then not $\angle A > \angle B$.

From V' and I' there follows:

$$\text{If } \angle B > \angle A, \text{ then not } BC > AC.$$

From this and III' we have:

$$\text{If } \angle B > \angle A \text{ and if not } BC = AC, \text{ then } AC > BC.$$

From IV' and II' there follows:

$$\text{If } \angle B > \angle A, \text{ then not } BC = AC.$$

From the last two sentences we have:

$$\text{If } \angle B > \angle A, \text{ then } AC > BC.$$

At no point in this proof have we entertained 'not $AC > BC$' even as a mere hypothesis.

In an investigation of the *foundations of geometry* it may also look as if consequences are being drawn from something false or at least doubtful. Can we not put to ourselves the question: How would it be if the axiom of parallels didn't hold? Now there are two possibilities here: either no use at all is made of the axiom of parallels, but we are simply asking how far we can get with the other axioms, or we are straightforwardly supposing something which contradicts the axiom of parallels. It can only be a question of the latter case here. But it must constantly be borne in mind that what is false cannot be an axiom, at least if the word 'axiom' is being used in the traditional sense. What are we to say then? Can the axiom of parallels be acknowledged as an axiom in this sense? When a straight line intersects one of two parallel lines, does it always intersect the other? This question, strictly speaking, is one that each person can only answer for himself. I can only say: so long as I understand the words 'straight line', 'parallel' and 'intersect' as I do, I cannot but accept the parallels axiom. If someone else does not accept it, I can only assume that he understands these words differently. Their sense is indissolubly bound up with the axiom of parallels. Hence a thought which contradicts the axiom of parallels cannot be taken as a premise of an inference. But a true hypothetical thought, whose condition contradicted the axiom, could be used as a premise. This condition would then be retained in all judgements arrived at by means of our chains of inference. If at some point we arrived at a hypothetical judgement whose consequence contradicted known axioms, then we could conclude that the condition contradicting the axiom of parallels was false, and we should thereby have proved the axiom of parallels with the help of other axioms. But because it had been proved, it would lose its status as an axiom. In such a case we should really have given an indirect proof.

If, however, we went on drawing inference after inference and still did not come up against a contradiction anywhere, we should certainly become more and more inclined to regard the axiom as incapable of proof. Nevertheless we should still, strictly speaking, not have proved this to be so.

Now in his *Grundlagen der Geometrie* Hilbert is preoccupied with such questions as the consistency and independence of axioms. But here the sense of the word 'axiom' has shifted. For if an axiom must of necessity be true, it is impossible for axioms to be inconsistent with one another. So any discussion here would be a waste of words. But obvious though it is, it seems just not to have entered Hilbert's mind that he is not speaking of axioms in Euclid's sense at all when he discusses their consistency and independence. We could say that the word 'axiom', as he uses it, fluctuates from one sense to another without his noticing it. It is true that if we concentrate on the words of one of his axioms, the immediate impression is that we are dealing with an axiom of the Euclidean variety; but the words mislead us, because all the words have a different use from what they have in Euclid. At § 3[1] we

---

[1] The quotation here is from the first edition of the *Grundlagen der Geometrie*. Later editions give a different axiom in place of that which Frege cites under II.4 (ed.).

read '*Definition*. The points of a straight line stand in certain relations to one another, for the description of which we appropriate the word "between".' Now this definition is only complete once we are given the four axioms

II.1 If A, B, C are points on a straight line, and B lies between A and C, then B lies between C and A.

II.2 If A and C are two points on a straight line, then there is at least one point B lying between A and C, and at least one point D such that C lies between A and D.

II.3 Given any three points on a straight line, there is one and only one which lies between the other two.

II.4 Any four points A, B, C, D on a straight line can be so ordered that B lies between A and C and between A and D, and so that C lies between A and D and between B and D.

These axioms, then, are meant to form parts of a definition. Consequently these sentences must contain a sign which hitherto had no meaning, but which is given a meaning by all these sentences taken together. This sign is apparently the word 'between'. But a sentence that is meant to express an axiom may not contain a new sign. All the terms in it must be known to us. As long as the word 'between' remains without a sense, the sentence 'If A, B, C, are points on a straight line and B lies between A and C, then B lies between C and A' fails to express a thought.

An axiom, however, is always a true thought. Therefore, what does not express a thought, cannot express an axiom either. And yet one has the impression, on reading the first of these sentences, that it might be an axiom. But the reason for this is only that we are already accustomed to associate a sense with the word 'between'. In fact if in place of

'B lies between A and C'

we say

'B pat A nam C',

then we associate no sense with it. Instead of the so-called axiom II.1 we should have

'If B pat A nam C, then B pat C nam A'.

No one to whom these syllables 'pat' and 'nam' are unfamiliar will associate a sense with this apparent sentence. The same holds of the other three pseudo-axioms.

The question now arises whether, if we understand by A, B, C points on a straight line, an expression of the form

'B pat A nam C'

will not at least come to acquire a sense through the totality of these pseudo-sentences. I think not. We may perhaps hazard the guess that it will come to the same thing as

'*B* lies between *A* and *C*',

but it would be a guess and no more. What is to say that this matrix could not have several solutions?

But does, then, a definition have to be unambiguous? Are there not circumstances in which a certain give and take is a good thing?

Of course $a^2 = 4$ does not determine unequivocally what a is to mean, but is there any harm in that? Well, if a is to be a proper name whose meaning is meant to be fixed, this goal will obviously not be achieved. On the contrary one can see that in this formula there is designated a concept under which the numbers 2 and -2 fall. Once we see this, the ambiguity is harmless, but it means that we don't have a definition of an object.

If we want to compare this case with our pseudo-axiom, we have to compare the letter 'a' with 'between' or with 'pat-nam'. We must distinguish signs that designate from those which merely indicate. In fact the word 'between' or 'pat-nam' no more designates anything than does the letter 'a'. So we have here to disregard the fact that we usually associate a sense with the word 'between'. In this context it no more has a sense than does 'pat-nam'. Now to say that a sign which only indicates neither designates anything nor has a sense is not yet to say it could not contribute to the expression of a thought. It can do this by conferring generality of content on a simple sentence or on one made up of sentences.

Now there is, to be sure, a difference between our two cases; for whilst 'a' stands in for a proper name, 'pat-nam' stands in for the designation of a relation with three terms. As we call a function of one argument, whose value is always a truth-value, a concept, and a function of two arguments, whose value is always a truth-value, a relation, we can go yet a step further and call a function of three arguments whose value is always a truth-value, a *relation with three terms*. Then whilst the 'between-and' or the 'pat-nam' do not designate such a relation with three terms, they do indicate it, as 'a' indicates an object. Still there remains a distinction. We were able to find a concept designated in '$a^2 = 4$'.

What would correspond to this in the case of our pseudo-axioms? It is what I call a second level concept. In order to see more clearly what I understand by this, consider the following sentences:

> 'There is a positive number'
> 'There is a cube root of 1'.

We can see that these have something in common. A statement is being made, not about an object, however, but about a concept. In the first sentence it is the concept *positive number*, in the second it is the concept *cube root of 1*. And in each case it is asserted of the concept that it is not empty, but satisfied. It is indeed strictly a mistake to say 'The concept *positive number* is satisfied', for by saying this I seem to make the concept into an object, as the definite article 'the concept' shows. It now looks as if 'the concept *positive number*' were a proper name designating an object and as if the intention were to assert of this object that it is satisfied. But the truth is that we do not have an object here at all. By a necessity of language, we have to use an expression which puts things in the wrong perspective; even so there is an analogy. What we designate by 'a positive number' is related to what we designate by 'there is', as an object (e.g. the earth) is related to a concept (e.g. planet).

I distinguish concepts under which objects fall as concepts of first level from concepts of second level within which, as I put it, concepts of first level fall. Of course it goes without saying that all these expressions are only to be understood metaphorically; for taken literally, they would put things in the wrong perspective. We can also admit second level concepts within which relations fall. E.g. in the sentence:

'It is to hold for all A, B, C that if A stands in the p-relation to B and if A
stands in the p-relation to C, then $B = C$',

we have a designation of a second-level concept within which relations fall and 'stands in the p-relation to ...' here stands in for the argument-sign—for, that is, the designation of the relation presented as argument. If we substitute e.g. the equals sign, we get

'It holds for all A, B, C that if $A = B$ and if $A = C$, then $B = C$'.

If this is true, then it follows that the relation of equality falls within this second level concept.

As we call a function of one argument, whose value is always a truth value, a concept, and as we call a function of two arguments, whose value is always a truth value, a relation, so we could introduce a special name for a function of three arguments, whose value is always a truth value. Provisionally, such a function may be called a relation with three terms. That designated by the words 'lies between ... and ...' would be of this kind, if these words were understood as we should ordinarily understand them when used in speaking of Euclidean points on a Euclidean straight line. However, they are not used in our pseudo-axioms as a sign which designates, but only as one which indicates, as are letters in arithmetic. So in this context they do not designate such a three-termed relation: they only indicate such a relation. Even if we wish, for the time being, to understand the actual words 'point' and 'straight line' in the Euclidean sense, still the words 'lies between ... and ...' are not to be regarded, strictly speaking, as words with a sense, but only as a stand-in for an argument, as is the letter 'a' in 'a^2'. But the function, whose arguments they stand in for, is a second level function within which only relations with three terms can fall.

My basic logical Insights[1]

[1915]

The following may be of some use as a key to the understanding
of my results.

Whenever anyone recognizes something to be true, he makes a judgement.
What he recognizes to be true is a thought. It is impossible to recognize a
thought as true before it has been grasped. A true thought was true before it
was grasped by anyone. A thought does not have to be owned by anyone.
The same thought can be grasped by several people. Making a judgement
does not alter the thought that is recognized to be true. When something is
judged to be the case, we can always cull out the thought that is recognized
as true; the act of judgement forms no part of this. The word 'true' is not an
adjective in the ordinary sense. If I attach the word 'salt' to the word 'sea-
water' as a predicate, I form a sentence that expresses a thought. To make it
clearer that we have only the expression of a thought, but that nothing is
meant to be asserted, I put the sentence in the dependent form 'that sea-
water is salt'. Instead of doing this I could have it spoken by an actor on the
stage as part of his role, for we know that in playing a part an actor only
seems to speak with assertoric force. Knowledge of the sense of the word
'salt' is required for an understanding of the sentence, since it makes an
essential contribution to the thought—in the mere word 'sea-water' we
should of course not have a sentence at all, nor an expression for a thought.
With the word 'true' the matter is quite different. If I attach this to the words
'that sea-water is salt' as a predicate, I likewise form a sentence that
expresses a thought. For the same reason as before I put this also in the
dependent form 'that it is true that sea-water is salt'. The thought expressed
in these words coincides with the sense of the sentence 'that sea-water is
salt'. So the sense of the word 'true' is such that it does not make any
essential contribution to the thought. If I assert 'it is true that sea-water is
salt', I assert the same thing as if I assert 'sea-water is salt'. This enables us
to recognize that the assertion is not to be found in the word 'true', but in the
assertoric force with which the sentence is uttered. This may lead us to think
that the word 'true' has no sense at all. But in that case a sentence in which
'true' occurred as a predicate would have no sense either. All one can say

---

[1] According to a note by Heinrich Scholz on the transcripts on which this edition
is based, this piece is to be dated around 1915 (ed.).

is: the word 'true' has a sense that contributes nothing to the sense of the whole sentence in which it occurs as a predicate.

But it is precisely for this reason that this word seems fitted to indicate the essence of logic. Because of the particular sense that it carried any other adjective would be less suitable for this purpose. So the word 'true' seems to make[1] the impossible possible: it allows what corresponds to the assertoric force to assume the form of a contribution to the thought. And although this attempt miscarries, or rather through the very fact that it miscarries, it indicates what is characteristic of logic. And this, from what we have said, seems something essentially different from what is characteristic of aesthetics and ethics. For there is no doubt that the word 'beautiful' actually does indicate the essence of aesthetics, as does 'good' that of ethics, whereas 'true' only makes an abortive attempt to indicate the essence of logic, since what logic is really concerned with is not contained in the word 'true' at all but in the assertoric force with which a sentence is uttered.

Many things that belong with the thought, such as negation or generality, seem to be more closely connected with the assertoric force of the sentence or the truth of the thought.[2] One has only to see that such thoughts occur in *e.g.* conditional sentences or as spoken by an actor as part of his role for this illusion to vanish.

How is it then that this word 'true', though it seems devoid of content, cannot be dispensed with? Would it not be possible, at least in laying the foundations of logic, to avoid this word altogether, when it can only create confusion? That we cannot do so is due to the imperfection of language. If our language were logically more perfect, we would perhaps have no further need of logic, or we might read it off from the language. But we are far from being in such a position. Work in logic just is, to a large extent, a struggle with the logical defects of language, and yet language remains for us an in-dispensable tool. Only after our logical work has been completed shall we possess a more perfect instrument.

Now the thing that indicates most clearly the essence of logic is the assertoric force with which a sentence is uttered. But no word, or part of a sentence, corresponds to this; the same series of words may be uttered with assertoric force at one time, and not at another. In language assertoric force is bound up with the predicate.

---

[1] A different version of the manuscript has 'to be trying to make' in place of 'to make' (ed.).

[2] This sentence and the one following are crossed out in the manuscript (ed.).

[Notes for Ludwig Darmstaedter][1]

[July 1919]

I started out from mathematics. The most pressing need, it seemed to me, was to provide this science with a better foundation. I soon realized that number is not a heap, a series of things, nor a property of a heap either, but that in stating a number which we have arrived at as the result of counting we are making a statement about a concept. (Plato, *The Greater Hippias*.)

The logical imperfections of language stood in the way of such investigations. I tried to overcome these obstacles with my concept-script. In this way I was led from mathematics to logic.

What is distinctive about my conception of logic is that I begin by giving pride of place to the content of the word 'true', and then immediately go on to introduce a thought as that to which the question 'Is it true?' is in principle applicable. So I do not begin with concepts and put them together to form a thought or judgement; I come by the parts of a thought by analysing the thought. This marks off my concept-script from the similar inventions of Leibniz and his successors, despite what the name suggests; perhaps it was not a very happy choice on my part.

Truth is not part of a thought. We can grasp a thought without at the same time recognizing it as true—without making a judgement. Both grasping a thought and making a judgement are acts of a knowing subject, and are to be assigned to psychology. But both acts involve something that does not belong to psychology, namely the thought.

False thoughts must be recognized too, not of course as true, but as indispensable aids to knowledge, for we sometimes arrive at the truth by way of false thoughts and doubts. There can be no questions if it is essential to the content of *any* question that that content should be true.

Negation does not belong to the act of judging, but is a constituent of a thought. The division of thoughts (judgements) into affirmative and negative is of no use to logic, and I doubt if it can be carried through.

Where we have a compound sentence consisting of an antecedent and a consequent, there are two main cases to distinguish. The antecedent and consequent may each have a complete thought as its sense. Then, over and

---

[1] This piece is dated at the end by Frege himself. It is one of the few manuscripts of Frege which have come down to us in the original and is in the possession of the *Staatsbibliothek der Stiftung Preußischer Kulturbesitz* where it forms part of the collection of the historian of science Ludwig Darmstaedter, ref. number 1919–95 (ed.).

above these, we have the thought expressed by the whole compound sentence. By recognizing this thought as true, we recognize neither the thought in the antecedent as true, nor that in the consequent as true. A second case is where neither antecedent nor consequent has a sense in itself, but where nevertheless the whole compound sentence does express a thought—a thought which is general in character. In such a case we have a relation, not between judgements or thoughts, but between concepts, the relation, namely, of subordination. The antecedent and consequent are here sentences only in the grammatical, not in the logical, sense. The first thing that strikes us here is that a thought is made up out of parts that are not themselves thoughts. The simplest case of this kind is where one of the two parts is in need of supplementation and is completed by the other part, which is saturated: that is to say, it is not in need of supplementation. The former part then corresponds to a concept, the latter to an object (subsumption of an object under a concept). However, the object and concept are not constituents of the thought expressed. The constituents of the thought do refer to the object and concept, but in a special way. There is also the case where a part doubly in need of supplementation is completed by two saturated parts. The former part corresponds to a relation.—An object stands in a relation to an object.—Where logic is concerned, it seems that every combination of parts results from completing something that is in need of supplementation; where logic is concerned, no whole can consist of saturated parts alone. The sharp separation of what is in need of supplementation from what is saturated is very important. When all is said and done, people have long been familiar with the former in mathematics ($+$, $:$, $\sqrt{}$, sin, $=$, $>$). In this connection they speak of functions, and yet it would seem that in most cases they have only a vague notion of what is at stake.

A general statement can be negated. In this way we arrive at what logicians call existential judgements and particular judgements. The existential thoughts I have in mind here are such as are expressed in German by '*es gibt*'.[1] This phrase is never followed immediately by a proper name in the singular, or by a word accompanied by the definite article, but always by a concept-word (*nomen appellativum*) without a definite article. In existential sentences of this kind we are making a statement about a concept. Here we have an instance of how a concept can be related to a *second level concept* in a way analogous to that in which an object is related to a concept under which it falls. Closely akin to these existential thoughts are thoughts that are particular: indeed they may be included among them. But we can also say that what is expressed by a sentence of the particular form is that a concept stands in a certain *second level relation* to a concept. The distinction between first and second level concepts can only be grasped clearly by one who has clearly grasped the distinction between what is in

---

[1] i.e. judgements that are expressed in English by 'there is' or 'there are' (trans.).

need of supplementation and what is saturated. A saturated part obtained by analysing a thought can sometimes itself be split up in the same way into a part in need of supplementation and a saturated part. The sentence 'The capital of Sweden is situated at the mouth of Lake Mälar' can be split up into a part in need of supplementation and the saturated part 'the capital of Sweden'. This can further be split up into the part 'the capital of', which stands in need of supplementation, and the saturated part 'Sweden'. Splitting up the thought expressed by a sentence corresponds to such a splitting up of the sentence. The functions of Analysis correspond to parts of thoughts that are thus in need of supplementation, without however being such.

A distinction has to be drawn between the sense and meaning of a sign (word, expression). If an astronomer makes a statement about the moon, the moon itself is not part of the thought expressed. The moon itself is the meaning of the expression 'the moon'. Therefore in addition to its meaning this expression must also have a sense, which can be a constituent of a thought. We can regard a sentence as a mapping of a thought: corresponding to the whole-part relation of a thought and its parts we have, by and large, the same relation for the sentence and its parts. Things are different in the domain of meaning. We cannot say that Sweden is a part of the capital of Sweden. The same object can be the meaning of different expressions, and any one of them can have a sense different from any other. Identity of meaning can go hand in hand with difference of sense. This is what makes it possible for a sentence of the form '$A = B$' to express a thought with more content than one which merely exemplifies the law of identity. A statement in which something is recognized as the same again can be of far greater cognitive value than a particular case of the law of identity.

Even a part of a thought, or a part of a part of a thought, that is in need of supplementation, has something corresponding to it in the realm of meaning. Yet it is wrong to call this a concept, say, or a relation, or a function, although we can hardly avoid doing so. Grammatically, 'the concept of God' has the form of a saturated expression. Accordingly its sense cannot be anything in need of supplementation. When we use the words 'concept', 'relation', 'function' (as this is understood in Analysis), our words fail of their intended target. In this case even the expression 'the meaning', with the definite article, should really be avoided.

It is not, however, only parts of sentences that have meaning; even a whole sentence, whose sense is a thought, has one. All sentences that express a true thought have the same meaning, and all sentences that express a false thought have the same meaning (the *True* and the *False*). Sentences and parts of sentences with different meanings also have different senses. If in a sentence or part of a sentence one constituent is replaced by another with a different meaning, the different sentence or part that results does not have to have a different meaning from the original; on the other hand, it always has a different sense. If in a sentence or part of a sentence one constituent is replaced by another with the same meaning but not with the same sense, the different sentence or part that results has the same meaning as the original, but not the same sense. All this holds for direct, not for indirect, speech.

A thought can also be the meaning of a sentence (indirect speech, the subjunctive mood)[1]. The sentence does not then express this thought, but can be regarded as its proper name. Where we have a clause in indirect speech occurring within direct speech, and we replace a constituent of this clause by another which has the same meaning in direct speech, then the whole which results from this transformation does not necessarily have the same meaning as the original.

The miracle of number. The adjectival use of number-words is misleading. In arithmetic a number-word makes its appearance in the singular as a proper name of an object of this science; it is not accompanied by the indefinite article, but is saturated. Subsumption: 'Two is a prime,' not subordination. The combinations 'each two', 'all twos' do not occur.

Yet amongst mathematicians we find a great lack of clarity and little agreement. Is number an object that arithmetic investigates or is it a counter in a game? Is arithmetic a game or a science? According to one man, we are to understand by 'number' a series of objects of the same kind; according to another, a spatial, material structure produced by writing. A third denies that number is spatial at all. Perhaps there are times when arithmeticians merely delude themselves into thinking that they understand by 'number' what they say they do. If this is not so, then they are attaching different senses to sentences with same wording; and if they still believe that they are working within one and the same discipline, then they are just deluding themselves. A definition in arithmetic that is never adduced in the course of a proof, fails of its purpose. With almost every technical term in arithmetic ('infinite series', 'determinant', 'expression', 'equation') the same questions keep cropping up: Are the things we see the subject-matter of arithmetic? Or are they only signs for, means by which we may recognize, the objects to be investigated, not those objects themselves? Is what is designated a number? and, if it isn't, what else is? Until arithmeticians have agreed on answers to these questions and in their ways of talking remain in conformity with these answers, there will be no science of arithmetic in the true sense of the word—or else a science is made up of series of words where it doesn't matter what sense they have or whether they have any sense at all. Since a statement of number based on counting contains an assertion about a concept, in a logically perfect language a sentence used to make such a statement must contain two parts, first a sign for the concept about which the statement is made, and secondly a sign for a second level concept. These second level concepts form a series and there is a rule in accordance with

---

[1] In German clauses in indirect speech are often put into the subjunctive mood (Trans.).

which, if one of these concepts is given, we can specify the next. But still we do not have in them the numbers of arithmetic; we do not have objects, but concepts. How can we get from these concepts to the numbers of arithmetic in a way that cannot be faulted? Or are there simply no numbers in arithmetic? Could the numerals help to form signs for these second level concepts, and yet not be signs in their own right?

Bad Kleinen, 26th July, 1919.   Dr. Gottlob Frege,
                                                 formerly Professor at Jena.

Logical Generality[1]

[Not before 1923]

I published an article in this journal on compound thoughts, in which some space was devoted to hypothetical compound thoughts. It is natural to look for a way of making a transition from these to what in physics, in mathematics and in logic are called *laws*. We surely very often express a law in the form of a hypothetical compound sentence composed of one or more antecedents and a consequent. Yet, right at the outset, there is an obstacle in our path. The hypothetical compound thoughts I discussed do not count as laws, since they lack the generality which distinguishes laws from particular facts, such as, for instance, those we are accustomed to encounter in history. In point of fact the distinction between law and particular fact cuts very deep. It is what creates the fundamental difference between the activity of the physicist and of the historian. The former seeks to establish laws; history tries to establish particular facts. Of course history tries to understand the causes of things too, and to do that it must at least presuppose that events conform to laws.

This may be enough by way of preliminary to show the necessity of a closer study of generality.

The value a law has for our knowledge rests on the fact that it comprises many—indeed, infinitely many—particular facts as special cases. We profit from our knowledge of a law by gathering from it a wealth of particular pieces of information, using the inference from the general to the particular, for which of course a mental act—that of inferring—is still always required. Anyone who knows how to draw such an inference has also grasped what is meant by generality in the sense of the word intended here. By inferences of a different sort, we may derive new laws from ones we already acknowledge.

What, now, is the essence of generality? Since we are here concerned with laws, and laws are thoughts, the only thing that can be at issue in the present context is the generality of a thought. Every science progresses by recognizing a succession of thoughts as true; but here it is seldom thoughts that are the object of our investigation, what we make statements about. What figure as such are for the most part the objects of sense perception. In

---

[1] Frege in the first sentence refers to the article *Gedankengefüge* that appeared in 1923, as the third part of the *Logischen Untersuchungen* published in the journal *Beiträge zur Philosophie des deutschen Idealismus*. This establishes the date. We may accept further that Frege intended to develop this fragment into a fourth part of this series of essays (ed.).

predicating something of these, we utter thoughts. And this is the usual way in which thoughts figure in science. Here, in predicating generality of thoughts, we are making them the objects of our investigation and they take over the place normally occupied by the objects of sense perception. These latter, which elsewhere, and in particular in the natural sciences, are the objects of enquiry, are essentially different from thoughts. For thoughts cannot be perceived by the senses. To be sure, signs which express thoughts can be audible or visible, but not the thoughts themselves. Sense impressions can lead us to recognize the truth of a thought; but we can also grasp a thought without recognizing it as true. False thoughts are thoughts too.

If a thought cannot be perceived by the senses, it is not to be expected that its generality can be. I am not in a position to produce a thought in the way a mineralogist presents a sample of a mineral so as to draw attention to its characteristic lustre. It may be impossible to use a definition to fix what is meant by generality.

Language may appear to offer a way out, for, on the one hand, its sentences can be perceived by the senses, and, on the other, they express thoughts. As a vehicle for the expression of thoughts, language must model itself upon what happens at the level of thought. So we may hope that we can use it as a bridge from the perceptible to the imperceptible. Once we have come to an understanding about what happens at the linguistic level, we may find it easier to go on and apply what we have understood to what holds at the level of thought—to what is mirrored in language. Here it isn't a question of the day to day understanding of language, of grasping the thoughts expressed in it: it's a question of grasping the property of thoughts that I call logical generality. Of course for this we have to reckon upon a meeting of minds between ourselves and others, and here we may be disappointed. Also, the use of language requires caution. We should not overlook the deep gulf that yet separates the level of language from that of the thought, and which imposes certain limits on the mutual correspondence of the two levels.

Now, in what form does generality make its appearance in language? We have various expressions for the same general thought:

> 'All men are mortal'
> 'Every man is mortal'
> 'If something is a man, it is mortal'.

The differences in the expression do not affect the thought itself. It is advisable for us to confine ourselves to using one mode of expression, so that we do not take incidental differences, in the tone of the thought, say, to be differences of thought. The expressions involving 'all' and 'every' are not suitable for use *wherever* generality is present, since not every law can be cast in this form. In the last mode of expression we have the form of the hypothetical compound sentence—a form we can hardly avoid using in other cases too—together with the indefinitely indicating parts of the sentence, 'something' and 'it'; and these really contain the expression of generality. From this mode of expression we may easily make the transition to the particular, by replacing the indefinitely indicating parts of the sentence by one that designates definitely:

> 'If Napoleon is a man, Napoleon is mortal.'

In view of this possibility of the transition from the general to the particular, expressions of generality with indefinitely indicating parts of the sentence are alone of use to us, but if we were restricted to 'something' and 'it', we would only be able to deal with the very simplest cases. Now it is natural to copy the methods of arithmetic by selecting letters for indefinitely indicating parts of a sentence:

> 'If *a* is a man, *a* is a mortal.'

Here the equiform letters cross-refer to one another. Instead of letters equiform with '*a*' we could just as well take ones equiform with '*b*' or '*c*'. But it is essential that they should be equiform. However, taken strictly, we are stepping outside the confines of a spoken language designed to be heard and moving into the region of a written or printed language designed for the eye. A sentence which an author writes down is primarily a direction for forming a spoken sentence in a language whose sequences of sounds serve as signs for expressing a sense. So at first there is only a mediated connection set up between written signs and a sense that is expressed. But once this connection is established, we may also regard the written or printed sentence as an immediate expression of a thought, and so as a sentence in the strict sense of the word. In this way we obtain a language dependent on the sense of sight, which, if need be, can even be learnt by a deaf man. In this, individual letters can be adopted as indefinitely indicating parts of a sentence. The language we have just indicated, which I will call the *object-language*,[1] is to serve for us as a bridge from the perceptible to the imperceptible. It contains two different *constituents*: *those with the form of words and the* individual *letters*. The former correspond to words of the spoken language, the latter have an indefinitely indicating role. This object-language is to be distinguished from the language in which I conduct my train of thought. That is the usual written or printed German, my *meta-language*. But the sentences of the object-language are the objects to be talked about in my meta-language. And so I must be able to designate them in my meta-language, just as in an article on astronomy the planets are designated by

---

[1] The German editors see the distinction Frege here draws between a '*Hilfssprache*' and a '*Darlegungssprache*' as anticipating the distinction subsequently drawn by Tarski between an 'object-language' and a 'meta-language', and certainly the resemblance is close: close enough for us to have decided to avail ourselves of the expedient of using Tarski's way of speaking to translate Frege's two notions: the reader is not to suppose that Frege anticipates this actual terminology and may judge for himself how far he anticipates Tarski's thought (trans.).

their proper names 'Venus', 'Mars', etc. *As* such *proper names of the sentences of the object-language I use these very sentences, but enclosed in quotation marks.* Moreover it follows from this that the sentences of the object-language are never given assertoric force. 'If *a* is a man, *a* is mortal' is a sentence of the object-language in which a general thought is expressed. We move from the general to the particular by substituting for the equiform indefinitely indicating letters equiform proper names. It belongs to the essence of our object-language that equiform proper names designate the same object (man). Here empty signs (names) are not proper names at all.*
By substituting for the indefinitely indicating letters equiform with '*a*', proper names of the form 'Napoleon', we obtain

> '*If Napoleon is a man, Napoleon is mortal.*'

This sentence is not however to be regarded as a conclusion, since the sentence 'If *a* is a man, *a* is mortal' is not given assertoric force, and so the thought expressed in it is not presented as one recognized to be true, for *only a thought recognized as true can be made the premise of an inference.* But an inference can be made of this, by freeing the two sentences of our object-language from quotation marks, thus making it possible to put them forward with assertoric force.

The compound sentence '*If Napoleon be a man, then is Napoleon mortal*'[1] expresses a hypothetical compound thought, composed of one condition and one consequence. The former is expressed in the sentence '*Napoleon is a man*', the latter in '*Napoleon is mortal*'. Strictly, however, our compound sentence contains neither a sentence equiform with '*Napoleon is a man*' nor one equiform with '*Napoleon is mortal*'. In this divergence between what holds at the linguistic level and what holds at the level of the thought, there emerges a defect in our object-language which is still to be remedied. I wish now to dress the thought that I expressed above in the

---

* I call proper names of our object-language *equiform*, if they are intended to be so by the writer and are meant to be of the same size, if we can recognize this to be the writer's intention even if it is imperfectly realized.

---

[1] In German, unlike English, the order of the words in a sentence is altered when it is made into the antecedent or consequent of a hypothetical. The compound sentence with antecedent 'Napoleon is a man' and consequent 'Napoleon is mortal' transliterates 'If Napoleon a man is, is Napoleon mortal'. Throughout the preceding discussion we have translated such hypothetical sentences into natural English. Here, where Frege is concerned with the deviation between the vernacular (German) and a language which reflects more accurately 'the level of thought', it has proved necessary to resort to a clumsy English rendering of the hypothetical sentence. The fact that English *happens* not to have what Frege here argues is a defective correspondence between the level of language and that of the thought, does not, of course, detract from the force or interest of the point he is here making (trans.).

sentence '*If Napoleon be a man, then is Napoleon mortal*', in the sentence '*If Napoleon is a man, Napoleon is mortal*'; which, in what follows, I wish to call the second sentence. Similar cases are to be treated in the same way. So I want also to transform the sentence '*If* a *be a man, then is* a *mortal*' into '*If* a *is a man*, a *is mortal*', which in what follows I will call the sentence.* In the first sentence I distinguish the two individual letters equiform with '*a*' from the remaining part.

---

* The first sentence, unlike the second, does not express a compound thought, since neither '*a is a man*' nor '*a is mortal*' expresses a thought. We have here really only parts of a sentence, not sentences.

[Diary Entries on the Concept of Numbers][1]

[23.3.1924–25.3.1924]

23.3.1924   My efforts to become clear about what is meant by number have resulted in failure. We are only too easily misled by language and in this particular case the way we are misled is little short of disastrous. The sentences 'Six is an even number', 'Four is a square number', 'Five is a prime number' appear analogous to the sentences 'Sirius is a fixed star', 'Europe is a continent'—sentences whose function is to represent an object as falling under a concept. Thus the words 'six', 'four', and 'five' look like proper names of objects and 'even number', 'square number', and 'prime number', along with 'number' itself, look like concept-words. So the problem appears to be to work out more clearly the nature of the concept designated by the word 'number' and to exhibit the objects that, as it seems, are designated by number-words and numerals.

24.3.1924   From our earliest education onwards we are so accustomed to using the word 'number' and the number-words that we do not regard our way of using them as something that stands in need of a justification. To the mathematicians it appears beneath their dignity to concern themselves with such childish matters. But one finds amongst them the most different and contradictory statements about number and numbers. Indeed, when one has been occupied with these questions for a long time one comes to suspect that our way of using language is misleading, that number-words are not proper names of objects at all and words like 'number', 'square number' and the rest are not concept-words; and that consequently a sentence like 'Four is a square number' simply does not express that an object is subsumed under a concept and so just cannot be construed like the sentence 'Sirius is a fixed star'. But how then is it to be construed?

25.3.1924   At first, however, I was still captive to the error that language gives rise to. It is easy to see that a number is not a collection of things. What is a collection? A collection is a thing, a thing that is made up of things. The mathematician couples the word 'one' with the definite article

---

[1] These remarks were taken from a diary that Frege kept from 10.3.24 to 9.5.24; the other entries are simply statements of political attitudes which cannot be counted as part of the scientific *Nachlaß* (ed.). For further details concerning the nature and content of this Diary, readers are referred to Michael Dummett, *Frege: Philosophy of Language*, London 1973, p. xii. See also the article on Frege in the *Encyclopaedia Brittanica* (fifteenth edition) Trans.

and speaks of 'the number one'. If now a number is a thing, we must produce the thing that is called the number one. Many people even want to call numerals numbers. If this were true, we should have to be able to specify which of these numerals was the number one. What a calamity it would then be if this One were ever to be destroyed by fire! It is already a step forward when a number is seen not as a thing but as something belonging to a thing, where the view is that different things, in spite of their differences, can possess the same One, as different leaves can, say, all possess the colour green. Now which things possess the number one? Does not the number one belong to each and every thing?

Number[1]

[September 1924]

My efforts to throw light on the questions surrounding the word 'number' and the words and signs for individual numbers seem to have ended in complete failure. Still these efforts have not been wholly in vain. Precisely because they have failed, we can learn something from them. The difficulties of these investigations are often greatly underrated. Anyone who can regard a number of a series of objects of the same kind shows that he is so far from having any real understanding that he does not yet have even an inkling of the task involved.

First of all we need to come to an understanding about the words 'number', 'numeral', 'number-word'. In everyday life one often calls the numerals numbers. In the present context we must exclude this way of speaking. The simplest thing seems to be to understand by a numeral a sign that designates a number and by a number-word a word which designates a number. Then numerals and number-words will have the same role, namely that of designating a number; only the vehicle used will be different.

What, then, are numbers themselves? What sort of thing is it that one means to designate by a number-word or numeral? Obviously it is not anything that can be perceived by the senses. A number can neither be smelt, nor tasted, nor seen, nor felt. It jars to speak of warm or yellow or bitter numbers, just as it would jar if one chose to speak of yellow or warm or bitter points in geometry. We may seek to discover something about numbers themselves from the use we make of numerals and number-words. Numerals and number-words are used, like names of objects, as proper names. The sentence 'Five is a prime number' is comparable with the sentence 'Sirius is a fixed star'. In these sentences an object (five, Sirius) is presented as falling under a concept (prime number, fixed star) (a case of an object's being subsumed under a concept). By a number, then, we are to understand an object that cannot be perceived by the senses. Even the

---

[1] According to a remark made by the previous editors on the transcripts on which this edition is based, these comments stem 'from two drafts of which the first is dated: Sept. 1924 to 23.III.1924'. The date 23.III.1924 apparently refers to the remarks which Frege made in his diary on that day (cf. p. 263). It is also clear from remarks made by the previous editors that the first three paragraphs come from the second draft, and the last two paragraphs from the first (ed.).

The curious dating may mean that Frege added, on Sept. 1924, the last two paragraphs to a re-working of the diary entry of 23.III.1924 (trans.).

objects of geometry, points, straight lines, surfaces etc. cannot really be perceived by the senses.

These investigations are especially difficult because in the very act of conducting them we are easily misled by language: by language which is, after all, an indispensable tool for carrying them out. Indeed one might think that language would first have to be freed from all logical imperfections before it was employed in such investigations. But of course the work necessary to do this can itself only be done by using this tool, for all its imperfections. Fortunately as a result of our logical work we have acquired a yardstick by which we are apprised of these defects. Such a yardstick is at work even in language, obstructed though it may be by the many illogical features that are also at work in language.

In pre-scientific discourse what are called numbers are often no more than numerals. These signs are ordered in a series beginning with the sign '1'. In this series each sign, with the exception of the last, has an immediate successor, and each sign, with the exception of the first (the sign '1') an immediate predecessor. For example 1*2*3*4*5, in which I have separated the individual numerals by asterisks.

Sources of Knowledge of Mathematics and the mathematical natural Sciences[1]

[1924/5]

When someone comes to know something it is by his recognizing a thought to be true. For that he has first to grasp the thought. Yet I do not count the grasping of the thought as knowledge, but only the recognition of its truth, the judgement proper. What I regard as a source of knowledge is what justifies the recognition of truth, the judgement.

I distinguish the following sources of knowledge:

1. Sense perception
2. The logical source of knowledge
3. The geometrical and temporal sources of knowledge.

Each of these is subject to its own disturbances, which detract from its value.

A. Sense Illusions

A sense impression is not in itself a judgement, but becomes important in that it is the occasion for our making a judgement. When this happens, we may be misled: in such cases we talk of 'sense illusions'. Since for the mathematical natural sciences sight is the most important sense, we will examine it in greater detail. To our consciousness, the line of vision from the eye to the object is straight. In the majority of cases, the corresponding light

---

[1] From the correspondence between Frege and Richard Hönigswald (cf. the letter from Hönigswald to Frege of 24/4/1925), it emerges that Frege submitted this article to Bruno Bauch for the series edited by Hönigswald and Bauch, *Wissenschaftliche Grundfragen*. In the letter mentioned Hönigswald gave a very favourable judgement on Frege's article, but suggested that it be essentially enlarged, 'Our concern in our venture *isn't* to produce a philosophical *journal*, in which in each issue many articles are put together, but a series of parts, each comprising between 4 to 6 sheets, and appearing *on their own in book form*'. He asked Frege to resubmit the article for the *Wissenschaftliche Grundfragen* affer enlarging it, and listed a number of points where further reworking appeared to him to be desirable. Because of his death three months later, Frege was obviously only able to do some of the preliminary work required for this. In the *Nachlaß* three sheets, now lost, with notes pointing in this direction were to be found, as may be learnt from a note of the earlier editors to the Frege–Hönigswald correspondence. Cf. further, Frege's letters to Hönigswald of 26/4/1925 and later (ed.).

ray from the object to our eye is also straight, or the deviation from a straight line is too slight to matter to us. If we notice the deviation, we speak of an optical illusion. We encounter such cases with the reflection of the light in a mirror, with diffraction or refraction of the light. Because of these illusions we might from the very outset regard visual perception as a source of knowledge that is unreliable and hence of little value, and yet it is precisely sense perception that is regarded by many as the most reliable, if not the only, source of knowledge. Of course a mirror appears to be an opening in the wall giving us a view of a neighbouring room; of course a calm stretch of water gives us the illusion of a sun which seems to be looking up at us; but people are no longer deceived by such cases, because there are at our disposal a diversity of means for correcting the judgement gained from the first impression. Of course, if there were no laws governing events, or if the laws governing events in the physical world were unknowable for us, we would lack the means for recognizing illusions for what they are and thus for rendering them harmless. The laws of nature we already know enable us to avoid being misled by sense illusions. Thus knowledge about the refraction of light tells us that many of the images we see through the microscope are wholly unreliable. In order to know the laws of nature we need perceptions that are free from illusion. And so, on its own, sense perception can be of little use to us, since to know the laws of nature we also need the other sources of knowledge: the logical and the geometrical. Thus we can only advance step by step—each extension in our knowledge of the laws of nature providing us with a further safeguard against being deceived by the senses and the purification of our perceptions helping us to a better knowledge of the laws of nature. We must be careful not to overestimate the value of sense perception, for without the other sources of knowledge, which protect us from being deceived, we could hardly get anywhere with it. We need the perceptions, but to make use of them, we also need the other sources of knowledge. Only all taken in conjunction make it possible for us to penetrate ever deeper into mathematical physics.

For mathematics on its own, we don't need sense perception as a source of knowledge: for it the logical and geometrical sources suffice.

At times sense perception has been an outright hindrance to the advancement of knowledge. For a long time the idea of the spherical shape of the earth was almost universally held to be completely absurd, since if it were true, on the bottom side of the earth men's heads would dangle downwards from their feet. People had been led by their senses to regard the upwards direction as everywhere the same; and even today there are difficulties in such considerations which children find difficult to surmount. It was a long time before the idea of the spherical shape of the earth gained sufficient ground for Columbus to put his trust in it and be able to embark on his famous voyage. Its success and the subsequent circumnavigations of the earth were the victory of scientific reflection over the old view: a view that was almost overwhelmingly suggested by, and apparently unassailably grounded in, sense perception.

B. The logical Source of Knowledge and Language

The senses present us with something external and because of this it is easier to comprehend how mistakes can occur than it is in the case of the logical source of knowledge which is wholly inside us and thus appears to be more proof against contamination. But appearances are deceptive. For our thinking is closely bound up with language and thereby with the world of the senses. Perhaps our thinking is at first a form of speaking which then becomes an imaging of speech. Silent thinking would in that case be speech which has become noiseless, taking place in the imagination. Now we may of course also think in mathematical signs; yet even then thinking is tied up with what is perceptible to the senses. To be sure, we distinguish the sentence as the expression of a thought from the thought itself. We know we can have various expressions for the same thought. The connection of a thought with one particular sentence is not a necessary one; but that a thought of which we are conscious is connected in our mind with some sentence or other is for us men necessary. But that does not lie in the nature of the thought but in our own nature. There is no contradiction in supposing there to exist beings that can grasp the same thought as we do without needing to clad it in a form that can be perceived by the senses. But still, for us men there is this necessity. Language is a human creation; and so man had, it would appear, the capacity to shape it in conformity with the logical disposition alive in him. Certainly the logical disposition of man *was* at work in the formation of language but equally alongside this many other dispositions—such as the poetic disposition. And so language is not constructed from a logical blueprint.

One feature of language that threatens to undermine the reliability of thinking is its tendency to form proper names to which no objects correspond. If this happens in fiction, which everyone understands to be fiction, this has no detrimental effect. It's different if it happens in a statement which makes the claim to be strictly scientific. A particularly noteworthy example of this is the formation of a proper name after the pattern of 'the extension of the concept a', e.g. 'the extension of the concept *star*'. Because of the definite article, this expression appears to designate an object; but there is no object for which this phrase could be a linguistically appropriate designation. From this has arisen the paradoxes of set theory which have dealt the death blow to set theory itself. I myself was under this illusion when, in attempting to provide a logical foundation for numbers, I tried to construe numbers as sets. It is difficult to avoid an expression that has universal currency, before you learn of the mistakes it can give rise to. It is extremely difficult, perhaps impossible, to test every expression offered us by language to see whether it is logically innocuous. So a great part of the work of a philosopher consists—or at least ought to consist—in a struggle against language. But perhaps only a few people are aware of the need for this. The same expression—'the extension of the concept *star*'—serves at the same time to illustrate, in yet another way, the fatal tendency of language to form apparent proper names: 'the concept *star*' is, of itself, one such. The definite article creates the impression that this phrase is meant to designate an object, or, what amounts to the same thing, that 'the concept *star*' is a proper name, whereas 'concept *star*' is surely a designation of a concept and thus could not be more different from a proper name. The difficulties which this idiosyncrasy of language entangles us in are incalculable.

But, isn't thinking a kind of speaking? How is it possible for thinking to be engaged in a struggle with speaking? Wouldn't that be a struggle in which thinking was at war with itself? Doesn't this spell the end to the possibility of thinking?

To be sure, if you search for the emergence of thinking in the development of an individual, you may well describe thinking as an inaudible inner speaking; but that doesn't capture the true nature of thinking. Can't a mathematician also think in formulae? The formula-language of mathematics is as much a human creation as spoken language, but is fundamentally different from it. Here those traits of spoken language which, as we have seen, lead to logical errors, can be avoided. Yet the influence of speech is so great that they aren't always avoided. Thus if we disregard how thinking occurs in the consciousness of an individual, and attend instead to the true nature of thinking, we shall not be able to equate it with speaking. In that case we shall not derive thinking from speaking; thinking will then emerge as that which has priority and we shall not be able to blame thinking for the logical defects we have noted in language.

In the formula-language of mathematics an important distinction stands out that lies concealed in verbal language. Of course mathematicians themselves are still so strongly influenced by verbal language that even in their discipline the distinction I have in mind doesn't stand out as clearly as all that. Mathematicians are compelled by the nature of their discipline to grasp a concept to which they have given the name 'function'. As early as in the upper forms of high school, pupils are introduced to trigonometric functions, and if they should then go on to study mathematics, they hear a great deal about functions, without it becoming clear to them what people mean by the word. Their teachers take great pains but in vain, and it is precisely the most gifted pupils who perhaps will understand it least, since they will notice that the definitions given do not agree with the teacher's own way of speaking. One surely has some right to expect that a definition, once given, will not straightway be thrown in a corner to gather dust, but that it will be drawn upon when the expression it defines is used.

But this expectation is disappointed because the alleged definition cannot begin to provide what one expects of it. For not everything can be defined; only what has been analysed into concepts can be reconstituted out of the parts yielded by the analysis. But what is simple cannot be analysed and hence not defined. If, nevertheless, someone attempts a definition, the result is nonsense. All definitions of function belong to this category. How does a child learn to understand grown-ups? Not as if it were already endowed with an understanding of a few words and grammatical constructions, so that all you would need to do would be to explain what it did not understand by means of the linguistic knowledge it already had. In reality of course children are only endowed with a capacity to learn to speak. We must be able to count on a meeting of minds with them just as in the case of animals with whom men can arrive at a mutual understanding. Neither is it possible, without a meeting of minds, to make designations of a logically unanalysable content intelligible to others. The word 'function' is such a designation. The way in which designations for functions are used can come to our assistance here. The sign '*sin*' which we say designates the sine function, only occurs in mathematics in close combination with other signs, as in 'sin 10°', 'sin 0° 11''', 'sin α', and so is a sign in need of supplementation and therein is different from a proper name. Its content is correspondingly also in need of supplementation and therein is different from any object, for instance, even from any number; for a number, by which I don't want to understand a numerical sign, appears in mathematics as an object, e.g. *the* number 3.

Now it is usual in higher mathematics to permit the sign 'sin' to be followed simply by a numerical sign or a letter standing in for one. For instead of defining the size of an angle A in degrees, minutes and seconds, it can simply be defined by a number as follows: Let C be a circle in the plane of A whose centre is at the vertex of A. Let the radius of C be r. Let the sides of A include an arc of C, whose length is b, say. Let C_1 be a circle in the plane of A, whose centre is at the vertex of A. Let the radius of C_1 be r_1 and the sides of A include an arc of C_1 whose length is b_1. Then $b_1 : r_1 = b : r$. Thus b/r is the same number as b_1/r_1, and this number depends on the size of the angle A and defines that size. If instead of A we take the angle A', then b'/r say, takes the place of b/r, and b_1'/r_1, that of b_1/r_1 and in fact $b' > b$ if $A' > A$. And so in that case $b'/r > b/r$. And so the size of the angle A is defined by the number b/r, which coincides with b_1/r_1, and what's more a larger number corresponds to a larger angle. Thus b/r is greater than, less than or equal to b'/r according as A is greater than, less than or equal to A'. From this we may see how the number b/r (which coincides with b_1/r_1) defines the angle A. If $b/r = 1$, then $b = r$. Thus the number 1 defines an angle for which the length b is equal to r, that is the length of the arc of C included by the sides of A is then equal to the radius of A. In the same way an angle is defined by the number 2, in which case the arc of C included by the sides of A is twice the length of the radius of C etc. We may also say: the number that in this way defines the size of angle is the number yielded by measuring the arc of *C* included by its sides with the radius of *C*. In this way it is in every case fixed which number is meant when the sign 'sin' is completed by the sign for a real number. The only thing presupposed is that you know how an angle is related to its sine.

In the same way the sign 'cos' (cosine) is also in need of supplementation: it is to be completed by numerical signs, and cos 1, cos 2 and cos 3 are numbers. Thus 'cos' is neither a proper name, nor does it designate an object; but you can't deny the sign 'cos' some content. If, however, you wished to say, using the definite article, '*the* content of the sign "cos"', you would convey the wrong idea, that an object was the content of the 'cos' sign. Perhaps it can be seen from this how difficult it is not to allow ourselves to be misled by language. Just because this is so difficult, it is hardly to be expected that a run-of-the-mill writer will take the trouble to avoid being misled, and linguistic usage will, to be sure, always remain as it is.

Added to this, there is also the following: mathematicians use letters to express generality, as in the sentence '$(a + b) + c = (a + c) + b$'. These letters here stand in for numerical signs and you arrive at the expression of a particular thought contained in the general one by substituting numerical signs for the letters. If one has in fact admitted functions, one will feel the need to express generality concerning functions too. As one uses letters instead of numerical signs so as to be able to express general thoughts concerning numbers, one will also introduce letters for the specific purpose of being able to express general thoughts concerning functions. It is customary for this purpose to use the letters *f*, *F*, *g*, *G* and also ϕ and Φ, which we may call function-letters. But now the function's need of supplementation must somehow or other find expression. Now it is appropriate to introduce brackets after every function-letter, which together with that letter are to be regarded as one single sign. The space within the brackets is then the place where the sign that supplements the function-letter is to be inserted. By substituting for the function-letter in $f(1)$ a particular function by means of the sign 'sin', you obtain 'sin 1', just as you obtain '3^2' from 'a^2' by substituting '3' for the letter '*a*'. In each case, in so doing, you make the transition from an indefinitely indicating sign, that is, a letter, to one that designates determinately. If this happens in a sentence, this corresponds to the transition from a general thought to a particular one contained in it. An example of this is the transition from '$(a - 1) \cdot (a + 1) = a \cdot a - 1$' to '$(3 - 1) \cdot (3 + 1) = 3 \cdot 3 - 1$'. I cannot give here a similar example in which a function-sign that designates definitely is substituted for an indefinitely indicating letter, since to do so I would have to presuppose certain elements of higher analysis: even so it will be clear enough what I mean, and you will at least be able to gain some idea of the importance of the introduction of functions into mathematical investigations, and of the introduction of function-signs and function-letters into the sign-language of mathematics. It is here that the tendency of language by its use of the definite article to stamp as an object what is a function and hence a non-object, proves itself to be the source of inaccurate and misleading expressions and so also of errors of thought. Probably most of the impurities that contaminate the logical source of knowledge have their origins in this.

C. The geometrical Sources of Knowledge

From the geometrical source of knowledge flow the axioms of geometry. It is least of all liable to contamination. Yet here one has to understand the word 'axiom' in precisely its Euclidean sense. But even here people in recent works have muddied the waters by perverting—so slightly at first as to be scarcely noticeable—the old Euclidean sense, with the result that they have attached a different sense to the sentences in which the axioms have been handed down to us. For this reason I cannot emphasize strongly enough that I only mean axioms in the original Euclidean sense, when I recognize a geometrical source of knowledge in them. If we keep this firmly in mind, we need not fear that this source of knowledge will be contaminated.

From the geometrical source of knowledge flows the infinite in the genuine and strictest sense of this word. Here we are not concerned with the everyday usage according to which 'infinitely large' and 'infinitely many' imply no more than 'very large' and 'very many'. We have infinitely many points on every interval of a straight line, on every circle, and infinitely many lines through every point. That we cannot imagine the totality of these taken one at a time is neither here nor there. One man may be able to imagine more, another less. But here we are not in the domain of psychology, of the imagination, of what is subjective, but in the domain of the objective, of what is true. It is here that geometry and philosophy come closest together. In fact they belong to one another. A philosopher who has nothing to do with geometry is only half a philosopher, and a mathematician with no element of philosophy in him is only half a mathematician. These disciplines have estranged themselves from one another to the detriment of both. This is how eventually formal arithmetic became prevalent—the view that numbers are numerals. Perhaps its time is not yet over. How do people arrive at such an idea? If someone is concerned in the science of numbers, he feels an obligation to say what is understood by numbers. Confronted by the task of explaining the concept he recognizes his inability, and without a moment's hesitation settles on the explanation that numerals are numbers. For you can of course see these things with your eyes, as you can see stones, plants and stars. You certainly have no doubt there are stones. You can have just as little doubt there are numbers. You must only banish completely from your mind the thought that these numbers mean something or have a content. For you would then have to say what this content was, and that would lead to incredible difficulties. Just this is the advantage of formal arithmetic, that it avoids these difficulties. That is why it cannot be emphasized strongly enough that the numbers are not the content or sense of certain signs: these very numerical signs are themselves the numbers and have no content or sense at all. People can only talk in this way if they have no glimmer of philosophical understanding. On this account, a statement of number can say nothing, and the numbers are completely useless and worthless.

It is evident that sense perception can yield nothing infinite. However many stars we may include in our inventories, there will never be infinitely many, and the same goes for us with the grains of sand on the seashore. And so, where we may legitimately claim to recognize the infinite, we have not obtained it from sense perception. For this we need a special source of knowledge, and one such is the geometrical.

Besides the spatial, the temporal must also be recognized. A source of knowledge corresponds to this too, and from this also we derive the infinite. Time stretching to infinity in both directions is like a line stretching to infinity in both directions.

Numbers and Arithmetic[1]

[1924/25]

When I first set out to answer for myself the question of what is to be understood by numbers and arithmetic, I encountered—in an apparently predominant position—what was called formal arithmetic. The hallmark of formal arithmetic was the thesis 'Numbers are numerals'. How did people arrive at such a position? They felt incapable of answering the question on any rational view of what could be meant by it, they did not know how they ought to explain what is designated by the numeral '3' or the numeral '4', and then the cunning idea occurred to them of evading this question by saying 'These numerical signs do not really designate anything: they are themselves the things that we are inquiring about.' Quite a dodge, a degree of cunning amounting, one might almost say, to genius; it's only a shame that it makes the numerals, and so the numbers themselves, completely devoid of content and quite useless. How was it *possible* for people not to see this? Time and again the same cunning idea occurs to people and it's very possible that there are such people to be found even today. They usually begin by assuring us that they do not intend the numerals to designate anything—no, not anything at all. And yet, it seems, in some mysterious way some content or other must manage to insinuate itself into these quite empty signs, for otherwise they would be useless. That, then, is what formal arithmetic used to be. Is it now dead? Strictly speaking, it was never alive; all the same we cannot rule out attempts to resuscitate it.

I, for my part, never had any doubt that numerals must designate something in arithmetic, if such a discipline exists at all, and that it does is surely hard to deny. We do, after all, make statements of number. In that case, what are they used to make an assertion about? For me there could be no doubt as to the answer: in a statement of number something is asserted about a concept. I was using the word 'concept' here in the sense that I still attach to it even now. To be sure, among philosophical writers this word is used in a deplorably loose way. This may be all very well for such authors, because the word is then always at hand when they need it. But, this aside, I regard the practice as pernicious.

If I say 'the number of beans in this box is six' or 'there are six beans in

---

[1] Similarities in content to the paper 'Sources of Knowledge of Mathematics and the mathematical natural Sciences', in particular the claim of the priority for mathematics of a source of knowledge that is geometrical in nature, make it highly probable that this piece also dates from the last year of Frege's life (ed.).

this box', what concept am I making an assertion about? Obviously 'bean in this box'.*

Now numbers of different kinds have arisen in different ways and must be distinguished accordingly. To begin with, we have what I call the kindergarten-numbers. They are, as it were, drilled into children by parents and teachers: here what people have in mind is the child's future occupation. The child is to be prepared for doing business, for buying and selling. Money has to be counted, and wares too. We have the picture of a child sitting in front of a heap of peas, picking them out one by one with his fingers, each time uttering a number-word. In this way something like images of numbers are formed in the child's mind. But this is an artificial process which is imposed on the child rather than one which develops naturally within him. But even if it were a natural process, there would be hardly anything to learn about the real nature of the kindergarten-numbers from the way they originate psychologically. All the same, we can go as far as to say that the series of kindergarten-numbers forms a discontinuous series, which because of this discontinuity is essentially different from the series of points on a straight line. There is always a jump from one number to the next, whereas in a series of points there is no such thing as a next point. In this respect nothing is essentially altered when the child becomes acquainted with fractions. For even after the interpolation of the rationals, the series of numbers including the rationals still has gaps in it. Anything resembling a continuum remains as impossible as ever. It is true that we can use one length to measure another with all the accuracy we need for business life, but we can do this only because the needs of business will tolerate small inaccuracies. Things are different in the strict sciences. These teach that there are infinitely many lengths that cannot be measured by a given unit of length. This is what makes the kindergarten-numbers extremely limited in their application. The labours of mathematicians have indeed led to other kinds of numbers, to the irrationals, for example; but there is no bridge which leads across from the kindergarten-numbers to the irrationals. I myself at one time held it to be possible to conquer the entire number domain, continuing along a purely logical path from the kindergarten-numbers; I have seen the mistake in this. I was right in thinking that you cannot do this if you take an empirical route. I may have arrived at this conviction as a result of the following consideration: that the series of whole numbers should eventually come to an end, that there should be a greatest whole number, is manifestly absurd. This shows that arithmetic cannot be based on sense perception; for if it could be so based, we should have to reconcile ourselves to the brute fact of the series of whole numbers coming to an end, as we may one day have to reconcile ourselves to there being no

---

* If something is asserted of a first level concept, what is asserted is a second level concept. And so in making a statement of number we have a second level concept.

stars above a certain size. But here surely the position is different: that the series of whole numbers should eventually come to an end is not just false: we find the idea absurd. So an *a priori* mode of cognition must be involved here. But this cognition does not have to flow from purely logical principles, as I originally assumed. There is the further possibility that it has a geometrical source. Now of course the kindergarten-numbers appear to have nothing whatever to do with geometry. But that is just a defect in the kindergarten-numbers. The more I have thought the matter over, the more convinced I have become that arithmetic and geometry have developed on the same basis—a geometrical one in fact—so that mathematics in its entirety is really geometry. Only on this view does mathematics present itself as completely homogeneous in nature. Counting, which arose psychologically out of the demands of business life, has led the learned astray.

A new Attempt at a Foundation for Arithmetic[1]

[1924/25]

A.)[2] I first repeat earlier assertions of mine that I still regard as true.

Grundgesetze I, p. 1. Arithmetic does not need to appeal to experience in its proofs. I now express this as follows: *Arithmetic does not need to appeal to sense perception in its proofs.*

Grundgesetze I, p. 3. A statement of number contains an assertion about a concept.

B.) Secondly, I retract views I have expressed previously which I can no longer hold to be correct.

I have had to abandon the view that arithmetic does not need to appeal to intuition either in its proofs, understanding by intuition the geometrical source of knowledge, that is, the source from which flow the axioms of geometry. Recently, a vicious confusion has arisen over the use of the word 'axiom'. I therefore emphasize that I am using this word in its original meaning.

C.) I distinguish the following sources of knowledge for mathematics and physics:

1. Sense perception
2. The Geometrical Source of Knowledge
3. The Logical Source of Knowledge.

---

[1] According to early descriptions of the Frege archives the original manuscript was found in the *Nachlaß* together with a copy of a hand-printed version of the article *Gedankengefüge* which appeared in 1923—it might indeed have been written on the back of this copy. And so the earliest possible date for its composition is 1923. On the other hand there is no mention of a 'geometrical' foundation for arithmetic in Frege's brief remarks on the concept of number written in 1924. We do however find such mention in the essay 'Sources of Knowledge in Mathematics and the mathematical Natural Sciences' (pp. 267 ff. of this volume)—possibly not written before the beginning of 1925—and also, more plainly, in the short piece 'Numbers and Arithmetic (pp. 275 ff.). This suggests that we should assign Frege's last attempt to provide a foundation for arithmetic to the same date or later (if we regard them as an attempt to fill out what he says on pp. 267 ff., 275 ff.) An alternative possibility would be to date Frege's new account earlier—say in Autumn 1924; that is, as a train of thought which Frege found promising, and that lies behind the later remarks about the power of 'the geometrical source of knowledge' for arithmetic (ed.).

[2] In the manuscript the letter 'A' together with the phrase 'preliminary remarks' appears as a heading (ed.).

The last of these is involved when inferences are drawn, and thus is almost always involved. Yet it seems that this on its own cannot yield us any objects. From the geometrical source of knowledge flows pure geometry. In the case of arithmetic, just as in the case of geometry, I exclude only sense perception as a source of knowledge. Everyone will grant that there is no largest whole number, i.e. that there are infinitely many whole numbers. This doesn't imply there has ever been a time at which a man has grasped infinitely many whole numbers. Rather, there are probably infinitely many whole numbers which no man has ever grasped. This knowledge cannot be derived from sense perception, since nothing infinite in the full sense of the word can flow from this source. Stars are objects of sense perception. And so it cannot be asserted with certainty that there are infinitely many of them: no more can it be asserted with certainty that there are not infinitely many stars. Since probably on its own the logical source of knowledge cannot yield numbers either, we will appeal to the geometrical source of knowledge. This is significant because it means that arithmetic and geometry, and hence the whole of mathematics flows from one and the same source of knowledge—that is the geometrical one. This is thus elevated to the status of the true source of mathematical knowledge, with, of course, the logical source of knowledge also being involved at every turn.

The Peculiarity of Geometry

Now in geometry we speak of straight lines, just as in physics people speak of solids, say. 'Solid' is a concept and you may point at a thing, saying 'This is a solid'; by so doing you subsume the thing under the concept 'solid'. We may surely call subsumption a logical relationship.[1]

D.) We may begin by outlining my plan. Departing from the usual practice, I do not want to start out from the positive whole numbers and to extend progressively the domain of what I call numbers; for there's no doubt that you are really making a logical error if you do not use 'number' with a fixed meaning, but keep understanding something different by it. That this was how the subject evolved historically is no argument to the contrary, since in mathematics we must always strive after a system that is complete in itself. If the one that has been acknowledged until now proves inadequate, it must be demolished and replaced by a new structure. Thus, right at the outset I go straight to the final goal, the general complex numbers.

If one wished to restrict oneself to the real numbers, one could take these to be ratios of intervals on a line, in which the intervals were to be regarded as oriented, and so with a distinction between a starting point and an end point. In that case one could in fact shift the interval along the line at random without altering it in a way that has any mathematical significance, but

---

[1] It is impossible to determine whether the heading 'Peculiarity of Geometry' and the paragraph that follows it are placed here in accordance with Frege's own instructions or at the instigation of the previous editors. We only have a note of theirs saying that this passage 'is to be inserted before D' (ed.).

not switch it round. If we want to include the complex numbers in our considerations, we must adopt as our basis not a straight line, but a plane.

I call this the *base plane*.

I take a point in it that I call the *origin*, and a different point that I call the *endpoint*. Then there can in fact be shifts of an interval in the base plane which have no significance for our reflections, namely shifts in a parallel direction, but not rotations of the interval. If, in the way that Gauss proposed, one lets these oriented intervals in the base plane correspond to complex numbers, then the ratio of two such intervals is a complex number which is independent of the interval originally chosen as the unit length. Thus I wish to call a ratio of intervals a number; by this means I have included the complex numbers from the very outset. I say this to make it easier for the reader to see what I'm after, but in so doing I don't wish to presuppose either a knowledge of what I want to call a complex number, or a knowledge of what I want to call a ratio. These are supposed only to be explained in the exposition which follows. The reader should therefore try to forget what he hitherto thought he knew about ratios of intervals and about complex numbers; for this 'knowledge' was probably a delusion. The fundamental mistake is that people start out from the numbers they acquired as children, say through counting a heap of peas. These numbers leave us completely in the lurch even when we encounter the irrational numbers. If you take them seriously, there are no irrational numbers. Karl Snell, a man, long since dead, who was deeply revered by me at Jena, often enunciated the principle: in mathematics, everything is to be as clear as $2 \times 2 = 4$. The moment there appears anything at all which is mysterious, that is a sign that not everything is in order. But he himself, when he employed Gauss's method of introducing the complex numbers, could not avoid altogether the mysterious, and he also felt this himself and was dissatisfied with the account he gave.

E.) The ideas[1] I have adopted as basic are *line* and *point*. The primitive relation between points and a line which I take as basic is given by the sentence:

The point A is *symmetric* with the point B with respect to the line l.

F.) Definitions.

1. If the point P is symmetric with itself with respect to the line l, then I say

the point P is on the line l.

2. If the point A is a symmetric with the point A' with respect to the line l, and if the point B is symmetric with the point B' with respect to the line l, and if the point C is symmetric with the point C' with respect to the line l, then I say

The triangle ABC is symmetric with the triangle A'B'C' with respect to the line 1.

---

[1] Against 'ideas' the previous editors have the note: in the MS as a second correction of 'primitive objects'—the first being 'concepts' (ed.).

3. If there is a line, with respect to which the triangle *ABC* is symmetric with the triangle *DEF*, then I say

The triangle ABC is symmetric with the triangle DEF.

4. If the triangle *ABC* is symmetric with the triangle *DEF*, and if the triangle *DEF* is symmetric with the triangle *GHI*, then I say

The triangle ABC is congruent to the triangle GHI.

5. If there is a line, which the point *A* is on, and which the point *B* is on and which the point *C* is on, then I say

A, B and C are collinear.

6. If the point *A* is symmetric with the point *B* with respect to the line *l* and if *B* is symmetric with the point *C* with respect to the line *m*, and if *A*, *B* and *C* are collinear, then I say

l is parallel to m.

7. If the point *A* is on the line *l* and if the point *A* is on the line *m* and if *l* is different from *m*, then I say

A is the intersection of l and m.

8. If *A* is the intersection of *l₁* and *l₃*, *C* the intersection of *l₁* and *l₄*, *B* the intersection of *l₂* and *l₃*, *D* the intersection of *l₂* and *l₄*, if *l₃* is parallel to *l₄*, if *M* is the intersection of *l₁* and *l₂*, if *M* is different from *A*, and *B* and from *C*, and if the triangle *MCD* is congruent to the triangle *PQR*, then I say

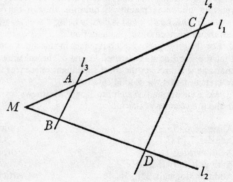

The triangle MAB is similar to the triangle PQR

or, as meaning the same,

The ratio of MA to MB is the same as the ratio of PQ to PR.

If *P*, *Q* and *R* are points, I write the ratio of *PQ* to *PR* in the form *PQ:PR.*

9. If *O* is the origin and *A* the endpoint (in the base plane) and the triangle *OAC* is similar to the triangle *PQR*, then I say

The point C corresponds to the ratio PQ:PR.

10. Theorem: If the triangle *OAC* is similar to the triangle *PQR*, and if the triangle *OAD* is similar to the triangle *PQR*, *D* is the same point as *C*; or

If the point *C* corresponds to the ratio *PQ:PR* and the point *D* corresponds to the ratio *PQ:PR*, then *D* is the same point as *C*.

INDEX

This index is largely based on the index prepared for the German edition by Gottfried Gabriel, the main difference being that it contains no references to editorial matter. Thus the present index—with the exception of one or two references to translators' footnotes—treats *only* of Frege's text. Since Frege's thought revolves around relatively few basic concepts, so that terms such as *concept, object, meaning, sense* recur again and again throughout these writings, there is a danger of making the index too comprehensive and of course some attempt has to be made to confine references under a given term to the more significant of its occurences. In this respect, although we have made a few additions, we have in general adopted a slightly more restrictive policy than that of the German edition, believing that this would produce a more useful index. Possibly the index as it stands now is still too long, and we are, of course, aware that there will be no general agreement about which occurrences of a term are the more significant and about the point at which references become too numerous to be of much use.

We have sometimes included, under a given word, references to parts of the text where the relevant notion is plainly in question though the word itself does not occur there. For instance, *unsaturatedness* is clearly being discussed when Frege uses phrases like 'predicative nature' or 'in need of supplementation'.

For the most part, cross references in this index are to main catchwords, and signify *either* that the word at stake is used in one of the subsidiary catchwords under that main one, *or* that one will discover the most significant references to the notion involved by looking up the references under the second catchword.

We are extremely grateful to Roger Matthews for the generous assistance he has given us in the preparation of this index.